T0377410

SACRED ART OF

TAROT

SACRED ART OF
TAROT

An Essential Guide for
**READING THE CARDS TO
ENHANCE YOUR INTUITION** and
REVEAL LIFE'S MEANINGS

LIZ DEAN

FAIR WINDS

Quarto.com

© 2015, 2025 Quarto Publishing Group USA Inc.
Text © 2016 Liz Dean

First Published in 2025 by Fair Winds Press, an imprint of The Quarto Group,
100 Cummings Center, Suite 265-D, Beverly, MA 01915, USA.
T (978) 282-9590 F (978) 283-2742

Fair Winds Press titles are also available at discount for retail, wholesale, promotional, and bulk purchase. For details, contact the Special Sales Manager by email at specialsales@quarto.com or by mail at The Quarto Group, Attn: Special Sales Manager, 100 Cummings Center, Suite 265-D, Beverly, MA 01915, USA.

29 28 27 26 25   1 2 3 4 5

ISBN: 978-0-7603-9902-6

Digital edition published in 2025
eISBN: 978-0-7603-9964-4

Library of Congress Cataloging-in-Publication Data available

The content in this book was previously published in *The Ultimate Guide to Tarot* by Liz Dean (Fair Winds Press, 2015) and *The Ultimate Guide to Tarot Spreads* by Liz Dean (Fair Winds Press, 2016).

Design, Cover Image, and Page Layout: Merideth Harte

Printed in China

This book is dedicated to all students of tarot.
May your unique journey through the cards
bring you great rewards.

CONTENTS

1

INTRODUCING
THE TAROT

Welcome to *Sacred Art of Tarot*. Whether you're a novice or an expert reader, this book offers everything you need to know to read tarot cards for daily affirmation, prediction, and intuitive and spiritual development. It's also a compendium of card layouts that addresses virtually every question you may ask your tarot cards—from relationships to business dilemmas, and from angelic guidance to house moves—using both simple and developed patterns of cards.

Tarot is a system of archetypes, a picture book of the human condition, reflecting our states of mind and stages of life. Over the past six hundred years, people have consulted the cards for religious instruction, spiritual insight, self-knowledge, and divining the future. The ancient symbols we see on the cards are designed to stimulate our intuition, connecting us with our higher selves or our divine or spiritual aspect. With regular tarot practice, you may experience increased self-awareness, enhanced creativity, better-honed intuition and psychic ability, and the ability to empower others to find their spiritual path.

We begin with the basics—the structure of a tarot deck, how to choose your cards and connect with them, and how to prepare for a tarot reading. Next, you'll learn how to lay out the cards for a reading with both the traditional spreads on pages 20–28 and original mini layouts. The aim is to help you be creative with tarot and experiment and find ways to read the cards that work for *you*. There's no right or wrong way to lay out cards, just the way that's right for you.

The interpretations chapters follow. In the detailed major arcana card interpretations, you will see listed the card's alternative names, number, and numerological association—this is the number that the card's number reduces to, which gives additional insight. For example, XXI, The World, reduces as follows: 2 + 1 = 3, or III, The Empress. Also listed is the card's astrological sign or planet, element, Hebrew letter and Tree of Life pathway, chakra, and key meanings. I also highlight and explain the key symbols of each card, along with each major arcana card's "Reflection" in the minor arcana, which guides you toward the minor cards that hold similar meanings to the major card. For example, major card IV, The Emperor, is reflected in the four kings of the minor arcana because as kings they reflect the "father" aspect of the Emperor.

The minor arcana interpretations are divided by suit and list for cards Ace through Ten each card's suit, element, astrological association, number, and Tree of Life position and key meaning. Page and Knight court cards list just their element and key meaning, while the Queens and Kings also include zodiac signs and associated chakras. You'll also find further information on chakras' and crystals' associations with tarot in the Appendices (pages 329–331).

If you're already familiar with tarot, you'll find that there are additional tips throughout that will spark your imagination and invite you to view familiar techniques or spreads in a new light. My hope is that you will find something in these pages that sparks your creativity and offers a new perspective.

A NOTE ON THE RIDER-WAITE TAROT

Myriad versions and styles of tarot decks have been created through the years. The tarot deck shown throughout this book is the Universal Waite, an enhanced Rider-Waite deck. The original Rider-Waite was devised by A. E. Waite, one of the key members of the Hermetic Order of the Golden Dawn (see page 10), and published by Rider, London. It is considered the most influential contemporary deck and has inspired many variants, which use the same symbols and similar compositions of people, objects, and landscapes. The deck should properly be known as the Rider-Waite Smith, to honor the illustrator, Pamela Colman Smith, a fellow member of the Golden Dawn.

EARLY CARDS: COURT AND CLERGY

The earliest surviving tarot cards date to the fifteenth century, probably created in Northern Italy. (It's likely that the word "tarot" derives from *tarocchi*, an Italian card game that preceded tarot.) These cards, known as the Visconti-Sforza tarots, were commissioned by the Duke of Milan, Francesco Visconti, as early as 1415. Although the Church called early cards "the devil's picture book"—possibly because some printed versions were used for gaming purposes—these original hand-painted cards have predominantly Christian themes and imagery. Their sequence tells a story of a youth who symbolically dies and is reborn, embodied in 0, The Fool, and XXI, The World (see pages 30 and 114; for this reason, the sequence of cards known as the major arcana is often referred to as "The Fool's Journey"). The cards feature angels, the four virtues, the Devil, and a male and female Pope, along with other characters we would associate more with fairytales than a satanic manifesto: the wise woman, the mother, the father, the innocent youth, the old man, lovers, kings, queens, knights, and a magician. Yet knowledge of the tarot may have preceded even the Duke, as in 1377 a German monk, brother Johannes von Rheinfelden, described a series of painted cards that worked as an allegorical journey of life and the soul. It's also believed that gnostic sects may have used the cards to teach illiterate people about dualism, or the interplay of opposites—which we see in many of the card's meanings. In this way, the cards may have been used to express and possibly teach Christian beliefs.

HIDDEN KNOWLEDGE: ASTROLOGY AND KABBALA

The word *occult* may have dark connotations, but it actually means "hidden knowledge." The tarot's reputation as an occult practice crept in during the eighteenth century with the French Freemason Antoine Court de Gébelin's treatise *Monde Primitif* (1781) in which he claimed tarot cards were in effect an ancient Egyptian book of wisdom; he named the tarot *The Book of Thoth*, after the Egyptian god of healing, wisdom, and the occult. De Gébelin's beliefs emerged as a part of the occult revival of the late 1800s when ancient knowledge was popularized by Napoleon's invasion of Egypt in 1798 and tomb artifacts made their way to the West. De Gébelin's work was continued by a Parisian barber, Jean-Baptiste Alliette (know by his pseudonym Etteilla), who developed the tarot's possible links with Kabbalah, the esoteric belief system based in Hebrew tradition. The story continues with the French Rosicrucian Eliphas Levi, who made the connection between the twenty-two cards of the major arcana and the twenty-two letters of the Hebrew alphabet, which correspond to pathways on the Tree of Life.

Levi's research influenced A. E. Waite, the creator of the Rider-Waite cards, who was a leading light of the Hermetic Order of the Golden Dawn, a British occult society founded in 1888 by freemasons William Wynn Westcott, William Robert Woodman, and Samuel Liddell Mathers. The order brought together kabbalistic, astrological, and Egyptian wisdom, creating a theory of tarot associations that have become generally accepted today (see the Appendices for a list of these associations for the major and minor arcanas).

While tarot has collected many occult associations over the years, essentially these magical cards reflect the beliefs of their creators. Tarot's ability to adapt and survive has lead to a plethora of decks from Wiccan tarots to steampunk, angel tarots to vampires, and fairies to da Vinci. While these may be contemporary tastes, tarot ultimately speaks to us through its archetypes, the infinite mirrors of the self.

CHOOSING YOUR CARDS

First of all, there are no rules when it comes to choosing tarot cards. You might use your personal interests to guide you toward a particular tarot. There are endless possibilities—and endless tarot decks to choose from. Go with your gut instinct: You'll know intuitively whether they feel right for you. Your tastes change over time, and so can your tarot cards. Many readers have upward of twenty decks, and, while they may stick with one deck pretty consistently, they're always open to experimenting with new, ingenious, or beautiful decks.

EXPLORING THE DECK: THE MAJOR AND MINOR ARCANA

A standard tarot deck has seventy-eight cards divided into two groups: twenty-two major arcana cards and fifty-six minor arcana cards. The word *arcana* means "secret." The major arcana denote important life events or shifts, while the minor arcana cards reflect day-to-day events. The minor arcana cards can be seen as being more detailed aspects of the major arcana cards.

THE MAJOR ARCANA CARDS

Numbered from 0 (The Fool) to XXI (The World), the twenty-two major arcana cards can be referred to singularly as arcanum and collectively as keys or trumps. Although no one knows the provenance of the tarot's major arcana cards for sure, some suspect the word *trump* derives from triumphs, from the old card game Trionfi, popular initially in Italy and France. In the game, trump cards approximating the major arcana outranked other cards in the deck. For example, the Fool is trumped by the clever Magician, who is trumped by the wisdom of the High Priestess. Well-known librarian Gertrude Moakley also suggested that the major arcana characters and symbols derived from a Milanese carnival based on the Roman festival of Saturnalia: City folk dressed as tarot trumps and processed in chariots throughout the city. As the Duke of Milan is believed to have commissioned some of the first tarot cards in the fifteenth century (the Visconti-Sforza tarots, some of which survive today), the festival explanation may be plausible.

THE FOOL. · THE MAGICIAN. · THE HIGH PRIESTESS.

THE EMPRESS. · THE EMPEROR. · THE HIEROPHANT.

THE LOVERS. · THE CHARIOT. · STRENGTH.

THE HERMIT. · WHEEL *of* FORTUNE. · JUSTICE.

THE HANGED MAN. · DEATH. · TEMPERANCE.

THE DEVIL. · THE TOWER. · THE STAR. · THE MOON. · THE SUN. · JUDGEMENT. · THE WORLD.

The remaining fifty-six cards are known collectively as the minor arcana, and they are arranged into four suits: Wands, Pentacles, Cups, and Swords. Each suit has fourteen cards, from Ace to Ten, plus four court cards: Page, Knight, Queen, and King.

The four suits each have a ruling element, and each corresponds to specific areas of life:

- **Cups:** the element of Water; emotions and relationships

- **Pentacles:** the element of Earth; property, money, and achievement

- **Swords:** the element of Air; the intellect and decisions

- **Wands:** the element of Fire; instinct, travel, and communication

Psychologist Carl Jung famously distilled humankind's mental processes into his theory of four functions, and it sums up the suit meanings neatly:

- **Swords/Air:** I think.

- **Wands/Fire:** I desire.

- **Pentacles/Earth:** I possess.

- **Cups/Water:** I feel.

Another way of remembering the suits' elements is as follows:

- **Swords/Air:** I think—the mind

- **Wands/Fire:** I desire—the soul

- **Pentacles/Earth:** I possess—the body

- **Cups/Water:** I feel—the heart

The court, or people, cards of the minor arcana bring an additional element:

- **Knights:** Fire

- **Queens:** Water

- **Kings:** Air

- **Pages:** Earth

Note that the alignment of Knights with Fire and Kings with Air differs from the traditional link between Knights with Air and Kings with Fire: To me, the Kings, as holders of wisdom and authority, align with the mind-oriented suit of Swords with its element of Air, while Knights, ever-moving, align with the fast energy of Fire and its suit of Wands.

Understanding the basic concepts of the elements offers a meaning for the card. So, the Queen of Wands, combining Water and Fire, suggests emotions and intuition (Water) with communication and energy (Fire).

MAKING FRIENDS WITH YOUR DECK

Studying your cards without the pressure of reading with them immediately helps you become familiar with your deck and form a bond with it. You might also like to choose a card at random each day and intuit its meaning without looking at its standard interpretation right away. A great way to do this is to pick a card each morning and allow the image to impress itself upon your imagination. What does it suggest to you? How does it make you feel? Do you have a sense of its meaning? Write down your insights in a tarot journal. At the end of the day, review your journal, then look up the card's interpretation in the back of the book. You'll find similarities, and you'll understand that you're inherently aware of some essential aspects of that card's traditional meaning. Remember, the meanings given in this book are a guide only. Your personal impressions of a card can be more valid because they are personal to you—which is why it's very helpful to note down your intuitive responses to your new cards.

ACE of CUPS.

PAGE of CUPS.

KNIGHT of CUPS.

QUEEN of CUPS.

KING of CUPS.

ACE of SWORDS.

PAGE of SWORDS.

KNIGHT of SWORDS.

QUEEN of SWORDS.

KING of SWORDS.

ACE of PENTACLES.

PAGE of PENTACLES.

KNIGHT of PENTACLES.

QUEEN of PENTACLES.

KING of PENTACLES.

2

HOW TO BEGIN

Tarot cards, like people, draw in energy. During readings, tarot cards absorb your energies and those of anyone else who touches them. For this reason, it's important not to let other people touch your cards casually; the cards hold your energies and intentions and are personal to you. Here are tried-and-tested ways to attune to your new deck, cleanse the cards before a reading session, and protect them when you are not using them.

ATTUNING TO A NEW DECK

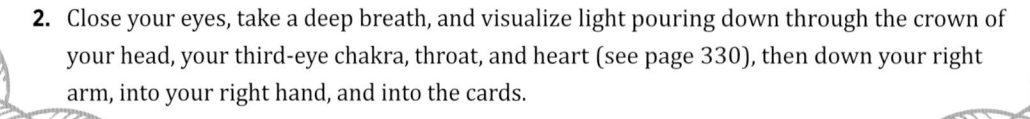

The process of connecting with your cards is called attuning. The more connected you feel to your cards, the more accurate, insightful, and inspiring your readings can be.

Before you begin reading a new deck of tarot cards, attune to them for exactly seven days by sleeping with your cards under your pillow. Also, get to know them by looking at the cards daily, touching them so your energy becomes imprinted upon them. Some readers attune to their cards through visualization. Try this:

1. Hold your cards in your right hand. This is known as the giving hand—and you are about to give the cards your energy.

2. Close your eyes, take a deep breath, and visualize light pouring down through the crown of your head, your third-eye chakra, throat, and heart (see page 330), then down your right arm, into your right hand, and into the cards.

3. Imagine your cards filling with pure light. If you work with spirit guides or angels, ask them to come close and to help and protect you during the reading.

4. Open your eyes when you are ready.

CLEANSING YOUR DECK
BEFORE A READING SESSION

When you take out your cards, clear away any old energy by blowing on and knocking on your cards:

1. Hold the cards in one hand and fan them out.

2. Gently blow on the card edges. You can do this in one breath.

3. Next, put the cards back in a neat pile, still holding them in one hand, and then knock firmly once on the top of the deck. Now the deck is cleansed of old energy and ready to use.

PROTECTING YOUR CARDS
WHEN THEY'RE NOT IN USE

Your cards hold your energy imprint. Like people, cards may pick up extraneous or negative energy from people and spaces, which can affect your readings. So when you are not using your cards, protect them from the environment, both physically and energetically. Keep them wrapped in a cloth of a dark color, such as deep purple cotton or silk, and in a tarot bag or a box. You can also store them with a favorite crystal—such as a clear quartz (known as the master crystal, which keeps energies clear) or amethyst (for healing, insight, and protection)—to keep them energetically cleansed and safe.

CREATING A SPACE FOR READINGS

First, find a peaceful space you feel relaxed and comfortable in. Make sure your space has a flat, clean surface you can lay your cards on. Most readers put down a reading cloth first to protect the cards both physically and energetically from direct contact with the surface you're working on. The reading cloth is usually the silk cloth you wrap your cards in when they're not in use, but any piece of fabric you like will do.

You might like to perform a short ritual before you lay out the cards to honor the ancient practice of tarot-reading that you are about to embark upon. Our thoughts create reality and help manifest a strong connection between our cards, ourselves, the person you are reading for, and if you are aware of them, your spiritual guides who may help you during your reading.

Here's a suggestion to get you started, and you can personalize your own ritual as you read more:

1. Light a candle in your reading space and place it on a safe surface.

2. Close your eyes and take a few calming breaths.

3. Visualize white light flowing from the crown of your head into your cards, as described in the attuning exercise, or simply set the intention to enjoy the best tarot reading you can.

4. When you have finished your reading, affirm in your mind that the reading is over, feel gratitude for the insights your cards and intuition have given you, and put your cards away.

5. Blow out the candle.

> TIP: After cleansing the deck, store your cards with a small clear quartz crystal. This helps keep the cards' energy pure. You'll also need to keep your "tarot" crystal cleansed, too, by running it under water or by blowing, smudging, or using incense (see previous page).

CHOOSING CARDS FOR A READING

1. SHUFFLING THE DECK

After you've cleansed the deck, shuffle the cards for a few moments. Relax and allow your feelings and questions to surface. To choose the cards for a reading, you can use either the fan method or cut the deck. The fan method is best when you want just a few cards for a reading, while cutting the deck suits more elaborate layouts that need lots of cards, such as the Celtic Cross or Tree of Life.

Fan Method
When reading for yourself: Spread all the cards facedown in a fan shape. Choose the cards one by one with just your left hand (known as the hand of fate), from anywhere in the fan, and place them in front of you, still facedown, following the spread layout you have chosen.

When reading for another person: Have the person shuffle the deck. Take the deck from the recipient and fan out the cards for him or her. Ask the recipient to choose the cards from the fan with his or her left hand and pass them to you so you can lay them out, keeping the cards facedown.

Cutting the Deck
When reading for yourself: Cut the deck twice with your left hand so you have three piles facedown on the table. Choose one pile to become the top of the deck and gather up the other two piles underneath it. Lay out the cards according to the spread you have chosen (see pages 20–28) by dealing the cards from the top of the deck and placing them facedown in front of you.

When reading for another person: Ask the recipient to shuffle the cards. Have the recipient split the deck into three piles using his or her left hand and then choose one pile. Gather up the remaining two piles for the person and place their chosen pile on top. Then you lay out the cards.

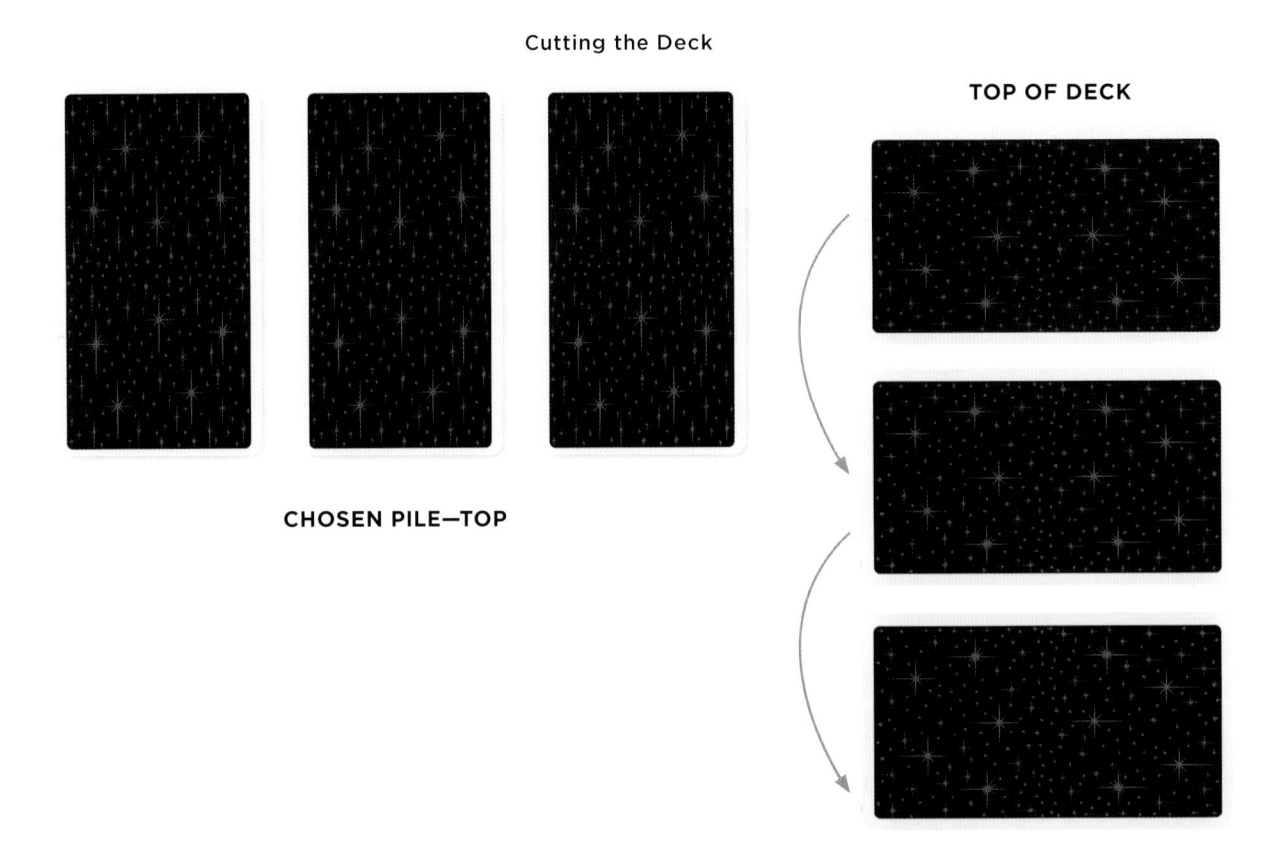

Cutting the Deck

CHOSEN PILE—TOP

TOP OF DECK

When turning over the cards, always flip them sideways—from left to right—not from top to bottom or vice versa, or you may be turning the card upside down. Doing so can give it a different meaning (see What About Reversals on page 19).

USING THE CARD INTERPRETATIONS

As you will see throughout this book, the cards—particularly the major arcana cards—have lots of symbols and possible meanings. Consider the cards before you look up their meaning; think about what aspect of a card you are drawn to first. This is your internal guidance directing you to the most relevant meaning of the card for your reading. This also means that the cards can offer a varying significance each time you look at them. Similarly, when you read for other people, you will find that you don't give a card the same interpretation for every person who gets that card in a reading—you are personalizing the reading according to your intuition.

Sometimes you'll begin a reading and can't make sense of what the cards are telling you. If this happens, here's what to do:

- Shuffle and lay out the cards again. If the same or similar cards come up this time, go with the reading. Relax and tune in to the card images; don't worry about reading the traditional interpretations. Say what comes into your head straight away, and the words will flow.

- Did the Ten of Wands come up? If so, this often means there's too much going on just now and it's not the right time to read your cards. Wait a day or two and try again.

- If you're reading for someone else, feeling blocked can indicate the recipient's state of mind. Here's an example: During a recent beginners' workshop, one of my students said, "My mind is blank. I've laid out the cards for Rosa, but I just don't know what's going on here—can you help me?" Before I could respond, Rosa said, "But that's just how I feel—totally confused. I can't think." If this happens to you, acknowledge the recipient's feelings and begin the reading again, asking him or her to let go of expectations.

> **TIP:** If any cards are dropped during shuffling, look at them: This often gives an indication of the theme of the reading to come. If lots of cards are dropped during shuffling, there's a lot going on! And if you're reading for another person and they drop the cards while shuffling the deck, make a mental note of the dropped cards, if possible, then return them to the inquirer so they can shuffle them back into the deck.

SIX EASY WAYS TO BEGIN YOUR TAROT READING

These six techniques helped me learn tarot over the years—and I wish I'd known them all when I first began. Tarot is a journey, and you learn as you go. Try starting with just one or two of the following tips and see which ones fire your intuition.

1. GET INTUITIVE: WORK WITH IMAGES FIRST

You will be guided to notice certain symbols on the cards. Each card is full of symbols—but you will find that you notice one or two features that really stand out in each picture. These are what I call your intuition hooks. Once you hone in on these, go deeper and connect with how they make you feel. Don't worry about the written card meanings in this book just yet. Say whatever comes to your mind straight away—before you begin to think what the symbols mean—and imagine yourself telling a story.

To develop the reading, trying looking at the quick-reference meanings only (see pages 29, 118, and 119) and then go back to the card images. Staying with the image as long as you can stimulates your intuition, which is essential to a reading, whereas reading the words engages your logical left brain, which often becomes the judge, questioning if you've got it "right."

There's no right or wrong—just your interpretation. You can read the detailed card meanings when you're not giving a reading to develop knowledge. But to begin with, look at the pictures first; this technique can help you read any deck of cards, not just Rider-Waite tarot.

2. USE JUST THE MAJOR ARCANA FIRST

Start with the major arcana cards and progress to the full seventy-eight-card deck when you're more confident. The major arcana are the prime energies, whereas the minors are more incidental influences. As many minor cards are dilutions of the majors, you won't be missing out on any vital information by beginning with majors-only readings. The majors will give you or the person you are reading for the essential messages.

3. IGNORE REVERSED CARD MEANINGS

As you're learning, work with the upright card meanings; if you get reversed cards, turn them the right way up and focus on your responses to the card in this position. Some tarot readers use reversals religiously, while others do not—no matter how great their experience and knowledge. It's a matter of preference; go with what feels right for you.

4. READ THE SUIT CARDS BY THEIR ELEMENT

Try this minor arcana shortcut: Learn just the meaning of the element of each of the four suits. For example, Pentacles, the Earth element, tells you that security (home and finances, structure and planning) is the focus. Wands, for Fire, reveals talking, creating, and action. Cup cards, of the element Water, ask us to tend to our emotions and relationships. Swords, of the element Air, ask for mental clarity and the need for resolution and decisions.

5. READ THE SUIT CARDS BY THEIR NUMBERS

In numerology, the ancient art of mystical number interpretation, numbers have the following meanings, which correspond to the suit cards:

- **Ones (Aces):** Beginnings; new energy
- **Twos:** Partnerships, balance, and division
- **Threes:** Acknowledgment and activity
- **Fours:** Stability and boundaries
- **Fives:** Instability and challenges
- **Sixes:** Harmony and improvement
- **Sevens:** Potential and ambitions
- **Eights:** Rewards and progress, gateways
- **Nines:** Intensity
- **Tens:** Culmination; endings, but also beginnings; and completion

The numbers are modified by the element of the suit—so the Three of Swords, in the sharp suit of Swords, means sorrow or betrayal (three Swords compete against one another), while the Three of Cups, in the loving suit of Cups, means celebration (three people make a happy crowd). Try putting together the suit element and the number and devise your own interpretations.

6. READ ANY CARD BY ITS COLORS

You may be drawn to one or more colors on a card when you are interpreting it. Here's a general guide to color meanings:

- **Yellow, for vitality:** Conscious action, enlightenment, ideals, virtue, happiness, good health, self-expression

- **White, for purity:** Innocence, openness, divinity

- **Orange, for warmth:** Communication, flow, creativity, impulse, self-control

- **Red, for fire:** Drive, energy, passion, practical and material concerns

- **Blue, for truth:** Truth, clarity, integrity, spirituality, balance; "true blue"

- **Purple, for intuition:** Intuition, mysticism, spirituality, other realities, problem solving, royalty, leadership

- **Green, for nature:** Growth, healing, nature, abundance, new life

- **Gray, for decisions:** Stress, doubt, procrastination, unknown outcomes; the need for refuge and protection; can also reveal neutrality

- **Brown, for the earth:** Security, fecundity, necessity and basic needs; can also show stubbornness; "stuck in the mud"

- **Black, for the shadow:** Intensity, disruption, protection, oppression; the dark side of life; that which is hidden or unknown

WHAT ABOUT REVERSALS?

You will see that all the card interpretations in this book contain both upright and reversed card meanings. An upright card is just that—when you turn it over, it is upright. A card is known as reversed when it is upside down.

There are lots of books dealing solely with reversed meanings. With a few exceptions, a reversed card's meaning is generally more negative than the positive, or upright, meaning. However, many tarot professionals ignore reversals in a reading and just turn the cards the right way up if they come out reversed; they use their intuition to interpret the card in a positive or negative light. Do whatever feels right for you.

3

CARD LAYOUTS

THE SPREADS IN THIS SECTION HAVE BEEN USED BY MANY READERS OVER THE YEARS, and they form the blueprint for lots of other layouts. You will find, over time, that you use two or three spreads regularly. Try them all and see which you prefer. Master them and you'll find yourself naturally progressing to the spreads in the remaining chapters, and you'll feel confident enough to try more complex or focused layouts.

THE ONE-CARD DAILY READING

Giving yourself a daily one-card reading is a great way to get to know your tarot. Shuffle the deck, cut it or fan out the cards (see page 16), and choose one card with your left hand. Now contemplate your question. It's best to avoid "closed" questions that demand a yes or no answer. You'll find it more helpful to phrase your question as follows:

- What do I need to know about this (name it) situation?

- What's going on with this (name them) person?

- What's my potential for success with (name the endeavor, such as a relationship, a new job, or a new hobby)?

- What might happen with (name the event or issue, such as a vacation, a relationship, or finances)?

Work with the card's image for an interpretation or turn to the card interpretations starting on page 29. Display the card where you can see it during the day or carry it with you. You can also choose the crystal associated with that card (see the list in the Appendices, pages 329–331).

PAST, PRESENT, FUTURE

This easy spread is perfect for mini-readings. Shuffle the deck, fan the cards or cut the deck, and then lay three cards as shown:

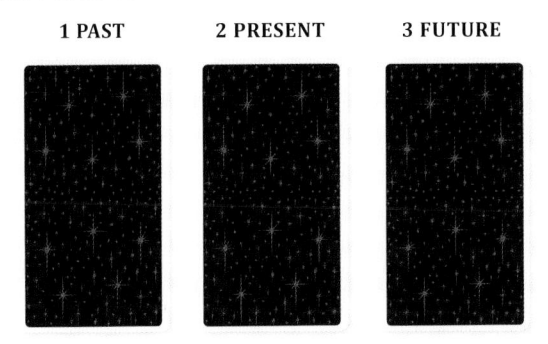

1 PAST **2 PRESENT** **3 FUTURE**

For more insight, you can lay an extra card for each position:

1 PAST **2 PRESENT** **3 FUTURE**

4 **5** **6**

You can also create your own three-card reading to look at different life aspects—for example, Mind, Body, Spirit; or Love, Money, Home. You can also lay a card known as a Significator (this comes up in the Week Ahead and Year Ahead spreads, too—see pages 27 and 28). A Significator is a card that first sums up the theme of a reading that you then lay down. For example:

1 SIGNIFICATOR

2 LOVE **3 MONEY** **4 HOME**

If you'd like to lay cards on one theme, such as love, you can choose a Significator from the deck, rather than laying it out randomly as the first card that comes up after shuffling. For example, for a love reading, you might take out the Lovers card and then shuffle the deck and lay down three cards around it as follows:

THE LOVERS

1. PAST INFLUENCES   **2. PRESENT SITUATION**   **3. OUTCOME**

For a legal question, choose Justice as your Significator; for questions about education, choose the Hierophant; for psychic development, the High Priestess; for family and fertility, choose the Empress; and so on.

THREE CARDS: WHAT SHALL I DO?

"What Shall I Do?" is a great three-carder for your repertoire. Here's how to do it:

1 What to say no to
2 The situation
3 What to say yes to

ASK THREE TIMES: YES OR NO?

When you have a question and you need a fast answer, try this three-card oracle:

1. Shuffle the cards and then spread them facedown in a fan shape.

2. Ask your question aloud or in your mind. With your left hand, choose one card and place it to the left.

3. Ask the question again and choose a second card. Place it in the center, as shown.

4. Now ask your question a final time and choose a third card, placing it to the right.

Turn over the cards and look at the list below to determine if they are yes, no, or neutral cards. If you get three yeses, your answer is certain; two yes cards (with one no or neutral) mean a positive outcome is most likely, but it may take time to come about; and all no or a mix of no/neutral cards means the answer to your question is, of course, negative.

If you are reading reversals: Reversed cards mean no. If you're not using reversals, turn any reversed cards the right way up and read the list below to find out if your question is a yes or no answer.

YES CARDS

All cards apart from those listed here as no, neutral, or exceptions

NO CARDS

- **Swords:** Three, Five, Six, Seven, Eight, Nine, Ten, and Knight

- **Cups:** Five, Seven, and Eight

- **Pentacles:** Five

- **Death**

- **The Devil**

- **The Tower**

- **The Moon**

NEUTRAL CARDS

- **Swords:** Four

- **Cups:** Four

- **The Hermit**

- **The Hanged Man**

EXCEPTIONS

- **Two of Swords or Ten of Wands:** The answer is not yet known.

- **Five and Seven of Wands:** The answer is yes, but you must fight for your prize.

THE TREE OF LIFE

This layout reflects the pattern of the ten sephirots, or spheres, of the Tree of Life, the central motif of Kabbala (see page 328). The sephirots express the story of creation: The divine will flowed from the source, creating the top three sephirots, which overflowed and created more sephirots beneath. The sephirots are containers of the divine will of creation and the pathways on the Tree of Life a representation of the downward flow of the divine will from the top sephirot, Kether, to the lowest, Malkuth. The interpretation of each sphere, or card position, has been adapted to give a clearer path for using the tarot for divination, but also included are the traditional sphere meanings if you'd like to use this layout to look purely at your spiritual development.

1 Your situation
2 Responsibilities
3 Limitations and the past
4 What supports you
5 What opposes you
6 Achievements
7 Attraction and relationships
8 Work, health, and communication
9 What is hidden
10 The future environment; the outcome

FOR SPIRITUAL INSIGHT

1 **Kether:** Unity; spiritual growth
2 **Chockmah:** Wisdom; the male principle
3 **Binah:** Understanding; the female principle
4 **Chesed:** Love; universal love, peace, and the law
5 **Geburah:** Power and destruction; judgement and negative aspects
6 **Tiphareth:** Beauty; the child, rebirth, and progress
7 **Netzach:** Endurance; relationships and instinct
8 **Hod:** The mind; communication, creativity, and intelligence
9 **Yesod:** The unconscious mind; dreams, mysteries, and intuition
10 **Malkuth:** The kingdom; the environment

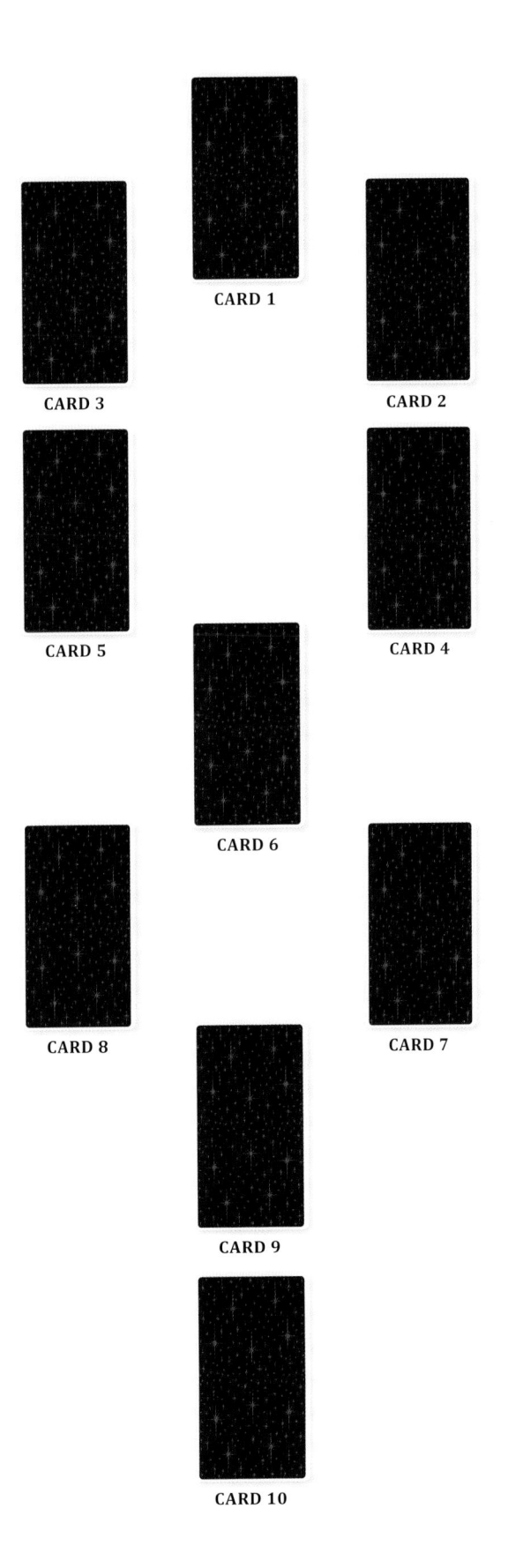

CARD 1

CARD 3

CARD 2

CARD 5

CARD 4

CARD 6

CARD 8

CARD 7

CARD 9

CARD 10

THE CELTIC CROSS

The Celtic Cross is one of the most popular tarot spreads in use today because it answers a question or, if you don't have an immediate question, gives an overview of your life just now. Set your intention before you begin, asking your question or for an overview as your shuffle.

Shuffle and choose the cards and then lay them out as shown below.

Many readers lay out the Celtic Cross, then add cards around card 10 for more insight into the future. You can also choose any card from the layout and begin a Past, Present, and Future layout, using the card from the Celtic Cross in the card 2/Present position of that layout (see page 21) and adding two new cards surrounding it, with the next new card in the past position and the final new card in the future position.

Tip: If the tenth card is a court card—a Page, Knight, Queen, or King—then the outcome of the question is up to you or the person you are reading for.

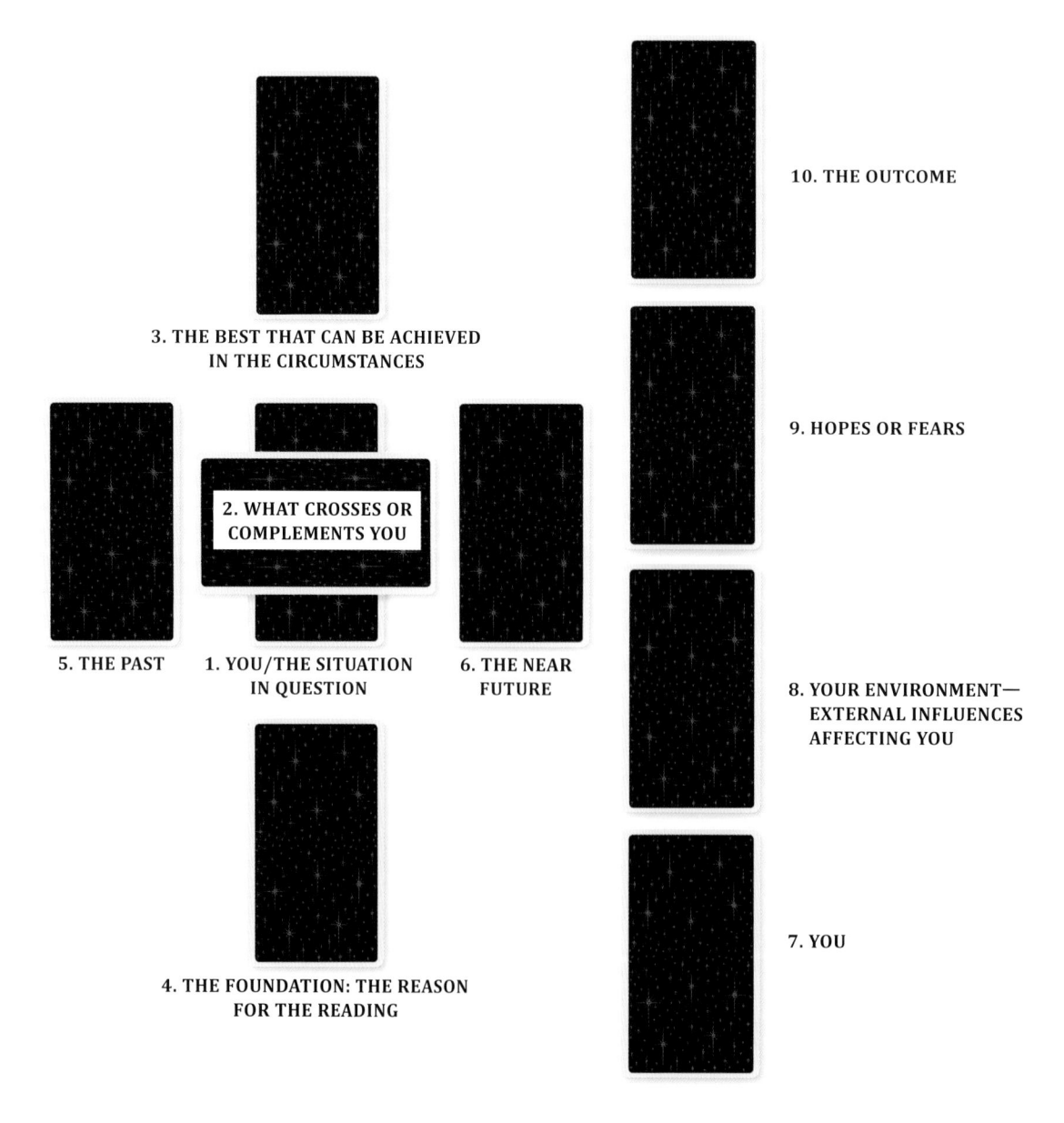

3. THE BEST THAT CAN BE ACHIEVED IN THE CIRCUMSTANCES

10. THE OUTCOME

2. WHAT CROSSES OR COMPLEMENTS YOU

9. HOPES OR FEARS

5. THE PAST

1. YOU/THE SITUATION IN QUESTION

6. THE NEAR FUTURE

8. YOUR ENVIRONMENT— EXTERNAL INFLUENCES AFFECTING YOU

4. THE FOUNDATION: THE REASON FOR THE READING

7. YOU

FINDING THE QUINTESSENCE

When you've finished a reading using any layout, here's a way to glean further insight: Add up the major arcana cards by number and then reduce it to a single digit. For example, if you had three cards—II, The High Priestess; XXI, The World; and XIV, Temperance—this gives 2 + 21 + 14 = 37. Reduce this number further by adding its two digits together: 3 + 7 = 10, or X, The Wheel of Fortune. The meaning of this card—a change for the better (see page 70)—offers an additional dimension.

THE WEEK AHEAD

For a look at your week ahead, shuffle and lay down one card for each day, as shown. Note that the cards do not flow chronologically—card 1, for example, is Monday while card 2 represents Wednesday. This is because the sequence is based on the order of the seven classical planets according to their speed of orbit (see the Spread of the Seven Planets, page 271).

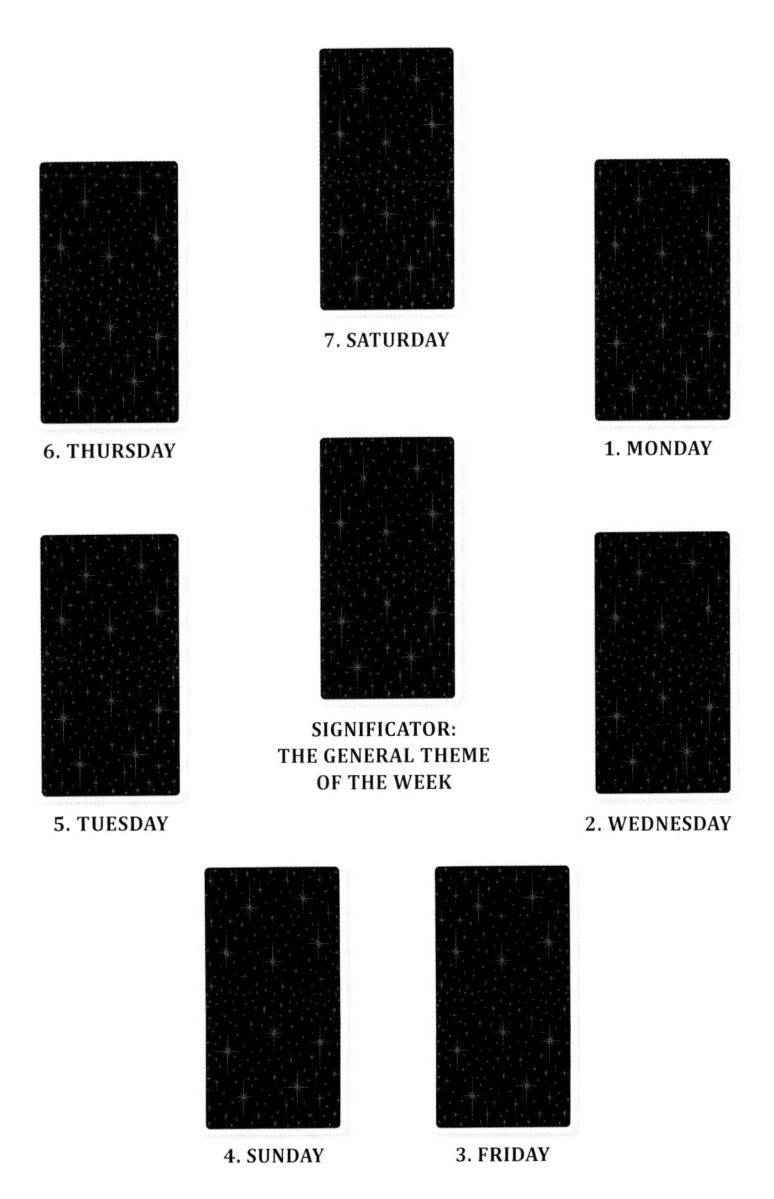

7. SATURDAY

6. THURSDAY

1. MONDAY

SIGNIFICATOR:
THE GENERAL THEME
OF THE WEEK

5. TUESDAY

2. WEDNESDAY

4. SUNDAY

3. FRIDAY

THE MONTH AHEAD

Here's how to see the influences over the next four weeks by laying two cards per week, side by side, as follows.

WEEK ONE

1   5

WEEK TWO

2   6

WEEK THREE

3   7

WEEK FOUR

4   8

THE YEAR AHEAD

For the Year Ahead, lay down one card for each month in sequence, beginning with the current month, in the position of numbers on a clock face. Again, you'll need a Significator card, so lay this first facedown in the center of the clockface, followed by your month cards—so if it were August, you would begin with an August card, then September, October and so on.

4

CARD INTERPRETATIONS: THE MAJOR ARCANA

QUICK-REFERENCE MEANINGS

0 THE FOOL	Beginnings; risks	**XI JUSTICE**	Decisions; balance, legal affairs
I THE MAGICIAN	Action, ambition, and manifesting	**XII THE HANGED MAN**	Waiting; sacrifice
II THE HIGH PRIESTESS	Secrets, intuition, and learning	**XIII DEATH**	Transformation, change, new beginnings
III THE EMPRESS	Creativity, resources, motherhood	**XIV TEMPERANCE**	Negotiation
IV THE EMPEROR	Order, power, and boundaries	**XV THE DEVIL**	Restriction
		XVI THE TOWER	Breakdown and illumination
V THE HIEROPHANT	Unity, marriage, and education	**XVII THE STAR**	Hope and guidance
VI THE LOVERS	Love; decisions	**XVIII THE MOON**	Crisis of faith; deep emotions
VII THE CHARIOT	Progress; determination	**XIX THE SUN**	Growth and recovery
VIII STRENGTH	Management; endurance	**XX JUDGEMENT**	The past; second chances
IX THE HERMIT	Analysis; solitude	**XXI THE WORLD**	Success and completion
X THE WHEEL OF FORTUNE	Luck; fate		

0 THE FOOL

Alternative Names: The Jester, The Idiot

Number: 0 (can also be considered XXII or unnumbered, depending on the deck)

Numerology Link: None of and all of the other major arcana cards

Astrological Sign or Planet: Uranus

Element: Air

Hebrew Letter: *Aleph*

Symbol: The ox

Meaning: Instinct

Tree of Life Pathway: First, between Kether and Chockmah

Chakra: Crown, for spiritual connection, and base, for survival

Key Meanings: Innocence, risk, and beginnings

UNDERSTANDING THE FOOL

The Fool is the innocent adventurer, about to begin an important journey. With a head full of hope, he is idealistic rather than practical; he is certainly not dressed for travel. The little dog at his heels tries to warn him of impending peril, but the Fool is blissfully ignorant of the risk he takes in stepping off a cliff. He is about to encounter danger, but how else can he make his way in the world?

We all begin life as a zero, a tiny egg of potential. The Fool is the cosmic egg, symbolized by the shape of his number, 0. As he journeys through the major arcana sequence, he is a part of every card, but he also stands outside the sequence without a formal value. An absolute beginner, he is about to explore the world, gain experience, and leave behind his status as a zero, a no-being. He will travel lightly, without the baggage of commitment. The Fool is the dreamer, lead only by his needs and desires.

Usually depicted as a youth, the Fool must grow to become a man in the next card in the tarot sequence: the Magician—an individual who knows life and has identified what he needs to succeed in it. The Fool on his journey will collect, in his bag, the four symbols of the minor arcana suits (the Cup, Sword, Pentacle, and Wand): These items are the essence of his survival—the Cup to drink from; the Sword to defend himself; the Pentacle, a coin, for victuals; and the Wand to connect him with his higher self. At this stage of his journey, he is yet to discover the power and meaning of these objects; when he fully understands their purpose, he may progress to the next stage of life, ready to morph into card I, the Magician. Even though his number is zero, his preceding card is the World, card XXI. Some tarotists even assign him number XXII/0, to show that the Fool is both the end and the beginning of the card sequence.

THE FOOL'S ASTROLOGY

The Fool's element is Air, which is fitting, given he is about to step off a precipice into the ether and on his travels will go wherever the wind blows. While the Fool is not linked with a zodiac sign, he does have a planet, Uranus, which symbolizes independence and a free spirit.

THE FOOL AND KABBALA

The Fool's letter is *Aleph*, the first letter of the Hebrew alphabet. It has no sound—it is the breath, the chi, the life force of the universe. Life begins with a breath, as the Fool is the beginner in life. *Aleph* commonly means ox, for endurance, and also instinct, which drives the Fool on his journey.

On the Tree of Life, he is placed on the first pathway between the spheres of Kether and Chockmah—denoting his journey from creation to wisdom.

UPRIGHT MEANING

The upright fool signifies calculated risk. It's never too late to begin anew and follow your heart's desire. The journey ahead is not without danger, but it is time to take a leap of faith. This card augers well for those embarking on new enterprises and educational courses, provided sensible planning is in place; this is a time for optimism and a fresh perspective.

The Fool brings an opportunity to start over and feel young again or excited at the prospect of a new way of living; the Fool is an embodiment of your spirit, whether male or female, ready to explore and discover. Whatever you start now will go well, provided you do look before you leap—but once the decision is made, it's time to push forward and not look back; have courage, commit to your path, and be fully in the moment. The Fool's appearance in a reading can bring a sigh of relief, in that there is now a way ahead. Welcome in the new and travel lightly.

Here are some insights the Fool can offer in particular areas of life:

- **Home:** The Fool can show a young person leaving home for the first time. Also, surprise visitors could call. You may also have younger guests in your home.

- **Relationships:** A new relationship—go with the flow at this point.

- **Career and money:** You may have sabbatical or a new opportunity in your current job or a new career or enterprise. Prioritizing your workload is also the key to moving ahead swiftly.

REVERSED MEANING

Is what you're proposing—or a situation offered to you—a leap too far? The Fool reversed brings out his irresponsible side, as his mouth works ahead of his brain. Without thinking through the downsides, the Fool makes decisions that are not wise. The reversed Fool leaps without awareness and so becomes the literal idiot, sabotaging his chances due to desperation and irrationality. Think carefully before agreeing a new approach to work and hold back from emotional commitments until you are sure of your ground.

HIS WISDOM MESSAGE

Leap, but look first.

THE FOOL'S SYMBOLS

In the Rider-Waite tarot, the Fool appears with these magical symbols. Some of them reappear in other major arcana cards, so learn to recognize them and you'll soon find you can apply your knowledge throughout the deck.

- *The dog* represents instinct and self-preservation. The animal tries to warn the Fool that he is about to walk off a cliff, but the Fool is oblivious to his warning.

  See this symbol on card XVIII, The Moon.

- *The white rose or butterfly:* The white rose stands for purity and innocence. Some cards show the Fool with a butterfly, a symbol of dreams and spirit.

  See the white rose symbol on card XIII, Death.

- *The bundle:* The Fool carries little in his bundle—just his essentials and four talismans, the symbols of the minor arcana.

- *The white sun:* This is a symbol of consciousness, of the workings of the mind that are directly expressed. As the sun rises, it illuminates the Fool's world, showing it all in the best possible light. The sun is white, which links with the Fool's chakra of the crown and his purity of spirit.

  See the golden sun on card VI, The Lovers; XIV, Temperance; XIII, Death; XVIII, The Moon; and XIX, The Sun.

- *The red feather:* The red feather in the Fool's cap denotes his life force.

  See this symbol on card XIX, The Sun, and XIII, Death.

THE HISTORICAL FOOL: IDIOT AND JOKER

In the earliest tarots, the Visconti-Sforza, the Fool looks very different from the jester-boy we see on twentieth-century decks. With feathers in his hair and his breeches down to his knees, the historical Fool is a figure of ridicule—the village idiot, without dignity—yet the overarching theme of the Fool of Renaissance Europe was as a signifier of Lent. The seven chicken feathers in his hair and his traveler's bundle represent a poor man. He is not a court jester but rather a symbol of poverty, a temporary reminder that worldly goods are not everything; what is in our hearts is more important.

The Fool archetype was part of the Roman festival of Saturnalia (see page 11) in which the major arcana characters paraded in chariots while the Fool ran around to tease and torment them. This is another reason why he is unnumbered—he had no official place in the procession. The Fool survives today as the Joker in the standard fifty-two pack of playing cards.

THE FOOL'S REFLECTIONS

The beginner aspect of the Fool is held in the minor arcana's four Aces: the Ace of Cups (new love), the Ace of Pentacles (new money), the Ace of Wands (new initiatives), and the Ace of Swords (new success); see pages 120, 148, 204, and 176. He is also reflected in the Three of Wands, for travel, and the Eight of Wands, for movement, messages, and activity.

TRY A READING WITH THE FOOL

Take the Fool from your deck and set him before you. Now shuffle the remaining cards and cut the deck or fan the cards out facedown. Choose five cards with your left hand and lay them out, as shown. You could ask, "What do I need to do to follow my path in life?" or "Is this risk worth taking?"

- **Card 1:** You and your situation

- **Card 2:** The risks

- **Card 3:** The potential rewards

- **Card 4:** What you can gain

- **Card 5:** Advice and likely outcome

CARD 2   CARD 3

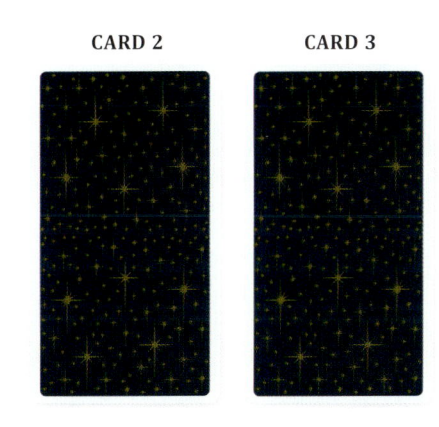

CARD 5

CARD 1   CARD 4

I THE MAGICIAN

THE MAGICIAN.

© 1990 U.S. Games Systems, Inc.

Alternative Names: The Magus, The Juggler, The Mountebank

Number: I

Numerology Links: X, The Wheel of Fortune, and XIX, The Sun

Astrological Sign or Planet: Mercury

Element: Air; also ether, the quintessence

Hebrew Letter: *Beth* (*Beit*)

Symbol: House

Meaning: Creativity

Tree of Life Pathway: Second, between Kether and Binah

Chakra: The palm chakras, for manifesting

Key Meanings: Action, creativity, and success

UNDERSTANDING THE MAGICIAN

Here we have a Magician in action, complete with magic wand and the implements of his trade on the table before him: the suit symbols of the Pentacle or coin, Cup, Sword, and Wand, representing the four elements of earth, water, air, and fire, respectively. With these base materials, he sets an intention to transmute them to create the fifth element of ether, or the quintessence—the mythological "breath of the gods." The Magician, who once journeyed as the Fool, is now ready to manifest his desires by aligning spirit and matter. As the conduit between earth and heaven, the Magician stands for decisions and creativity. The roses and lilies growing above and below him tell us that life can be beautiful when we commit to our passions.

In the major arcana sequence, the Magician comes after 0, The Fool, although the Magician can also be seen as the first card of the cycle, as some tarotists place the Fool after the World card as XXII. The Magician is the natural successor to the Fool as we move from 0, the cosmic egg, to I, the individual: The Fool's bundle contains the Magician's four symbols, ready to be activated. After the singular purpose of the Magician we meet II, The High Priestess, who introduces us to the duality of life—the now and the hereafter.

The Magician's number, I, is the first prime number, which stands for primal energy, the individual, and oneness with the divine spirit or God. The card is related to X, The Wheel of Fortune (10 reduces to 1), and XIX, or 19, The Sun, which reduces to 10 then 1, the Magician's number. Both these cards link with an awareness of realms beyond the earthly plane.

THE MAGICIAN'S ASTROLOGY

The Magician's ruling planet is Mercury, also the Roman god of magic—and the Greek Hermes, god of communication, linked with the Egyptian god Thoth. In alchemy, mercury's form as quicksilver was associated with transformation or the fifth element of ether. The element could also be signified by the symbol of a snake, shown on the Magician's serpent-girdle (see The Magician's Symbols).

THE MAGICIAN AND KABBALA

The Hebrew letter of the Magician is *Beth*, symbolized by a house, meaning creativity. On the Tree of Life pathway, the Magician is placed on the second pathway between the spheres of Kether and Binah. Kether stands for unity, echoing the card's number, I, while Binah is the sphere of experience—indicating practical magic and singular direction.

UPRIGHT MEANING

It's time for action—for communicating and expressing your ideas and desires. This is the card of the inventor, the traveler, the self-employed, and the entrepreneur, as it beckons you to broaden your horizons. You will have the drive to spur your plans forward, and, perhaps, to take new, creative approaches: to think laterally, ask questions, trust your internal guidance, and let go of procrastination.

Blessed with a magic wand, you have the ability to transform whatever you choose, and in this way, the Magician is a very positive card in a reading. He directs you to make the most of your skills and talents and step into your power; focus on your projects and capitalize on your personal strengths. Spiritually, the Magician shows you connecting with your higher, or true, self and acting with pure intention.

This card can also show a significant journey. Here are some other possibilities:

- **Home:** A house sale is completed, or you decide it is time to move forward with remodeling plans. This is a sociable time, with lots of visitors and entertaining.

- **Relationships:** If you are single and want love, it is coming. If you are in a relationship, the Magician shows love in action, so you will begin to see commitment. Communication between you is excellent and you reach an even deeper understanding of each other's needs. The card can also show you acting as one, so a joint project may be on the horizon, too.

- **Career and money:** There will be a new beginning, either finding new employment or a new direction in your existing work. This card can also show inspired leadership from a grounded and enthusiastic individual.

REVERSED MEANING

When the good Magician is reversed, he turns trickster, so this card can show you being mislead by a charming manipulator. What you see is not what you get, and it's all show, not truth. In your projects, the Magician reversed can show a creative block as you feel torn between two paths or choices that get in the way of progress. It's time to choose one option and commit to it fully. The reversed card can also reveal delays to travel plans and miscommunication in general.

HIS WISDOM MESSAGE

Manifest your desires.

THE MAGICIAN'S SYMBOLS

In the Rider-Waite tarot, the Magician appears with the following magical symbols. Some of them reappear in other major arcana cards, so learn to recognize them and you'll soon find you can apply your knowledge throughout the deck.

- *The lemniscate or infinity symbol:* balance, activity, and renewal

    See this symbol on card VIII, Strength.

- *The magic wand:* The wand is double-ended and reflects the Hermetic concept "As above, so below," or heaven and earth as mirrors. The wand's symbolism reflects that of the Magician's pose (see below).

    See this symbol on cards VII, The Chariot, and XXI, The World.

- *The four suit symbols:* These are the Magician's resources. He draws upon the four elements of the suits to create the quintessence, the fifth element.

- *The red cloak:* energy and action; practicality; and being grounded in the material world

    See this symbol on IV, The Emperor; V, the Hierophant; and XI, Justice.

- *The headband:* the mind and the intention to manifest desires

- *The Magician and his pose:* The Magician is the conduit of energy between earth, which he draws from with his downward left hand, and heaven, symbolized by his raised hand and wand.

- *The serpent-girdle:* The belt around the Magician's waist is a serpent, a symbol of the element of Mercury, the Magician's ruling planet (see The Magician's Astrology). To function as a belt, the serpent or snake must hold its tail in its mouth. This is the alchemical symbol of the ouroboros, which like the lemniscate stands for infinity and constant renewal—just as the snake continually sheds its skin.

THE HISTORICAL MAGICIAN: MAN AND GOD

Historically, the Magician has had many guises. In the fifteenth-century Visconti-Sforza tarots, he was a wealthy merchant seated at a table. By the nineteenth century, the Dotti tarot of Milan assigned him as a cobbler—*Il Bagatto.* By the twentieth century, he had transformed into a magus, then a god.

Most early tarots show the Magician seated at a table, while a standing pose appears to have been generally accepted by the sixteenth and seventeenth centuries, as seen in Marseilles-style tarots. But in our Rider-Waite deck, the standing Magician takes on a spiritual dimension, pointing to heaven and earth. Aleister Crowley takes the Magician a step further in his Thoth deck, showing his Magus card as the winged messenger-god Hermes, or Mercury, also the ruling planet of the card. Hermes as a god represented wisdom and was believed to be the architect of the pyramids and the creator of mathematics, astrology, and other arts. The Magician today embodies this spirit of invention, enterprise, and expression.

- *The roses and lilies:* The red roses symbolize love and the lilies, truth of purpose. The Magician acts with pure intention.

    See red roses on the gown in card III, The Empress, and on the gown of the supplicant on the left on card V, The Hierophant; roses are also around the waist of the maiden on VIII, Strength.

- *Yellow background:* consciousness, clear sight and support

    See this on III, The Empress; VII, The Chariot; VIII, Strength; and XI, Justice.

THE MAGICIAN'S REFLECTIONS

Because the Magician has all four suits represented on his table—Cup, Pentacle, Sword, and Wand—he can be seen as the ruler of the entire minor arcana. His appearance in a reading can ask you to pay particular attention to the minors—note which suits or elements they represent, as this will give you an instant over-view of which life area is important now.

TRY A READING WITH THE MAGICIAN: THE MAGIC WAND

Take the Magician from your deck and lay him before you, as shown. Now shuffle the remaining cards and cut the deck or fan out the cards facedown. Choose four cards with your left hand and place them around the Magician in the positions below. You could ask, "What can I manifest?" or "What do I need to do to make my idea work?"

- **Card 1:** Your situation

- **Card 2:** Emotional strengths

- **Card 3:** Practical skills and resources

- **Card 4:** The outcome

CARD 4

CARD 3

CARD 2

CARD 1

THE MAGICIAN.

II THE HIGH PRIESTESS

THE HIGH PRIESTESS.

Alternative Name: The Papess

Number: II

Numerology Links: XI, Justice, and XX, Judgement

Astrological Sign or Planet: The Moon

Element: Water

Hebrew Letter: *Gimel*

Symbol: Camel

Meaning: Wisdom

Tree of Life Pathway: Third, between Kether and Tiphareth

Chakra: Fifth eye, also known as the angelic or soma chakra, for psychic activation

Key Meanings: Secrets, wisdom, and the spiritual world

UNDERSTANDING THE HIGH PRIESTESS

The High Priestess stands in an enclosed chamber or temple between two great pillars labeled *B* and *J*. Behind her is a veil decorated with pomegranates and date fruit; she wears a horned moon headdress like the Egyptian goddess Hathor, and at her feet lies a crescent moon. She holds a scroll that is partly hidden, bearing the letters *t*, *o*, *r*, and *a*, indicating the Torah, the Jewish sacred text.

She represents the principle of the divine feminine; historically, she is the female Pope, a virgin priestess, signified by her blue-and-white robes. Today, she might be the psychic, astrologer, or spiritual teacher. Her spiritual path is above material values and earthly relationships. Her gift is wisdom; and knowledge of the world beyond the veil, the realms of gods, guides, and angels.

The number of the High Priestess is II, echoed in the two pillars of the temple of Solomon (see The High Priestess's Symbols). Her counterpart in the major arcana sequence is card V, The Hierophant or High

Priest. Like the High Priestess, he is a mentor, but he works in public office—the High Priestess, however, tends her inner garden of the spirit in secret, walking between the earth plane and the celestial realms beyond, separated by the pomegranate veil. She lives a dual life. She comes after I, The Magician, card of unity and outward expression, and before card III, The Empress. The High Priestess reveals that we need superconsciousness and awareness of the self before we can wholly engage in abundant relationships with others, which are embodied by the mother-goddess Empress.

She is numerologically linked with cards XI, Justice (11; 1 + 1 = 2), and XX, Judgement (2 + 0 = 2). Both these cards illuminate the need for discernment, wisdom, and discretion.

THE HIGH PRIESTESS'S ASTROLOGY

The High Priestess's element is Water, the element of the emotions, and her planet is the moon. The moon relates to intuition, the feminine cycles, and the rhythms of nature. She wears a crown showing the moon's waxing, waning, and full phases (see The High Priestess's Symbols).

THE HIGH PRIESTESS AND KABBALA

The High Priestess's kabbalistic letter is *Gimel*, the third letter of the Hebrew alphabet, which literally means camel, but also suggests wisdom. On the Tree of Life, she is placed on the third pathway, between the spheres of Kether and Tiphareth, or oneness with God and harmony/rebirth—a journey to inner peace.

UPRIGHT MEANING

Hidden knowledge, intuition, psychic experience, and significant dreams are the gifts of the High Priestess. This is a time for incubation and privacy, to go inward, deepening your relationship with your higher self and trusting your internal knowing. In your everyday life, confidentiality is key. If you have a secret, or a project you are nurturing, it is better to keep your own counsel.

On your spiritual path, the High Priestess predicts learning and a mentor. As the card of psychic gifts (along with card X, The Wheel of Fortune), her arrival in your reading can be a sign to follow your intuition and connect with your guides. If the High Priestess shows up in one of your first tarot readings, this is often a sign that tarot is part of your spiritual journey.

Here are some other signs she can reveal:

- **Home:** It's a quiet time. Relations between family members may be calm but a little distant; you may be buried in your separate lives just now.

- **Relationships:** This can mean being single for a time or, if you are in a relationship, you or your partner choosing to keep a part of your life separate, or secret.

- **Career and money:** Success is coming, but contracts and new work are taking time to nurture. You can only be patient.

REVERSED MEANING

When reversed, the High Priestess can show an inappropriate mentor or choosing a temporarily wrong path. You might be listening to bad advice or someone might try to persuade you to go against your intuition. It can also indicate secrets that need to be out in the open; knowledge locked up too long may be potentially harmful.

HER WISDOM MESSAGE

Explore your spiritual side.

THE HIGH PRIESTESS'S SYMBOLS

In the Rider-Waite tarot, the High Priestess appears with these magical symbols. Some of them reappear in other major arcana cards, so learn to recognize them and you'll soon find you can apply your knowledge throughout the deck.

- *The two pillars:* The initials B and J refer to Boaz and Jachin, names on pillars in the Temple of Solomon in the Old Testament, which were decorated with pomegranate designs (see pomegranate below). Boaz represents the elements of Water and Earth, and Jachin, Fire and Air. The pillars are black and white, to show duality—male and female, darkness and light, and the earthly and heavenly dimensions that the High Priestess inhabits. The pillars form a portal to otherworldly experience and a deeper experience of the self.

> See this symbol on cards V, The Hierophant, and XI, Justice, to symbolize balance.

- *The scroll:* The High Priestess holds the Sefer Torah, a hand-written scroll central to the study of Kabbala. It symbolizes the High Priestess's spiritual knowledge.

  > See the book as a symbol on card X, The Wheel of Fortune.

- *The pomegranate:* On the High Priestess's veil, the pomegranate denotes female fertility, linking with her aspect as the Egyptian goddess Hathor (see the moon below). The pomegranate can also be a sym-

bol of the Jewish sacred text—it has been taught that the fruit has 613 seeds, echoing the Torah's 613 biblical commandments.

> See this symbol on card III, The Empress.

- *The veil:* The veil symbolizes the otherworld beyond the material world.

- *The date:* masculinity, complementing the female pomegranate.

- *The moon:* This is a symbol of the subconscious and the emotions that lie beneath the solar or external persona. The moon is shown in three phases as a crown to echo Hathor/Isis, the Egyptian goddess of life and fertility who gave birth to Ra, god of the sun.

  > See this symbol on card XVIII, The Moon.

- *The blue-and-white robes:* White is for purity, relating to the traditional virginity of the nun. Blue is for truth, as in "true blue."

THE HISTORICAL HIGH PRIESTESS: FEMALE POPES

In the Visconti-Sforza tarots (see page 10), the High Priestess bears the likeness of Maria Visconti, a relative of the Duke of Milan, who commissioned some of the earliest tarot cards. Maria was a nun and a member of the Guglielmite sect, which believed that Christ would return to earth in 1300 and a female pope would rule. Maria, also known as Sister Manfreda, was chosen to become the first female pope—hence the card's alternative name, The Papess. Before her ambition could be realized, she was burned at the stake as a heretic in 1300.

The High Priestess as the Papess also links with the legend of St. Joan, chronicled in the thirteenth century by the Dominican monk Stephen of Bourbon. His myth tells of a ninth-century Englishwoman named Joan who eloped with a Benedictine monk. To disguise herself, she dressed as a man and named herself John of England. Her lover died, but she traveled to Rome, became a highly respected educator, and eventually was elected Pope. However, during the coronation procession she collapsed with labor pains, and her true identity as a woman was exposed. How she died varies according to different accounts—from instant demise after the birth, to being stoned to death, to being deposed and punished. Her child survived, and in the legend he was identified as the Bishop of Ostia, one of the diocese of Rome.

In Marseilles-style tarots of the seventeenth and eighteenth centuries, the High Priestess wears a papal crown, but otherwise this learned woman is very much as we see her in the Rider-Waite card, seated and robed, holding a holy book.

THE HIGH PRIESTESS'S REFLECTIONS

- The Queen of Swords, for strength of will and following your path

- The Eight of Pentacles, for study, knowledge, and reward

TRY A READING WITH THE HIGH PRIESTESS: THE ORACLE

Take the High Priestess from your deck and lay her before you on your left-hand side. Now shuffle the remaining cards and cut the deck or fan out the cards facedown. Choose three with your left hand and place them as shown. You could ask, "What do I need to know now?" or "Is this person a positive influence?"

- **Card 1:** The person or situation you are inquiring about

- **Card 2:** What you need to know

- **Card 3:** The outcome

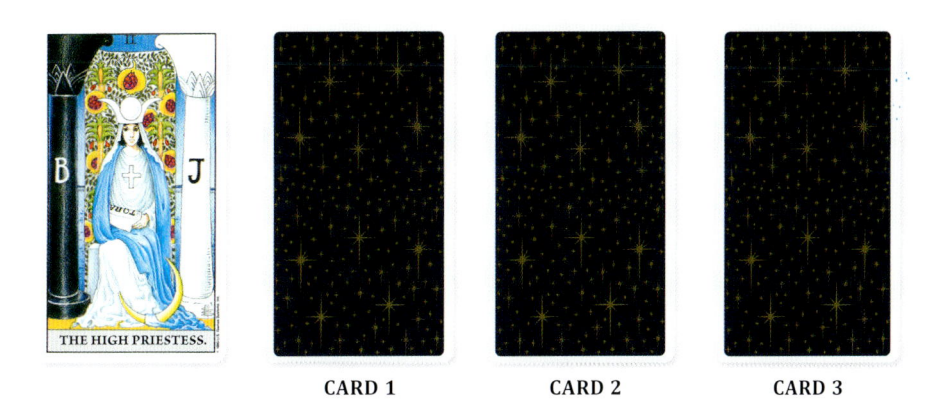

CARD 1 CARD 2 CARD 3

III THE EMPRESS

THE EMPRESS.

Alternative Name: The Mother

Number: III

Numerology Links: XII, The Hanged Man, and XXI, The World

Astrological Sign or Planet: Venus

Element: Earth

Hebrew Letter: *Daleth*

    Symbol: Door

    Meaning: Attainment

Tree of Life Pathway: Fourth, between Binah and Chockmah

Chakras: Heart, for love, and sacral, for fertility

Key Meanings: Abundance, generosity, and creativity

UNDERSTANDING THE EMPRESS

The Empress is the mother archetype, symbol of creativity and abundance. She bears the symbol of Venus on her shield, relating to her planet, Venus, and the Roman goddess of love. In pre-Roman times, Venus was much more than the ruler of relationships: She was the earth mother, nature herself.

She is seated in an earthly paradise, where corn grows at her feet. A river meanders then flows into a waterfall, forming an abundant pool. All the trees are in full leaf. This is summer, a time of harvest and plenty. The Empress leans slightly back, supported by a cushion and bolster, as if she has transplanted herself from indoors to her garden. While living in the material world, she stays connected to her roots and goes with the flow of life. Her pose and lose gown may suggest she is pregnant, and some decks show an obviously pregnant Empress. While the High Priestess is lunar and virginal, incubating herself spiritually to connect with the twilight realms beyond, the Empress manifests her femininity. She is the solar, earthly, and fertile aspect of womanhood, also indicated by the rich yellows, reds, oranges, and green colors of her card.

Her number, III, is dynamic and creative and stands for the triad of mother, father, and child. In early decks such as the Visconti-Sforza tarots, she is shown with a black eagle, matching the insignia of card IV, The Emperor—she is clearly an empress rather than a queen; the four Queens are her aspects (see The Empress's Reflections). As the consort of card IV, The Emperor, the Empress also represents the wife and traditional relationships. She is numerologically connected with XII, The Hanged Man—time suspended, presumably during pregnancy—and XXI, The World, expressing the joy of birth or creation.

THE EMPRESS'S ASTROLOGY

The Empress is linked with Venus, planet of love, and with warmth, relationships, light, and abundance.

THE EMPRESS AND KABBALA

The Empress's Hebrew letter is *Daleth*, or door, and attainment. As a mother, she represents the gateway to new life. This also complements the Hebrew letter of her tarot partner, the Emperor, which is *Hei*, the window: two aspects of the house of the soul.

On the Tree of Life, she is placed on the fourth pathway between the spheres of Binah and Chockmah. Binah is female intelligence, while Chockmah is male wisdom. The seeds of male and female within the Empress conceive new life.

UPRIGHT MEANING

The gifts of the Empress are abundance and material comfort, sensuality and security, and emotional support. This is an auspicious card for children and families, showing harmony at home; if you are hoping to begin a family, the Empress symbolizes fertility and femininity. Your creative projects thrive and you prosper financially now, too. The Empress is resourceful, so when she appears in your reading, you can feel assured that your needs will be met. This card, therefore, shows the influence of a nurturing mother figure who supports you. As the you/your situation card in a reading, it reveals you are a good mother to others—and to yourself.

Here are some additional possibilities:

- **Home:** renovation and extensions, home improvements; considering a move to a larger home; tending a garden

- **Relationships:** Happiness—If single, this indicates a good time to begin a relationship. Harmonious relationships exist within the family.

- **Career and money:** Security; money flows—In work, you are resourceful, able to support others, and come up with inventive ways to manage your projects.

REVERSED MEANING

When reversed, the Empress shows financial issues and domestic strife. This may take the form of a controlling and disruptive influence at home. She can also show a creative block in your projects and someone who is needy and takes too much from you. The result of these challenges and demands is stressful, and there may be an impact on fertility if this is an issue for you now—literally in terms of conceiving a child or figuratively in terms of finding the time and peace of mind to grow an idea.

HER WISDOM MESSAGE

Life is abundant.

THE EMPRESS'S SYMBOLS

In the Rider-Waite tarot, the Empress appears with these magical symbols. Some of them reappear in other major arcana cards, so learn to recognize them and you'll soon find you can apply your knowledge throughout the deck.

- *The starry crown:* The half-crown, or diadem, holds twelve stars, a common emblem on paintings of the Virgin Mary; the Book of Revelation 12:1–2 mentions a woman, interpreted as Mary, as, "Clothed with the sun, and the moon under her feet, and on her head a crown of twelve stars." The twelve stars may signify the twelve tribes of Israel, and some tarotists associate them with the twelve astrological signs. The number twelve signifies unity.

- *The laurel wreath:* The wreath the Empress wears just below her crown shows peace and success.

  See this victory symbol on the Six of Wands, the Two of Cups, the Seven of Cups, and the King of Pentacles.

- *Pomegranates:* The pomegranate design on the Empress's dress denotes fertility, death, and rebirth and relates to the myth of the Greek goddess of the harvest, Demeter. The fate of her daughter, Persephone, was determined by Persephone eating the seeds of the pomegranate in the underworld (see The Historical Empress). Another interpretation is that the symbol on the dress is a rose, for love.

  See this symbol on card II, The High Priestess.

- *The pearl necklace:* The seven pearls, meaning wisdom, also represent the seven major chakras in harmony—base, sacral, solar plexus, heart, throat, third eye, and crown (see pages 329–331). The seven pearls also link with the seven classical planets.

- *The shield with the sign of Venus:* The Venus sign—the circle with the cross beneath—is associated with the goddess Venus, for love, beauty, and creativity. It embodies the sun and the earth.

- *The scepter:* This is an emblem of state. The Empress is ruler of her own land and is secure in her authority. The orb atop it and the Empress's hand position echoes the shape of the sign of Venus. (See Venus above.)

- *The corn:* The ripe corn, ready for harvest, stands for rewards, fertility, and abundance. (See The Historical Empress.)

- *Yellow background:* consciousness, clear sight, and support

  See this on the I, The Magician; VII, The Chariot; VIII, Strength; and XI, Justice.

THE HISTORICAL EMPRESS: ROOTS OF THE GODDESS

The Empress is the great mother goddess at the heart of many ancient beliefs: the Roman Venus and Diana; the Sumerian Innana, Queen of Heaven; the Celtic goddess Brigid; the Egyptian deities Hathor and Isis; the Virgin Mary; the Nordic goddesses Freyja and Frigg; the Greek Aphrodite and Gaia; and the Hindu Parvati.

The ripe corn shown in the foreground of the card also associates the Empress with Demeter, the "grain mother," Greek goddess of the harvest and the cycles of nature. When Demeter's daughter, Persephone, was abducted by Hades, Demeter bargained to get her back by threatening to withhold the grain harvest. It was agreed that Persephone could return to her mother, but only if she had not eaten anything when with Hades. Alas, Persephone had eaten six seeds of the pomegranate (the fruit depicted on the dress of the Empress). And so Persephone was allowed to return to her mother and the earth for six months of the year, through spring and summer, but cursed to spend the other six months of fall and winter in the darkness that was Hades—a metaphor for the rhythms of the seasons that the mother-goddess Empress embodies.

THE EMPRESS'S REFLECTIONS

- The Queen of Cups, for love and nurturing—the heart aspect

- The Queen of Pentacles, for generosity and security—the physical body

- The Queen of Swords, for the intellect—the mind aspect

- The Queen of Wands, for creativity and communication—the soul aspect

- Nine of Pentacles, for money, luxury, and self-authority

TRY A READING WITH THE EMPRESS: GROWING CREATIVITY AND ABUNDANCE

Take the Empress from your deck and lay her before you. Now shuffle all the remaining cards and then cut the deck or fan out the cards facedown. Choose three with your left hand and place them around the Empress as shown. You could ask, "How can I develop my ideas/be more creative?" or "How do I have more abundance in my life?"

- **Card 1:** You/your present situation

- **Card 2:** The source of abundance—where to focus your expectation and attention

- **Card 3:** The outcome

CARD 2

CARD 1

CARD 3

IV THE EMPEROR

THE EMPEROR.

Alternative Name: The Grandfather

Number: IV

Numerology Link: XIII, Death

Astrological Sign or Planet: Aries the Ram

Element: Fire

Hebrew Letter: *Hei* (*Heh*)

> **Symbol:** Window
>
> **Meaning:** Progress

Tree of Life Pathway: Fifth, between Tiphareth and Chockmah

Chakra: Base, for security

Key Meanings: Control, security, order, and ambition

UNDERSTANDING THE EMPEROR

The Emperor is the father archetype, a symbol of male power and virility. His beard shows he is a man of maturity and wisdom, a forerunner of the Hermit, the other bearded man of the tarot, whom the Emperor will become in later years. Yet at this time of his existence, he is still full of vigor and ready to take action to defend his realm, as we see from the battle armor showing beneath his robes of state.

His number is IV, for the four compass points and for stability and order. The Emperor is sure of his position, and he sits squarely in place on his throne of stone, high-backed and secure in a landscape that appears to be little more than barren rock. Yet the mountains, almost equal in height on each side, seem to protect him, and his throne, higher than the peaks of the rocks, suggests he is in control of this strange environment. A tiny river runs behind him, perceptible at the base of the mountains—a sign of the potential for growth and cultivation of the land as he directs. The Emperor is a pioneer and a true Aries, shown by the rams' heads on his throne; his will drives him forward.

And as the Emperor knows the boundaries of his territory, he is realistic about the sphere of his influence. He also maintains and defends his boundaries appropriately, through rational negotiation rather than force.

In the major arcana sequence, the Emperor comes after his consort card III, The Empress, and before card V, The Hierophant. In traditional societies, this sequence reflected power status, from mother under father and priest at the top, being closest to God. The Emperor corresponds in numerology with card XIII, Death, perhaps linking with the Emperor's warrior aspects in that physical death would have been very much part of life as a feudal ruler. The Emperor and Death are the only two major arcana cards that show figures with visible leg armor.

THE EMPEROR'S ASTROLOGY

The Emperor's astrological sign is Aries, the Ram, the first sign of the zodiac (March 21–April 20). He has fire and determination, the qualities of leadership. Aries is ruled by Mars, planet of war, indicated by the Emperor's armor. It is known as the fiery planet, echoed in the color orange in the landscape behind the Emperor's throne and his red robes, which are also a sign of his sovereignty.

THE EMPEROR AND KABBALA

The Emperor's Hebrew letter is *Hei*, which means progress. Another meaning of *Hei* is window, or portal, through which streams the light of consciousness. He is fully aware of who he is and of his place in the world. Placed on the fifth Tree of Life pathway between the spheres of Tiphareth, for beauty and rebirth, and Chockmah, male principle.

UPRIGHT MEANING

In a reading, the Emperor can denote a powerful man, and the traditional male aspects of rulership and ambition. As the consort of card III, The Empress,

he signifies the husband or other intimate partner who is constant and trustworthy. He is in control of his emotions, and comfortable with who he is. Less appealing, depending on your perspective, is his need for conformity. Although he may have ambition, tradition is essential to his happiness.

As a general influence or symbol of the self he brings balance, security, and conventional values. He reveals mastery of life and control over territory, and predicts that problems can be overcome with careful planning and single-mindedness. He shows a return to order, so his arrival in your reading is a welcome sign of improvement in your circumstances. You may be offered protection from someone you trust; you can also trust yourself to make the right decisions.

It's time to live in the here and now and use what practical resources you possess—wisdom, determination, and the skills of others—to realize your next steps. Be the leader.

Here's what he represents in specific areas of your life:

- **Home:** Order and smooth running. However, it is also important to set boundaries and protect what is yours.

- **Relationships:** A new partner, or focusing on practical matters and future planning in established partnerships. Loyalty in love.

- **Career and money:** Finances get organized and you plan how to balance expenditures. You can expect to have fairness at work and to be sure of your goals; you will either enjoy this new structure or feel it stifles your creativity.

REVERSED MEANING

When reversed, the Emperor is power-hungry and excessive in his demands, and represents the negative traits associated with traditional masculinity, such as being domineering, controlling, and even cruel. Greed is another aspect of the Emperor reversed. Whereas the upright Emperor knows his boundaries, the reversed Emperor does not know where to draw the line and may use excessive force or persuasion to get what he wants. This card therefore shows issues with authority figures and other potentially domineering individuals who are run by their egos.

HIS WISDOM MESSAGE

Take control; you are protected.

THE EMPEROR'S SYMBOLS

In the Rider-Waite tarot, the Emperor appears with these magical symbols. Some of them reappear in other major arcana cards, so learn to recognize them and you'll soon find you can apply your knowledge throughout the deck.

- *The rams' heads:* There are four ram's heads on the card, echoing his number IV: two forward-facing on the front of his throne and two in profile on the top corners. They are the symbol of the Emperor's sign, Aries the Ram. In Egyptian mythology, Khnum, an aspect of the sun god, Ra, was depicted with the head of a ram. Khnum was a god of creation, also known as the Divine Potter, who molded children from the clay of the Nile.

- *The golden apple and ankh:* The stylized ankh, the Egyptian symbol for life and reproduction, stands for masculine virility. The Emperor holds the ankh in his right hand—the hand associated with giving.

In his left hand, he shows what he receives: the golden apple, symbol of love and sexuality associated with the Roman goddess Venus. Venus's symbol appears on the Empress, the Emperor's partner. In this way the ankh and apple denote their relationship and the male and female archetypes.

- *Armor:* The armor is a symbol of strength, defense, and action in the world. Battle is a quality of the planet Mars, ruler of the Emperor's sign of Aries.

  See this symbol on card VII, The Chariot.

- *The red cloak:* energy and action; being in the material world

  See this symbol on card I, The Magician; V, The Hierophant; and XI, Justice.

- *The crown:* A power symbol, the Emperor's crown sits on the crown chakra of the head, the connection point with the higher self. It shows autonomy and self-direction. The crown is closed, showing the Emperor's self-containment and self-reliance.

  See variants of the crown on II, The High Priestess; III, The Empress; V, The Hierophant; VII, The Chariot; VIII, Strength; XI, Justice; XVI, The Tower; the Six of Wands; the Ace of Swords; the Four of Pentacles; and the Kings and Queens of the minor arcana suits.

THE HISTORICAL EMPEROR: WENCESLAS AND CHARLEMAGNE

One of The Emperor's historical emblems is the black eagle, which appears on his hat in the Visconti-Sforza tarots (see page 10)—the bird was an insignia of the Visconti family and the Holy Roman Empire, which gave the family official permission to bear it. The historical Emperor may be Wenceslas of Bohemia (1205–1253), who married into the family of Roman Emperor Frederick I; other sources suggest the original Emperor may be Charlemagne, the first Holy Roman Emperor (c. 742–814). The Marseilles tarot (1701–1715) shows the Emperor side-on, just as we would see the profile of kings and other dignitaries on coins and playing cards.

THE EMPEROR'S REFLECTIONS

We can see aspects of the Emperor in these minor arcana cards:

- The Four of Pentacles, for financial stability

- The King of Cups, for love and intuition—the heart aspect

- The King of Pentacles, for generosity and security— the physical body

- The King of Swords, for the intellect—the mind aspect

- The King Wands, for creativity and communication—the soul aspect

TRY A READING WITH THE EMPEROR: KNOWING YOUR BOUNDARIES

Take the Emperor from your deck and lay him before you in the center of the spread, as shown. Now shuffle the remaining cards and cut the deck or fan the cards out facedown. Choose four cards with your left hand and place them around the Emperor, as shown. You could ask, "Should I consider moving house?" or "How can I feel more secure?"

- **Card 1:** You/your situation

- **Card 2:** Past issues

- **Card 3:** Hopes or fears

- **Card 4:** Outcome

CARD 3

CARD 4

CARD 1

CARD 2

V THE HIEROPHANT

THE HIEROPHANT.

Alternative Names: The High Priest, The Pope

Number: V

Numerology Link: XIV, Temperance

Astrological Sign or Planet: Taurus the Bull

Element: Earth

Hebrew Letter: *Vau* (*Vav*, *Wav*)

> **Symbol:** Nail or connector

> **Meaning:** Kindness

Tree of Life Pathway: Sixth, Chesed and Chockmah

Chakra: Causal, or fourth eye, for spiritual connection

Key Meanings: Education, unity, and spiritual direction

UNDERSTANDING THE HIEROPHANT

The Hierophant appears as a figure of religious orthodoxy. Wearing the papal crown and holding the scepter, he makes the hand gesture of blessing to two supplicants kneeling before him. He is the leader of the Catholic faith and symbolizes unity. One of his titles, Pontifex Maximus, means "The Great Bridge-Builder"; he is the bridge between heaven and earth. He shows us the potential for integrating our internal and external worlds, bringing together body and soul as well as our male and female self-aspects. As the priest, he officiates at weddings, joining two people together in physical and spiritual union.

The Hierophant is also a symbol of education. Also know as the Priest or the Pope, in the Rider-Waite tarot, he is named Hierophant after the *hierophantes*, or priests who guarded the Eleusinian Mysteries (see The Historical Hierophant). Through him, we may find and follow a higher path through learning. He may be a lecturer or inspiring leader, priest or magus, shaman or established esoteric teacher.

In the major arcana sequence, the Hierophant appears between card IV, The Emperor, and VI, The Lovers. We are moving from the Emperor's worldly domain to an encounter with the spiritual through a teacher-priest. After the Hierophant, we meet the Lovers and see God's messenger, Archangel Raphael, and then—through the sequence of these three cards—sense a progression from the earth realm to a glimpse of the divine.

The Hierophant's number is the indivisible V, the number of mankind, which indicates that he is the communicator between man and God, which is also shown by his hand gesture, symbolizing heaven and earth (see The Hierophant's Symbols). He is numerologically linked with card XIV, Temperance (14; 1 + 4 = 5, or V). The Angel of Temperance and the Hierophant are both channels for the message of God.

THE HIEROPHANT'S ASTROLOGY

The Hierophant's sign is Taurus, the Bull the second sign of the zodiac (April 21–May 21), ruled by sensuous planet Venus and the element of Earth, which is also represented by his red robes (see The Hierophant's Symbols). This fixed sign of the zodiac has the attributes of commitment and loyalty, groundedness, and practicality.

THE HIEROPHANT AND KABBALA

The Hierophant's kabbalistic letter is *Vau*, meaning nail or connector—the Hebrew letter resembles an *I* with a pen stroke to the left. *Vau*'s esoteric meaning is kindness.

On the Tree of Life, he is placed on the sixth pathway between the spheres of Chesed, meaning mercy and divine love, and Chockmah, or wisdom and the male principle. Chockmah is also known as the Father of Fathers and points to the Hierophant as the eternal father-god, spiritual counterpart to the mother-goddess embodied in card III, The Empress.

UPRIGHT MEANING

In the upright position, the Hierophant shows support, self-realization, and expansion. This is a time to develop emotionally and spiritually—to commit to relationships; to think and philosophize; and to become more spiritually aware. In this way, the Hierophant offers an opportunity to integrate mind and spirit and ascend to a higher plane of awareness. Day to day, this means nurturing your talents through learning and heeding good advice.

While the Hierophant offers wise counsel, he does represent institutions and traditional values—which may be a comfort to you or a test of how much you are willing to conform. Even if his conventions are not for you, the Hierophant offers an opportunity to question and define your values.

As a spiritual leader, the Hierophant shows you the path to follow in a community, such as joining a study group or class through which you may learn a new skill. He also represents good judgement and fairness: The Hierophant asks you to tune your moral compass, so if you have been questioning a decision, it is time to do what is right.

Here's what else the Hierophant can symbolize:

- **Home:** Expanding your current property; inviting people into your home to share your interests

- **Relationships:** Committed partnerships; marriage; celebrating the sacred in your relationship

- **Career and money:** Progress in your organization; direction and decisions; inspired leadership and growth

REVERSED MEANING

When reversed, the Hierophant shows poor leadership. You may be mislead by an incompetent or egotistic individual at work or on your spiritual path. This is the card of the bad guru—the judgemental teacher who is more interested in furthering his ambitions than supporting you in yours. In work, the Hierophant reversed can also show institutions that need restructuring: poor advice, mistrust, and wrong decisions with moral repercussions. It is better to seek your own path than to stay with a mentor or plan that doesn't suit your needs. Be a free spirit.

HIS WISDOM MESSAGE

Make the most of your gifts.

THE HIEROPHANT'S SYMBOLS

In the Rider-Waite tarot, the Hierophant appears with these magical symbols. Some of them reappear in other major arcana cards, so learn to recognize them and you'll soon find you can apply your knowledge throughout the deck.

- *The papal crown:* The triple crown is the symbol of papal authority. Its three layers stand for the holy trinity.

- *The papal staff, or crosier:* The three crosses on the Hierophant's staff stand for the Holy Trinity of Father, Son, and Holy Ghost; earth, heaven, and the spirit world; and the self, higher self, and the Christ/fully actualized self. We also see the three crosses on the Hierophant's papal robes, which are red, for earth, while the crosier is gold, for heaven.

- *The crossed keys:* The golden crossed keys represent the keys to the kingdom of heaven given by Jesus to St. Peter. Jesus said to Peter, "Whatever you bind on earth shall be bound in heaven." Heaven and earth are as one, a reminder of the Hierophant's key meaning of unity.

- *The hand gesture of blessing:* The blessing shows two fingers bent and two extended, representing what is seen and what is hidden from view—our visible earthly existence and the invisible heaven. The fingers are part of the same hand and, like the crossed keys, illustrate how our known and unknown worlds unite.

- *The red cloak:* energy and action; being in the material world
    See this symbol on cards I, The Magician; IV, The Emperor; and XI, Justice.

- *The roses and lilies:* The red roses symbolize love and the white lilies, purity.
    See this symbol on cards I, The Magician; the roses around the waist of the maiden on VIII, Strength; and red roses on the gown of card III, The Empress.

THE HISTORICAL HIEROPHANT: SECRET RITES

The Hierophant was named in the Rider-Waite tarot after *hierophant*, a general term meaning someone who introduced others to holiness—*hierophant* in Greek was *ta hiera* and *phainen*, meaning to show. Hierophantes was also the title of the High Priests of the Greek religion of Eleusis, who officiated at the Eleusinian Mysteries. This was a famous initiation ceremony and festival that took place at Eleusis, near Athens. The rites were secret, but involved the afterlife and the retelling of the story of Demeter the grain mother and her daughter, Persephone, who was abducted by Hades (see the Empress, page 42). The Hierophant was always chosen from a family named Eumolpidae, who had a mythical ancestor, Eumolpus, whose parents were the gods Poseidon and Chione. The Hierophant was the keeper of sacred mysteries, and he was renowned for his beautiful and hypnotic voice—which perhaps explains the emphasis on listening in many Hierophant card interpretations.

In early tarot cards, the Hierophant card was the Pope. The card's title changed in some seventeenth- and eighteenth-century decks in response to religious sensitivity. For example, Jupiter replaced the Pope in the Tarot de Besancon of 1818, and Bacchus, god of wine, is the Pope of the Belgian tarot of 1770.

THE HIEROPHANT'S REFLECTIONS

We can see aspects of The Hierophant in these minor arcana cards:

- The Nine of Wands, for defending your faith at any cost; protecting what is known

- The Six of Cups, for familiarity, harmony, and the past

- The Two of Cups, for love partnerships

TRY A READING WITH THE HIEROPHANT: FINDING A MENTOR OR SOUL MATE

Take the Hierophant from your deck and lay him before you. Now shuffle the remaining cards and cut the deck or fan out the cards facedown. Choose three cards with your left hand and place them around the Hierophant as shown. You could ask, "Will I find a mentor at this time?" or "Will I have a soul connection with this person?" Interpret card 3, the outcome, using the yes/no list of major arcana cards on page 23.

- **Card 1:** Your situation

- **Card 2:** The mentor you need or the person in question

- **Card 3:** The outcome

CARD 1

CARD 2

CARD 3

VI THE LOVERS

THE LOVERS.

Alternative Names: The Lover, Love

Number: VI

Numerology Link: XV, The Devil

Astrological Sign or Planet: Gemini the Twins

Element: Air

Hebrew Letter: *Zain*

> **Symbol:** Sword

> **Meaning:** Soulfulness

Tree of Life Pathway: Seventh, between Tiphareth and Binah

Chakra: Heart chakra, for love and healing

Key Meanings: Love and relationships, maturity, and decisions

UNDERSTANDING THE LOVERS

Two Lovers arrive in a magical garden where strange flowers bloom and snakes talk. The full sun beams behind a luminous Archangel Raphael, angel of love and healing, who presides over their union.

The Lovers stand in the Garden of Eden together, yet the woman, Eve, is gazing up at Archangel Raphael, who is holding up his right hand, explaining to them that they will be cast out of the garden if they eat the fruit from the Tree of Knowledge of Good and Evil. Their innocent paradise will end—a metaphor for the seeming perfection of a new relationship before we must negotiate the practicalities. The man, Adam—who could also be the Fool on his journey through the tarot—gazes directly at Eve. They may be called the Lovers, but they are not Lovers yet: See the clouds between them? The clouds predict the Fall and the hurdles they will overcome as their relationship becomes grounded in reality. All looks perfect in Eden, but Eve and Adam are only just about to recognize each other and know love. From this point onward, we know the snake will tempt Eve to eat the fruit, and their relationship will change forever.

In the major arcana sequence, the Lovers arrive after card V, The Hierophant. One of his meanings is marriage and the integration of male and female aspects. After the Lovers comes card VII, The Chariot—we have made our love decision, and the tension released drives us forward.

The Lovers' number is VI, the number of harmony, love, and growth. It is also associated with healing and so links with the healing Archangel Raphael. The card's numerological link is XV, The Devil, who stands for the shadow side of love, when issues of control and possessiveness take hold.

THE LOVERS' ASTROLOGY

The Lovers' sign is Gemini, the Twins (May 22–June 21), or the dual aspects of male and female, light and shadow. Loving our whole selves, in all our aspects, raises our consciousness to love God/the universe/the Great Spirit as the creator of the divine spark within. Eve is also Adam's twin, as she was created from him.

THE LOVERS AND KABBALA

The Lovers' Hebrew letter is *Zain*, or sword—it can also connote the penis. As swords are the suit of Air in the tarot and symbolize clear thought and action, this relates to the card's meaning of decisions. The tarotist Jonathan Dee also comments, "It is also interesting to note that Adam and Eve were expelled from the Garden [of Eden] by an angel with a sword." *Zain* can also mean soulfulness or living with an awareness of our higher selves.

The Lovers is placed on the seventh pathway on the Tree of Life between the spheres of Tiphareth, for beauty, rebirth, and ascending consciousness, and Binah, for understanding, the goddess, and the female principle.

UPRIGHT MEANING

The Lovers show relationships and a decision. The card can predict meeting a new partner or a career opportunity, and your choice now will have a significant effect on your future. In the upright position, the person coming into your orbit now has a positive influence and offers true love—provided you follow the guidance of your heart rather than your head. If you are willing to take a risk rather than stay with a safe choice, you may soon discover your own Garden of Eden, which is fertile and rich with possibility.

If you are already in a relationship, a decision whether to take your partnership to a deeper level will be made. The issue that the Lovers card raises is your ability to make a decision based on your long-term future rather than short-term gains. In this way, you are being asked to make a mature decision that supports your true needs—respect, intimacy, love, and trust—and to connect with a partner who is emotionally available to you.

Whatever your situation, the message is to follow your heart's desire.

An additional meaning of the Lovers card is a young person leaving home and making independent decisions.

- **Home:** If you're not living in your dream home, now is the time to work toward a property and location that will support your dreams and desires.

- **Relationships:** A love decision—Look at your patterns in previous relationships and see what your current love, or prospective new partner, can offer you that is different and ultimately more fulfilling. If you are single, love yourself first to manifest the right relationship when the time comes.

- **Career and money:** Career choices—One option may seem easier, but look carefully to ensure you are making the best decision in the long term. Look beyond money to your future development and ambitions.

REVERSED MEANING

When the Lovers card reverses, relationships go out of balance and the shadow side of your personalities enters the equation. A relationship is in crisis, and you may question your initial attraction as the values you once held as a couple feel corrupted. There may be inequality, betrayal, and dishonesty. The Lovers reversed is also an aspect of card XV, The Devil, which reveals lust, materialism, and addiction to negative patterns.

THEIR WISDOM MESSAGE

Follow the wisdom of your heart.

THE LOVERS' SYMBOLS

In the Rider-Waite tarot, the Lovers appear with these magical symbols. Some of them reappear in other major arcana cards, so learn to recognize them and you'll soon find you can apply your knowledge throughout the deck.

- *Archangel Raphael:* The archangel of love and healing symbolizes spiritual wisdom and the healing power of love. Following the heart and committing to love as a life purpose heals us and heals others.

  See other Archangels on XIV Temperance (Archangel Michael), and XX Judgement (Archangel Gabriel).

- *The Tree of Life:* Find this on the right of the card, behind the man; it stands for the male principle. It has twelve fruits representing the twelve signs of the zodiac.

- *The Tree of Knowledge of Good and Evil:* You can see this on the left of the card, behind the woman; it stands for the female principle. The tree's fruit is sexual experience.

- *The snake:* Risk and wisdom—In Christianity, it is the Fall of Man: Adam and Eve's banishment from Eden when they ate the fruit of the Tree of Knowledge of Good and Evil.

THE HISTORICAL LOVERS: WEDDINGS AND AFFAIRS

In Renaissance Italy, the Visconti family commissioned an artist to paint a set of tarot cards to commemorate the marriage of Bianca Maria Visconti and Francesco Sforza, and the joining together of two of the most powerful families in Northern Italy. Married in 1441, portraits of Bianca and Francesco were painted on the Lovers card, in which they are shown holding hands under a canopy decorated with heraldic shields and symbols with a blind cupid hovering above. The Visconti-Sforza tarots were almost a family album, featuring not only Bianca Maria and Francesco, but Bianca Maria again on the Chariot and Sister Manfreda, believed to be a relative of the Visconti family, as the High Priestess (see page 40).

In the Marseilles tarots, which may date from the fifteenth century, we see three people—two women and a man in the center. Cupid, who is not blindfolded, is about to shoot love's arrow at the couple on the right—indicating that the man will have to choose one of the women as his partner. In the tarots of Court de Gébelin (Antoine Court, 1725–1784), which appeared in his book *Le Monde Primitif* (1781), cupid favors the couple on the left of the card. The French occultist Etteilla (Jean-Baptiste Alliette, 1738–1791) created a deck with a different structure to that of traditional tarot, but with a card equivalent to the Lovers numbered 13 and named "Mariage," or marriage. Here, the central figure is a priest conducting a wedding ceremony. A. E. Waite's card holds this structure of three people, but transformed the priest or cupid into the angel and draws upon the Lovers' biblical lineage as Adam and Eve.

THE LOVERS' REFLECTIONS

We can see aspects of the Lovers in these minor arcana cards:

- The Ace of Cups, for love

- The Two of Cups, for a new partnership

TRY A READING WITH THE LOVERS: THE LOVE DECISION

Take the Lovers card from your deck and lay the card before you. Now shuffle the remaining cards and cut the deck or fan out the cards facedown. Choose six cards with your left hand and place them around the Lovers, as shown. You could ask, "What are my choices, and how do I choose?"

- **Card 1:** The question

- **Card 2:** Background to the present situation

- **Cards 3 and 4:** The choices

- **Card 5:** The best action to take

- **Card 6:** The outcome

CARD 6

CARD 3   CARD 4

THE LOVERS.

CARD 2   CARD 5

CARD 1

VII THE CHARIOT

Alternative Name: Victory

Number: VII

Numerology Link: XVI, The Tower

Astrological Sign or Planet: Cancer the Crab

Element: Water

Hebrew Letter: *Heth* (*Chet*, *Cheth*)

  Symbol: Fence or enclosure

  Meaning: Guidance

Tree of Life Pathway: Eighth, between Geburah and Binah

Chakra: Throat, for truth

Key Meanings: Determination, victory, and a journey

UNDERSTANDING THE CHARIOT

The Chariot—or the charioteer—is the traveler, standing strong in his carriage of stone and flanked by two resting sphinxes. With the city and its river behind him, he is about to move on; with determination and self-control, he will keep his vehicle on the road and be successful in his quest. At this point, his concerns are practical and material rather than mystical, yet he is aware of the heavenly realms above him, shown by his canopy of stars and the astrological symbols on his belt.

  The Chariot is a culmination of the cards that precede him, and some symbols from cards 0 to VI are included on the card as evidence. About to embark on a journey, the Chariot echoes the youth aspect of the Fool. On the Chariot's shoulder armor are crescent moons, for II, The High Priestess. His starry crown is like that of III, The Empress. The stone chariot resembles the Emperor's throne, and its pillars those of the Hierophant's chamber. The landscape evokes the Garden of Eden, home to card VI, The Lovers.

The charioteer will soon find his karmic life path. To stay on it, he needs to draw together all his past experiences.

Indivisible by any other number, VII is a number of unification, mirrored in the seven days of the week, the days of the creation of the universe, and, in classical wisdom, the then-seven planets of the solar system. Seven is also the sum of three and four, which tells us that the Chariot is the child of cards III and IV, the Empress and Emperor, wearing his mother's crown and standing astride his father's throne. His numerological correspondence is card XVI, The Tower. The shadow side of the Chariot is ego—which leads to destruction, or the Tower.

THE CHARIOT'S ASTROLOGY

The Chariot's astrological sign is Cancer the Crab (June 22–July 23), ruled by the moon. The crab has a shell, a protective vehicle for the body, like the chariot itself. The Charioteer's gauntlets have a shell-like frill at the forearms.

The card also indicates the four fixed signs of Aquarius, Scorpio, Leo, and Taurus and their elements, which are symbolized by the sphinx.

THE CHARIOT AND KABBALA

The Chariot's Hebrew letter is Chet, for fence or enclosure, a descriptor of the vehicle itself. The symbol of the square on the charioteer's breastplate may also reference the square form of the Hebrew letter *Mem*, which, in the ancient kabbalistic text the *Sefer Yetzirah*, means King over Water and Formed Earth in the Universe—suggesting the Chariot's crossing of the river and reaching dry land, from where he commences his journey.

In the kabbalistic Tree of Life, the Chariot is positioned on the eighth pathway between the spheres of Geburah, power and destruction, and Binah, meaning understanding and the female principle or creation.

UPRIGHT MEANING

The Upright Chariot signifies success and a major departure. This is a time for determination and focus as you travel in a new direction. A decision is made,

and now you can begin to experience real progress in your affairs. Ready to take control and navigate your path, you are poised to learn as your horizons rapidly expand. Just as the charioteer has his wand to drive him onward, you will need willpower to fuel your desires.

The Chariot can indicate a move or an important journey, and, on a mundane level, it shows you driving a car on your travels or getting a new vehicle.

Following are some other possibilities:

- **Home:** Travel away from home is the focus now, rather than on extending or improving your home. You may also welcome travelers from other states or countries. Any disagreements with those you live with will be quickly overcome.

- **Relationships:** A relationship progresses at a pace; if the cards around the Chariot show endings, you may be moving on alone—but this is your rightful path.

- **Career and money:** Swift progress in business affairs—the opportunity coming your way will be challenging and exciting. Financially, you are on the road to success.

REVERSED MEANING

When reversed, there is arrogance and self-indulgence. This can show a person or event spiraling out of control. Ego is at work, and selfish needs come before the greater good, so the Chariot reversed can indicate recklessness and poor leadership. When the Chariot reverses and is tipped off the road, travel plans and house moves are disrupted or delayed.

HIS WISDOM MESSAGE

Take charge and reach for the stars.

THE CHARIOT'S SYMBOLS

In the Rider-Waite tarot, the Chariot appears with these magical symbols. Some of them reappear in other major arcana cards, so learn to recognize them and you'll soon find you can apply your knowledge throughout the deck.

- *The chariot:* the vehicle for the personality and self-expression; protection and progress.

- *The black and white sphinxes*: The sphinx is a symbol of unity in diversity because it embodies a human face, eagle wings, the body of a lion, and the tail of a bull, which relate also to the four elements, the four suits of the minor arcana, and the four fixed signs of the zodiac (see The Chariot's Astrology).

  See this symbol on card X, The Wheel of Fortune.

- *The armor and breastplate:* The charioteer's armor symbolizes protection on his journey. On his breastplate, the alchemical symbol of the square signifies the four corners of the earth. The moon faces on the shoulder armor represent the divination stones, urmin and thummin, which in the Old Testament were used to divine God's will; it is suggested that the stones were cast to answer to a serious matter, such the decision to go to war.

- *The robes:* The written characters on the charioteer's robe are protective talismans. On the belt are some undefined symbols, believed to be signs of the zodiac.

- *The crown:* This is a symbol of authority. This crown has an eight-pointed star—this is the star from card XVII, The Star, a symbol of hope (see page 98).

A laurel wreath is worn underneath it, symbolizing victory.

  See this symbol on III, The Empress, and XVII, The Star.

- *The winged sun disk:* The winged sun belonged to the Egyptian god Horus and later to the sun god, Ra; the symbol may also relate to the Greek sun god, Helios, who rode the skies in his sun chariot. In this card, the symbol denotes solar power and the conscious mind.

- *Yoni-lingham:* This Hindu symbol, under the wing emblem on the front of the chariot, shows the feminine organ, the yoni, and the male lingam, pictured joined to symbolize the harmonious union of male and female aspects.

- *The canopy of stars:* This is a symbol of hope and direction and a link with the celestial realms, seen also on the zodiac symbols on the charioteer's belt.

  See this symbol on card XVII, The Star.

- *The magic wand:* power, creativity, and initiative

  See this symbol on card I, The Magician, and XXI, The World.

- *Yellow background:* consciousness, clear sight, and support

  See this symbol on card I, The Magician; III, The Empress; VIII, Strength; and XI, Justice.

THE HISTORICAL CHARIOT: THE PROCESSION OF TRIUMPHS

The Chariot dates back to the victory parades of ancient Rome, when victors processed through the streets in their triumphal chariot—*triumph,* from which the word *trump* (*trionfi*) is derived, also another term for the major arcana cards of the tarot. The charioteer of this parade of heroes was probably recognized by the Roman spectators as their sun god, Sol, shown by the bright yellow sunlight on the Rider-Waite card.

The people of Renaissance Italy continued this tradition, known as the procession of triumphs, during which allegorical figures appeared in triumphal carts to represent all the major arcana cards. The Visconti-Sforza tarot of the fifteenth century shows a chariot pulled by two white winged horses and in it a queen resembling Bianca Maria Visconti, the woman in the Lovers card (see The Historical Lovers, page 56).

THE CHARIOT'S REFLECTIONS

We can see aspects of the Chariot in these minor arcana cards:

- The Three of Wands, for broadening horizons and travel

- The Eight of Wands, for travel and communication

TRY A READING WITH THE CHARIOT: MOVING ON

Take the Chariot from your deck and lay the card in the center of the spread, as shown. Now shuffle the remaining cards and cut the deck or fan out the cards facedown. Choose seven cards with your left hand and place them around the Chariot, as shown. You could ask, "What do I need to take me forward?" or "What can I experience on this new path?"

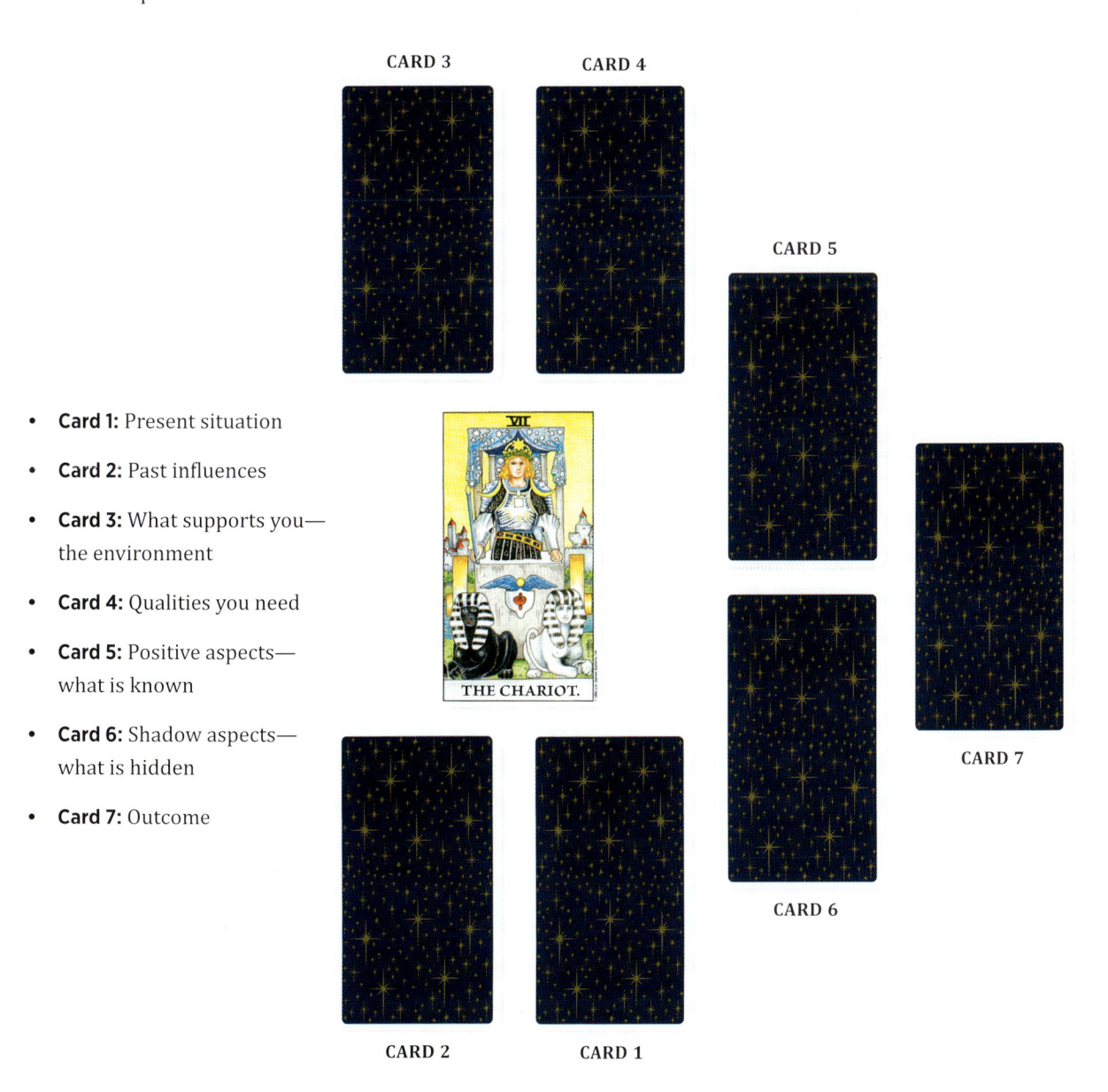

- **Card 1:** Present situation

- **Card 2:** Past influences

- **Card 3:** What supports you—the environment

- **Card 4:** Qualities you need

- **Card 5:** Positive aspects—what is known

- **Card 6:** Shadow aspects—what is hidden

- **Card 7:** Outcome

VIII STRENGTH

Alternative Names: Fortitude, Force

Number: VIII (can also be numbered XI in some decks)

Numerology Link: XVII, The Star

Astrological Sign or Planet: Leo the Lion

Element: Fire

Hebrew Letter: *Teth*

Symbol: The serpent

Meaning: Courage

Tree of Life Pathway: Ninth, between Geburah and Chesed

Chakra: Solar plexus, for self-empowerment

Key Meanings: Patience, tension, and strength

UNDERSTANDING STRENGTH

This card shows strength in action: A woman in white stands calmly over a lion, holding its jaws open midway. She stays in control by holding her position, symbolized by the infinity symbol above her head. The lion signifies passion and base instincts, and the woman, civility. Although her position is precarious, she does not show fear. She communicates with the lion through her calm presence; she is not denying his power. In this way, one of the card's messages is having the courage to listen to and accept our shadow voices, our own emotional turmoil, without the fear that it will eat us up. Yet Strength personified does more than hold on: She transmutes the beast's fierce energy to a higher purpose. As one of the four cardinal virtue cards of the major arcana sequence (see page 75), Strength implies a moral victory.

As a mediator of opposite qualities, Strength is not dissimilar to card II, The High Priestess, who stands between earth and the spirit world; V, The Hierophant, who intercedes between heaven and earth; and VII, The Chariot, who precedes her in the major arcana sequence, in which the charioteer reins in the light and dark aspects of the self. Although apparent rivals, these opposites derive from one source and, like the yin-yang symbol, are in essence each other. Armed with Strength's experience, card IX, The Hermit, is bold enough to go into the wilderness alone to find himself intellectually, emotionally, and spiritually.

Strength's number, VIII, stands for stability and renewal and was first assigned to the card by the Golden Dawn card correspondences. In earlier tarots, she was numbered XI, or the digits 11, for duality, and so links to II, The High Priestess. Strength as VIII is numerologically linked with card XVII, The Star (17, as 1 + 7 = 8). This too is a card of hope and high intention.

STRENGTH'S ASTROLOGY

Strength's zodiac sign is Leo the Lion (July 24–August 23), a natural alignment as the lion is shown on the card. The card's element is dynamic Fire, linked with energy and enterprise.

STRENGTH AND KABBALA

Strength's kabbalistic letter is *Teth*, meaning courage, as well as serpent or snake, referencing the wisdom of experience. The astrological glyph for Strength's sign of Leo resembles a snake. On the Tree of Life, Strength is placed on the ninth pathway between the spheres of Geburah and Chesed, meaning power linked with universal love and order. In Strength, we maintain order, despite the potential for chaos.

UPRIGHT MEANING

Strength shows that you turn to your higher self for self-guidance; she also demonstrates strength of character when dealing with pressure. Courage, determination, and patience are needed now, as it is time to get a situation—or individual—under control. You will need to act with grace and sensitivity, however, rather than using brute force. This is a good card for leadership, as it signifies you are ready to take on a challenge and stand firm; others may resist, but be consistent in your actions and results will come. In creative projects, Strength shows you taking a raw idea and developing it. You refine it without sacrificing its spirit or depleting your energy. This concept may take physical form as a document, piece of artwork, or prototype.

On a psychological level, Strength shows the integration of masculine and feminine traits and finding balance between the two. In terms of health, Strength shows resilience and vitality, recovery from illness, and the willpower to break bad habits.

Here are some specifics:

- **Home:** There's a need to support and direct those with strong opinions. You may need to take the role of mediator.

- **Relationships:** The need for balance—there is a danger that physical attraction masks emotional or other commitment issues that need to be addressed. This card is also a message of hope if your relationship has been tested, as the situation will soon improve.

- **Career and money:** Tension at work—resolution comes gently and without force.

REVERSED MEANING

When reversed, Strength turns to weakness of will and avoidance of risk, conflicts, and decision-making. This can refer to you ignoring your instincts altogether or allowing fear of conflict to stop you from taking action. This avoidance is holding back your personal growth; in this situation, you can only learn through experience. Whatever you resist persists, so take charge and take on the challenge.

Strength reversed is an obvious message about weakness, so be aware that indolence and overthinking can be more exhausting than confrontation.

HER WISDOM MESSAGE

With strength, you can discover your higher purpose.

STRENGTH'S SYMBOLS

In the Rider-Waite tarot, Strength appears with these magical symbols. Some of them reappear in other cards, so learn to recognize them and you'll soon find you can apply your knowledge throughout the deck.

- *The lemniscate, or infinity symbol:* Balance, activity, and renewal—The flow of this never-ending symbol also suggests consistency and patience. The eight-shape mirrors VIII, Strength's number.

  See this symbol on card I, The Magician.

- *The lion:* The lion is a universal symbol of power, courage, majesty, and leadership. In alchemy, the lion stands for base matters that can be turned into gold as well as enlightenment.

  See this symbol on card X, The Wheel of Fortune, and XXI, The World.

- *The garland of roses/rose briar:* civility, celebration, and protection

  See this symbol on cards I, The Magician; the Queen of Pentacles; and the Four of Wands.

- *The white robe:* a symbol of purity

  See this symbol on cards II, The High Priestess, and XIII, Death.

- *Yellow background:* consciousness, clear sight and support—applying strength, being courageous, is a conscious action

  See this symbol on cards I, The Magician; III, The Empress; VII, The Chariot; and XI, Justice.

HISTORICAL STRENGTH: THE LION-KILLERS

The image of woman or man and a lion is embedded in many of humanity's myths and legends. Some are stories of healing, such as the fairytale beauty and the beast. Another example is the classical fable of Androcles, a fugitive slave who heals the paw of a wounded lion. Androcles is later recaptured and condemned to public death by mauling by a lion. Yet the lion Androcles faces in the stadium is his old friend, who recognizes Androcles and refuses to kill him. The slave is given his freedom by the Emperor of Rome, and man and lion parade the streets together in celebration. Flowers are strewn upon them—echoed, perhaps, in the rose garlands shown on our Rider-Waite Strength card.

In other myths, taking on the lion shows our power over nature. The huntress Cyrene, the "girl lionkiller" according to Greek poet Nonnus, killed many a beast to protect her father's cattle; her exploits caught the attention of the god Apollo, who fell in love with her. The Visconti-Sforza tarots of the Renaissance show Hercules with a raised club, defeating the terrifying lion of Nemea. He brought the animal's skin back to King Eurystheus, and with this trophy proved he had succeeded in his first labor.

The Griggoneur tarot cards of the mid-fifteenth century include an unusual Strength card: a courtly lady sitting comfortably holding a broken pillar. It's unclear if she is supporting the two pieces, stopping them from falling, or actually breaking the pillar. This image may relate to Samson's destruction of the temple of the Philistines or the legend of the Pillars of Hercules, which, according to Plato, guarded the entry to the mysterious lost world of Atlantis. This was the border of civilization, so this lady and her pillar may symbolize the defense of boundaries. She is literally a pillar of strength.

In the Tarot of Marseilles (1701–1715), we see a woman restraining the lion's jaws and wearing a wide floppy hat—the brim makes the shape of the leminscate, or infinity symbol, shown also on the Rider-Waite card (see Strength's Symbols).

STRENGTH'S REFLECTIONS

We can see aspects of Strength in these minor arcana cards:

- The Seven of Wands, for endurance

- The Nine of Wands, for relentless effort

- The Ace of Swords, for decisiveness

- The Eight of Pentacles, for commitment

TRY A READING WITH STRENGTH: A TEST OF COURAGE

Take Strength from your deck and lay the card before you. Now shuffle the remaining cards and cut the deck or fan out the cards facedown. Choose five cards with your left hand and place them around Strength, as shown. You could ask, "What should I hold on to?" or "What could I let go of?" To hold or release—both actions require courage.

- **Card 1:** The issue

- **Card 2:** You in this situation

- **Card 3:** What to hold on to

- **Card 4:** What to let go of

- **Card 5:** The outcome

CARD 5

CARD 4

CARD 3

CARD 1

CARD 2

IX THE HERMIT

Alternative Names: The Old Man, Time, The Poor Man

Number: IX

Numerology Link: XVIII, The Moon

Astrological Sign or Planet: Virgo the Virgin

Element: Earth

Hebrew Letter: *Yod*

    Symbol: The hand

    Meaning: Prudence

Tree of Life Pathway: Tenth, between Chesed and Tiphareth

Chakra: Heart seed, for soul remembrance

Key Meanings: Healing and self-exploration

UNDERSTANDING THE HERMIT

The Hermit is a man all alone, old and bearded, with just his staff and lantern as his companions in a snowy wilderness. Inside his lantern is a glowing star, a symbol of guidance that lights his way ahead. The Hermit needs privacy, time for silence and discretion, so he can think and plan. He may be in the wilderness, but this space is essential to him. In this way, the Hermit tells us it is time to go it alone, to break with convention and find our soul's path.

In the major arcana sequence, the Hermit appears after VIII, Strength, and before X, The Wheel of Fortune. Having learned the lessons of Strength, he takes time out to contemplate his experiences. The Hermit can be seen as the Fool grown, the youth now as an old man, and his arrival marks the near-end of the first half of the tarot journey marked by X, The Wheel of Fortune. In the second half of the major arcana cycle, the material world fades and the spiritual quest beckons.

The Hermit's number is IX, or three groups of dynamic three. The Hermit needs time to integrate his experience in mind, body, and soul. Nine is also the last single-digit number in the major arcana sequence and a pause in activity before he aligns with fate, symbolized by the Wheel of Fortune. The Hermit is numerologically linked with card XVIII, The Moon (18; 1 + 8 = 9)—a card of imagination and self-reflection.

THE HERMIT'S ASTROLOGY

The Hermit's zodiac sign is Virgo the Virgin. It suggests the Hermit has this attribute—perhaps he is a chaste monk. The Hermit's number, IX, gives us the ninth month of the year, September, and the sign of Virgo (August 23–September 22).

THE HERMIT AND KABBALA

The kabbalistic letter of the Hermit is *Yod*, which means hand and also prudence. *Yod* is the foundation of all other letters in the Hebrew alphabet, just as the Hermit's retreat helps him establish his priorities.

On the Tree of Life, the Hermit is placed on the tenth pathway between Chesed and Tiphareth, or love and beauty aligned with salvation.

UPRIGHT MEANING

There's an opportunity to take time away from routine to consider your options or advance a personal project. This card can show you enjoying solitude, as you need space to process your thoughts and feelings. The Hermit can show a physical journey, but more commonly he represents a state of mind in which you wisely withdraw and keep your own counsel. It can show breaking with tradition and finding a unique approach to a challenge. You may appreciate a mentor, and when you are ready, as the saying goes, the teacher will appear. Until that time, you have yourself to rely upon, and you do have the answers; all you need is the mental space to connect with your inner wisdom. If you are under pressure to make a decision, the Hermit shows you need more time.

There is also a healing aspect to the Hermit, and the card can appear in a reading to show self-healing and healing others. You may need to guide others and show them the way forward. Even if you are not entirely sure you can help, you are equipped to do so.

The Hermit can also indicate the following:

- **Home:** Consider all your options carefully and avoid making big decisions at present. Prioritize your tasks and focus on planning rather than immediate action.

- **Relationships:** Take time to invest in your current relationship or to work on your relationship with yourself. The card can also show a period of being single.

- **Career and money:** Take a different approach and stand back. You may be drawn to research and professional development courses now. A mentor may guide you.

REVERSED MEANING

When reversed, you may be feeling alone and unsupported. However, this is more an attitude than reality, so it's worth asking yourself if you are avoiding help. The card can also show accepting a role—perhaps victim or martyr—that you find hard to let go of due to habit or stubbornness. Alternatively, the card can show a time when you are cut off from your usual support systems or have been unfriended by those you trusted. If this chimes for you, go with the upright card meaning and withdraw for a while, relying on your own guidance.

HIS WISDOM MESSAGE

Live quietly for a time.

THE HERMIT'S SYMBOLS

In the Rider-Waite tarot, the Hermit appears with these magical symbols. Some of them reappear in other major arcana cards, so learn to recognize them and you'll soon find you can apply your knowledge throughout the deck.

- *The staff:* The staff symbolizes self-support. In some decks, the staff is entwined by a snake, making a single spiral to form the Rod of Asclepius, a signifier for the Greek deity of healing.

- *The lantern:* a sign of the divine light within that illuminates our life path

- *The six-pointed star:* The star is a mark of hope and guidance. Its six points comprise two triangles—heaven and earth, or man and God, in unity. It is also a symbol of Saturn, god of agriculture and time, the Hermit's ancestor (see The Historical Hermit).

  See this symbol on card XVII, The Star, and III, The Empress.

- *The old man:* The archetype of wisdom, the old man's beard, hood, and downward gaze symbolize retreat and discretion.

THE HISTORICAL HERMIT: FATHER TIME

On the Renaissance Visconti-Sforza tarots, the Hermit is entitled "The Old Man." On these and similar cards of that era, the hermit holds an hourglass in the traditional shape of the infinity symbol or lemniscate, illustrating the Hermit's alternate name, Time. By the eighteenth century, however, the Hermit's hourglass had become a lantern—a possible misinterpretation by later artists.

The Hermit is depicted differently in many cards. He is shown in cards of the late fifteenth and sixteenth centuries as an old man on crutches. In the Tarocchi of Mitelli (c. 1664) he has angel wings, suggesting he is facing death. On eighteenth-century minchiate cards, he is on crutches by a tomb with an hourglass, pierced by time's arrow. Beside him is a stag, a Christ symbol. And later, by the twentieth century, we see the Hermit's staff entwined with a snake in the shape of the Rod of Asclepius, a symbol of the Greek god of healing.

There is also evidence that the Hermit was associated with the Roman god Saturn (rather than Mercury, ruler of his sign of Virgo). Saturn was an aspect of the Titan god Chronos, who ate his own children because he believed the prophesy that one of them would overthrow him—a grisly way to stop the passage of time. In the Tarocchi of Mantegna (c. 1470), card 47 is Saturno, a bearded man with a staff, just like our traditional Hermit.

The Hermit may also embody the tarot's hidden virtue card of Prudence. It seems most likely that Prudence survived in modern decks as Justice (see page 74) or possibly the Hanged Man (page 78), but the Hermit may have first crept into the tarot in the Prudence card of the Tarocchi of Mantegna, a deck of fifty instructional cards that may be Florentine or Venetian in origin and date from around 1470. Prudence shows both an old bearded man and a young woman with a mirror and a dragon (which may have morphed into the snake shown on the Hermit on contemporary decks). The virtue of Prudence has survived in the meaning of the Hermit in his Hebrew letter, *Yod*, and in his meaning of discretion and careful planning.

THE HERMIT'S REFLECTIONS

We can see aspects of the Hermit in these minor arcana cards:

- The Seven of Wands, for standing alone and advocating your beliefs

- The Nine of Wands, for the need for protection

- The Nine of Pentacles, for independence and resourcefulness

- The Queen of Swords, for independence

TRY A READING WITH THE HERMIT: THE HOURGLASS

Take the Hermit from your deck and lay him before you. Now shuffle the remaining cards and cut the deck or fan out the cards facedown. Choose eight cards with your left hand and place them around the Hermit as shown. You could ask, "What or whom do I need time out from?" or "What can I learn on my journey?"

- **Card 1:** Past events

- **Card 2:** The impact of the past

- **Card 3:** Your emotions

- **Card 4:** Your ambition

- **Card 5:** What holds you back

- **Card 6:** What will help you go forward

- **Card 7:** Hopes and dreams

- **Card 8:** Outcome

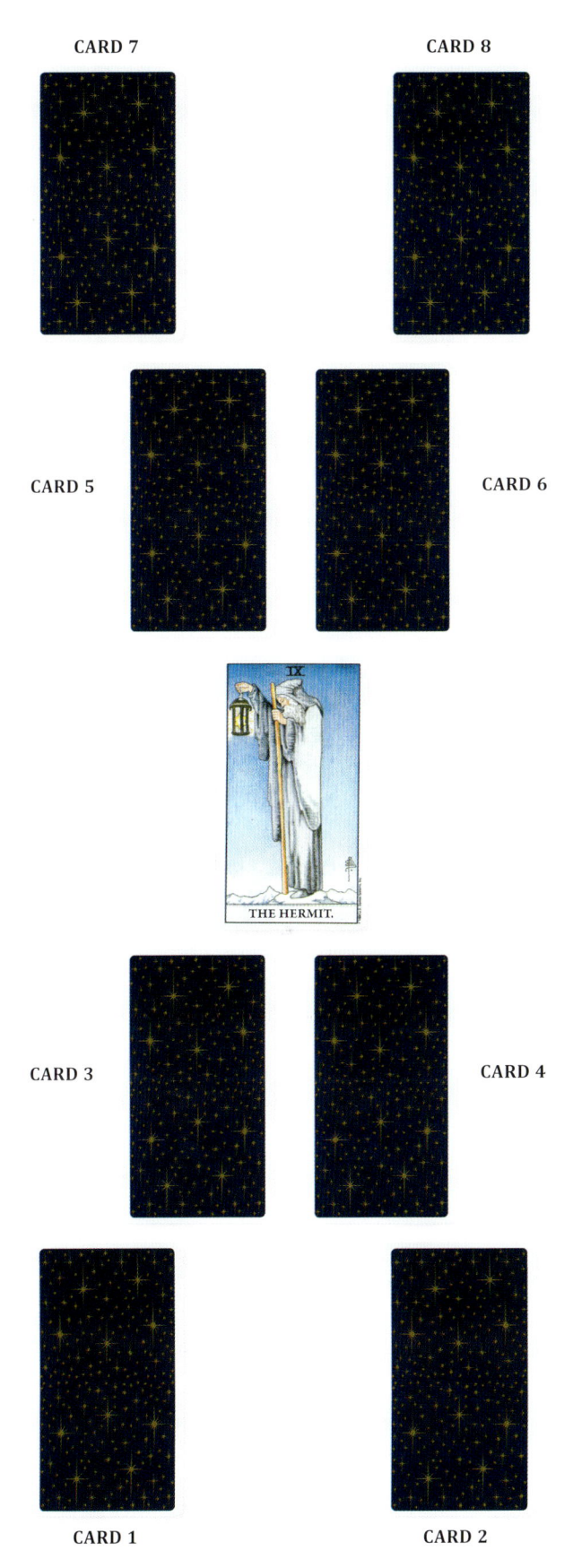

CARD 7   CARD 8

CARD 5   CARD 6

CARD 3   CARD 4

CARD 1   CARD 2

X THE WHEEL OF FORTUNE

WHEEL *of* FORTUNE.

© 1990 U.S. Games Systems, Inc.

Alternative Names: Fate, Destiny, The Wheel

Number: X

Numerology Links: I, The Magician, and XIX, The Sun

Astrological Sign or Planet: Jupiter

Element: Fire

Hebrew Letter: *Kaph*

> **Symbol:** The palms of the hand, or cup

> **Meaning:** Destiny

Tree of Life Pathway: Eleventh, between Chesed and Netzach

Chakra: Soul star, for soul connection

Key Meanings: Fate, change, intuition

UNDERSTANDING THE WHEEL OF FORTUNE

Flanked by three animals and a winged figure, the Wheel appears between the clouds in blue sky, symbolizing hope, clarity, and a breakthrough on a spiritual path. With The Wheel in motion is destiny at work: Divine law rules.

In the major arcana sequence, the Wheel of Fortune as card X marks the halfway point in our tarot journey. We now turn from the outward-looking phase, which focuses on our relationship with the external world, to another phase that begins our inner, spiritual journey. We learn the lesson of Justice, are transformed by Death, meet the Angel of Temperance, and then encounter the Devil and the Tower of destruction. After all this, we ascend to the cosmos with the Star, Moon, and Sun, look back on our lives with Judgement, and celebrate our achievements with the World before returning to begin all over again with card 0, The Fool.

The Wheel has a numerological link with card I, The Magician (10 reduces to 1), and card XIX, The Sun, (19; 1+ 9 = 10). Read together, these three cards assume the ritual of a spell or cosmic order: We set a singular intention with the Magician, align our wishes with the Wheel of Fortune, and enjoy the outcome with the Sun.

THE WHEEL OF FORTUNE'S ASTROLOGY

The Wheel corresponds to Jupiter, planet of luck, which rules religions and ideology, research and exploration. The angel and three animals around the wheel, embodied in the sphinx, can also be connected with the four elements and the fixed zodiac signs of Aquarius (the angel, element of Air), Taurus (bull, Earth), Scorpio (eagle, Water), and Leo (lion, Fire): They are shown on the Wheel as the primal elements of life.

THE WHEEL OF FORTUNE AND KABBALA

The Hebrew letter of the Wheel is *Kaph*, which means the palms of the hand and also destiny. On early tarot cards, a youth at the top of the Wheel is shown with one cupped hand.

On the Tree of Life, the Wheel is placed on the eleventh pathway between the spheres of Chesed, for law and love, and Netzach, for the forces of nature.

UPRIGHT MEANING

When the Wheel is upright, anything is possible—and usually positive. Chance meetings, unexpected offers, and news arrive in force. If life has been difficult recently, the Wheel shows a turn for the better.

Under this influence, your intuitive powers heighten, and you may find yourself tuning in to people from the past—who magically reappear. This is also an auspicious card for communication with family and friends who live some distance away. Additionally, the Wheel reveals psychic ability, either within you or someone close, and a chance to discover all your hidden aspects—both light and dark. You can use the Wheel's positive message wisely now to listen to your intuition and also to manifest your wishes, as your

energy aligns with your guides, angels, and other spirit helpers who help you on your path. Your quest for knowledge is heightened now and, while you cannot control the forces of the universe, you can certainly come to a better understanding of your role within the universe.

The Wheel also suggests the following:

- **Home:** An unexpected change in your living arrangements will happen; it will be surprising but beneficial in the long term.

- **Relationships:** An ex-partner or love interest comes back, but you will need to decide if this time your relationship will succeed. Don't try to make it work; if it is right, love will go smoothly.

- **Career and money:** News is coming that will improve your situation. However, you will need to prioritize the demands upon yourself and quickly adapt to new challenges.

REVERSED MEANING

When the Wheel is reversed, you may suffer some bad luck, but thankfully this marks the end of a run of challenges. In this way, the simple interpretation of the reversed Wheel is closure. The benefits of the upright Wheel will come—it will just take a little longer to gather momentum and move you forward. On a spiritual level, this card can also show a lack of confidence in your intuitive messages or a false start when choosing a way to spiritually develop. Vow to adapt, begin again, and keep on working toward your goal.

ITS WISDOM MESSAGE

Surrender to fate.

THE WHEEL'S SYMBOLS

In the Rider-Waite tarot, the Wheel of Fortune appears with these magical symbols. Some of them reappear in other major arcana cards, so learn to recognize them and you'll soon find you can apply your knowledge throughout the deck.

- *The wheel and its inscription:* In ancient Egypt, the wheel was a symbol of the sun. The wheel is inscribed with the letters *t*, *a*, *r*, and *o*, which can be arranged as *rota*, Latin for wheel. The *t*, *a*, *r*, and *o* can also be arranged as *Tora*, the visible letters on the scroll of the High Priestess.

  See this inscription on card II, The High Priestess.

- *The wheel's alchemical symbols:* The four symbols on the wheel spokes are Mercury, at the top, sulfur on the right, water below, and salt to the left. Mercury, sulfur, and salt were believed to be the secret ingredients used to create the mystical philosopher's stone.

- *The wheel's Hebrew letters:* These form the tetragrammaton: the four letters *Y, H, V, H*, or Yahweh—the name of God in Judaism.

- *The sphinx:* Meaning unity in diversity, the creature is traditionally composed of a human face (the angel), the body of a lion, the tail of a bull, and the wings of an eagle (the eagle is represented on the sphinx with a sword rather than wings). The four beings the sphinx embodies are illustrated around the Wheel, which also relate to the four fixed zodiac signs (see The Wheel of Fortune's Astrology).

  See this symbol on card VII, The Chariot.

- *The snake:* According to A. E. Waite, the snake is the legendary serpent-monster Typhon. He appears on the card with his head downward to show the negative aspect of fate.

  See this symbol on card I, The Magician, and VI, The Lovers.

- *The god Anubis:* Anubis is the jackal-headed Egyptian god of the afterlife and overseer of the rites of mummification. Placed on the lower right-hand side of the wheel with his head upright, we sense he travels all the way around the wheel, through life, death, and rebirth, echoing his role as protector of the dead.

- *The angel and three animals:* The angel, the lion, the bull, and the eagle are the symbols of the four evangelists, Matthew, Mark, Luke, and John—associated with the Four Gospels of the New Testament. They also symbolize the four elements and, by association, the four suits of the minor arcana.

  See these symbols on card XXI, The World.

THE HISTORICAL WHEEL OF FORTUNE: THE FOOL AND THE HERMIT

The Wheel of Fortune was a common motif of fickle fate in medieval times. The *Carmina Burana*, a manuscript of 254 poems dating from the eleventh to thirteenth centuries, later set to music by Carl Orff, contains an illustration of a wheel almost identical in composition to that shown in the very first tarot cards of the Renaissance era.

On the Visconti-Sforza card's Wheel of Fortune, a regal youth sits on a platform above the wheel. The youth has ass's ears, like early renditions of the Fool (see page 30). A bearded old man—the Hermit—is crouched under the Wheel. As with the *Carmina Burana*'s wheel, there is annotation for each of the four figures around the wheel. Words appear on the Visconti-Sforza card that translate as "I shall reign," "I am reigning," "I have reigned," and "I am without reign."

THE WHEEL OF FORTUNE'S REFLECTIONS

We can see aspects of the Wheel of Fortune in these minor arcana cards:

- The Six of Swords, for moving on

- The Nine of Cups, for a wish come true

TRY A READING WITH THE WHEEL: THE FOUR ELEMENTS OF FORTUNE

This reading uses just the minor arcana cards to reveal how best to harness your potential on four different levels. Take the Wheel from your deck and lay it before you. Now take out all the minor arcana cards and arrange them in their suits in four piles. Shuffle each pile. Choose the top card from each pile with your left hand and place them as shown. You could ask, "What opportunity is coming?"

- **Card 1:** What grounds you (Earth)

- **Card 2:** What inspires you (Fire)

- **Card 3:** Your wish (the angel; Air)

- **Card 4:** What will come—the future (Water)

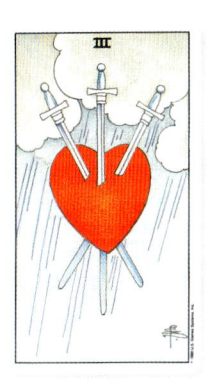

CARD 3: SWORD

CARD 4: CUP

THE WHEEL

CARD 1: PENTACLE

CARD 2: WAND

XI JUSTICE

Alternative Name: Adjustment

Number: XI (in some decks, numbered VIII and swapped with Strength)

Numerology Link: II, The High Priestess

Astrological Sign or Planet: Libra the Scales

Element: Air

Hebrew Letter: *Lamed*

> **Symbol:** The whip

> **Meaning:** Fairness

Tree of Life Pathway: Twelfth, between Tiphareth and Geburah

Chakra: Earth star, for spiritual grounding

Key Meanings: Balance, perception, and objectivity

UNDERSTANDING JUSTICE

Justice is one of the simplest cards to understand at first glance. A female figure is seated between two pillars on a ceremonial podium. This is the judge, or the virtue Justice personified, holding the traditional symbols of the law—an upright sword in her right hand and the scales in her left. Clad in the red robes of office, her right foot is forward and her pose is alert, as if she is about to pronounce judgement in court. Unlike traditional justice figures, tarot's Justice is not blindfolded. Her vision is clear.

The card favors those who are deserving (shown by the scales of mercy), but seeks retribution for past wrongs (symbolized by the sword of retribution). Justice is delivered through logical procedures and is focused on the mind rather than the emotions—just like the suit of Swords in the minor arcana (see page 176). However, there is, perhaps, more to Justice than meets the eye. Although Justice wears red, symbolizing the material world she lives in, the card's background is yellow, for enlightenment, suggesting the guidance of a higher, divine power. The card design, with a central figure between two pillars, is intentionally similar to those of V, The Hierophant, and II, The High Priestess, suggesting duality and knowledge.

Justice is one of the four cardinal, or essential, virtue cards of the tarot. The others are Strength, Temperance, and Prudence. The original Prudence card of early tarots has disappeared, but its meaning may be preserved in Justice. An old interpretation of *prudence* is wisdom, rather than caution—for example, in the conjunct word *jurisprudence*, the theory and study of law.

The number of Justice is XI. If XI is expressed as 11, we have two numbers with the same value, symbolizing balance and fairness. II is also the number of the High Priestess, Justice's numerological partner.

In traditional decks of the nineteenth century and earlier, Justice usually swapped places with Strength, number VIII. The VIII also suggests balance, as it comprises two sets of four, which is the number of stability.

JUSTICE'S ASTROLOGY

Justice takes the sign of Libra the Scales (September 22–October 23), which begins at the autumn equinox when the hours of daylight and darkness are equal, reflected in Libra's symbol, the scales. Justice's element, Air, also reminds us of the scales, which hang midair.

JUSTICE AND KABBALA

Lamed is the twelfth letter of the Hebrew alphabet and falls halfway within the sequence of twenty-two letters. *Lamed* means to whip or to goad—to assert authority; its esoteric meaning is fairness.

On the Tree of Life, Justice is placed on the thirtieth pathway between the spheres of Tiphareth, for beauty and consciousness, and Geburah, or power. In this way, the card's kabbalistic association suggests power, perfectly wielded.

UPRIGHT MEANING

There will be a positive outcome. This is a time when past errors or imbalances can be redressed. You benefit from a fair system, provided you are

accountable, honest, and deserving. Equally, you may be the judge in your own life, using your perspective and integrity to make good decisions that will safeguard your future. You may take a moral stand on an issue that affects you and those around you. In legal matters, a decision is made or a ruling given, which goes in your favor; justice will be done and order restored. On a spiritual level, Justice shows the working out of karma, or actions and consequences.

Justice shows a logical, considered influence. It is a welcome arrival in your reading if life has felt chaotic. It is a card of empowerment, advising you to take a left-brain approach to take control. Influential people favor you now, and your projects get support. Listen to advice from people around you whom you respect.

Justice can also indicate the following:

- **Home:** Legal issues concerning property are resolved. Contracts are signed and you can make progress.

- **Relationships:** While balance and practical issues are important now, take care that your emotional needs are met. Find the right balance between work and relationships.

- **Career and money:** At work you may be tested, but the outcome is positive; job interviews and negotiations are successful. Financially, you are coming to the end of a frugal period—money matters are set to improve.

REVERSED MEANING

Life goes out of balance as work, relationships, and money issues spiral out of control. A decision may go against you, so there may be dishonesty or a miscarriage of justice. You are treated unfairly, which is compounded by bad advice from a trusted individual. You are not able to speak your truth and feel overruled by those who don't understand your predicament. It is important to find your voice and stay strong to your values—if you are in the right.

HER WISDOM MESSAGE

With the right values, reward comes.

JUSTICE'S SYMBOLS

In the Rider-Waite tarot, Justice appears with these magical symbols. Some of them reappear in other major arcana cards, so learn to recognize them and you'll soon find you can apply your knowledge throughout the deck.

- *The stone pillars:* Boundaries and permanence—Justice's ruling is given within the boundaries of the law.

    See this symbol on card II, The High Priestess; V, The Hierophant; and VII, The Chariot.

- *The sword:* The sword shows the action that results from judgement. Like the Ace of Swords, it is held upright (see page 176) and signifies success.

    See this symbol on the Suit of Swords; X, The Wheel of Fortune; and I, The Magician.

- *The scales:* The scales represent the thought process involved in making a judgement—in that both sides of a story must be weighed up. The weight in the center of the scales resembles a ring through a sword, an ancient Celtic symbol of justice.

- *The crown:* An authority symbol, Justice's crown is known as a mural crown. Crenelated like castle walls, it suggests that justice is part of a civilized society. The square jewel in its center represents order.

- *The veil:* This appears to be a darkish red on the Rider-Waite card and is often shown as violet in later Rider interpretations. Some say this violet symbolizes spirituality, but consider it first as a soft boundary between the judge's court and the everyday world—when a ruling has been given, the veil is dropped and words become action.

    See this symbol on card II, The High Priestess, as a sign of the spirit world beyond her chamber.

- *Yellow background:* consciousness, clear sight, and support

    See this symbol on I, The Magician; III, The Empress; VII, The Chariot; and VIII, Strength.

HISTORICAL JUSTICE: THE WISDOM OF ASTREA AND MA'AT

The figure of justice so familiar to the courthouse derives from the ancient Greek goddess Astrea (the Roman Justitia), daughter of Themis. Both Astea and Themis were personifications of justice in the classical world. In statues depicting them, they raise the scales of justice and point the sword downward, and the goddesses were usually shown without blindfolds.

Historically, there are few variations on the card design. The Visconti-Sforza Justice cards, painted in fifteenth- and sixteenth-century Italy, show the likely figure of Maria Bianca Visconti (see page 40) with her scales and upright sword. However, a knight in black armor on a white charger is jumping over the throne, perhaps implying the result—or action—of her ruling; there may be a resonance with the horseman in the Death card (see page 82).

In the Classic Tarot, a reproduction of a Milanese tarot from around 1835, Justice has wings, echoing Ma'at, the ancient Egyptian goddess of cosmic wisdom and one of the earliest winged figures we have evidence of in art. Ma'at's influence is also suggested in card XX, Judgement. As Ma'at weighed the souls of the dead, in Judgement we evaluate our own soul (see page 110).

JUSTICE'S REFLECTIONS

We can see aspects of Justice in these minor arcana cards:

- The Ace of Swords, for clarity of thought and success

- The Two of Swords, which shows two swords, means a stalemate; a pending decision

TRY A READING WITH JUSTICE: THE BALANCE OF POWER

Take Justice from your deck and lay the card before you. Now shuffle the remaining cards and cut the deck or fan out the cards facedown. Choose four cards with your left hand and place them around Justice, as shown. You could ask, "How do I make this decision?" or, as a prediction, "Will a decision go in my favor?"

- **Card 1:** Present situation

- **Card 3:** The sword: what action to take/what events will occur

- **Card 2:** The scales: what needs to be weighed up

- **Card 4:** The outcome

XII THE HANGED MAN

THE HANGED MAN.

Alternative Name: The Traitor

Number: XII

Numerology Link: III, The Empress

Astrological Sign or Planet: Neptune

Element: Water

Hebrew Letter: *Mem*

> **Symbol:** Water and the oceans
>
> **Meaning:** Transition

Tree of Life Pathway: Thirteenth, between Hod and Geburah

Chakra: Third eye, for intuition

Key Meanings: Waiting, sacrifice, and enlightenment

UNDERSTANDING THE HANGED MAN

This card, with its strange image of a man suspended from a tree, seems deadly by name. Yet when we examine the man's face, he appears perfectly calm—content, even, regardless of his precarious situation. He hangs by one leg yet his expression is beatific, and he has been given a halo. What exactly is going on?

The Hanged Man is on a tree rather than a hangman's scaffold, and the tree is the Tree of Life, symbol of the world at an esoteric level. This tree is in bud and alive with future possibility. The Hanged Man also appears safely tethered, and it's as if he knows he cannot fall. Suspended in midair, he is content to wait out his fate.

The Hanged Man has numerous possible identities (see The Historical Hanged Man); he may even be Christ himself—we have a halo and a kind of cross, after all. In the Paris Eadwine Psalter, which dates from the twelfth century, Christ is shown upside down on a cross, attended to by angels and two men binding his wrists. This may relate one of the card's meanings, which is sacrifice. The T-shaped cross is also a symbol of salvation and indicated those who suffered through the crucifixion of Christ. It is natural to connect at first with the otherworldly situation of the Hanged Man in his happy suspension, rather than his identity. The Hanged Man is not about to die. Rather, he is hanging around until his circumstances change.

In the major arcana sequence, the Hanged Man falls after XI, Justice, and before XIII, Death. We had our values on trial in Justice, and now we must hold on until Death, when we can figuratively let go. Death brings transformation, while the Hanged Man prepares to make the sacrifice Death needs so he can move on. This may sound rather grim, but Death is ongoing change and transformation, and any big shift requires preparation—and in some cases, the waiting time that the Hanged Man represents.

The Hanged Man's number, XII, comprises 1 and 2, adding up to III for the Empress. Both cards are about incubation: The Hanged Man's waiting is a spiritual incubation, relating to the legend of Odin (see The Hanged Man's Symbols), whereas the Empress's equivalent is the gestation time for her babies (see III, The Empress, page 42).

THE HANGED MAN'S ASTROLOGY

Neptune is the planet of the Hanged Man. Ruler of the oceans, Neptune links with the element of the card, Water. Also associated with mystical states and the imagination, Neptune indicates the different facets of the card when reversed—the aspect of fantasy and the raised state of consciousness that a period of reflection can bring.

THE HANGED MAN AND KABBALA

The Hebrew letter of the Hanged Man is *Mem*, which means the oceans as well as transition. On the Tree of Life, the Hanged Man is placed on the thirteenth pathway between the spheres of Hod and Geburah, or the logical mind versus power. Hod is also concerned with creativity and insight while Geburah has a violent, destructive aspect. The hanged man is suspended

between these two energies, and perhaps he must use his clever mind to balance his frustration as he exists in limbo.

UPRIGHT MEANING

The obvious meaning of the card at first glance is hanging around: Events are not moving with speed, but all you can do is wait patiently in the knowledge that the universe has its own plan. The card can also indicate that you may have made sacrifices just now and are eager to see rewards. Unfortunately, you cannot force an outcome that fits with your timetable. There are many other factors about which you can have no knowledge or influence. Therefore, you may also expect delays to travel plans and projects.

On a creative level, this card can appear frequently when a person is feeling frustrated with their progress. However, the message of the Hanged Man is incubation—your project needs time to evolve. Use this time to develop perspective on your work and your ambitions.

Another message from the Hanged Man is to try to see things from a new angle. If your approach isn't working, ask yourself if you can think laterally or find a way to turn a situation around.

The Hanged Man can also suggest the following:

- **Home:** Waiting and delays may affect remodeling or house moves. Try to invest your time wisely while you wait—there may be a creative solution.

- **Relationships:** You are unable to get the commitment you need from a partner, or you may be the one unwilling to commit. Traditionally, it can also show hanging around for a lover to acknowledge you as a partner rather than friend. If you're waiting too long, you may decide it's not worth the emotional investment.

- **Career and money:** Hold back on signing contracts or dealing with legal matters just now. With work, decisions may be going on that will affect your position, but you are protected. If you are looking for work, there may be delays and frustration.

REVERSED MEANING

The Hanged Man reversed can be a sign of rigid thinking and martyrdom. You may need to revise your expectations; what you think you want may not be possible. In the position, the card asks you if you are hanging on to a fantasy that may make you a victim rather than a victor. Take another view and liberate yourself from a contract or other obligation that cannot offer you what you want.

HIS WISDOM MESSAGE

Use your time wisely.

THE HANGED MAN'S SYMBOLS

In the Rider-Waite tarot, the Hanged Man appears with these magical symbols. Some of them reappear in other major arcana cards, so learn to recognize them and you'll soon find you can apply your knowledge throughout the deck.

- *The Tree:* This represents the World Tree that the Norse god Odin hung from and the Tree of Life, central motif of the Kabbalah, the Judaic mystical belief system.

- *The Tree as the Tau Cross: Tau* is the last letter of the Hebrew alphabet and refers to the shape of a cross, a T-shape, upon which Christ was crucified.

- *The figure:* According to A. E. Waite, the figure's right bent leg suggests part of the shape of the fylfot cross, an early Christian symbol.

- *The halo:* A symbol of enlightenment and a spiritual signifier, around the Hanged Man, the halo is also a symbol of protection.
  See this symbol on card XIV, Temperance, crowning Archangel Michael.

THE HISTORICAL HANGED MAN: SOLDIER OF FORTUNE

The historical Hanged Man may be Muzio Attendolo Sforza, an Italian condottiere or mercenary connected with the Visconti family, who commissioned the early tarot decks (see page 10). Attendolo killed the tyrant Ottobuono Terzo, an opponent of the Pope, but claimed that Pope John had not paid him for his services, so he defected to fight for King Ladislaus of Naples. According to scholar Geoffrey Trease, the Pope was so incensed by Attendolo's turnabout that he commissioned a satirical illustration showing him as a traitorous hanged man, which the tarot illustration references.

Another possible inspiration for the Hanged Man is the Norse God Odin, who hung from the World Ash tree for nine days and nights and at the end of his ordeal was granted the gift of prophecy. The eighteenth-century occultist Court de Gébelin suggested that the Hanged Man may actually be a printer's error, and that the card was intended to be the other way up. Upright, it resembles a French tarot of around 1720 with a Prudence card showing the Hanged Man's pose, upright with one knee bent. However, given the earliest Hanged Man cards were hand-painted, it's more likely that the figure is correctly positioned—and that the original Hanged Man was actually Muzio Attendolo Sforza.

THE HANGED MAN'S REFLECTIONS

We can see aspects of the Hanged Man in these minor arcana cards:

- The Eight of Wands reversed, for delay with moving and communication

- The Two of Wands reversed, for delays to plans

- The Three of Wands reversed, for delays to travel

TRY A READING WITH THE HANGED MAN: AN ALTERED PERSPECTIVE

Take the Hanged Man from your deck and lay him before you. Now shuffle the remaining cards and cut the deck or fan out the cards facedown. Choose five cards with your left hand and place them as shown. You could ask, "What am I waiting for?" or "What supports me at this time?"

- **Card 1:** Your situation

- **Card 2:** What supports you emotionally

- **Card 3:** What supports you practically

- **Card 4:** An alternative view of the situation

- **Card 5:** Outcome

CARD 5

CARD 2

CARD 3

CARD 1

CARD 4

XIII DEATH

Alternative Names: Mortality, Transformation, Thirteen; sometimes unnamed

Number: XIII

Numerology Link: IV, The Emperor

Astrological Sign or Planet: Scorpio the Scorpion

Element: Water

Hebrew Letter: *Nun*

> **Symbol:** The fish

> **Meaning:** Decline and rebirth

Tree of Life Pathway: Fourteenth, between Netzach and Tiphareth

Chakra: Alta Major, for the past and past lives

Key Meanings: Transformation and change

UNDERSTANDING DEATH

Death's image is unmistakable. Unlike the Hanged Man—a common motif in the fifteenth century but a puzzle to us today—Death's grim reaper is eternally understood as an immutable part of our earthly existence. Triumphant with his scythe and hood, sometimes riding a horse, skeletal Death is a reminder of our human frailty. Yet Death is also the bringer of necessary change and is not a sign of the physical death of a person in the present or future. He heralds the end of an era, when what is not needed is taken so the next phase can begin. Without him, we could have no clear sight of what might be possible.

Death as the reaper brings in the harvest, which is shown by the five ears of corn on his standard, or flag. Whatever is worth having will be saved, but what is irrelevant will be taken. On the Rider-Waite card, Death's influence affects all people regardless of status, shown by the people on the card at various stages of death or surrender, from the bishop to the child, the king to the maiden. This is the medieval Dance of Death, a common subject in paintings of that era. His black armor and pale horse follow the description of Death, one of the four horsemen of the apocalypse described in the New Testament's Book of Revelation.

In the major arcana sequence, Death arrives after card XII, The Hanged Man, a logical progression in that death must be the consequence of hanging, but this is spiritual death and rebirth after a time of contemplation. The card that follows Death is Temperance, when we begin to assimilate our past, present, and future to come to a greater understanding of our potential.

Death's number, XIII, is traditionally unlucky, but in numerology it reduces to 4 (1 + 3 = 4)—or IV, The Emperor, which promises that a new order will come after Death has cleared the way. A sun silhouettes the city: This is both sunset and sunrise, or simultaneous endings and beginnings.

DEATH'S ASTROLOGY

Scorpio is named after the scorpion, which kills with a swift sting—and, unsurprisingly, it is the astrological sign associated with Death. Its dates (October 23–November 22) mark the period after the harvest when leaves fall and we stock up for the winter. Scorpio is associated with death and sex, dying and creation, just as Death brings an ending before fertile new life with the spring.

DEATH AND KABBALA

The Hebrew letter associated with Death is *Nun*, which means fish, a symbol of sexuality and sperm; in climax this is *le petit mort*, the Little Death, which leads us to *Nun*'s connotations of decline and rebirth.

On the Tree of Life, Death is placed on the fourteenth pathway, between the spheres of Netzach and Tiphareth, or the cycles of nature—rebirth and growth.

UPRIGHT MEANING

Death brings endings and beginnings—sometimes all at once. This a time of fast and deep transformation and an opportunity to let go of whatever you no longer need. Unlike card XX, Judgement, which signals a process of self-examination, Death's impact is sudden and may be shocking. You have little control over external events when Death looms, but in time you will be able to see this sharp change in circumstances as a blessing. A break with the past—from relationships and friendships to work that is no longer satisfying—is the only way forward. In this sense, Death can be a release and a relief. Death, after all, is the ultimate reality check, and he leaves you with the bare bones, the truth.

In certain areas of life, Death can signify the following:

- **Home:** You need to find a new home; the place you are living no longer meets your needs. New circumstances may offer an opportunity to relocate.

- **Relationships:** A relationship ends or there is a period of necessary separation. In friendships, there will be an opportunity to reconnect when the time is right.

- **Career and money:** Signifying a career change or the ending of business partnerships or ways of bringing in an income, Death also suggests new opportunities are on the horizon. Financially, this is a tough time, but money matters will improve, so hold tight.

REVERSED MEANING

Death reversed has virtually the same meaning as the card in the upright position, but the difference is in your reaction. You may feel anxious and stressed, unable to comprehend what is happening, rather than being accepting. When Death is reversed, the universe is telling you that there is no way back—a relationship cannot be mended, or an employer won't change their mind. If you do a second reading and ask the question again, this card can appear after you have already had Death upright, as a final confirmation of your question.

ITS WISDOM MESSAGE

Swift change brings new beginnings.

DEATH'S SYMBOLS

In the Rider-Waite tarot, Death appears with these magical symbols. Some of them reappear in other major arcana cards, so learn to recognize them and you'll soon find you can apply your knowledge throughout the deck.

- *The standard:* The standard, or flag, shows a white rose and five ears of corn. The rose symbolizes renewal and the corn, the harvest. Death takes his harvest of souls and leaves the grain—the truth of his decision.

  See the flag of St. George on card XX, Judgement.

- *The black armor:* Black symbolizes loss and endings. Death is protected by his armor, whereas his chosen ones have no protection from his scythe.

- *The pale horse:* The pale horse of Death, one of the four horsemen of the apocalypse, links the Death card with Judgement: The four horsemen bring an apocalypse upon the world before the Last Judgement.

- *The red feather:* Symbolizing the life force, here it is shown wilted and dying.

  See this symbol as a positive on cards 0, The Fool, and XIX, The Sun.

- *The bishop and child:* The innocent child and godly bishop are both shown in yellow to symbolize their piety. They look directly at the figure of Death, their purity protecting them from fear, while the other victims turn away.

- *The city gates:* Death's rampage takes place outside the city walls because, traditionally, burial grounds were established away from cities for hygiene reasons. On the card, the city gates represent the gates of heaven. The sun rising and/or setting shows the dawn of a new era and the closing of a present era.

  See this symbol on card XVIII, The Moon.

- *The ship:* The boat or ship is a signifier in many ancient beliefs for the journey the soul takes to the afterlife. The riverbed is marshlike and suggests the Styx, the mythological Greek river over which the souls of the dead were carried to the underworld; this also links to Death's element of Water. In Christianity, the boat is an old symbol for Christ and the church.

HISTORICAL DEATH: DANSE MACABRE

The Visconti di Modrone tarot (1441–1447) shows Death on horseback with a bandage around his head, wielding a huge scythe—very like our Rider-Waite card, as it too shows a bishop or king and children, all about to succumb. In the Visconti-Sforza tarots, Death is a skeletal archer who holds a vertebra in the shape of an archer's bow. The clear message is that death, just like love, strikes at random.

The Black Death, famine, and the Hundred Years War in Europe in the thirteenth and fourteenth centuries made death a very common part of life in medieval times, and paintings showing Death were a common reminder of our frailty: Painter and printmaker Pieter Bruegel the Elder's 1562 *The Triumph of Death* depicts a Dance of Death, or Danse Macabre, showing Death as an animated skeleton slaying people from all walks of life, again, like the randomness shown in the Rider-Waite card. Later, Death's dance became a subject for satire, and Death became an almost comic figure, leading unwilling and random citizens to their demise.

DEATH'S REFLECTIONS

We can see aspects of the Death card in these minor arcana cards:

- The Ten of Swords, for endings

- The Four Aces, for beginnings

TRY A READING WITH DEATH: LOOKING AT TRANSFORMATION

If you are uncomfortable with the Death card, focus on the meaning of transition and change—and get comfortable with the image. Take Death from your deck and lay him before you. Now shuffle the remaining cards, and cut the deck or fan out the cards facedown. Choose two cards with your left hand and place them as shown. You could ask, "What needs to go?" or "What will be transformed?"

- **Card 1:** Past issues: what is to be released

- **Card 2:** The outcome

CARD 1   CARD 2

XIV TEMPERANCE

Alternative Name: Art

Number: XIV

Numerology Link: V, The Hierophant

Astrological Sign or Planet:
Sagittarius the Archer

Element: Fire

Hebrew Letter: *Samekh*

  Symbol: Support or crutch

  Meaning: Patience

Tree of Life Pathway: Fifteenth, between Yesod and Tiphareth

Chakra: Solar plexus, for personal power

Key Meanings: Moderation, reconciliation, healing, and angelic guidance

UNDERSTANDING TEMPERANCE

An angel holds two cups flowing with water. He has one foot on a rock and the other in the pool of water, showing the present, conscious mind (the rock, or earth), and the past, emotions and the unconscious mind (water). A clear path runs from the pool through two mountains and toward a potential future: a luminous rising sun. A new horizon or perspective is in sight. The riverbank is lush and verdant, and two yellow irises bloom there, symbols of hope. The angel, by moderating the flow of water in his cups, creates a harmonious flow, a new reality.

In the major arcana sequence, the angel of Temperance sits between card XIII, Death, and XV, The Devil; it is the antithesis of Death's loss and the Devil's enslavement to materialism and base urges. The angel is Archangel Michael, the protector warrior-angel, who offers us spiritual help and guidance while we strive to pacify or temper volatile forces. If we look closely, we see that the water from Michael's cups could be running upward or downward. Alchemy is at work, suggesting that a little magic may be needed if we are to reconcile all the demands upon us.

Temperance is one of the tarot's four virtues. Numerically between VI, The Lovers, and XX, Judgement, Temperance is also the second angel card in the major arcana sequence; it's a call to spiritual connection and service. This is shown by the symbol of the sun on Archangel Michael's forehead and the amulet on his chest (see Temperance's Symbols). Angels in the tarot are also connected with time. With Temperance, we are dealing with issues of the past, present, and future. With the Lovers, Archangel Raphael calls time on a present decision with future impact; with Judgement, Archangel Gabriel calls time on the past.

Temperance's number is XIV, the double of prime number 7, the magical number of creation. In numerology, the sum of XIV (14; 1+4 =5) gives 5, or V, The Hierophant. The Hierophant and Temperance's Archangel Michael are divine meditators.

TEMPERANCE'S ASTROLOGY

Sagittarius the Archer (November 23–December 21) is Temperance's sign. The archer is sometimes known as the centaur—half-man, half-beast—showing the blending of opposites. The glyph for Sagittarius is the crossed arrow, like that of the archer. It is a symbol of precision, just as Archangel Michael pours the water between goblets at a precise angle so no liquid is spilled. Temperance's element is Fire, for action and energy.

TEMPERANCE AND KABBALA

The Hebrew letter associated with Temperance is *Samekh*, meaning support and patience. Temperance is placed on the Tree of Life on the fifteenth pathway, between the spheres of Yesod and Tiphareth, linking together the qualities of change and salvation.

UPRIGHT MEANING

Temperance shows you dealing with a potentially volatile situation, and you need to temper your thoughts and actions to find balance and harmony. This means choosing neither one nor the other, but blending two opposing forces to create an inspired solution. The card also asks you not to resist, but to accept both sides of a situation and be guided by what feels most natural to you. It is time to reconcile any area of your life that is out of kilter. Be hands-on; you can analyze what you might do for eons, but what matters now is action.

Temperance also shows you are connecting with your guides and angels. You may be given a sign, such as advice from a friend or even a stranger whom the angels have sent to help you. This may also be the beginning of a spiritual journey for you. In your projects, what you imagine you can create. You may also be inspired by an invention or work of art from the past.

Here are some other interpretations:

- **Home:** Running a household and dealing with demanding children or partners is a fine balancing act, but you have the financial and emotional resources to succeed.

- **Relationships:** This is a stage in a relationship when you can reach a new level of trust. If you are single, you may be guided toward a new partner; it's an emotionally intense time.

- **Career and money:** You may be dealing with difficult or highly sensitive individuals. Be the diplomat, and you can work a miracle. In money terms, pay extra attention to your income and outgoings.

REVERSED MEANING

Temperance reversed shows imbalance and unfairness in relationships and problems with money; what you pour into your relationships and work isn't rewarded. This card can also show you struggling with change, and the past dominating your present and future. In this position, difficult old memories can resurface and you feel held back. Try to look at what you need now, in the present.

ITS WISDOM MESSAGE

You are guided to find peace.

TEMPERANCE'S SYMBOLS

In the Rider-Waite tarot, Temperance appears with these magical symbols. Some of them reappear in other major arcana cards, so learn to recognize them and you'll soon find you can apply your knowledge throughout the deck.

- *The triangle and square:* The triangle within the square denotes the element of Fire (the upward-pointing triangle) and the Earth (the square). This, said A. E. Waite, is the symbol of the septenary—the seven principles of man according to nineteenth-century Theosophists. The seven principles are the physical body, the astral body, the breath, desire, thought, the spirit, and "I am." Above this amulet are the four Hebrew letters *Y*, *H*, *V*, and *H*, the tetragrammaton for the Lord or, when spoken, Yahweh.

- *The cups:* A cup represents the vessel of our experience. In Temperance, one cup is for the past and one is for the present, and the water running between the two symbolizes the present—what we create from the past and our future expectations. The cups also show focus on the task in hand.

- *The sun symbol:* The dotted circle on the archangel's head is the astrological symbol for the sun and spiritual illumination. It is also the alchemical symbol for gold.

  See this symbol on card XIX, The Sun; 0, The Fool; and VI, The Lovers; as a halo, see card XII, The Hanged Man.

- *Archangel Michael:* Archangel Michael is the protector-archangel who deals with cutting through fear and letting go of the past.

  See the Archangels Raphael and Gabriel on card VI, The Lovers, and XX, Judgement.

- *The irises:* The irises refer to Iris, the Greek goddess of rainbows and hope.

- *The water-pool:* The water symbolizes purification and regeneration in cultural practice and is also a signifier of the flow of emotions and unconscious mind.

  See this symbol on card XVII, The Star, and XVIII, The Moon.

- *Rising sun over mountain/volcano:* Symbolizing renewal, it's a new dawn after a period of stress, shown by the mountains.

  See the sun rising over the city on card XIII, Death.

HISTORICAL TEMPERANCE: FINDING CHARITY

Temperance has few variations in its card design throughout history. Early tarot cards of the Renaissance show a woman without wings, and after the 1700s, the woman becomes an angel; the two cups, however, have always been present.

It's likely that Temperance embodies more than just one virtue. Prudence, Faith, Hope, and Charity are the "lost" cards of the tarot, which once appeared in variations of the Visconti-Sforza tarots of fifteenth-century Italy as well as earlier tarots. It's likely that Temperance became a natural home for Charity, as the Catholic catechism states, "The virtue of chastity comes under the cardinal virtue of Temperance, which seeks to permeate the passions and appetites of the senses with reason."

TEMPERANCE'S REFLECTIONS

We can see aspects of Temperance in these minor arcana cards:

- The Two of Coins, for weighing up a decision, or money flow

- The Six of Cups, for harmony

- The Page of Cups, for magical thinking

- The Queen of Cups, for nurturing a situation

- The Six of Pentacles, for fairness and generosity

TRY A READING WITH TEMPERANCE: MAKING PEACE

Take Temperance from your deck and lay the card at the top of the spread as shown. Now split the deck into the minor and major arcana and shuffle each pile. Choose the first two cards from the minor arcana pile and lay them out as shown, then choose cards 3, 4, and 5 from the major arcana pile. You could ask, "What do I need to temper?" The suit element of the minor cards will show you which life area needs attention. The majors give you a deeper insight into how the situation may be transformed.

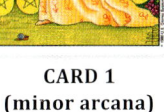

CARD 1
(minor arcana)

CARD 3
(major arcana)

- **Card 1:** What factors are in balance (minor arcana)

- **Card 2:** What factors are out of balance (minor arcana)

- **Card 3:** What guidance do I need? (major arcana)

- **Card 4:** Action to take (major arcana)

- **Card 5:** The outcome (major arcana)

CARD 5
(major arcana)

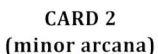

CARD 2
(minor arcana)

CARD 4
(major arcana)

TIP: For cards 1 and 2, you can use the general minor arcana suit meanings to begin with:
Swords: work, focus, decisions—the mind
Wands: projects, inspiration, travel—the soul
Cups: emotions, relationships—the heart
Pentacles: money, home, security—the physical body

XV THE DEVIL

Alternative Names: Pan, Temptation

Number: XV

Numerology Link: VI, The Lovers

Astrological Sign or Planet: Capricorn the Goat

Element: Earth

Hebrew Letter: *Ayin*

    Symbol: Eye

    Meaning: Clear vision

Tree of Life Pathway: Sixteenth, between Hod and Tiphareth

Chakra: Base for base instincts

Key Meanings: Enslavement and temptation

UNDERSTANDING THE DEVIL

A bearded man-beast sits above a door to which two demons, a man and woman, are chained. With an inverted pentacle rising from his third eye, he appears to be the epitome of evil, complete with horns, clawed feet, and batlike wings. He is half-man, half-goat, an archetype with roots in many ancient gods. He may be the faun Pan, god of excess; Satan, son of God gone bad; Baphomet, the dark idol the Knights Templar were accused of worshipping; or perhaps Cernunnos, the horned Pagan deity. All are attributed with great virility and sexual power.

The goat-god's abode is black, like a cave. We are in a dark place here, save for his fiery torch. His right hand raised asserts his control over the two small figures that stand before him. The couple is Adam and Eve, who, banished from paradise, find themselves enslaved and corrupted—they are becoming demons, shown by the tiny horns growing from their heads. Yet when we look closely, we can see that the chains around their necks are not at all tight; if they wished, they could walk away from the Devil altogether. The fruit near Eve reminds us of the Garden of Eden and the forbidden fruit. Adam's tail has a devilish fork, showing that these two have certainly given in to temptation.

In the major arcana sequence, the Devil falls between XIV, Temperance, and XVI, The Tower. If the lessons of Temperance are not learned, we fall from the grace of Temperance's angel and into the arms of the Devil. When we do finally turn our back on him, the lesson is profound. We must find a whole new way of living as the Tower—the ego—struck by lightning is destroyed.

The Devil's number, XV, reduces to card VI (1 + 5 = 6), or the Lovers. The Devil is the shadow side of the Lovers, fallen to materialism, greed, and lust. The Devil is also a symbol for other negative behavior patterns, such control, dangerous affairs, and addiction.

THE DEVIL'S ASTROLOGY

The Devil's zodiac sign is Capricorn the Goat (December 22–January 20), linking with his identities as Pan and Satan. Capricorn's element is Earth, for material needs, and its planet is Saturn. Saturn was the Roman god of time. Time, like the Devil himself, is traditionally the ultimate enemy of man (see The Historical Devil).

THE DEVIL AND KABBALA

The Devil's kabbalistic letter is *Ayin*, meaning eye, and also clear vision—a clue to be vigilant and all-seeing in the Devil's presence. On the Tree of Life, the card is placed on the sixteenth pathway between the spheres of Hod and Tiphareth. Hod stands for the mind and Tiphareth, beauty and rebirth, which shows us how our insight into a particular situation may just release us from the Devil's grip.

UPRIGHT MEANING

You may be enslaved to an ideal or a relationship that demands too much. What started positively, or even pleasurably, has reversed, and now you are seeing a situation for what it is. This is a destructive situation, and you may be feeling controlled and under a bad influence. This is a card of greed, temptation, and

materialism. Yet to change the situation, you will need to think laterally and use a little cunning. It's never worth confronting the problem, as the negativity is endemic— hence the Devil card often appears to describe situations that are not worth trying to fix or heal. The message is to simply walk away, to escape in the best way you can, regardless of the temptation of staying.

The Devil often arrives in a relationship reading to show lust and negative ways of relating, in that one partner is gaining much more that the other. By extension of this, additional meanings of the Devil are addiction—issues with sex, food, substance abuse, and overall negative thinking patterns.

Some other specifics include the following:

- **Home:** Here, the Devil may indicate living with domineering people or dealing with a difficult landlord. Psychic vampires and generally negative people may drain your energy. You may feel controlled and invaded just now.

- **Relationships:** Difficult relationships are indicated here, such as controlling partners, lust-over-love situations, affairs, and codependent patterns. For separated partners, the Devil may show financial dependency or other ongoing money or property issues that keep you tied to the past.

- **Career and money:** You're experiencing bad financial contracts, careers that are unsatisfying, domineering bosses, or a toxic work environment— but you stay because you are financially trapped.

REVERSED MEANING

When reversed, this is one of the few cards whose meaning becomes more hopeful. With the upright Devil, it's time to acknowledge how you may be trapped and to begin to search for the light. When reversed, the Devil suggests the decision you need to make will be easier than you think. When the card is upside down, the chains around the couple are more lax than they appear, so a situation is not quite as drastic as you first thought. Now is the time to make your move.

In terms of health, a difficult cycle is about to end. Addiction and bad habits become easier to manage and eventually banish, and you or those close to you can look forward to recovery.

HIS WISDOM MESSAGE

In one leap, you can be free.

THE DEVIL'S SYMBOLS

In the Rider-Waite tarot, the Devil appears with these magical symbols. Some of them reappear in other major arcana cards, so learn to recognize them and you'll soon find you can apply your knowledge throughout the deck.

- *The devil:* He is a symbol of internal or external oppression. Showing the shadow side of human nature, he suggests base instincts at work rather than the higher self.

- *The tails:* The tails show lower instincts taking shape in our lives. The woman's tail shows fruit, echoing the forbidden fruit of the Garden of Eden, which she has now eaten. The man's tail is devil-like and appears to be catching the color of the Devil's torch, symbolizing corruption.

- *The chains:* Representing control and dependency, the chains illustrate emotional and material bonds that are habitual but not necessary.

- *The torch:* The torch is not held up to illuminate the scene, or situation; the Devil keeps his knowledge and his power for himself.

- *The inverted pentagram:* The upright pentagram stands for humanity and being humane. When reversed, it is a sign of cruelty and dark forces. The symbol can also be seen as a representation of the Devil's head, with the pointed beard at the lowest point of the pentagram and his ears and horn the middle and upper points.

THE HISTORICAL DEVIL: DARK ARCHETYPES

In the Visconti-Sforza tarots of the Renaissance, the Devil is a terrifying monster with two heads—one devil, one human—and the Devil's mouth is busy devouring a small naked man. While the man-eating beast was a popular motif in early paintings showing the Last Judgement, myths of devilish gods date back to the Greeks and Romans. The Greek Cronos, god of time, ate his own children. He is associated with aspects of Roman god Saturn, who appears in the fifteenth-century Tarocchi of Mantegna cards as Saturno, a man holding a serpent biting its tail—making the shape of the ouroboros, the alchemical symbol for never-ending time. With his other hand, he is raising a child to his mouth, about to consume it. Four other children await their fate at his feet.

In the mid-fifteenth-century Griggoneur tarots, the Devil is an upright figure with a human body. Goatlike and bearded, with horns and clawed feet, he has a strange devil's face painted on his groin to show the dangers of lust. The devil-in-the-pants motif is also seen in the painting *Devils Waiting for the Last Judgement* (Livre de la vigne nostre Seigneur, France 1450–1470). Here, the devil head over the genitals has a big laviscious tongue, making the message of lust and sexual temptation all the more evident.

The Rider-Waite's devil is the traditional Pan or Satan, an embodiment of the Devil archetype across the ages.

THE DEVIL'S REFLECTIONS

We can see aspects of the Devil in these minor arcana cards:

- The Two of Swords, for being stuck

- The Eight of Swords, for restriction

- The Three of Swords, for conflict and betrayal

TRY A READING WITH THE DEVIL: BREAKING THE SPELL

Take the Devil card from your deck and lay it before you. Now shuffle the remaining cards and cut the deck or fan out the cards facedown. Choose four cards with your left hand and place them around the Devil as shown. You could ask, "What's controlling me?" or "How can I get out of this situation?"

- **Card 1:** Present situation

- **Card 2:** What or who is trapping you

- **Card 3:** What action to take

- **Card 4:** Outcome

CARD 3

CARD 2 THE DEVIL CARD 4

CARD 1

XVI THE TOWER

THE TOWER.

Alternative Names: The House of God, Fate, The Lightning

Number: XVI

Numerology Link: VII, The Chariot

Astrological Sign or Planet: Mars

Element: Fire

Hebrew Letter: *Peh (Pei)*

Symbol: Mouth

Meaning: Chaos

Tree of Life Pathway: Seventeenth, between Hod and Netzach

Chakra: Crown and base, for heaven and earth

Key Meanings: Destruction and enlightenment

UNDERSTANDING THE TOWER

The Tower is aflame, struck by lightning that has thrown two figures to the ground. A crown, once atop the Tower, is blasted in to the darkness as nature asserts her power over Earth. In early French tarots, the card is named *la Maison Dieu*, the House of God, calling to mind the burning of the Tower of Babel as divine retribution for our sins, a story told in the rabbinic text the *Midrash*. Genesis offers an alternative story: The Tower and city were abandoned, not burned, when God made the Babylonians speak in incomprehensible languages.

As with the other supposedly dark cards in the major arcana—Death and the Devil—there is always a way forward, provided we can accept a force that is higher than us and adapt to a new way of living and relating to each other. If we've been cossetting ourselves away in ivory towers, it's time to come back down to earth.

The Tower marks a point of awakening. In the major arcana sequence, it falls after the Devil. If the Devil is pride, ego, and arrogance, then the Tower is a fall from grace. It is a necessary stage of breakdown and rebuilding so our horizons can expand. We must look for a new place to be, physically or spiritually, and engage with new concepts and people if we are to progress to card XVII, The Star, which offers hope and the chance to follow a dream.

The Tower's number, XVI, comprises two number 8s, for renewal. Also, in numerology, XVI reduces to VII (1 + 6 = 7), or the Chariot, which is powered by the charioteer's determination. With the Tower, our willpower has no effect. Only the will of God determines the outcome. In this sense, the Tower, along with the Wheel of Fortune (see page 70), is a card of fate.

THE TOWER'S ASTROLOGY

The Tower's planet is Mars, fiery and masculine, forceful and warlike. Although Mars's energy can bring destruction, with this comes a release, a breakthrough.

THE TOWER AND KABBALA

The kabbalistic letter of the Tower is Peh, which means mouth, and also expression, words, and speech, perhaps relating to the Babyloneans' speaking in different tongues. Another meaning of Peh is chaos—the impact of the falling Tower.

On the Tree of Life, the Tower is placed on the seventeenth pathway between the spheres of Hod and Netzach, or the logical mind and the forces of nature. Whatever we think, we are always subject to higher forces.

UPRIGHT MEANING

The Tower hits us with sudden change: the collapse of an ideal, a dream, an organization, or a relationship. This is inevitable and is due to forces beyond your control. The Tower can represent shattered ego, so you may feel vulnerable and confused. Yet you can only surrender to the power of the Tower and work on accepting the huge shift in awareness it offers—although the benefits may not be obvious just yet.

The upside of the Tower is its message of release. The walls come tumbling down, but in the moment of destruction, everything is illuminated. You can see inside the Tower and look at how you built it—how you lived in your psychological tower and what it protected you from. Now, you can experience a flash of deep insight. With the Tower gone, you can begin to sense how the future might evolve. What you build next can have more foundation.

Some readers find the Tower an apt descriptor of migraines, with the buildup of pressure and intense pain. The Tower's lightning bolt has also been likened to sexual tension and earth-shattering release.

Here are some other possibilities the Tower may signify:

- **Home:** The Tower can illustrate an abrupt change to your circumstances. A property you hoped to move into does not materialize, or you encounter delays to building projects, for example.

- **Relationships:** A secret comes to light, which may be shocking. It is time to let go of past patterns of relating. Equally, you may experience an intense physical or spiritual attraction, which has a profound impact on your orderly existence.

- **Career and money:** Restructuring in businesses, possible redundancies that may mean a move to alternative premises—the Tower signifies change. A person in a position of power makes tough decisions, and a leader may be ousted from their post.

REVERSED MEANING

When the Tower is reversed, you may find yourself taking responsibility even when you are blameless. It can also show you have held on to a career, project, or relationship that is not strong enough to stand the test of time. If you have clung to the past to protect yourself from reality, your fears may materialize. The Tower's collapse is inevitable, so do not feel responsible for forces outside your control. Its impact is sudden and dramatic, and soon you will know exactly where you stand.

ITS WISDOM MESSAGE

Surrender.

THE TOWER'S SYMBOLS

In the Rider-Waite tarot, the Tower appears with these magical symbols. Some of them reappear in other major arcana cards, so learn to recognize them and you'll soon find you can apply your knowledge throughout the deck.

- *The tower:* Illustrating society, protection, and the ego, a lone tower can also symbolize the past.

  See the symbol of the watchtowers on card XVIII, The Moon.

- *The falling figures:* The figures symbolize humanity at the mercy of God and the power of nature. They also represent the fallout that disaster can bring—emotional, physical, and financial.

- *Fire:* Fire is the element associated with Mars, both the planet and the Roman god of war. It symbolizes change, rebirth, and purification.

  See this symbol as a negative aspect in card XV, The Devil, on his torch, and as a positive symbol of growth on card XIX, The Sun.

- *The golden droplets:* On the Rider-Waite card, the flames emit golden droplets in the form of the Hebrew letter *J*, meaning fire. There are twenty-two, the number of letters in the Hebrew alphabet and the number of major arcana cards in a traditional tarot deck.

  See this symbol on card XVIII, The Moon.

- *Lightning bolt:* The lightning bolt is a symbol of enlightenment and purification, revealing what has been hidden. In a flash, we are spiritually awakened and cleansed of negative karma.

- *The falling crown:* The crown is a symbol of power and sovereignty. The falling crown shows that worldly power no longer holds—nature is a far greater force. We are not in control or protected by our ego anymore.

THE HISTORICAL TOWER: PUNISHMENT AND PURIFICATION

Throughout the years of tarot history, the Tower has always been burning, although with minor variations. The Visconti-Sforza cards of the Renaissance era show a cross at the bottom of the Tower, a symbol of resurrection after chaos. This may reference attacks on the Catholic faith by heretics, which were common in the fifteenth century. The Tower, a symbol of the power of the Church, is not struck down by God—the flames appear to have been created by the intense heat from two suns, symbols of diverse political forces. On our Rider-Waite card, the burning Tower links with Midrash's account of the fall of the Tower of Babel. It may also be a depiction of God's punishment of the cities of Sodom and Gomorrah, which were burned to the ground in retribution for the people's sins.

The lightning bolt is a magical symbol in many myths and belief systems: A flash of lightning from Zeus impregnated Semele, Princess of Thebes, with her son, Dionysus, the god of wine—thus the lightning bolt is a nod to the shift in consciousness that the Tower brings. Buddhism has its own sacred lightning bolt, a *djore* (Tibet region of China) or *vajra* (India), a symbol for the purification of the mind, which, in a flash, releases the negative karma with which we are born.

THE TOWER'S REFLECTIONS

We can see aspects of the Tower in these minor arcana cards:

- The Seven of Swords, for loss

- The Three of Swords, for sorrow and pain

- The Five of Cups, for loss and upset

- The Eight of Cups, for emotional upheaval

- The Ten of Wands, for overwhelm and burdens

TRY A READING WITH THE TOWER: LETTING GO

Take the Tower from your deck and lay it before you. Now shuffle the remaining cards and cut the deck or fan out the cards facedown. Choose six cards with your left hand and place them around the Tower, as shown. You could ask, "What will be released?" or "Is my present position in my career/relationship/ home secure?"

- **Card 1:** The foundation: the past

- **Card 2:** Emotional reasons for your tower

- **Card 3:** The financial benefits of your tower

- **Card 4:** What needs to be released

- **Card 5:** Emotional outcome

- **Card 6:** Practical outcome

CARD 4

CARD 5

CARD 6

CARD 3

CARD 2

CARD 1

THE TOWER.

XVII THE STAR

Alternative Names: Hope, The Stars

Number: XVII

Numerology Link: VIII, Strength

Astrological Sign or Planet:
Aquarius the Water Carrier

Element: Air

Hebrew Letter: *Tzaddi*

   Symbol: The fishhook

   Meaning: Hope

Tree of Life Pathway: Eighteenth, between Yesod and Netzach

Chakra: Higher heart, for universal love

Key Meanings: Hope, guidance, inspiration, and creativity

UNDERSTANDING THE STAR

Like the water carrier of her zodiac sign of Aquarius, a maiden is pouring water from two vessels, one onto the earth and the other into a pool. It is twilight, but we can see clearly a tree and a tiny bird on the right of this serene landscape. At one with the natural world, this woman is a maiden aspect of the earth goddess, or card III, The Empress. Her nakedness under the stars shows purity and truth, and she is connected with the cosmos and the divine. There are eight stars above her, and one of them, a guiding star, is much bigger than the others. The Star card reveals hope and guidance.

In the major arcana sequence, the Star comes after XVI, The Tower, and before XVIII, The Moon. After the Tower's destruction, the maiden and her stars are a sign of hope for a new world. The cycles of nature continue, present in the four elements represented on the card: Earth, Air, and Water, with Fire suggested by the yellow guiding star. Pouring calming water onto the earth and into the pool, she heals the past and the present.

The Star's number, XVII, comprises 7 and 1, adding up to 8, or VIII, Strength. Strength shows a clothed woman holding the jaws of a lion, in a bid to control dangerous instincts.

In the Star, the maiden has ascended to a more conscious state of awareness. She can let the water flow, trusting that she is on her path. In some decks, this card may show a winged maiden to illustrate angelic guidance.

THE STAR'S ASTROLOGY

The Star's sign is Aquarius the Water Carrier (January 21–February 19), and the element of the card is Air. Water represents insight, consciousness, and healing and Air, thought and idealism, suggesting the social conscience with which Aquarians are so often attributed.

THE STAR AND KABBALA

The Hebrew letter of the Star is *Tzaddi*, meaning the fishhook; it also takes the meaning of hope. On the Tree of Life, the Star is placed on the eighteenth pathway, between the spheres of Yesod and Netzach. Yesod is the sphere of magic and the moon, while Netzach stands for sensual passion and instinct. The Star is therefore the result of both these aspects, bringing together the qualities of the sun and moon to create a new Earth.

UPRIGHT MEANING

The Star offers hope and guidance, so if things have felt difficult recently, have faith that your luck is about to change for the better. The Star is a powerful symbol of hope, and you can begin to appreciate everything life has to offer, including better physical and spiritual well-being. The Star supports beauty, and creativity flows like the star-maiden's water. In your projects and relationships, you can be fully expressed, sharing your love, gifts, and talents. The Star allows you to shine and show your Star quality, so your efforts are appreciated. You may also feel more intuitive and insightful under the Star's influence and have more trust in messages from your angels and guides.

The Star also shows good health. It is the card of the healer and is traditionally associated with astrology.

The Star can also indicate the following:

- **Home:** You feel inspired to create beauty and style in your home, so craft projects and design are especially favored now. If you have your eye on a dream home, it will come to you.

- **Relationships:** The Star shows that you are destined to be with someone; it is time to find a soul mate. Other existing relationships are calm and harmonious.

- **Career and money:** The Star brings money luck. Work you do begins to pay off, as you have considered your long-term goals and given attention to what matters most. Entrepreneurs may be guided to begin a new business, or you find you have a hidden talent you can put to good use. The Star can also show awards and fame.

REVERSED MEANING

In the reversed position, the Star can show giving up too easily in your projects and experiencing a creative block. You may be too attached to a fantasy scenario—after all, starlight is bewitching—while overlooking the details. Alternatively, you may feel lulled into a false sense of security in a venture that has no foundation and little chance of success. An additional meaning is feeling alone just now, without the support you need.

ITS WISDOM MESSAGE

Be inspired—dreams come true.

THE STAR'S SYMBOLS

In the Rider-Waite tarot, the Star appears with these magical symbols. Some of them reappear in other major arcana cards, so learn to recognize them and you'll soon find you can apply your knowledge throughout the deck.

- *The eight stars:* Hope and divine guidance are embodied by the stars. The central yellow star, according to A. E. Waite, is a symbol of Freemasonry called the Flamboyant Star, or Seal of Solomon. (Waite had become a Freemason in 1901.) However, this talisman is usually shown with six rather than eight points, so perhaps this was to be just one aspect of its meaning. The star may also represent Sirius, or Venus (see The Historical Star). The eight stars each have eight points, symbolizing renewal. Eight is also the sum of the Star's number, 17.

  See the star crown and canopy of stars on card VII, The Chariot.

- *The maiden:* A symbol of eternal youth and the creative soul, she may be the Greek Aphrodite or the Egyptian deity Isis (see The Historical Star).

  See the maiden as a symbol of civilization on card VIII, Strength.

- *The bird:* The bird may symbolize the dove of Aphrodite or the ibis of Isis (see History). The ibis may be an intentional link with the card's Hebrew letter *Tzaddi*, which, according to tarot scholar Jonathan Dee, is "the perfect fishhook." The ibis also links with the Egyptian god Thoth, who was sometimes shown with the head of an ibis, one of his sacred creatures. In general, birds are symbols of freedom and the soul.

- *Flowing water:* This is the water of life, symbolizing resourcefulness and healing. The star-maiden pours water into the pool and onto the earth to nourish it, just as the goddesses Venus and Isis brought fertility to the land.

THE HISTORICAL STAR: GODDESSES AND ANGELS

The image of the maiden and star has altered little over the centuries, from its simplest form in the Visconti-Sforza tarots—a woman holding a star—to the more illustrative Rider-Waite image, to which is added a pool, tree, and bird.

The star maiden herself may be Greek love and fertility goddess Aphrodite, the Roman Venus, who is often pictured with a dove. If so, the star above her is Venus, the Morning Star. An alternative identity is the Egyptian Isis, queen of magic and fertility, associated with the Ibis bird. If this is so, the big star is her symbol, Sirius, also known as the Star of Isis, fertility omen of the Nile. Legend has it that when Sirius, the brightest star in the night sky, appeared, the Nile flooded, watering the crops growing on the silt bed of the delta.

In some decks, the star-maiden is an angel. The card also embodies Faith, one of the "lost" virtue cards of the tarot that existed in early decks. The early Faith cards of the fifteenth and sixteenth centuries show a female figure holding in one hand one cup and in the other hand a cross. In this way, perhaps Faith's cup became subsumed into the two vessels of the Star, and her cross, symbol of religious guidance, went up to the heavens to become one of the eight stars in the sky.

THE STAR'S REFLECTIONS

We can see aspects of the Star in these minor arcana cards:

- The Three of Pentacles, for creativity

- The Six of Cups, for harmony

- The Nine of Cups, for luck and a wish come true

- Ace of Wands, for creativity and inspiration

- Six of Wands, for victory and acknowledgment

- The Ace of Pentacles, for beginnings and money luck

- The Nine of Pentacles, for comfort and contentment

TRY A READING WITH THE STAR: WISH UPON A STAR

Take the Star from your deck and lay it before you. Now shuffle the remaining card, and cut the deck or fan out the cards facedown. Choose five cards with your left hand and place them around the Star, as shown. You could ask, "What will inspire me?" or "Will my wish come true?"

- **Card 1:** You/your present situation

- **Card 2:** Your wish

- **Card 3:** The outcome

- **Card 4:** What hinders you

- **Card 5:** What helps you

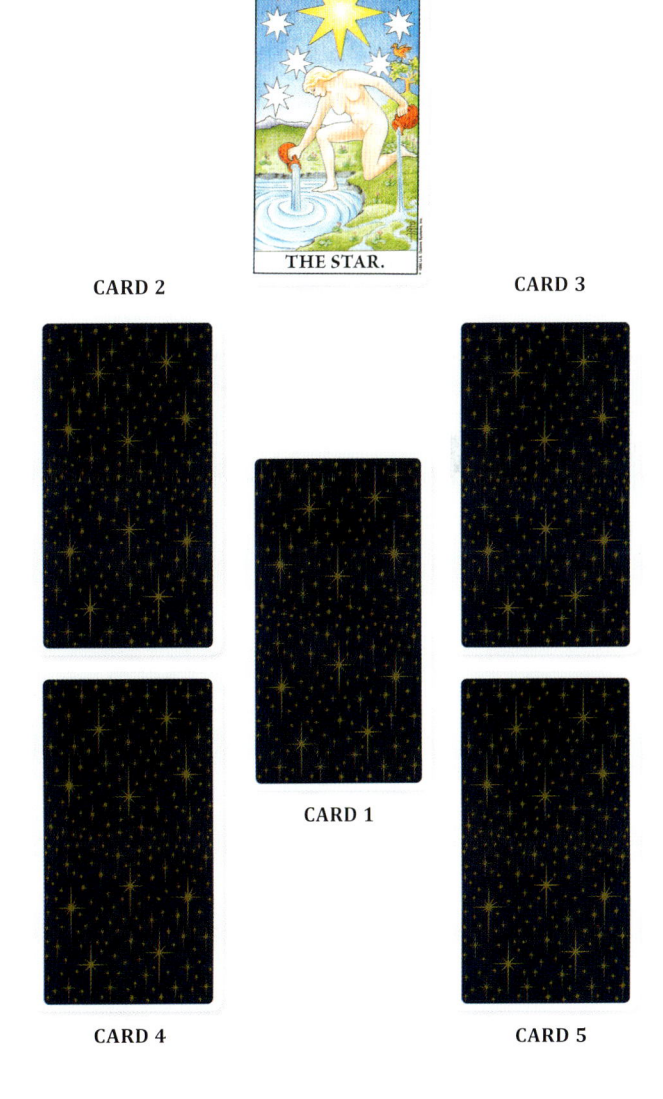

CARD 2

CARD 3

CARD 1

CARD 4

CARD 5

XVIII THE MOON

Alternative Names: Illusion, Luna

Number: XVIII

Numerology Link: IX, The Hermit

Astrological Sign or Planet: Pisces the Fish

Element: Water

Hebrew Letter: *Qoph* (*Kuf*)

   Symbol: The back of the head

   Meaning: Hidden problems

Tree of Life Pathway: Nineteenth, between Malkuth and Netzach

Chakra: Third eye, for intuition

Key Meanings: Illusion, dreams, and crisis

UNDERSTANDING THE MOON

The Moon is a card of duality and emotional turmoil, with its two foreboding towers and two howling dogs. One dog appears domesticated while the other is wild—a wolf, even—representing the dual aspects of internal conflict. The sun-moon above appears to gaze upon the scene below, but the eyes are closed; the solar aspect, the perspective of daylight, is blind under moonlight. The central crayfish appears to struggle halfway between the water toward land. Something very important is about to surface.

The crayfish stands for the fearful self. He can just glimpse the long and winding road that yawns beyond the dogs and the towers. He senses that others have trodden this path before, but can he follow? And if he does, is there reward for taking this risk? Under the light of the sun-moon, what he is seeing may be an illusion, pure fantasy. As A. E. Waite says, "The card represents the life of the imagination apart from the life of the spirit." This is the dark night of the soul, a lonely time when there is little but moonlight to guide us. We, like the crayfish, will need to make a decision in order to resolve the conflict between staying safe in a place we know and taking on the challenge of the unknown.

In the major arcana sequence, the Moon rises after card XVII, The Star, and before XIX, The Sun. With the Star, we have realized our guidance, the path we must follow, and the Moon shows the hidden impact of this realization, when deep-seated doubts and fears are realized. The Sun is the resolution of this dark night, a sanctuary before we make our final Judgement on our actions before the ending and beginning of our journey with the World. To heal the conflict of the Moon, we need to embody our higher self, our soul wisdom.

The Moon's number, XVIII, or 18, adds up to 9—IX, the number of the Hermit. Both the Moon and the Hermit show being alone and a time for self-reflection.

THE MOON'S ASTROLOGY

The Moon's sign is Pisces, the Fish (February 20–March 20), whose element is emotional Water. In astrology, the Moon in Pisces means compassion and intuition. Pisces the Fish and stands for the soul as well as sexuality and creativity.

THE MOON AND KABBALA

The Hebrew letter of the Moon is *Qoph* or *Kuf*, meaning the back of the head and hidden problems. On the Tree of Life, the Moon is on the nineteenth pathway between the spheres of Malkuth and Netzach, or the logical mind and the unseen forces of nature—or what is ruminating under the surface.

UPRIGHT MEANING

The Moon's traditional meaning is a crisis of faith and a period of emotional vulnerability. It reveals misgivings about a situation, as you cannot be sure if what you are seeing is the truth. Under the light of the Moon, is what you are seeing an illusion? Or does the Moon bring to light the essence of a problem that needs attention? This may be a time of deep emotional conflict, and the struggle is private rather than shared.

You have a decision to make, and to choose wisely, you need to rely on your senses rather than logic. Take note of your intuitive messages and dreams now and acknowledge them as valid sources of information that will lead you in the right direction. The Moon can show you being asked to take a risk, to broaden your life experience. The prospect may make you uncomfortable, but the Moon asks you to dive deep and examine the real cause of unrest.

The Moon can also suggest the following:

- **Home:** You could be feeling disillusioned about your current living situation or having second thoughts about a move or home improvement project that is proving more costly than anticipated. On a positive note, you may intuitively find an object you thought was lost.

- **Relationships:** Confusion and disappointment reign as someone lets you down. A lack of trust that a relationship will work leads you to a love decision.

- **Career and money:** You may achieve a goal but ultimately feel it was not worth the effort. With colleagues, emotions run high, and you may need to protect yourself from others' negativity. Money matters are stable, but you want more satisfaction from work than just the paycheck.

REVERSED MEANING

When the Moon is reversed, you may avoid difficult emotions and confrontations, so your needs are not expressed or recognized. A trauma is ignored again rather than explored, so the Moon reversed can show you going back to old ways of coping with the past. The card can also show you feeling stuck in an old emotional pattern that keeps arising—until you give it attention.

ITS WISDOM MESSAGE

Be guided by messages from your unconscious.

THE MOON'S SYMBOLS

In the Rider-Waite tarot, the Moon appears with these magical symbols. Some of them reappear in other major arcana cards, so learn to recognize them and you'll soon find you can apply your knowledge throughout the deck.

- *The crayfish:* This creature is a symbol of the primal self, which in this environment is not at peace and is struggling to surface, like subconcsious fears.

- *The wolf and dog:* The canines show fear of the unknown. They also are guardians of experience, representing a rite of passage. The wolf is wild instinct and the dog, the tamed self.
  See the dog on card 0, The Fool.

- *The watchtowers or gates:* These are the gates of Hades in classical mythology (see The Historical Moon). In a reading, these represent the boundary between the unconscious and conscious self.
  See this symbol on card XIII, Death.

- *The sun-moon:* A full moon, crescent moon, and sun are merged. The moon is the subconscious aspect that affects how we behave in the solar world, which dominates the sleeping sun.
  See the sun on card XIX, The Sun; VI, The Lovers; and 0, The Fool.

- *The golden droplets:* There are fifteen droplets in the shape of the Hebrew letter *J*, which means fire. This creates a strong tension with the water below the sun, which in combination symbolize conflict. A. E. Waite calls these droplets "the dew of thought" that emanate toward the world of the moon, or intuition and imagination.
  See this symbol on card XVI, The Tower.

- *The path:* The unknown—the path is poorly lit and only reflected light may guide us upon it.
  See this symbol on card XIV, Temperance.

THE HISTORICAL MOON: URANIA, DIANA, AND HECATE

As early tarot cards developed, three distinct Moon cards evolved, inspired by lunar goddesses. The Tarocchi of Mantegna has two lunar goddess cards, Luna and Urania. Luna holds a crescent moon while riding her chariot across the skies, while Urania shows a goddess with a blank circle and astronomer's compass.

Luna is closely identified with the lunar goddess Diana the huntress (Artemis), often shown in traditional art with a bow and arrow. The Moon card of the Visconti-Sforza tarots shows Luna-Diana: She holds a crescent moon and what appears to be the skein from her bow, loose and useless—a symbol of failure and confusion. The fifteenth-century Griggoneur cards, however, took Urania as their inspiration. Urania, the muse of astronomy, carries a compass and globe in traditional paintings and statuary. On the Griggoneur Moon card, two astrologers stand under a waning moon; one holds his compass up while the other rests his on a book, as if making a calculation.

On the surface, the Rider-Waite card with its strange crayfish has a very different ancestry, dating back to a deck of around 1750 made by Joannes Palegius Mater, and Court de Gébelin's book *Le Monde Primitif* of 1781—yet, like the Moon card itself, a peek beneath the surface shows more than expected. The two towers and dogs are the symbols of Hecate, dark deity of magic—who is a shadow aspect of Luna-Diana. Hecate is the guardian of the gates of Hades, indicated by the card's two towers. The dogs are Hecate's companions—ancient statues of the goddess show her with hounds, and in her form as a triple goddess, she appeared with the head of a dog.

THE MOON'S REFLECTIONS

We can see aspects of the Moon in these minor arcana cards:

- The Two of Pentacles, for weighing up your options

- The Five of Pentacles, for insecurity

- The Nine of Swords, for anxiety

- The Seven of Cups, for fantasy and possibility

- The Three of Swords, for distress—what your heart is telling you

- The Two of Swords, for indecision

TRY A READING WITH THE MOON: WHAT LIES BENEATH

Take the Moon from your deck and lay it before you. Now shuffle the remaining cards and cut the deck or fan out the cards facedown. Choose four cards with your left hand and place them around the Moon, as shown. You could ask, "What needs to come to the surface?" or "What will be the outcome of this crisis/ soul-searching?"

- **Card 1:** Significator—a card that represents you

- **Card 2:** What needs to be addressed—past or childhood issues

- **Card 3:** What needs to be addressed—present challenges or fears

- **Card 4:** Outcome

CARD 4

THE MOON.

CARD 2

CARD 3

CARD 1 SIGNIFICATOR

XIX THE SUN

Alternative Name: The Children

Number: XIX

Numerology Links: X, The Wheel of Fortune, and I, The Magician

Astrological Sign or Planet: The Sun

Element: Fire

Hebrew Letter: *Resh*

> **Symbol:** The front of the head, or face

> **Meaning:** Success

Tree of Life Pathway: Twentieth, between Yesod and Hod

Chakra: Solar plexus, for physical health and soul wisdom

Key Meanings: Success, good health, and a holiday

UNDERSTANDING THE SUN

In a sunny a walled garden, we are back in what appears to be the earthly paradise of card VI, The Lovers—yet now we are reaching higher levels of consciousness and awakening. With the Sun, we are seeing the cosmic light. The child on his horse is ready to return home, uniting his spirit with the spirit of the world. He is open-armed and full of joy, and his nakedness shows him as a child of nature. Psychiatrist Carl Jung saw the archetype of the child as an aspect of our developing personality. In this way, the Sun holds echoes of our own childhoods, revealing an opportunity to recapture our early days—an idealized time of innocence and happiness, free for a time from adult, worldly anxieties. In this sense, the Sun is one of the happiest cards of the tarot, offering sanctuary, growth, success, and happiness.

The child is in direct sunlight, in full awareness of himself and his place in the universe. He can see his way ahead—his world so unlike the darker world of the preceding card, the Moon, which can only offer reflected light. In the major arcana sequence, the Sun rises after card XVIII, The Moon, and before cards XX, Judgement, and XXI, The World. Having faced the fears of the Moon, we, like the child, now see the light of the world and make ready to ride toward it before our reincarnation as 0, The Fool.

The Sun's number, XIX, comprises 1 and 9, adding up to 10, or X for the Wheel of Fortune, which further reduces to I, The Magician. The Sun embodies action and the creative power of the Magician in the earthly realm and the dawning spiritual realization of the Wheel, at which point in our tarot journey we turn toward the higher aspects of life and our spiritual ascension.

THE SUN'S ASTROLOGY

Naturally, the Sun is the planet of this card. The Sun is concerned with the solar, or outward aspects of the self, and renewed vitality after the dark night of soul encountered under the Moon. In the past, the card has been linked with Gemini the Twins as printed decks such as the Marseilles-style tarots show two children on the card rather than one child, as on the Rider-Waite.

THE SUN AND KABBALA

The Hebrew letter of the Sun is *Resh*, meaning the head and also success. On the Tree of Life, the Sun appears on the twentieth pathway between the spheres of Yesod and Hod. Yesod governs the moon and the unconscious mind, and Hod is the sphere of the rational mind. The Sun integrates these two aspects, suggesting happiness and spiritual growth.

UPRIGHT MEANING

The Sun brings success and achievement and is one of the most positive cards in the major arcana. If you have had a challenging time, the Sun shows that every aspect of your life will improve. You'll also enjoy more energy, and if you or someone close has suffered from health problems, the card predicts recovery and a return to good health. As a card of energy and growth, all your projects benefit now, so the Sun heralds a good time to nurture your creative endeavors, your business, and the relationships you value.

This card is also associated with children and family. It reveals good news about children in general and also about spending happy times with friends who make you smile. You may be reunited with an old friend, partner, or family member. In terms of a state of mind, the Sun shows you feeling carefree and creative, nurturing your inner child.

In a layout with "negative" cards, the sun has the power to shed a positive light on the whole reading.

Here's some other good news the Sun can predict:

- **Home:** You feel comfortable and secure in your home—you may also feel more like entertaining others. In particular, the Sun shows children coming into your home.

- **Relationships:** Partnerships bloom under the sun as your relationship grows and you enjoy every minute together. You may also take a trip away to a sunny place to escape everyday pressures.

- **Career and money:** The Sun does not specifically predict money but does show success and a position from which you can generate money. The Sun shines on your career, too, as you get the acknowledgment you deserve. Now is the time to bask in your success.

REVERSED MEANING

It's virtually impossible to see any negative side to the Sun, even when reversed. The only glitch could be a delay to travel plans, but you will enjoy a happy and content period regardless.

ITS WISDOM MESSAGE

Enjoy your success.

THE SUN'S SYMBOLS

In the Rider-Waite tarot, the Sun appears with these magical symbols. Some of them reappear in other major arcana cards, so learn to recognize them and you'll soon find you can apply your knowledge throughout the deck.

- *The sun:* The sun is a symbol of consciousness, happiness, and self-expression. The solar power of the sun signifies energy and good health. In numerology, the 21 rays of the sun reduce to III, The Empress—perhaps a link to the Empress as the mother of the divine child.

  See this symbol on XVIIII, The Moon; VI, The Lovers; XIV, Temperance; and 0, The Fool.

- *The child or children:* Simplicity, innocence, purity, and wholeness—These are all elements of the happy inner child. The child appears to have six small flowers in his or her hair in the spirit of celebration.

- *The sunflowers:* Growth, beauty, and strength—The sunflowers grow tall above the level of the wall, reaching upward to see what is beyond the boundaries. The four sunflowers may symbolize the four elements of Air, Water, Fire, and Earth—everything that is needed for life. The sunflower is a symbol of Clytie, a nymph who turns into a sunflower when mourning the loss of her lover, the sun god, Helios (the Greek Apollo). She always faces the sun, hoping to see Apollo's sun-chariot return. The sunflower is also a symbol of the Spiritualist church—as the sunflower when young turns its head to capture the sun throughout the day, so this tells us the search for the light is our true nature.

- *The walled garden:* Boundaries, security, and protection—A. E. Waite calls this "the walled garden of the sensitive life."

- *The white-gray horse:* He represents the vehicle for our soul—the physical body.

  See this symbol on card XIII, Death.

- *The red flag:* This illustrates energy and vitality.

- *The red feather:* This familiar image represents the life force.

  See this symbol on card 0, The Fool; on card XIII, Death, the red feather is withered.

THE HISTORICAL SUN: SPINNING AND SUNFLOWERS

One of the oldest Sun cards from the Visconti-Sforza tarots shows a male cherub holding aloft a glowing sun-face. The figure has one leg outstretched and the other rests on a deep-blue cloud over a landscape of blue mountains, water, and a grassy plain that ends in a cliff edge. All four traditional elements are present: Water, Earth, Fire (the sun), and Air, represented by the cherub's cloud.

The fifteenth-century Griggoneur cards show a version of the Renaissance Moon card (see The Historical Moon in XVIII, The Moon), but his time Artemis-Diana carries an arrow and she is stretching a thread or skein from hand to hand, perhaps part of her bow—or as has been suggested by the tarot scholar Stuart Kaplan, she is spinning yarn. This suggests the Norse deity Frigg, protector of spinning and women, later associated with Artemis. Another interpretation is a connection with the Greek goddesses known as the Fates, who spin the thread of life, measure it, and cut it when life is over: the story of birth, lifetime, and death.

Seventeenth- and eighteenth-century cards in the Marseilles style show two children in the garden, rather than one child, with a wall behind them. Flowers begin to appear in the nineteenth century, in the Fanciful Tarot (1852) and the Gaudais deck (c.1860). However, it appears that the Rider-Waite tarot's Sun card was the first to include prominent sunflowers as symbols of strength, light, and energizing solar power.

THE SUN'S REFLECTIONS

We can see aspects of the Sun in these minor arcana cards:

- The Four of Wands, for happiness and freedom

- The Ace of Cups, for love and nurturing

- The Three of Cups, for celebration

- The Six of Wands, for success

- The Six of Cups, for harmony and old friends

TRY A READING WITH THE SUN: FOUR WAYS TO SHINE

This reading takes the four elements symbolized by the four sunflowers to divine your situation in terms of Earth, Air, Fire, and Water. Take the Sun from your deck and lay it at the top, as shown. Now shuffle the remaining cards and cut the deck or fan out the cards facedown. Choose four cards with your left hand and lay them from left to right as shown.

- **Card 1:** Earth: finances and property—what grounds you

- **Card 2:** Air: decisions—action to take

- **Card 3:** Fire: how projects will fare—communication

- **Card 4:** Water: letting emotions flow

CARD 1 CARD 2 CARD 3 CARD 4

XX JUDGEMENT

Alternative Names: The Angel, Fame, Time

Number: XX

Numerology Links: II, The High Priestess, and XI, Justice

Astrological Sign or Planet: Pluto

Element: Fire

Hebrew Letter: *Shin*

   Symbol: The tooth

   Meaning: Renewal

Tree of Life Pathway: Twenty-first, between Malkuth and Hod

Chakra: Alta major, for the past and past lives

Key Meanings: Assessment, and letting go of the past

UNDERSTANDING JUDGEMENT

Judgement depicts Judgement Day, prophesized by the apostle Paul in his letter to the Thessalonians when the souls of men would be awakened by an archangel's trumpet call and judged before God. The figures may be holding up their arms to embrace the moment of resurrection before judgement. Judgement is a personal wake-up call to consider our past actions. How do we judge ourselves?

The archangel who blows the trumpet is Gabriel, and his wake-up call is a moment of revelation, when we can discover the truth of our relationship with ourselves. We may also be awakened to a new relationship with God, with our spirit guides, or with the angels—as one of the three Angel cards of the tarot, along with the Lovers and Temperance (see pages 54 and 86), Judgement can be a call to spiritual service.

In the major arcana sequence, Judgement comes after card XIX, The Sun, and before card XXI, The World. We have reached a sanctuary with the Sun, a reminder of the paradise of Adam and Eve of the

Lovers card, but before we can complete our cycle, we must make some decisions and gain some acceptance about the past. When this is done, we can evolve to a state of completion and rebirth, offered by the World, before we return to card 0, The Fool. When the Last Judgement of man is complete, a new world is created—which the Fool will discover when he incarnates once again and his journey begins anew.

Judgement's number, XX, is composed of two tens and implies balancing our past actions. It reduces to the number two, or II in the major arcana cards (10 + 10 = 20; 2 + 0 = 2), the number of The High Priestess, who stands between the earth plane and the world of the dead. Judgement also links with card XI, Justice (whose number, XI, also reduces to II). While Justice is an external judgement upon us, Judgement is how we judge ourselves. At this time, we can reflect on the past, assess our actions, and release the experience so we can move forward.

JUDGEMENT'S ASTROLOGY

Judgement is associated with Pluto, who was the Roman god of the dead and the underworld. The planet Pluto is also associated with transformation at a deep level. The element of Judgement is Fire, perhaps a reference to flames of purification and the burning of the physical body in rituals of cremation.

JUDGEMENT AND KABBALA

The kabbalistic number of Judgement is *Shin*, meaning tooth. The letter takes the form of three upright stokes, like a *W*, which could be interpreted as the three aspects of consciousness highlighted by Judgement—the past, present, and future. *Shin* also stands for Shaddai, a name for God. One of the meanings of *Shin* in the sacred ancient text *Sefer Yetzirah* is head in the soul, a perfect descriptor for Judgement, as we mentally assess our past actions. *Shin* also comes up in the phrase Sh'at haShin (the *Shin* Hour), which roughly translates as "the eleventh hour." Judgement certainly tells us that the time is now.

On the Tree of Life, Judgement is placed on the twenty-first pathway between the spheres of Malkuth, our perceived world, and Hod, wisdom and the

mind—just as Judgement asks us to assess our place in the world according to our deeds.

UPRIGHT MEANING

It is time to come to a decision about the past. Great changes and opportunities are on the horizon, but before you can decide on your direction, certain past issues need to be addressed. This process is purely about how you judge yourself on your past actions and attitudes. In the upright position, Judgement shows you will feel you have acted with integrity and did the best you could. As you accept yourself fully, you can blow your own trumpet and praise yourself for your achievements. An additional meaning is being in the public eye, hence Fame, the card's alternative title.

Judgement also predicts a spiritual awakening, as you feel called to explore your potential. You have learned much about yourself in this most recent phase and are ready to go further, developing your spiritual connection with your guides and angels. As you receive guidance on your path, your confidence and wisdom will grow.

Here's more insight:

- **Home:** You may be drawn to an old property or consider returning to a place that holds happy memories. You will soon need to make a major property decision.

- **Relationships:** Love is assessed and shifts into a new phase. There may be a need for reconciliation, if you deem the relationship worthwhile. If you are single, you may revisit an old relationship and decide if it is worth trying again. An old friend may reappear.

- **Career and money:** Acknowledgment for your successes is coming; finances also improve.

REVERSED MEANING

When reversed, you may be stuck in the past or refuse to learn the lessons that are there for you. You may find yourself in old patterns and not yet able to break free. Delays are also indicated, in terms of future plans, and you may be feeling trapped and unable to progress, without really understanding why. You have the ability to judge your actions and attitudes and then move on; the past cannot be changed, only accepted. Have compassion for the person you were then and for the decisions you made. You don't have to live with the results of these choices in the future; you can decide to be free.

ITS WISDOM MESSAGE
Look back with pleasure.

JUDGEMENT'S SYMBOLS
In the Rider-Waite tarot, Judgement appears with these magical symbols. Some of them reappear in other major arcana cards, so learn to recognize them and you'll soon find you can apply your knowledge throughout the deck.

- *The archangel:* Symbolizing awakening, the Archangel is Gabriel, but the flag on his trumpet is that of dragon-slaying St. George, patron saint of England, linked with Archangel Michael. Michael's element is Fire, the element of this card, although what we see on the card is Water, the element of Archangel Gabriel. The archangel, therefore, may be an amalgamation of both Michael and Gabriel.

  See archangels Raphael and Michael on card VI, The Lovers, and card XIV, Temperance.

- *The trumpet:* The call of the trumpet tells us it is time to resurrect the past and make a decision. Heralds blew on trumpets to announce war, and also the presence of royalty and other dignitaries, explaining the card's alternative title, Fame.

- *The dead rising:* The rising dead are resurrection and rebirth. The six figures are shown in two groups of three that reflect different phases of the past. They are man, woman, and child, asking us to look at our roles and relationships. Naked, they are about to be reborn. The child symbolizes the spirit of the new age.

- *The open coffins:* Transformation is illustrated by the figures rising from the restriction of their coffins into a new consciousness.

- *The flag of St. George:* The flag bears St. George's cross, for England's patron saint. The red and white symbolize the unification of opposites.

- *The sea and glaciers:* The water is a symbol of purification; the past can be forgiven and washed away. The glaciers feel like a paradise, a new world about to be born.

HISTORICAL JUDGEMENT: GOD AND GABRIEL

The oldest tarot decks show one or two angels calling the dead from their graves, usually three people at various stages of emergence. In the Visconti-Sforza tarot held at the Carey Collection at Yale University, we see the walls of a city, showing that the dead exist in another territory. Just discernable is a tiny bridge between the two angels and water running under it, perhaps indicating the river of souls or the Styx, which carried the souls of the dead to the otherworld.

In some Renaissance tarots, the angels are replaced by God. In most tarot decks, the dead are naked, as if being reborn, to resurrect the past in order to judge it, release it, and allow ourselves to be complete before we encounter the final card in the major arcana sequence, the World, before beginning our journey again with 0, The Fool.

JUDGEMENT'S REFLECTIONS

We can see aspects of Judgement in these minor arcana cards:

- The Six of Cups, for nostalgia and reunions

- The Nine of Cups, for contentment in achievement

TRY A READING WITH JUDGEMENT: THE SPIRITUAL AUDIT

Take Judgement from your deck and lay it before you. Now shuffle the remaining cards and cut the deck or fan out the cards facedown. Choose five cards with your left hand and place them, as shown. You could ask, "How do I judge myself?" or "What past situation can I let go of?"

- **Card 1:** Present situation

- **Card 2:** The recent past—what to look at and let go of

- **Card 3:** The distant past—what to look at and let go of

- **Card 4:** What may be blocking you

- **Card 5:** Outcome: what you can learn from this

CARD 3

CARD 2

CARD 4

CARD 5

CARD 1

XXI THE WORLD

Alternative Name: The Universe

Number: XXI

Numerology Link: III, The Empress

Astrological Sign or Planet: Saturn

Element: Earth

Hebrew Letter: *Tav (Tau)*

    Symbol: The cross

    Meaning: Completion

Tree of Life Pathway: Twenty-second, between Yesod and Malkuth

Chakra: Stellar gateway, the cosmic portal

Key Meanings: Completion, success, reward, and joy

UNDERSTANDING THE WORLD

One of the most positive cards of the major arcana, the World signals success and completion. In the center of an oval laurel wreath a figure dances, holding a wand in each hand. Protected by four figures from the Wheel of Fortune, who are symbols of the four evangelists of the gospels, the dancer is also the Fool. From his humble beginnings, he has traveled the world in body and spirit and is about to be reborn in his own card, 0. The dancer is obviously female from the waist up, but it is believed that the swathe of fabric conceals the male genitals of the Fool. This hermaphrodite dancer shows the perfect balancing of opposites, the sun and moon (two previous cards, XVIII and XIX), our male and female aspects, and the conscious and the unconscious minds. With the world at our feet, we are ascending to higher realms of understanding.

A. E. Waite explains in his *Pictorial Key to the Tarot* how the World "represents also the perfection and end of the Cosmos, the secret which is within it, the rapture of the universe when it understands itself in God. It is further the state of the soul in the consciousness of Divine Vision, reflected from the self-knowing spirit." We can see the World as a card of perfection and of peace. We are dancing all over the world, in harmony within ourselves and with all others.

The Wheel of Fortune as card X and the World as XXI mark two key points in the major arcana journey—the Wheel is halfway, when the Fool turns to the second, cosmic phase of his spiritual quest, while the World is the card of completion and renewal. Before the Wheel and the World are two cards of self-reflection—the Hermit and Judgement (see pages 66 and 110). The World's number, XXI, comprises 2 and 1, adding up to III for Mother Earth, the Empress. This fertility aspect is embedded in the World as the seed of new life and the new tarot cycle.

THE WORLD'S ASTROLOGY

The taskmaster planet, Saturn, is the ruler of the World. The planet symbolizes decisions and hard work and shows you deserve all your success. The four evangelists on the card (see The World's Symbols) link with the four elements, the four minor arcana suits of Cups, Wands, Pentacles, and Swords, and the four fixed signs of the zodiac—Aquarius (Air, the angel), Taurus (Earth, the bull), Leo (Fire, the lion), and Scorpio (Water, the eagle).

THE WORLD AND KABBALA

The Hebrew letter of the World is *Tav*, symbolized by a cross, which can represent the four directions and four elements of Fire, Air, Earth, and Water; the meaning of the character is completion, the card's message. On the Tree of Life, the World is placed on the twenty-second pathway between Yesod and Malkuth. Yesod means change and magic and Mulkuth, the earth itself: in combination, the ongoing cycle of birth, life, and rebirth.

UPRIGHT MEANING

The upright card denotes triumph, completion, and reward for your efforts—and for this reason, the World is one of the most welcome cards in a reading. It denotes deep joy and happiness, and now you can really feel your deserved success. Cherished projects fly, as your commitment and dedication pays off. Life feels balanced, too, as work, relationships, finances, and domestic affairs run smoothly.

A phase is coming to an end in a positive way, and you will be acknowledged publicly for what you do. Now is the time to enjoy your fame, and you will have the confidence to take center stage. If you have been waiting for a decision or opportunity to manifest, the World will soon turn in your favor. You may also benefit spiritually just now, living more mindfully and from the heart.

This is also a time for celebration, and in a reading, the World often reveals anniversaries, birthdays, and parties, so it is a great card for groups and positive group consciousness. You may also decide to venture out into the world and travel far afield.

The World could also mean the following:

- **Home:** A dream-home come true—whatever you have worked toward can be yours now, whether it's successful building work or other remodeling.

- **Relationships:** Happiness and joy—you have a relationship that is fulfilling and loving.

- **Career and money:** You're achieving your goals. An award at work, a new position and/or promotion—the World shows you rising in status and being given more authority. You may also receive gifts at this time.

REVERSED MEANING

When reversed, the World shows you are ready to move on but feel blocked or don't feel you are deserving of success. It can also show hanging on to one ambition that eludes you—and if so, it's time to redefine what you want and adjust your expectations, as you may be clinging on to a dream to the exclusion of all else. Alternatively, you may feel eclipsed by another's shining light. Overall, however, the negatives here are minor, and you will get what you deserve; it may just take a little longer to become obvious. In the meantime, keep the faith.

ITS WISDOM MESSAGE
Enjoy your success.

THE WORLD'S SYMBOLS
In the Rider-Waite tarot, the World appears with these magical symbols. Some of them reappear in other major arcana cards, so learn to recognize them and you'll soon find you can apply your knowledge throughout the deck.

- *The angel and three creatures:* The angel and the lion, bull, and eagle are the symbols of the four evangelists—respectively Matthew, Mark, Luke and John—associated with the Four Gospels of the New Testament. The animals also link with the four elements and four fixed signs of the zodiac (see The World's Astrology).

    See these symbols on card X, The Wheel of Fortune.

- *The laurel garland:* The laurel symbolizes victory. It is in the shape of the mandorla, an oval, which signifies heaven on earth and appears in religious icons to frame holy figures.

    See this symbol on card III, The Empress, and VII, The Chariot.

- *The garland's ribbons:* The two ribbons are tied at the top and bottom of the garland in a figure-eight, or lemniscate, the symbol for infinity, the never-ending cycles of time and rhythms of nature.

    See this symbol on card I, The Magician, and VIII, Strength.

- *The world dancer:* The dancer shows joy and celebration, the *animus mundi* or "soul of the world" (see The Historical World).

- *The wands:* The wands symbolize the perfect balance of opposites: complete self-expression and the ability to make magic happen.

    See this symbol on card I, The Magician.

THE HISTORICAL WORLD: THE CITY AND THE WORLD SOUL

There are two distinct styles of World card, one in the Renaissance tradition and the other dating from the 1700s—the latter is the influence for the Rider-Waite World and those of many other contemporary decks.

In the Renaissance Visconti-Sforza deck, two male cherubs hold aloft what appears to be a circular painting of an idealized city on an island, showing a twilight sky and stars—perfection on earth and in the heavens above. The composition for A. E. Waite's Rider-Waite card comes from the seventeenth- and eighteenth-century Marseilles-style cards, which show a dancer enclosed in a wreath with the four evangelists in each corner. The world dancer, and the belief that the world herself has a soul, is a part of Hermetic, Platonic, and Shamanic belief systems.

What unites both styles of World card is the concept of enclosure, from the idealized city as a circular portrait to the mandorla, or laurel garland, around the world dancer—a symbol of completion and return to the beginning, the cosmic egg that is O, The Fool.

THE WORLD'S REFLECTIONS

We can see aspects of the World in these minor arcana cards:

- The Ten of Pentacles, for families coming together in love and financial reward

- The Ten of Cups, for family love

- The Nine of Cups, for a dream come true

- The Six of Wands, for victory

- The Three of Cups, for friends and celebration

- The Six of Cups, for reunion and harmony

TRY A READING WITH THE WORLD: ELEMENTS OF SUCCESS

Take the World from your deck and lay it before you. Now shuffle the remaining cards and cut the deck or fan out the cards facedown. Choose five cards with your left hand and place them around the World, as shown. You could ask, "How will I achieve success?" or "What reward is coming my way?"

- **Card 1:** The bull: earth—security and possessions

- **Card 2:** The angel: air—thought and decisions

- **Card 3:** The eagle: water—emotions

- **Card 4:** The lion: fire—desires and goals

- **Card 5:** Outcome

CARD 2

CARD 3

CARD 5

CARD 1

CARD 4

5

CARD INTERPRETATIONS: THE MINOR ARCANA

QUICK-REFERENCE MEANINGS

CUPS

ACE	Love, fertility, beginnings	**EIGHT**	Departure
TWO	Partnerships	**NINE**	A wish come true
THREE	Celebration	**TEN**	Happiness and family
FOUR	Boredom; stasis	**PAGE**	Fun and socializing
FIVE	Loss, sadness	**KNIGHT**	A dreamer; a proposal
SIX	Peace; a visitor	**QUEEN**	An intuitive woman
SEVEN	Confusion; possibilities	**KING**	A warmhearted man

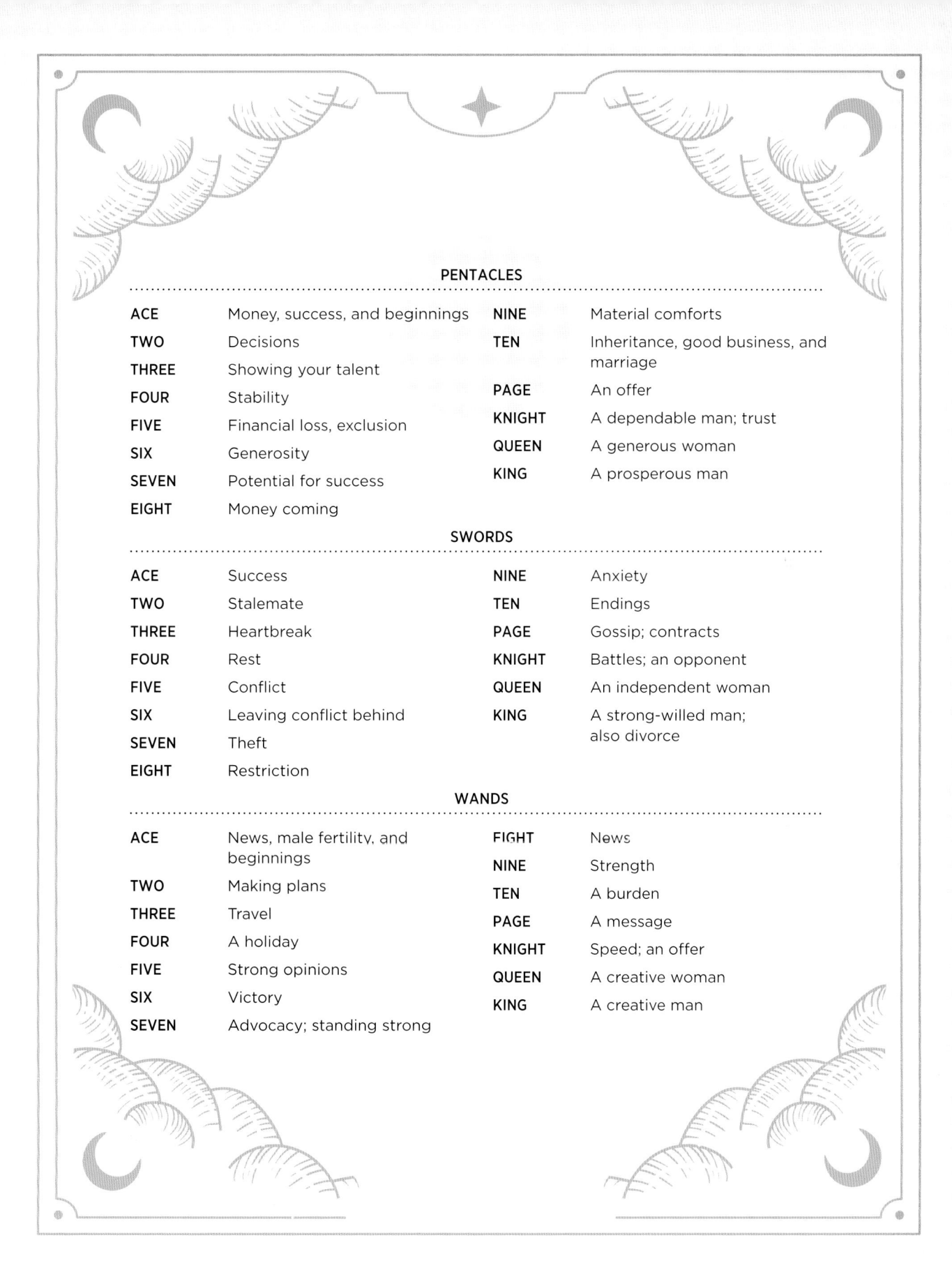

PENTACLES

ACE	Money, success, and beginnings	NINE	Material comforts
TWO	Decisions	TEN	Inheritance, good business, and marriage
THREE	Showing your talent		
FOUR	Stability	PAGE	An offer
FIVE	Financial loss, exclusion	KNIGHT	A dependable man; trust
SIX	Generosity	QUEEN	A generous woman
SEVEN	Potential for success	KING	A prosperous man
EIGHT	Money coming		

SWORDS

ACE	Success	NINE	Anxiety
TWO	Stalemate	TEN	Endings
THREE	Heartbreak	PAGE	Gossip; contracts
FOUR	Rest	KNIGHT	Battles; an opponent
FIVE	Conflict	QUEEN	An independent woman
SIX	Leaving conflict behind	KING	A strong-willed man; also divorce
SEVEN	Theft		
EIGHT	Restriction		

WANDS

ACE	News, male fertility, and beginnings	EIGHT	News
		NINE	Strength
TWO	Making plans	TEN	A burden
THREE	Travel	PAGE	A message
FOUR	A holiday	KNIGHT	Speed; an offer
FIVE	Strong opinions	QUEEN	A creative woman
SIX	Victory	KING	A creative man
SEVEN	Advocacy; standing strong		

ACE OF CUPS

Element: Water

Astrological Associations: The Water signs—Cancer, Scorpio, and Pisces

Number: 1

Tree of Life Position: Kether, for divine light

Key Meanings: Love, relationships, and beginnings

UNDERSTANDING THE ACE OF CUPS

A single chalice, offered from a hand extending from a cloud, is overflowing with five streams of water that pour into a lake below. Water lilies flourish on the lake's surface. There's also a bird, a white dove of peace, descending toward the chalice. In its beak is a wafer marked with the sign of the cross, for the Host, or Eucharist. This may symbolize Christ, or the spark of the Divine, the life force, entering the chalice or womb, for fertility at a physical, creative, or spiritual level, reflecting the card's Tree of Life sphere of Kether, for divine light. The bird, much like the folkloric stork bringing a baby in its beak, is about to deliver a gift. The chalice is offered with the right hand, the hand of giving (as opposed to the left hand, which traditionally is the receiving hand).

Twenty-six dewdrops appear to emanate around the top of the cup stem, which could be a representation of semen. They are similar in form to the droplets on the Aces of Swords and Wands; XVI, The Tower; and XVIII, The Moon (see pages 176, 204, 94, and 102). While the Rider-Waite tarot's originator, A. E. Waite, gives no specific meaning for the twenty-six droplets, this number may relate to the tetragrammaton of *Y, H, V, H*, the name of God in Hebrew, which is formed of the numeric values of the letters *Yod, Hei, Vau,* and *Hei,* adding up to twenty-six.

The Aces offer the pure energy of their suits. As number ones, they represent oneness with the divine spirit or God. Indivisible, their energy is singular, strong, and purposeful. They all represent beginnings, impulses, and new possibilities, in the most pure and obvious form.

Astrologically, this card is linked with the element of Water, which stands for the emotions and life—hence the Ace of Cups' association with pregnancy. The *W* on the cup appears like an upside-down *M*—and if so may stand for mother, or the Hebrew letter, *Mem,* whose associated symbol is water, for the emotions, reminding us of the traditionally feminine element of the suit of Cups.

UPRIGHT MEANING

The Ace of Cups brings the gift of love and key emotional events: fertility, pregnancy, birth, and motherhood; when not predicting a pregnancy, it can reveal that being a parent and/or partner takes priority over work, finances, and projects. In relationships, the card denotes falling in love, passion, and a significant new partnership. In existing relationships, it signifies loves and support. Positive emotions flow.

If you are nurturing a new project, this Ace heralds creativity and growth, so make time for activities you enjoy, and you will see them flourish. An enterprise you hold dear will come to fruition, so it's time to turn to your novel, business concept, or travel plan and give it your full attention. This is also a great card for spiritual growth, so you may find yourself discovering a belief system or other important way to explore your spirituality.

Generally, this is a time for love, kindness, conviviality, and good friends, the simple joy in living each day and appreciating every moment.

In a reading, one Ace brings a focus on the life area according to the suit, which can set the theme of the reading. If two or more Aces appear near each other in a reading, it means the following:

- **Two Aces:** An important partnership
- **Three Aces:** Good news
- **Four Aces:** Excitement, beginnings, and potential

REVERSED MEANING

As you might expect from the meaning of the upright card, when reversed, the Ace suggests fertility issues and creative block. There may be lack of space and time to nurture your relationships and projects, or you may be the one feeling neglected; conversely, you may be feeling exhausted due to others' emotional demands. If you are asking about a new relationship, sadly, the reversed One can indicate disappointment and confusion—a potential new love does not develop into something more lasting.

In general, the reversed card reveals insecurity and doubt, and you may not feel you can believe in those people you'd like to trust. Follow your instincts and hold on to your self-belief; thankfully, this influence will not last.

TWO OF CUPS

Element: Water

Astrological Association: Venus in Cancer

Number: 2

Tree of Life Position: Chockmah, the sphere of wisdom

Key Meanings: Love and partnerships old and new

UNDERSTANDING THE TWO OF CUPS

A man and a woman face each other, eye to eye, each offering the other a cup. Between them is a strange symbol: the caduceus of Hermes and a lion's head. The caduceus is a central rod entwined by two snakes, an ancient symbol of negotiation and balance associated with the winged Greek messenger-god, Hermes, the Roman Mercury. The lion, although not given a specific meaning by the card's creator, A. E. Waite, can be interpreted as a symbol of passion and protection.

The maiden is dressed in the colors of the High Priestess (see page 38)—blue and white—while the young man wears a tunic and boots similar to those of the Fool, card 0; even the colors of his tunic—yellow, red, and black—are similar to those of the Fool. The combination of the Fool's meaning of beginnings and risk along with the virginal High Priestess's intuition reveals that a brand-new relationship may be in the cards. The maiden is crowned with an olive garland, while our Fool sports a garland of red flowers;

together, the garlands signify success and love. Their cups tell us that they are showing their emotions, and the man's hand is reaching out toward the woman's cup—a signifier of sexual intention, as cups are traditionally a womb symbol, just as the wand is phallic. On the kabbalistic Tree of Life, the sphere associated with this card is Chockmah, the sphere of wisdom, the father, and male virility.

Astrologically, this card is linked with Venus in Cancer, a pairing that promotes intuition, love, and emotional support. There's also a sense of domestic bliss here, shown by the idyllic cottage and green fields behind the couple. The number of the card, two, is for two people: relationships and other significant partnerships.

UPRIGHT MEANING

The Two of Cups represents harmony, peace, partnership, and love. In relationships, the card signifies a deeper commitment in an existing relationship, such as an engagement, moving in together, or getting married (particularly when it appears with the "marriage" cards, V, The Hierophant, and the Ten of Pentacles). There's a great connection between you two, so your emotions are freely expressed and reciprocated; you feel whole and content. The Two of Cups also predicts new romance and strong passions, which may be all-consuming just now. Inspiring partnerships are favored too, so this is an auspicious card for getting together with a study partner or anyone with whom you share similar creative interests, such as writing, crafting, and other hobbies, or psychic and healing work. Whomever you hook up with, the relationship will be mutually supportive and understanding.

If friendships have been difficult territory for you recently, the Two of Cups shows harmony will return, and in general, this Two shows reconciliation. Old arguments will be resolved as you put the past behind you. Any ongoing negotiations will go in your favor, too—contracts, financial settlements, custody issues, or rearranging your working hours or schedule, for example.

If the Two represents you in your reading, the focus is on feelings and your intuition. Nurture all your relationships and enjoy the love and pleasure they bring. As a prediction card, it shows love: Deeper love is coming—and you deserve all that is on offer.

REVERSED MEANING

When reversed, the Two reveals relationship stress. A new romance may turn sour as your hopes for love are disappointed. Also, the card asks you to rely on your intuition; there may be a secret you don't yet know, and traditionally, the reversed Two can show infidelity. Although on the surface everything may appear to be ticking along, pay attention to your instincts; there's a reason for doubt, and it's time to communicate openly about any fears rather than ignore them.

Generally, in established relationships, the Two can also indicate an unavoidable glitch simply due to the ongoing stresses and strains of leading too-busy lives. If it seems like this is the case, try to keep communicating—there may be a lack of understanding between you just now, but with work on both sides, you can rekindle your connection. Passion may be on hold just now, but it can return.

THREE OF CUPS

Element: Water

Astrological Association: Mercury in Cancer

Number: 3

Tree of Life Position: Binah, the sphere of understanding

Key Meaning: Celebration, abundance, family, and friendships

UNDERSTANDING THE THREE OF CUPS

Three maidens are raising their cups in a joint toast. They are so close together they almost appear as one, and in this way perhaps represent the three aspects of the goddess: maiden, mother, and crone—the whole experience of life. They can also be seen as three of the tarot virtue cards, denoted by the colors of their robes. The woman in white is the maiden from VIII, Strength; the woman in red, with her back to us, is crimson-robed Justice, from card XI; and the woman in red and white links with the colors of Temperance's angel Gabriel. So Strength, Justice, and Temperance together give us parts of this card's meaning: vitality, balance, and reunion. The feminine aspect of the card is also expressed in the Tree of Life sphere Binah, which means understanding and represents the feminine principle.

The maidens are barefoot and free, their robes flowing, and together they appear to be dancing. Fully engaged with life, two women raise their cups with their right hands and the other toasts with her left hand. The right hand is the hand of giving and the left hand receives, so their poses shows they are able to both give and receive abundantly. The Three of Cups is also a card of earthly pleasures, symbolized by the garden of flowers and plentiful ripe fruits. Astrologically, the card is linked with Mercury in Cancer, which promotes sociability, fun, and going with the flow. The negative aspect of this conjunction is thoughtlessness and superficiality. So happy are these women in paradise that little else exists for them, but, quite rightly, they will enjoy their moment of happiness and success while they can.

The number three is dynamic—it is the number of creation. As the next card in the suit after the Two of Cups, for partnerships, the Three of Cups is naturally the next step as two people create three with a new baby or, symbolically, with the birth of a creative project. Three is also the number of the Empress, the goddess-mother archetype in the major arcana (see page 42).

UPRIGHT MEANING

It's time to celebrate! The Three shows parties and reunions—from anniversaries, christenings, weddings, and birthdays to a great night out or weekend away with friends and family. This is a time for indulgence and reward, to enjoy other's company, be carefree, and have simple fun. There's also a flirtatious air about this Three, so if you're looking for a relationship, you'll soon be in the perfect situation and mood for lighthearted love.

The cups on the card are raised in a toast: There's a feeling of abundance, but if you're a wine- rather than water-drinker, or you've got a sweet tooth, you may be tempted to overindulge. However, whatever your pleasure, the Three ultimately reveals emotional and/or physical healing. Spending time with people who make you feel good raises your vibration and

energy levels. This positive influence can also soothe physical ailments that are triggered or exacerbated by stress.

As three is the number of creation, this shows a creative time—literally, with a pregnancy or birth, or in your creative goals. Turn your focus to new ideas and share them, as whatever you do will be enjoyable and well received, and even rewarded, by others. It's time to let your talent shine.

REVERSED MEANING

When reversed, the Three of Cups can indicate a flirtation or indulgence gone too far, with affairs and heated emotions. In established relationships, there may be distance and a lack of cohesion and understanding. Someone close may be overly opinionated and egotistical, and the dynamics of a close relationship—romantic or friendship—become skewed. Emotional betrayal in friendships is also a common meaning of the Three of Cups.

Creativity takes a nosedive, too, as creative blocks abound; it may be hard to get started as you suffer a lack of motivation and support. If so, take a break and return to your projects when you feel more grounded and less affected by others' emotional demands.

This card can also show irritating or recurrent health problems that need your attention.

FOUR OF CUPS

Element: Water

Astrological Association: Moon in Cancer

Number: 4

Tree of Life Position: Chesed, the sphere of love

Key Meanings: Restlessness and boredom

UNDERSTANDING THE FOUR OF CUPS

A young man sits under a tree, his arms and legs crossed. Three cups are set out in a row before him. From a cloud, a hand holds out a fourth cup, resembling the one on the Ace of Cups, symbolizing a new start. Although the hand appears at his eye level, his eyes are downcast—he is refusing to acknowledge the offered cup. Disenchanted, he appears to be looking discontentedly at the three cups on the grass as if to indicate that the fourth cup, whatever it may represent, is bound to be just more of the same old thing. This is in sharp contrast to the Three of Cups, in which the cups are held aloft in celebration (see page 124). The young man's pose is defensive, and he has set himself apart from his own emotions and the possibility of change.

Regardless of his mood, the sky is blue and the outlook is bright. The tree that gives him refuge is in full leaf. If he were to stand up and move around, he could enjoy the abundant life going on all around him. In this way, the card shows the potential for others to see your light, to see you able to stand tall like a tree, rooted and firm, and with branches open to embrace whatever comes. On the kabbalistic Tree of Life, the individual sphere associated with this card is Chesed, for love. In the case of this Four, it shows that love and support are there, if one wants it.

Astrologically, this card is linked with the Moon in Cancer, which denotes sensitivity and deep intuition, which we see in the self-protective pose of the man, with his arms and legs crossed. The negative aspect of this conjunction is possessiveness and sentimentality—not wanting to let go of what we have, regardless of whether it makes us happy or not.

The number four is the number of stability, which in Cups, the suit of emotions, indicates inertia. Water needs to flow—if it rests too long, it stagnates. In this way, the Four of Cups shows an underlying restlessness, a feeling that something is not quite right, but habit keeps the young man from making a decision.

UPRIGHT MEANING

If you are looking for a relationship, the Four of Cups shows disillusion. This card often comes up if you have been hurt in the past and protect yourself with a checklist, instantly rejecting anyone who doesn't live up to your exacting standards—to the degree that even if your soul mate came along right now, you wouldn't recognize his or her potential. I call this the "Will I ever meet anyone I like?" card. The answer is: You can and will, but it's time to risk opening up emotionally again. You may think you're ready for love, but there may be some past issues still to heal. If you're in an established relationship, the Four of Cups shows a tinge of boredom. This may be a phase, and if so, it's time to inject some romance; otherwise, you may find yourself staying in a relationship out of habit.

In work and home life, the card shows a static situation—you may feel bored with your job or need to make a positive change to your environment. Even a small change will go a long way to making you feel you are going forward, so look around for some much-needed inspiration—it isn't far away.

REVERSED MEANING

The meaning of the reversed Four of Cups is generally the same as for the upright card, but with a higher degree of dissatisfaction—you may be yearning for change but don't yet know what you want. If so, it's important to try new tactics at work and address what needs to change in your relationship or environment. Try to express your needs now, rather than locking them up.

When the Four of Cups is reversed, the man's crossed legs echo the bent knee of card XII, The Hanged Man. One of this major arcana card's meanings is hanging around, feeling in limbo. Rather than wait for change, the message of the reversed Four of Cups is to take control and make life happen. Thankfully, this limbo is temporary—change is always possible.

FIVE OF CUPS

Element: Water

Astrological Association: Mars in Scorpio

Number: 5

Tree of Life Position: Geburah, the sphere of power

Key Meanings: Loss, leaving, and sorrow

UNDERSTANDING THE FIVE OF CUPS

A figure shrouded in black, for mourning, contemplates three overturned cups. These are the three standing cups from the Four of Cups, the previous card, which have been cast to the ground, spilling blood or wine and water. A small dwelling is set above a river, which flows under a bridge with two arches. This may be a home that he has left behind, a symbol of past happiness and security he is now separated from by water, evoking the mythical Styx that divided the world of the living from the otherworld of the dead. The river also suggests the saying "a river of tears," in keeping with the sorrowful feel of the card. The mourner is in unfamiliar territory, a place of sadness, away from comfort and emotional security—at least for the time being. On the kabbalistic Tree of Life, the sphere associated with this card is *Geburah*, which means power, destruction, and cruelty. The mourner is powerless in his loss, which may or may not be cruel; yet what he doesn't appear to notice are the two vessels behind him, still standing. Three cups are overturned, but there are two that he can grasp—all he needs to do is to turn around and see them. While he cannot change past events, it is up to him to make the best of what remains.

Astrologically, this card is linked with Mars in Scorpio, bringing warlike qualities to the passionate sign of Scorpio, also linked with death and the past. The mourner is engrossed with the spilled cups, and it's worth noting in a 1910 edition of the Rider-Waite deck, his face was strangely red, the same color as the spilled wine or blood. While this may just be the artist using the same blood red for consistency, the blush indicates shame—shame and embarrassment about past actions or humiliation caused by a person or situation.

The number five in the tarot's minor arcana usually indicates imbalance and upset. After the stable, if boring, four, five brings disruption—but this is often necessary and can be the only way to shift energy and bring about healing and change. Five is also the number of humanity. The sadness of this card is universal, shared by all of us at some point in our lives.

UPRIGHT MEANING

The Five of Cups is the card of upset and loss. It often shows sadness and confusion due to a breakup, disappointment or arguments in a close friendship, or the need to temporarily move away from a family member who has caused hurt. The card can also apply to leaving a job or home before you are ready to do so—you are forced to deal with whatever life throws your way, whether invited or not. This card can also refer to a loss of status or money. The gift of this five is that there is no mistaking what has happened because you feel it in every bone of your body. At this point, there is no going back. But all is not lost: You will be able to move onward and upward regardless. The two remaining cups on the card can show the support of friends, family, and colleagues.

The Five of Cups can also come up in a reading for a bereavement and the natural sense of loss and grief this brings. It's also an indicator that you or the person you are reading for is revisiting the past, trying to assimilate old stress and sorrow in order to make a fresh start.

REVERSED MEANING

The Five of Cups along with major arcana card XV, The Devil, are the only two cards in the tarot deck whose reversed interpretations are more positive than their upright meanings. The Five reversed reveals you have already experienced the lowest point in a downward cycle and, as a result, are close to recovery, finally letting go of painful past memories. Ready to pick up the pieces, you will be stronger than you were before, able to face reality and move forward.

An additional meaning of the card is meeting up with old friends and, socially speaking, coming back to life.

SIX OF CUPS

Element: Water

Astrological Association: Sun in Scorpio

Number: 6

Tree of Life Position: Tiphareth, the sphere of beauty and rebirth

Key Meanings: Harmony, childhood, reconciliation, and old friends

UNDERSTANDING THE SIX OF CUPS

The two figures on this card look odd—an overgrown child in a red cap offering a cup to a girl dressed liked an old woman in the garden of a manor house and tower. One cup stands on a stone podium with a heraldic shield, while four cups stand upright before them. There's a fairytale theme at work here, which reminds us of childhood tales: little red cap, or little red riding hood, or even a child-prince awakening a princess grown old after one hundred years of sleep. However we interpret this otherworldly scene, it is designed to remind us of childhood and the past.

The tower and watchman on the left of the card symbolize protection and the flowers, spiritual blossoming and love. The star-shaped blooms may be white datura, or apple-thorn flowers, once used in herbal potions as an aphrodisiac or poison, but they also resemble a species of morning glory, which blooms early in the day—linking with a return to the early part of our lives, childhood and the past. Whichever flower we prefer, both carry the meaning of an otherworldly state of mind: Both apple thorn and morning glory were used as hallucinogens. Our hearts and minds are certainly not in the present moment.

In astrology, the Six of Cups is linked with the Sun in Scorpio, which stands for loyalty and strong bonds with friends, family, and partners. Scorpio is a sign of deep emotions and the past, again suggesting the impact of childhood experience. The Six of Cups' Tree of Life sphere is Tiphareth, for beauty and rebirth, which emphasizes the card's meaning of reconnection with people from the past.

The number six stands for serenity and peace. The six-pointed Star of David is composed of two triangles, representing the concept of heaven on earth—a reminder that we can realize the heavenly and spiritual aspects of ourselves in our daily lives to enjoy harmony in mind, body, and spirit. In the Six of Cups, the two themes are the past and the present. The challenge is to integrate our experiences, reconciling our past memories with present reality to create the future—the perfection of this idea is summed up in the Ten of Cups, the card of family and full emotional expression. The diagonal cross, known as the saltire cross, on the podium in the Six of Cups' garden makes the shape of the roman number X, or 10—again, offering an ideal concept of love on earth.

UPRIGHT MEANING

The Six of Cups reveals happy memories and a time to recall childhood with fondness. Your children, if you have them, may help you reconnect with your own childhood, or you are able to give your inner child free rein to play and have fun without the usual burden of worries. This is a time for good things coming from the past—reunion parties, reconnecting with old friends and more distant family members, or literally going back to your roots. This card may predict a trip home or to a place with fond memories. In some way, the past returns to help you in the present, too, as conversations and reminiscing with old friends or contacts seeds a new idea or approach.

Overall, you will find the right balance in relationships and enjoy a period of peace and harmony. This Six of Cups also shows compassion and kindness, so if you have suffered poor treatment, your situation is set to improve. Sweet, happy times are ahead, and any disruptions or upsets will be soothed and remedied.

In love, an old flame comes back, and you may need to weigh up if it is worth going back to the relationship.

REVERSED MEANING

When the Six of Cups is reversed, nostalgia rules, and you may recall past events with more positivity than they deserve. The card can also show you feeling locked in the past as a way to avoid moving on. A particular relationship needs to stay in the past rather than be revived. Unexpected visitors or communications may stir up old memories, and if so, let the memories rest—these people have no place in your future just now.

SEVEN OF CUPS

Element: Water

Astrological Association: Venus in Scorpio

Number: 7

Tree of Life Position: Netzach, the sphere of endurance, instinct, and desire

Key Meanings: Opportunities and extremes

UNDERSTANDING THE SEVEN OF CUPS

Seven cups appear to float in the sky, and a dark, anonymous figure seems to behold or even command them. Each cup has its own mini-cloud, rather like the Ace of Cups itself. And like the Ace multiplied, this card offers us seven potential gifts or beginnings—but it is up to us to discern what is feasible. At the moment, we're like the foreground figure: in the shadows, trying to discern reality from fantasy.

Each cup has an emergent symbol. The first cup shows a male face with curly hair, which echoes that of Archangel Michael, the angel of Temperance, card XIV, indicating a higher force may be at work. It can also be seen as your own reflection, a sign of your future potential. The tiny covered figure in the central cup symbolizes what is hidden and can be regarded as a symbol of Christ and ascending consciousness—the shadow figure, perhaps, is sensing a divine plan yet to be revealed.

The snake in the third cup stands for wisdom and flattery. (The snake also appears on card VI, The Lovers, and X, The Wheel of Fortune.) The tower on the rock appears to be a fantasy castle—as A. E. Waite says, "the images are most especially those of the fantastic spirit." The fifth cup shows overflowing jewels, for riches and abundance. The sixth cup shows a victory wreath like that on the Six of Wands, but on the cup itself is a shadowy likeness of a skull, casting doubt on this positive meaning—even this wreath-cup, the most obvious of symbols, is not what it seems. The wreath can mean fame, or reputation, which triumphs over death, just as in the procession of triumphs in the major arcana sequence (see page 11). The seventh cup shows a salamander or dragon with a forked tongue. Who knows if what we hear are lies or truth?

All in all, this card's seven images, according to Waite, are those of "reflection, sentiment, imagination, things seen in the glass of contemplation." They are not real—yet.

In astrology, the Seven of Cups is linked with Venus in Scorpio, which stands for mad passions and extreme reactions. This meaning links with the interpretation for the reversed card, which can indicate obsessive thinking. Netzach, the card's Tree of Life sphere, means endurance and desire—in this card, we might interpret this as ongoing fantasy.

The number seven is a mystical number. It was sacred to the god Apollo, founder of the famous Delphic oracle, and is the number of the days of the week, the deadly sins, and the wonders of the world (see The Chariot, page 58). Seven represents possibilities: It comprises three, the number of heaven, and four, the number of earth—and so the potential to bring heaven down to earth, to manifest an ideal.

UPRIGHT MEANING

Choices and confusion—While the seven brings the potential for amazing opportunities, these options and offers are insubstantial. At present, it's not clear what's feasible and what is fantasy, as everything feels up in the air, just like the floating cups on the card itself. Be discerning and find out what you can about each possible path, but ultimately you'll need to choose by paying attention to your instincts and emotions. This is not a test of logic: Go with the flow and trust your inner knowing. Don't rush. In relationships, the card can show new doorways opening again as joint finances improve.

The Seven is also the card of the visionary and shows the beginning stages of a new project, when anything is possible. Dreams and visions are additional interpretations.

REVERSED MEANING

The reversed Seven of Cups has much the same meaning as the upright card, but here, extreme emotions are in play. Be aware of the danger of idealizing a situation and avoiding a difficult truth; in relationships, the card can mean being deceived by appearances—a new lover may not be faithful. This is not the right time for commitment. Avoid becoming embroiled in drama; step back until your options are clear.

EIGHT OF CUPS

Element: Water

Astrological Association: Saturn in Pisces

Number: 8

Tree of Life Position: Hod, the sphere of majesty and the mind

Key Meanings: Departure, change, and emotional intelligence

UNDERSTANDING THE EIGHT OF CUPS

Like card XVIII, The Moon, we see the sun and moon combined. Which will reign—the sun (the mind) or the moon (impulse and intuition)? This is nighttime, the moon's realm: Our hero turns away from his familiar surroundings under her light, guided by his instincts alone. The sun will have his time the next day, when it's time for plans and practicalities, but for now, he must go with the flow, following the water toward a new destination.

The cloaked man has found a way forward. He has navigated a ribbon of pathway by the low rocks, which gives way to a soft riverbank, where he walks purposefully, supported by his staff. This can be likened to the Magician's wand or the Hermit's staff, a symbol of internal guidance. His red cloak shows he has the ability to manifest his intentions. We also sense he left his cups just moments ago—the gap in the top line of three cups still puts him among them, as if he has only just said good-bye. With his back to us, he is firmly fixed on the mountain to the right, a symbol of challenges and new, great experiences to come. When he has journeyed around the mountain, we know that our hero will have an entirely different perspective.

This Eight of Cups' astrological association is Saturn in the sign of Pisces. Saturn, the task-master planet, in imaginative Pisces poses a potential conflict between practical needs and idealism. Perhaps the solution is found in the card's Tree of Life sphere, Hod. Its common meaning is majesty, and in this card, it refers to the mastery of the mind—finding solutions and direction.

Eight is the number of fulfilment. It comprises two fours, the number of stability, which, however, when interpreted in the suit of Cups, turns to dissatisfaction and boredom. The Eight of Cups therefore is boredom doubled—or at the very least, a situation that has become stagnant. Conversation, creativity, or money no longer flows, so it must be found elsewhere.

UPRIGHT MEANING

The upright Eight of Cups reveals a time of restlessness when it feels as if something is missing. Work and relationships may appear harmonious from the outside, but your intuition is nagging you. The result may be a departure. Traditionally, the Eight of Cups predicts you leave a situation or break an agreement that no longer gives you fulfilment. This should not be a hasty decision; only move on when you are sure that there is no more you can gain or contribute. When the timing is right, there's also less drama than you would expect: Like the figure on the card slipping away in the night, you can take your leave quietly and swiftly. Naturally, you may feel sadness but little regret—provided the timing is right.

Like the figure in red following the path of the river, it's now time to go with the flow. You'll soon feel energized to move on to where your interests and curiosity call. You can also feel content with what you have achieved.

This card often turns up in a reading to show that you have already left a situation emotionally, and action will follow as you now take your actual leave. It can also predict a time to travel, to explore physically or through spiritual journeying.

REVERSED MEANING

What are you holding on to? Take stock: Are you clinging in to the past when you really do know that your current living situation has to change? When reversed, the Eight of Cups shows errors of judgement, so you jump too soon or stay too long, unable to see that there's an alternative way to do things. At this point, there's no logical solution; like the Eight of Cups' sphere of Hod, for the mind and its strategies, an intellectual approach might make you feel in control, but the way ahead is to follow your instincts. Timing is important now, so trust yourself that you will know the right time to move on, without self-pressure. An additional meaning of the card is being abandoned, leaving you confused as others move on from you— with undignified haste.

NINE OF CUPS

Element: Water

Astrological Association: Jupiter in Pisces

Number: 9

Tree of Life Position: Yesod, the sphere of foundation and the unconscious mind

Key Meaning: Happiness

UNDERSTANDING THE NINE OF CUPS

A seated male figure is encircled by nine cups on a table. Radiant with pride, he shows off what he has in life: joy and achievement. The cups are trophies, rewards for his past efforts, on display for all to see. This is a card of true happiness; what the man possesses can be enjoyed to the full. As the table is covered with a cloth, there is also a sense of banqueting, the table set ready to welcome a party. Secure in his role as benefactor, it is the man's joy to share his riches with others. He is perfectly comfortable with this abundance, sitting squarely on a low bench wearing a cap and hose—both red for vitality and joie de vivre.

With lucky planet Jupiter in the idealistic sign of Pisces, astrologically the Nine of Cups has the meaning of good fortune, prosperity, fun, and the spirit of generosity. Piscean's natural humanitarianism comes to the fore, as what benefits our hero of the Nine of Cups will naturally be shared with others. The card's Tree of Life sphere, Yesod, means foundation. Ruled by the Moon, symbol of the unconscious, Yesod brings together intuition and logic in balance—an alignment with our life purpose.

As a nine of the suit of Cups, this card indicates emotions find their ultimate expression: Feelings flow. Nine also represents the triad of mind, body, and spirit, showing a perfect balance of all three aspects of our humanity. In this way, the Nine of Cups symbolizes joy that is perfectly expressed. The cups almost touch one another in a half circle symbolizing intimacy and connection.

UPRIGHT MEANING

The Nine of Cups is known as the wish card of the tarot because it foretells a dream come true. Whatever you hope for can now come to fruition. Joy comes from prosperity, generosity, and optimism, alongside parties and entertainment.

In relationships, the Nine of Cups reveals new romance and rewarding friendships. Whatever feelings have been nurtured in the past can now be expressed as others show their hearts. The time for waiting for love is over; if love has grown, it will be declared fully. Friends will step closer to you as you feel more connected to your own heart. When fully living your truth, others respond. In the spirit of sharing, there is now an easy connection with others as projects begin and existing work becomes more rewarding. This is a time to communicate, laugh, and appreciate all you have.

If you are nurturing a new project or idea, the Nine of Cups heralds its growth, so listen to your intuition, make time for the activities that make you happy, and see them flourish. Astrologically, this card is linked with Jupiter in Pisces, which promotes imagination, artistic flair, and generosity—so it is time, also, to share and own your ideas. Independence will also be important at this time.

The Nine also favors good health, as old tensions dissolve, flowing away in the waters of the past. Now is the time to appreciate the joy of the present.

REVERSED MEANING

When reversed, ego steps in—and with it self-centeredness and emotional disconnection. This can manifest as smugness. More commonly in readings, the Nine reversed tells a tale of narcissism: You are faced with others' inability to see beyond their own immediate needs. This influence can infect personal and professional relationships, which suffer as others forge ahead with their agendas for short-term gain, leaving you bruised. However, it's also worth asking yourself if you are the one overstriving for recognition, sidelining others in the process.

In personal and business projects, uncertainty rules due to misunderstandings, and your plans may be delayed. Creativity can suffer at this time, too, with stop-start-stop frustration. Focus on maintaining balance and routine to help you navigate these difficult waters and hold on to those dreams and schemes. This may not be the right time for new ideas idea to flourish, but this doesn't diminish your worth or the strength of your concepts.

Take extra care of yourself and your relationships now, as energy levels may be low; hibernate a little until that spark returns.

TEN OF CUPS

Element: Water

Astrological Association: Mars in Pisces

Number: 10

Tree of Life Position: Malkuth, the Kingdom, the sphere of experience

Key Meanings: Prosperity, joy, family, and contentment

UNDERSTANDING THE TEN OF CUPS

Here is an idealized family scene: mother, father, and their two children, who are dancing. We see their home, established above a river, and from the river plain below, the couple beholds ten glowing cups in the sky, arranged on a rainbow arc. The river flows, trees grow, and not one cloud can be seen. This family lives in abundance—shown also by their smart clothing—and they appear to be celebrating their achievement. This is their kingdom, their Malkuth, the card's Tree of Life sphere. What could be happier than this place of security and contentment?

The focus here is on the ideal of perfection. This is the perfect life, blessed by a vision of the ten cups; the rainbow is a symbol of hope and reward. We see only the backs of the couple and, although the children are in engrossed in their own game, they are happy entertaining themselves while their parents raise their arms in thanks for all they have been given.

In numerology, ten represents completeness and perfection. In the Ten of Cups, this gives the meaning of greatest happiness. Out of the ten cups, four are directly touching, perhaps reflecting the familial connection between the four figures.

The Ten of Cups' astrological association reveals that feeling, rather than intellect, is foremost: The warlike influence of Mars dissipates when in the sign of gentle, idealistic Pisces, so the focus is on intuition and the emotions.

UPRIGHT MEANING

One of the most positive cards of the minor arcana, the Ten of Cups reveals the benefits of love and the security of family; it favors children as an expression of love, and often reveals that children will do well socially and academically, succeeding in their studies. The card therefore predicts great happiness for couples and families or equivalent close friendship groups. In work, the Ten of Cups shows peace and harmony for business partnerships and other key networks. Togetherness, not competition, will be your strength. In fact, anything you do en masse will go well now, from sporting activities, committees, and choirs to group trips and collaborative projects.

In relationships, this is an emotional time, in wholly a positive way. Partnerships built on stability and trust become even more rewarding and supportive. Different generations of a family may come together and put aside old disagreements; it's a common card for forthcoming weddings, parties, and other significant celebrations. Communication between parents and children, children and grandparents, and other family members will grow stronger and be more fulfilling. If you have been searching for a new home, the Ten of Cups shows this will come to you, and it will be the right property in the right location for your needs.

In relation to projects, the card gives assurance that what you have worked hard for will finally come together. Financially, the Ten of Cups is a wonderful indicator of prosperity, which comes to you as a result of well-deserved achievement.

REVERSED MEANING

When reversed, the Ten of Cups retains much of its positive vibe, but with some irritating undercurrents and changes in friendships and family bonds. A family issue may need to be addressed as your routine is disrupted, or you sense discord in some relationships; also, you may feel that you're not getting an entitlement, from respect from different generations of the family to enjoying enough time with children. Your plans to bring friends and family together may falter due to miscommunication. Equally, the need to keep up appearances prevents authentic conversations and understanding.

Friends may also prove troublesome under the influence of the reversed Ten of Cups, and as a result, one or two confidants step back from your circle or introduce you to a new friend of theirs with whom you don't feel comfortable—which upsets your usually happy dynamic. However, other people you prefer will soon come into your orbit to take their place.

Do bear in mind, however, that these are temporary glitches, rather than major challenges—and that the reversed Ten of Cups' overriding meaning is still positive.

PAGE OF CUPS

Element: Earth of the suit of Water

Key Meaning: Love news

UNDERSTANDING THE PAGE OF CUPS

A fairytale page holds a cup, contemplating a fish within it—which appears to look up at him as if about to communicate. The fish is a symbol here of dreams and emotions that have taken form, so the Page is contemplating that which has come from the deep—or his desires and impulses. In folklore and Chinese myth, the fish is a prosperity symbol; in the ancient Celtic story of Fionn MacCumhail (pronounced *Finn MacCool*), the hero eats the salmon of knowledge and becomes the wisest person in all the land; and in Paganism, the fish has been a fertility symbol associated with female genitalia. A secret symbol of faith for persecuted Christians during Greek and Roman times, the fish is also a symbol of the soul. But the Page is not all deep symbolism—there's playful magic and lightheartedness here, too—one of the key meanings of the card.

The Page stands on dry land, and behind him water flows; perhaps the fish has sprung from this river or ocean. The card's element is Earth of Water, which suggests that emotions, thoughts, and ideas—the water—can become as substantial as earth, or matter. The Page's tunic is decorated with water lilies, and as lilies are traditional signifiers of purity, this Page is pure of heart. His colors, blue and pink, stand for spirituality and love. The scarf around his hat flows down around his shoulders, echoing the flow of the water. From this, we can tell that his emotions are on show. One side of the scarf forms a scallop shape, another echo of the fish's natural habitat.

Pages and Knights in tarot are generally regarded as people or influences, whereas the other court cards (the Queens and Kings) are assumed to be people. Let your intuition guide you toward the most appropriate meaning for the Page in a reading by working with the card's imagery first, then the written interpretations here (see also the Introduction, page 8).

UPRIGHT MEANING

As an influence: The Page represents sociability, good company, and fun. Whatever your age, the Page reveals you will feel young at heart. As Pages are messengers, the Page of Cups brings good news about the emotional aspects of your life: relationships, children, and finances (when this has a direct impact on your relationships). In love, he can show a new potential partner is coming. This is not the Page himself—he is simply the messenger—but he lets you know that love is once more on the horizon. While it will be tempting to rush into a new romance, it may be wise to hold back a little. Other responsibilities such as extra work and exams can't be abandoned just yet.

This card also favors imagination and creativity, and so augers well for new projects and opportunities to improve your home and lifestyle. If you have suffered periods of insecurity and doubt, the Page assures you that all is well and good times are ahead. Finances are also favored now.

As a person: An individual with an artistic temperament, this Page is a dreamer. He loves company, is highly emotional and intuitive, and is naturally generous, sometimes to a fault. He is a good friend and happy to introduce others into his circle. The Page can often indicate a sensitive child or other young person you care for.

As the "you" card in a reading: It's time to enjoy life's pleasures.

If two or more Pages fall close together in a reading, the meanings are as follows:

- **Two Pages:** Friendship if upright; rivalry if one or both cards are reversed

- **Three Pages:** Lots of social activities

- **Four Pages:** A social group of young people

REVERSED MEANING

When reversed, the Page brings frustration and irresponsibility. Offers do not materialize; you may feel that life is all work and no play. As a person, the reversed Page is emotionally immature and attention-seeking, so you cannot rely on his perspective—he can only obsess about his own needs. This person may be living in a dream world and become very defensive when challenged. In family relationships, a child may find it difficult to communicate his or her feelings.

An additional meaning of the reversed Page is intoxication—too much partying. It's time to calm down and get back to an ordered routine.

KNIGHT OF CUPS

Element: Fire of the suit of Water

Astrological Associations: Aquarius and Pisces

Key Meaning: A proposal

UNDERSTANDING THE KNIGHT OF CUPS

This is a proud knight indeed. With his heroic helmet topped with the wings of Hermes, Greek god of communication, he sits astride a dainty steed. Shiny and poised, he is dressed more for appearance than warfare. As traditionally knights all have a quest, this Knight's quest is love, signified by two elements on the card: his outstretched, empty cup, symbol of his quest for the holy grail of love; and the river flowing through the valley, which signifies that he will follow the course of his feelings. The blue of his armor links with the meaning of truth (shown also in card II, The High Priestess), while the red fish design on his tunic denotes passion, along with faith (see also the Page of Cups, page 140).

The card's element is Fire of the suit of Water. Together, this combination makes for conflicting feelings: Fire and Water cancel each other out, so the Knight veers between bravado and ultra-sensitivity. His words may be engaging, but he may hesitate when it comes to action—not the ideal quantities of a marital knight.

In truth, we would rather have the cutting Knight of Swords or action-hero Knight of Wands to protect us and defend the realm. The Knight of Cups's characteristics are more in keeping with the idealized knights of Chrétien de Troyes's medieval tales, *Le Morte d'Athur*—when courtship followed strict rituals. Love was an impossible ideal, and, often, an unattainable lady the object of obsession—a far cry from real, requited relationships in earthly life. Such is our Knight of Cups: full of potential, loud with declarations. But will his words of love translate into commitment?

Knights and Pages in tarot are generally regarded as people or influences, whereas the other court cards (the Queens and Kings) are assumed to be people. Let your intuition guide you toward the most appropriate meaning for the Knight in a reading by working with the card's imagery first, then the written interpretations here (see also the Introduction, page 8).

UPRIGHT MEANING

As an influence: The Knight of Cups heralds an emotional time—you may be bewitched by a new love interest (or even more than one), enjoy more romance with an existing partner, and/or other sweet things that capture your imagination: beauty, nature, time away from work or your usual routines, or creative pursuits. New friends may enter your circle.

As a person: Idealistic and dreamy, artistic and sensitive, this Knight is a true romantic. His arrival in a reading shows a love prospect and even a proposal—which is wonderful if you have an established relationship. However, as a new love interest, tread carefully. This Knight is an idealist and, while wanting a relationship, finds it hard to articulate his true feelings. He may be stuck behind a persona of the perfect partner—gallant and generous—but unable to drop the act to let you see who he really is. While this is understandable in the early days of a romance, if the actions don't match the words of passion, take care; don't be swept away just yet.

As the "you" card in a reading: Be open to real love; judge not by appearance.

If two or more Knights fall close together in a reading, the meanings are as follows:

- **Two Knights:** Friendship if upright; rivalry if one or both cards are reversed
- **Three Knights:** Men meeting up
- **Four Knights:** Lots of action; events speed up

REVERSED MEANING

The Knight reversed means disappointment—an offer that at first glance appeared perfect does not materialize, leaving you feeling confused and pushed out. As a person, the reversed Knight is untrustworthy and unreliable. He is hooked on the chase, the romantic or sexual ideal, but has no intention of going beyond the honeymoon phase of a relationship. He may also be looking for the thrill of new romance elsewhere, continuing the cycle of manipulation.

This card often appears in a reading to denote a lover who has intimacy and commitment issues. His behavior may be inconsistent and unpredictable, but when challenged, he may protest that this is not the case and try to deflect the problem onto you. It is of course best for you to step away, as this knight has little to offer other than ongoing drama.

QUEEN OF CUPS

Element: Water of the suit of Water

Astrological Associations: Gemini and Cancer

Chakras: Sacral, heart, and third eye, for creativity, love, and second sight

Key Meaning: An intuitive woman

UNDERSTANDING THE QUEEN OF CUPS

The Queen of Cups can be considered as an aspect of card III, The Empress, or a mother archetype who brings love, kindness, and abundance. She respectfully holds up her treasure, an ornate golden chalice. With a cross atop it and two praying angels fixed on either side, it is a signifier of faith and spirituality. The chalice is closed, suggesting the sacredness of the womb and the creation of life.

On the card are three water-babies: one holding the prosperity symbol of the fish and the other two a pair, like the Queen's sign of Gemini, sitting on each side of the throne top. The water-babies signify the Queen's maternal instinct. The choice of water-baby and beach may have been inspired by a Victorian tale still popular in the period during which the Rider-Waite cards were created.

Charles Kingsley's novel *The Water-Babies: A Fairy Tale for a Land Baby* (1863) tells the story of Tom the chimney sweep, who is taken by fairies and turned into a water-baby. Kinglsey tells the reader we must be open-minded to the existence of such things and that we know but "the very smallest" corner of the world—which can be likened to "only a child picking up pebbles on the shore of a boundless ocean." Perhaps the Queen is sitting at the edge of Kingsley's boundless ocean of knowledge, and the pebbles at her feet signify the elements of wisdom that come our way, washed up on the shore. These physical pebbles are repeated as a design on the Queen's crown and as a cluster on the chalice. They look like golden nuggets, symbols of her generosity.

The card's element is Water of Water, for intense emotions. The throne's scallop shape reflects this Water element, echoed in the scallop brooch fixed at her heart, pink for love. The scallop echoes Botticelli's *The Birth of Venus* (1486), which shows the goddess rising from the sea on a scallop shell—linking our Queen with Venus/Aphrodite, goddess of earthly and divine love. The fish-scale cloak falls into the water at the Queen's feet, while water-swirls decorate the lower segments of the throne so she appears as one with the water. Even the plait of the Queen's hair is scale-like, and the color is auburn, just like Botticelli's Venus.

Queens and Kings in tarot are traditionally regarded as people in your life or people about to come into your orbit. However, you can also read the Queen as a general influence, so this interpretation is included last.

UPRIGHT MEANING

As a person: The Queen of Cups predicts the positive influence of an intuitive, sensitive woman. She is nurturing and compassionate, with high emotional intelligence. Her work may be artistic, and she may also be drawn to medicine, caregiving, complementary therapies, certain types of sales work, or research in nonmainstream subjects. Given her sensitivity and natural empathy, this Queen has to choose her close friends carefully—but when she makes a connection with a person, she treasures him or her, just like her chalice.

This card often comes up in readings to show the ideal female partner, who is unafraid of intimacy while having stability and appropriate boundaries. It can predict motherhood and children, too.

As the "you" card in a reading: Loving and giving, you make the world a better place.

As an influence: Love and happiness are foremost—falling in love, loving behavior, and emotional honesty. All you need to do is follow your heart. Creative projects are favored, too. Pay attention, also, to your dreams, which hold messages for you.

If two or more Queens fall close together in a reading, the meanings are as follows:

- **Two Queens:** Rivalry
- **Three Queens:** Helpful friends
- **Four Queens:** Women meeting up

REVERSED MEANING

When the reversed Queen of Cups appears, you suffer emotional or financial pressure. There may be jealousy in a relationship, and most negatively, the card in this aspect can show that someone is unfaithful. As a person, the reversed Queen has obsessive tendencies, competes for attention, and needs to have her own way at all times. She drains those around her, so try not to facilitate her needs. She is not one to commit to love or contribute financially.

KING OF CUPS

Element: Air of the suit of Water

Astrological Associations: Libra and Scorpio

Chakras: Heart, third eye, and solar plexus, for love, intuition, and wisdom

Key Meaning: A charismatic man

UNDERSTANDING THE KING OF CUPS

The King of Cups can be considered as an aspect of card IV, The Emperor, or a father archetype who brings structure, order, and authority. His realm is the emotions.

He sits on a throne in the sea or ocean, comfortable but rock-steady despite the stormy outlook—the sailing ship on the horizon is listing in high winds, and waves are rising against a sky of white-gray. His throne is shell-shaped and, given this King's apparent cool despite his isolation, echoes Greek god Triton, the merman who blew through a conch shell to control the rise and fall of the waves.

His emblem is the fish, for prosperity and faith, or passion, worn as an amulet around his neck; a small dolphin or fish also leaps into the picture from the left. The water is green, turquoise, and gray—the many colors of the emotions. On his crown are waves and red jellyfish. The jellyfish may be an apt reference to one of the King's zodiac associations, Scorpio, a sign renowned for its deadly sting. The jellyfish may also link with the King as Perseus, the Greek god who beheaded the Gorgon Medusa—the "medusa stage" is a term describing a stage of the jellyfish's development. Jellyfish pulsate to move but have little power to propel themselves on their own, so they also symbolize acceptance and trust.

The card's element is Air of Water, for steam and clouds. As water evaporates with heat, so the King can convert Water to Air, transmuting feelings to ideas—the shift from heart to head. Like Triton, he is master of the waves and master of his emotions. This Air-Water combination can be challenging, however, as the King strives to find a balance between sharing his feelings and holding back.

Kings and Queens in tarot are traditionally regarded as people in your life or people about to come into your orbit. However, you can also read the King as a general influence, so this interpretation is included last.

UPRIGHT MEANING

As a person: The King of Cups shows a warmhearted, charismatic male. He might be an academic, lawyer, advisor, businessman, scientist, or artist. In his work, he follows his intuition. In friendships, he is sociable, but, like his counterpart the Queen of Cups, is sensitive and needs to choose his closest friends wisely. For this reason, he may have one or two confidants and a wide circle of acquaintances. While being empathic, at times he tries to control his feelings and can come across as distant. He often needs time to process his intense emotions before sharing them.

This card often comes up in readings to show the ideal romantic partner, who is unafraid of intimacy while having stability and appropriate boundaries. It can predict fatherhood and children, too.

As the "you" card in a reading: Follow your heart.

As an influence: A need exists to settle a conflict, either within yourself or between you and others, usually in a work or family situation. You are unsure whether to be logical or left-field, to go with the consensus or go with a hunch. If in doubt, follow your intuition and let your heart rule. In negotiations, use all your charm and empathy. When others feel that

you are really engaged with them, they will drop their defenses and communication will improve.

If two or more Kings fall close together in a reading, the meanings are as follows:

- **Two Kings:** A good partnership

- **Three Kings:** Influential men

- **Four Kings:** A power battle

REVERSED MEANING

The reversed King reveals emotional vulnerability. If this applies to an individual in your life, you may be dealing with someone who is volatile right now. This person may be secretive, ashamed, and uncommunicative when not blaming others for their predicament. Thankfully, this situation is temporary and will change.

An additional meaning of the reversed card is a person with destructive behavior patterns and possibly addiction issues (see also card XV, The Devil, page 90).

ACE OF PENTACLES

ACE *of* PENTACLES.

Element: Earth

Astrological Associations: The Earth signs—Taurus, Virgo, and Capricorn

Number: 1

Tree of Life Position: Kether, the sphere of divine light

Key Meanings: Prosperity, property, and beginnings

UNDERSTANDING THE ACE OF PENTACLES

A hand appears from a cloud, offering a single golden coin. It is the only card of the suit to show a coin with a double border, as if to emphasis its value. The scene below the coin and hand depicts cultivated lilies and a rose garden with an arch forming an oval window looking onto a mountain view. This is wealthy land, where the owners can afford to grow their own lilies, symbols of purity. The clear view beyond the roses to white peaks signifies challenge and the ambition to succeed without hindrance. The message, though, is that this wealth is being offered to us, the holder of the card. The perfect garden, abundant with beautiful blooms, is an example of the prosperous lifestyle that the gift of the Ace may bring. The coin is offered with the right hand, the hand of giving (as opposed to the left hand, which traditionally is the receiving hand).

The golden coin is engraved with the symbol of the pentagram, which appears on all the cards of this suit. The pentagram is an ancient symbol for the four elements, plus the fifth element, or quintessence—the magical element of ether (see card I, The Magician, page 34). The arrangement of the pentagram points can also represent heaven over the earth. Heaven is represented as the uppermost point of the pentagram, which also links with the card's Tree of Life sphere, Kether, for the divine light of God, or great spirit. The five points can also symbolize the body's five senses, which relate to the cards' element of Earth, which is concerned with our physical experience in the world as well as wealth and productivity.

The Aces offer the pure energy of their suits. As number ones, they represent oneness with the divine spirit or God. Indivisible, their energy is singular, strong, and purposeful. They all represent beginnings, impulses, and new possibilities, in the most pure and obvious form.

UPRIGHT MEANING

The upright meaning of the Ace of Pentacles is auspicious for every aspect of your life. In a spread, it overrules other minor arcana cards close by (just like XIX, The Sun). The Ace predicts happiness and contentment; you can have what you desire. Traditionally, it predicts prosperity, and you find money comes to you quickly, cither as a windfall or win, or you are shown the way to achieve it. In this sense, the card presents an opportunity for further attainment, so now is the time to receive the precious gift or opportunity on offer and use it to maximize your potential. You may find a way to use it to build for the future, as property is favored in the suit of Pentacles.

In readings, it commonly arises to show money is coming or a new property; it also predicts foundation and stability, so if you have questions concerning your home or relationship, you will receive what you need in abundance. One message of the card, too, is not to doubt your good fortune. You deserve it.

In a reading, one Ace brings a focus on the life area according to the suit, which can set the theme of the reading. If two or more Aces appear near each other in a reading, it means as follows:

- **Two Aces:** An important partnership
- **Three Aces:** Good news
- **Four Aces:** Excitement, beginnings, and potential

REVERSED MEANING

When the Ace reverses, it reveals greed and holding fast to one outcome. This desperation can cause materialistic thinking, and when you are fixed to one goal, other aspects of your life may suffer. The card can show unwise investment of time or money, so be aware of the motives of those you invest with or work for; this can be a difficult time when you are treated unfairly by an unscrupulous person or organization. Money for work you have done may not materialize. The reversed Ace of Pentacles also shows financial mismanagement and mistakes; as a prediction card in a reading, it advises not to make major financial decisions at present.

In personal relationships, the card can show that someone close becomes grasping and materialistic and selfishly wants to keep everything for themselves. The card can also show gambling and reckless spending.

TWO OF PENTACLES

Element: Earth

Astrological Association: Jupiter in Capricorn

Number: 2

Tree of Life Position: Chockmah, the sphere of wisdom

Key Meaning: Negotiation

UNDERSTANDING THE TWO OF PENTACLES

A young man appears to be dancing, holding two coins joined on a green thread in the shape of a figure-eight, for infinity and the continuity of life. The same symbol appears in card I, The Magician, and VIII, Strength, and stands for balance, activity, and renewal. The flow of this never-ending symbol also suggests consistency and patience. In the case of the Two of Pentacles, the youth's concern is cash flow; he appears to be dancing but is actually juggling his coins to respond to changing circumstances, shown by the two boats in the background that rise and fall on the waves.

At this point, he is considering two options. He needs to be practical and use his head to make a decision and find balance, which is symbolized by his tall red hat—at the moment, his dilemma is all in his mind and he has yet to take action. Hats of this style, known as acorn hats, were worn by artisans and courtiers in the fifteenth century but were usually shorter than that of our coin-dancer. It seems his hat was purposefully elongated by the card's artist, Pamela Colman Smith, to emphasize thinking, although another interpretation may be self-delusion, or big-headedness, which is evidenced by the reversed meaning of the card.

Two is the number of partnership, and in the Two of Pentacles, the focus is on two people or two opposing forces. The continual tension between these two forces keeps the coins spinning on the figure-eight, so the situation perpetuates. When a decision is made, the tension evaporates.

On the kabbalistic Tree of Life, the sphere associated with this card is Chockmah, the sphere of wisdom and the father, echoed in the phallic hat of the young man on the card. He needs to decide between two options or courses of action, and to do this, he needs to draw upon his wisdom.

The astrological association of Jupiter in Capricorn reveals strength and resourcefulness. The challenge of this combination for the Two of Pentacles is the pull between paying close attention to immediate detail and stepping back to see the long-term impact of the actions he takes.

UPRIGHT MEANING

In the upright position, the card shows making a decision and in particular, managing money. There may be temporary cash-flow issues, and you'll need consistent effort to balance the books. If your income is up and down, an unexpected expenditure can hit hard; this is a common card for freelancers whose income varies from month to month as well as for two people in business together. On a more positive note, the card says that if you pay close attention to financial and property matters, you will manage well, even on a tight budget. As a personality trait in the person/situation position in a spread, the Two of Pentacles indicates fairness and a willingness to find a good balance between work and personal life.

In readings, the card often comes up to show two properties and sometimes making a decision about where to live—in particular, a choice between home and a property abroad. This may also reveal a choice between two jobs in different places and weighing the pros and cons of each offer.

An additional meaning is news that comes in writing, so you may receive an important letter or email.

REVERSED MEANING

In the reversed position, egotism and pride can get in the way of practicality. Irresponsible spending may cause hardship, and these financial mistakes may be hidden—gambling is a common meaning here as well as a generally reckless attitude toward money.

In work, you may be dealing with an unreasonable boss who is unrealistic about what can be achieved, putting you under needless pressure.

The card can also show the ending of a business partnership due to financial difficulties; one of you may be investing more resources into the business than the other. The message is to observe closely just how committed you and your colleagues are and if the contribution is fair and equal.

THREE OF PENTACLES

Element: Earth

Astrological Association: Mars in Capricorn

Number: 3

Tree of Life Position: Binah, the sphere of understanding

Key Meanings: Enterprise and success

UNDERSTANDING THE THREE OF PENTACLES

The Three of Pentacles shows a stonemason at work on a church, following a plan held up by a figure clad in a strange orange cloak. Symbolizing lifelong vocation, a monk stands by, observing the work on his building. Our mason stands on a workbench, similar to that shown on the Eight of Pentacles; both the Three and the Eight show a craftsman at work. The man in Eight has finished his apprenticeship and graduated into the Three, the qualified craftsman who works independently. The three coins are a part of the church's design; his ideas are embedded in the structure of the building. His contribution will be lasting, set in stone.

The mason is working by a half-open door, signifying that his good work and reputation will open doors for him in the future. He wears a tunic of rich purple, the color of high office in the church, to show that he is spiritually in tune with his talents and beliefs. This also aligns with Binah, his Tree of Life sphere, which means understanding. He fully comprehends his brief and knows how to direct his skills to best effect.

It's also notable that the mason appears in a public space, where he can be seen. He is proud to show his work, and the art he creates is accessible to all—which is more important than the money he will be paid. Of note, too: This is the only Pentacles card that shows the coins in black; they are a representation of lasting satisfaction rather than a reward of literal golden coins.

In numerology, three is a dynamic number (see also card III, The Empress, page 42). We can interpret this as mother, father, child—with the mason as the mother (of his own inventions); the father, the mentor of his apprenticeship; and the child, the work the mason creates.

The Three of Pentacles is associated with Mars in Capricorn, which highlights strong ambition and often applies to people who are self-starters. The challenge with this combination is too avoid obsession and sidelining other life aspects with their drive to succeed.

UPRIGHT MEANING

The upright meaning of the Three of Pentacles is rewarding work. It often shows you are ready to let your talents shine in public, and the card often appears in readings to show launching a business, receiving a commission, giving a lecture or teaching, or presiding over an important event; specifically, it can also show making a speech at a graduation or wedding, for example.

In domestic affairs, the card can predict building or improvement work to your home or putting a property up for sale. The Three of Pentacles is also a good card for creatives, predicting that projects will be finished and appreciated. The work may also be displayed in a public space.

According to tarot scholar Jonathan Dee, the Three of Pentacles is sometimes called the Architect, which means you establish a lasting enterprise, a project that "causes you to stand head and shoulders above both friends and enemies alike." The downside, of course, as you succeed and become visibly successful, is the touch of envy you may sense around you; it may

feel uncomfortable, as you're not used to negative attention. This jealousy, as with elements of all minor arcana cards, is transitory and will not dint your confidence or harm your progress. Detractors can only make you stronger.

REVERSED MEANING

When the Three of Pentacles reverses, work is tiresome and you may not be willing to put in the groundwork—or indeed to work at all. This may be because you feel you've seen it all before and have become cynical about finding a career that will suit, or you take on a role for the perceived glamor—or the way it is sold to you—and later realize that the work is mostly tedium. You'll need to push through the dull details or make a swift decision to move on.

Another interpretation of the card is poor planning so a project doesn't succeed. In property affairs, it can show builders who do not finish the work they begin.

FOUR OF PENTACLES

Element: Earth

Astrological Association: Sun in Capricorn

Number: 4

Tree of Life Position: Chesed, the sphere of love

Key Meanings: Security, self-improvement, and holding on to money

UNDERSTANDING THE FOUR OF PENTACLES

The male figure we see on the Four of Pentacles has set himself up as a king, complete with a simple crown and stone throne, set just a little above the town behind him. His purpose is to elevate himself socially and financially and create a stable base for his future. The red colors of his gown show he has focused his energy in practical ways to create a firm foundation for himself, and now that he has achieved this, he wears a black cloak of protection to safeguard his assets. He needs to keep this money for himself.

The components of the card are almost symmetrical, expressing his number four, for the concept of balance. However, what is notable is how connected this man is to his money. He has a foot on each on two coins, one attached to his crown, and one held tight against center of his body. Symbolically, his money grounds him (at his feet); it is literally at his heart, at the center of his being; and at the crown of the head, it reflects his mind-set and beliefs. His arms, wrapped around the sides of the coin, almost look unnaturally twisted in his effort have physical contact with every part of its curve. He has made sure that no other hand can touch it, but it has also become a part of his identity. Wearing his coin on his crown means he is proud to show he is now a person of means and has risen through the ranks of the streets in the background to become a self-made man of note. He holds the central coin rather like a wheel—a sign that he believes money makes the world go round.

In numerology, four represents stability. On the kabbalistic Tree of Life, the individual sphere associated with this card is Chesed, for love. In the case of this Four of Pentacles, it indicates love for possessions and a strong desire for stability—even though there may be an emotional cost, which is reflected in the reversed meaning of the card.

The Four of Pentacles has an astrological association with the Sun in Capricorn, highlighting practicality and resilience, although super-solar Capricorn can be abrasive. Positively, Sun in Capricorn traits make for strong leadership and problem-solving.

UPRIGHT MEANING

The upright Four of Pentacles shows the need for stability and establishing a firm foundation. If you have suffered past hardship, the Four of Pentacles shows the tough times are over, as now your work pays off. While this doesn't indicate a huge windfall (look to the Ten of Pentacles for this), you will have enough money and acknowledgment to feel satisfied. The card also shows protection of assets and traditional values. Proving a strong foundation for a growing family may be important to you now, so you may consider moving to a new home or investing in a small business that will bring you future dividends. In work, you attain a position that is very secure, so if your work is temporary, for example, the Four of Pentacles can show you being offered a permanent contract.

An additional meaning of the card is the miser, as the male figure is clinging hard to his coin, but this money has come from hard work. You will value what you have achieved, and for now, want to keep it for yourself.

REVERSED MEANING

When reversed, the Four of Pentacles reveals an overly materialistic individual, a would-be king—male or female—who holds too fast to status and possessions. If this is you, try to let go of insecurity, as this can take up much of your head space—and feed an ongoing belief that you will never have enough. In work, the card can reveal that you miss opportunities because your confidence is low, and changes to your role may leave you feeling disempowered. It's therefore important to do well in any professional or educational tests now; you may need to put in more work than first anticipated.

The reversed Four of Pentacles can also suggest a person who is showy and even a little smug; in a position of power over you, you may find this individual controlling and self-centered.

FIVE OF PENTACLES

Element: Earth

Astrological Association: Mercury in Taurus

Number: 5

Tree of Life Position: Geburah, the sphere of power

Key Meaning: A test of resources

UNDERSTANDING THE FIVE OF PENTACLES

The Five of Pentacles features a snow scene showing two impoverished people suffering a harsh winter. It is reminiscent of Dickens's 1843 novel *A Christmas Carol* and its child character, Tiny Tim, a disabled boy on crutches. The beggar in the Rider-Waite deck appears to be a small grown man—an adult Tiny Tim, still struggling to survive years on. Around his neck is a bell, which in medieval times was worn by lepers to warn others of their approach. He has become untouchable and excluded from society.

The woman accompanying him is barefoot and gray-haired, wearing a red cloak. The color shows she will persist, despite their predicament—but what she cannot yet grasp is any possibility of change. The pair are fixed on surviving the elements and do not notice the window above, with its depiction of a money tree of five coins and a safe, solid property behind it. Even if the paupers could raise their heads to face the biting wind, this idyllic scene would seem a world away from their reality. The stained glass also reminds us of church windows. As the man and woman are not part of the church, and do not venture inside, there is a sense of being excluded from a spiritual community.

On the kabbalistic Tree of Life, the sphere associated with this card is Geburah, or power; its additional meaning is destruction and cruelty, echoing the suffering of the two beggars. We might also interpret this harsh sphere as a message to relinquish our victimhood and take back our power, whatever knocks we endure.

The astrological association of Mercury in Taurus is an uncomfortable, and often incompatible, combination. Mercury is lined with speed and communication, while the influence of Taurus is slow and steady. In the Five of Pentacles, this can reveal a contrary influence that brings frustration and at times the inability to make consistent progress.

Five is the number of mankind. Five is also the quintessence, or fifth element in alchemy. The five coins on the card give us the meaning that there is still something to be discovered that is not yet obvious—like the quintessence, it is invisible now, but may be revealed later.

UPRIGHT MEANING

The traditional meaning of this Five of Pentacles is financial loss, so when it shows up in a reading, it can mean losing a job or a relationship or experiencing some other financial or emotional hardship. The positive aspect is that you find support from others in a similar position. These contacts may become good friends whom you may never have met in your usual circumstances. Consider new options, and you may discover another resource or approach that will help you see a way forward.

However, this card often comes up in readings to show a fear of poverty and isolation, rather than actual poverty. It also commonly shows a fear of losing the

security of home and/or the aftermath of a relationship breakup, with one partner feeling alone and depleted. It occasionally reveals the impact of bereavement. While tarot cards do not predict death, the Five of Pentacles when in the present/situation position in a reading (rather than the future position) can reflect the feelings of sadness as a result of losing someone close.

REVERSED MEANING

There's a moral theme to the interpretation for the reversed Five of Pentacles, in that the card asks you to examine your values. If you're clinging to objects, people, or money, what are you avoiding? Fear of change could lead you to ignore debt or become oblivious to growing tension in a relationship. Hoarding old possessions and memories shows you need to feel safe for now and don't have the confidence or the faith that you will be supported in the future—at least, just at present. As with all minor arcana cards, though, this is a temporary influence.

In relationships, you may suffer due to a partner's selfish behavior. This person doesn't want to give to you emotionally, or he or she withholds money. The card can also show you being ill-treated by an ex-partner who doesn't pay what is due.

SIX OF PENTACLES

Element: Earth

Astrological Association: Moon in Taurus

Number: 6

Tree of Life Position: Tiphareth, the sphere of beauty and rebirth

Key Meaning: Property, family, inheritance

UNDERSTANDING THE SIX OF PENTACLES

Like the figure of card XI, Justice, the young nobleman on the Six of Pentacles holds a pair of scales, and he is dressed in red, the color of energy and practicality. His mantle is purple, the color of intuition and spirituality—and a sign that he acts in good faith. He wears a blue-striped tunic—the only other Pentacle card with this stripe is the Nine, in which the woman shows one blue stripe beneath her robe. Both these cards share the virtue of generosity. Our nobleman is judicious, weighing the situation with the scales of mercy in his left hand and giving out coins with his right hand.

The two figures kneeling before him are beggars. One is wounded, wearing sackcloth and a bandage around his head, the other, young and poor, his blue cloak bearing a patch. Because of his blue, we know he is experiencing true poverty and deserves help. The men exist in a barren place beyond the city walls and its greenery, and there is nothing to succor them. The white sky gives a feeling of uncertainty—it is not yellow and joyful, nor blue, for clarity—but this wealthy man gives money regardless of what the outcome might be.

Six is the number of harmony and passivity. For the beggars, this is the ability to surrender and accept, which brings some serenity, even temporarily. The particular arrangement of the coin symbols might be a representation of the Hebrew letter *Kaph* on its side—*Kaph* means palm and what might be in the palm. On this card, the palms give and receive coins. Six also has the meaning of the past creating the present and future, so money earned or saved in the past may now be shared.

The Tree of Life sphere associated with this card is Tiphareth, the sphere of beauty and rebirth, relating to the beauty of the generous soul. The Six of Pentacles has an astrological association with the Moon in Taurus, highlighting stability with sensitivity. This means being able to be generous without patronizing the recipient and also knowing how to receive help graciously.

UPRIGHT MEANING

The upright card shows that money is coming to you. It may arrive as a gift or an award and may be donated by an individual rather than an organization. This allows you to pay off any outstanding debt and/or invest the money wisely in your future. If you have been struggling financially, this card is a welcome sign that your circumstances will certainly improve. Equally, the card can show that you are the benefactor, so you may help a friend in need with a temporary cash-flow problem, or you feel drawn to support a charity that is close to your heart. Whomever you choose to help, you will consider carefully his or her needs and offer the right amount to make a difference.

Overall, this card brings genuine support and predicts you feeling connected and close to your usual circle of friends and family. Together, you may be exchanging small gifts of appreciation.

An additional meaning is receiving help or money from a person from your past or using savings to help another person.

REVERSED MEANING

When reversed, the Six of Pentacles shows money coming to you but you cannot keep it—usually due to carelessness or theft. A traditional meaning of the card is having your purse or wallet stolen, and this message is reinforced if the reversed card is placed close to the Seven of Swords, the "thief" card of the minor arcana (see page 188). Guard your possessions carefully and watch what you spend so that enough money stays in your pocket. The reversed card also suggests there may be envy due to money, so monitor your attitudes and the attitudes of people around you.

An alternative interpretation is an offer of money, but it comes with conditions that are not acceptable to you. The message here is not to compromise and to say no if you need to. There will be other options.

SEVEN OF PENTACLES

Element: Earth

Astrological Association: Saturn in Taurus

Number: 7

Tree of Life Position: Netzach, the sphere of endurance, instinct, and desire

Key Meanings: Work and the potential for success

UNDERSTANDING THE SEVEN OF PENTACLES

The Seven of Pentacles is a card of potential success. A young man considers his treasure, six coins arranged on a vine and a seventh at his feet. This is the same vine we see on the "bounty" cards of this suit—the prosperous Ace, luxury-loving Nine, the established Ten, and the wealthy King (see pages 148, 164, 166, and 174). Here, on the Seven of Pentacles, the vine is established, with large, healthy leaves—but there are no grapes. The plant is not mature enough yet to bear its full fruit. The man leans on his hoe, his magical object of transformation, as he painstakingly tends the land to nurture his vine. Slowly and with effort, it will bear him fruit. According to A. E. Waite, the creator of the Rider-Waite cards, "One would say that these are his treasures and that his heart was there." The six coins on the tree show what must be saved for the future, and the single coin represents his disposable income, or what he can spend now on himself. This is small reward for now, but there is more to come, provided he can keep going and not rest too long contemplating his situation.

Our grafter wears a tunic of red, to symbolize his energy, and blue, showing he is following his true purpose. His feet, like his vine, are firmly planted in the soil. He may be taking stock of his achievement as he gazes at his coins, but he will have to keep going if he is to see his ideas ripen and reward come. The purple mountains echo those on the Two and Three of Wands, and stand for goals and using our intuition.

The card's astrological association, Saturn in Taurus, means endeavor. The influence of the taskmaster planet Saturn leaves no room for fantastical plans and proposals—whatever you do must be grounded, organized, and nurtured with consistent effort. Netzach, the card's Tree of Life sphere, stands for endurance, so the combined astrological and kabbalistic meaning of the card is long-term dedication.

The card's number is the mystical number seven. Seven is composed of three, the number of heaven, and four, the number of earth, so the challenge is to bring heaven down to earth—to makes your dreams reality (see VII, The Chariot, page 58). In the Seven of Pentacles, this reward comes from work, work, work—and keeping your eye on the prize.

UPRIGHT MEANING

There's a goal in sight, and you are close to achieving it—but now is not the time to stop and reflect. The Seven of Pentacles is the card of doing, not philosophizing, so keep your focus on what you want and believe you can achieve it. This effort may feel relentless, but your hard work will pay off.

The card often comes up in readings to show the need to keep the focus on your career goals or to work through a particularly tedious stage in a current project that leaves you feeling tired and deflated. You might be tired of the relentlessness of it all, but the reward will come as long as you don't falter. Also, the

Seven can show saving for a home or accruing funds and clients to expand a business. In domestic affairs, the Seven of Pentacles can show there's not enough money left for the little luxuries that make all the effort of saving worthwhile. Whatever your situation, keep going—you are nearly there, and in the future, you will thank yourself for your dedication.

REVERSED MEANING

When reversed, the Seven of Pentacles means procrastination. Time is running out, so commit fully to the work you're doing or the lifestyle you have, regardless of the ups and downs—or put your energies elsewhere. This may mean considering a different job or career path. You may have become disheartened with slow—or no—progress in your work or improvement in your finances, but while you're in the doldrums, opportunities can slip away. Muster your willpower and take action now: Any decision is better than no decision at all.

An additional meaning of the card is anxiety about a loan or other financial agreement. If this is affecting your motivation, try to renegotiate terms, rather than give up now.

EIGHT OF PENTACLES

Element: Earth

Astrological Association: Sun in Virgo

Number: 8

Tree of Life Position: Hod, the sphere of majesty and the mind

Key Meanings: Education and achievement

UNDERSTANDING THE EIGHT OF PENTACLES

The Eight of Pentacles depicts an apprentice at work. He is highly productive, and the tree, a symbol for growth, displays his creations—he works hard, and has eight coins to show for it. Dressed in blue and red, for energy and truth of purpose, he also wears a black apron, the vestment of a mason or smith. While the apron gives him practical protection during his work, the color black figuratively symbolizes protection, just like the merchant's black cloak on the Four of Pentacles (see page 154). In the Eight, the apprentice's budding knowledge and expertise will afford him protection from financial vulnerability in the future. A solid education and skill will equip him to earn the good living he deserves. While the atmosphere he works in is uncertain—the impassive gray-white sky gives no clue to future trends, unlike other cards with blue or sunny skies to set the tone—he keeps his head down regardless, attentive to his task.

The city in the background is distant, so he may have made a conscious decision to study or work away from familiar comforts. He may have traveled for work away from home, which, while not a convenient choice, shows his ambition and dedication to walk his own path.

The apprentice's work is repetitive, doing the same job over and again until he has mastered his skill. He takes pride in his work. However, he could be overly perfectionist, as one coin seems to have been discarded and left on the floor, while the others are displayed. He has high standards and needs to achieve excellence at all times. This personality trait relates to the card's astrological association of the Sun in Virgo. Virgoan qualities include attention to detail and practicality, but there is also a tendency toward self-criticism. The apprentice is analytic and mindful, linking with the card's Tree of Life sphere, Hod. Its common meaning is majesty, and in this Eight of Pentacles refers to the mastery of the mind.

The card's number is eight, which stands for stability and renewal (see also card VIII, Strength, page 62). The eights in the minor arcana, as they are nearing the end of the numbered sequence, hold all our experiences up to that point. We have past knowledge to draw upon, which gives us wisdom and enables new choices—a time to renew our skills and find a fresh direction.

UPRIGHT MEANING

Money is on its way, often as a result of previous efforts or decisions rather than an unexpected bonus or gift. (Look to the Six or Ten of Pentacles for generosity and windfalls.) You may be offered an opportunity to gain new skills that will be profitable in the long term. You may also consider a new career direction or be working for promotion. In general, the card also reflects the need for a logical, diligent approach to your projects.

This card is often known as the apprentice. It comes up in readings to show education and gaining a qualification, particularly an undergraduate degree or diploma. The Eight of Pentacles also shows a personality aspect, so if it appears in the "you/situation" position in a spread, it reveals a hardworking, trustworthy, and dedicated individual who takes his or her responsibilities seriously.

REVERSED MEANING

The reversed Eight of Pentacles can show that you're feeling trapped. This may be because you've chosen an educational course that isn't for you and doesn't develop your particular talents or reflect your interests enough to be sustainable long term. In work, you may know you're only doing the job for the money. While this may be acceptable on a short-term basis, long term it feels soul-destroying. While supporting yourself financially, it may be time to look elsewhere rather than let the situation continue.

As a prediction card, the Eight of Pentacles shows a cycle is about to come to an end, so rather than wait for this to happen, conserve your energy and direct it toward finding a new career. Don't resign yourself to your present situation if there's no sense of achievement or appreciation.

NINE OF PENTACLES

Element: Earth

Astrological Association: Venus in Virgo

Number: 9

Tree of Life Position: Yesod, the sphere of foundation and the unconscious mind

Key Meanings: Comfort, accomplishment, and prosperity

UNDERSTANDING THE NINE OF PENTACLES

The Nine of Pentacles is a card of comfort, luxury, and attainment. Here we have a country idyll—a manor house protected by hills and before us, a woman standing proud in her vineyard. These are grapes she has cultivated herself, shown by the two green loops holding the vines to wooden supports on the right of the card. In this rich and plentiful land, the lady of the house tends her nine coins and lays her right hand over one coin protectively. Her treasure might remind us of hay bales, harvested and piled in summer fields, their circular ends stacked like the faces of coins. Note that the piles of coins are unequal: She keeps six to her right and three to her left. Those on her right feel like hers to keep, while those on the left might be coins to give away. By ensuring she gives away less than she receives, she will maintain her standard of living.

Her hat is red, for passion and energy, and the lining of her gown is also red. This red lining offers a connection with the womb and its implicit fertility. This woman is fertile in her thoughts and tends her garden with the utmost love and care. The flower symbol on her robe is similar in form to the glyph of Venus, for her ruling planet, also the symbol for the female.

The small bird on her gauntlet is curious—its head is covered with a red hood, showing that it is temporarily tamed; wild instincts are under control. Although birds are often symbols of spirit, when domesticated or restrained, they can also signify vanity. Because the bird is temporarily hooded (rather than chained or caged), we sense that this woman is alert to the dangers of using money to exert control. She guards against materialism and egotism. Her kabbalistic and astrological associations account for this level of self-awareness. Luxury-loving, passionate Venus is tempered by Virgo's conservatism and attention to detail. The card's Tree of Life sphere, Yesod, means foundation. Yesod is associated with the Moon, ruler of the unconscious mind.

The card's number is nine, or three sets of three. Three is a dynamic number and, when multiplied by itself, symbolizes intense productivity. It also holds the message of the three aspects of the goddess (maiden, mother, and crone), as well as the integration of mind, body, and spirit. In the Nine of Pentacles, this can show that the lady's financial security feeds her mentally and spiritually, allowing her to live abundantly and give generously to others.

UPRIGHT MEANING

The Nine ushers in a time of financial stability. You can feel safe in your home and proud of your achievements. At last, you can surround yourself with the material objects you love, and you may find yourself redecorating your home or tending your garden or yard. It's time to appreciate all that you have, so leisure time beckons; treat yourself to whatever makes you happy and enjoy the fruits of your work. You will be able to focus on your own needs without feeling guilty.

The Nine also brings a sense of serenity and relaxation, so the card predicts you can feel at home, and at one, with yourself.

This card often comes up in a reading to show a woman of independent means who is generous and well balanced. In this way, the Nine of Pentacles is similar to the Queen of Pentacles (see page 172), although the Queen's influence is generally greater. In work matters, the card can predict financial reward, such as a bonus, for your efforts.

REVERSED MEANING

When reversed, the card can show vanity and ego at large—the urge for material wealth gets out of control, so overspending (or dealing with a loved one's overspending) may need to be confronted. In general, the card can show financial dependence that is uncomfortable or misuse of money for selfish means.

An additional meaning is feeling that your home is somehow under threat because you are struggling with debt. Don't struggle alone—help is at hand.

TEN OF PENTACLES

Element: Earth

Astrological Association: Mercury in Virgo

Number: 10

Tree of Life Position: Malkuth, the Kingdom, the sphere of experience

Key Meanings: Property, family, and inheritance

UNDERSTANDING THE TEN OF PENTACLES

A happy couple and their dogs face each other under an archway, the formal entrance to a prosperous home. We spy a house in a walled courtyard, and there is a prominent high tower—possibly an obvious sexual symbol to show a love relationship or a signifier for the traditional, learning, and protection.

An older man looks on, seated in a thronelike chair. He is the King of Pentacles grown old, now with white hair, but still wearing his grapevine cloak (see page 174). By his presence alone, he appears to give the pair his blessing; it is now their turn to inherit the values of the family through marriage. We see three generations here, the grandfather-king, his son or daughter and their beloved, and a small child, presumably theirs or the offspring of another relative. Each generation seems quite separate from one another, but they happily share the same space.

All is in perfect balance. The ten coins on the card are symmetrical and represent the Tree of Life. The four elements are represented, too, equally. We see watery scenes on the coats of arms on the bridge; for the Earth element, there are grapevines; the woman's cloak is red, for Fire: and the sky over the bridge gives us the element of Air. All four elements exist in harmony.

In numerology, ten represents completeness and perfection. In the Ten of Pentacles, this shows happy stability, emotionally and financially. The ten coins are laid out in the shape of the kabalistic Tree of Life (see page 328)—each one representing a sphere on the tree and each sphere having an esoteric concept. The whole tree links with the card's meaning of maturity and completeness. The individual sphere associated with this card is Malkuth, for kingdom—so the Ten of Pentacles celebrates our personal kingdom or our material world.

The Ten's astrological association of Mercury in Virgo highlights practical affairs as well as the physical body. This combination also shows the ability to find specific solutions to problems.

UPRIGHT MEANING

The upright Ten of Pentacles shows an inheritance, generosity, and a love relationship that brings wealth and happiness—so if you are asking the question, "Will my current relationship get more committed?" the answer will be a resounding yes. The Ten of Pentacles often comes up in readings to show a wedding. What is even better is that the couple shares similar values and often has similar cultural backgrounds (and the two families actually like one another!).

An additional meaning is inherited property, buying a second home, or extending your current home, again with family support. At this time, you also benefit from sharing—your time, resources, skills, or money to help each other out. Note that *family* in this context signifies those you consider family and treat as such, so this could relate to a close circle of longtime friends.

This card also suggests maturity. You can interpret this in financial terms, with investments maturing, as well as in emotional terms, as the emotional maturity that comes with life experience. You may find that an older person in the family has wisdom to share in addition to resources.

REVERSED MEANING

When reversed, the Ten of Pentacles reveals communication problems in families as one generation tries to dominate another; children and parents disagree and have very different attitudes. The card can highlight contention over a specific issue, such as conflict over property or money. Equally, general attitudes toward finances may be at the heart of the problem. This card often comes up in readings to show overly strict parents who try to control their families with money.

There is also an issue with status here as traditional values block freedom of expression. Older people may find it hard to accept that their children want to do things differently.

In romantic relationships, money, property issues, and the demands of family get in the way of love. Ambition takes over; personal life comes second.

PAGE OF PENTACLES

PAGE *of* PENTACLES.

Element: Earth of the suit of Earth

Key Meanings: Talent shines and money news

UNDERSTANDING THE PAGE OF PENTACLES

Unlike the wary Page of Swords, the Page of Pentacles is entirely absorbed in his coin rather than in his surroundings. He holds the money lightly, like a precious object, a gift that will become an accolade, an award for his talents.

Around him are low mountains, ploughed fields, grass, and trees—a landscape of plenty—and this fertile place of possibility is his natural home. Four trees in the distance tell us that his good fortune has come from seeds he diligently tended. He can admire his coin in the knowledge that he will always be supported: Turning his attention to one issue does not mean any other life aspect will suffer, and he does not need to look over his shoulder for challengers hoping for a share of his glory. In this way, the Page is the opposite of poverty consciousness. With his youthful optimism, he assumes he will always have everything he needs.

The Page's red headgear stands for energy and passion. His scarf is draped over his shoulder and extends down his back, signifying his wholehearted motivation. The yellow background and coin symbolize the intellect and solar consciousness: this Page is proud to let his light shine.

Earth of Earth is the Page's elemental association. What he achieves comes from the ground up, like the card's trees, with solid roots and foundation. He begins with a solid plan and an aim to establish something great. As double Earth, he may not be idealistic, but he is practical, sees through his ideas, and is loyal to his purpose.

Pages and Knights in tarot are generally regarded as people or influences, whereas the other court cards (the Queens and Kings) are assumed to be people. Let your intuition guide you toward the most appropriate meaning for the Page in a reading by working with the card's imagery first, then the written interpretations here (see also the Introduction, page 8).

UPRIGHT MEANING

As an influence: This Page reveals progress and adventure as well as auspicious beginnings. This is a time to nurture your skills and abilities. There will be good news concerning finances, business, education, and travel. The Page of Pentacles also highlights the need for management, and in work matters, there may be an opportunity to manage people and projects. This Page often appears to show a job offer or an offer made on a property.

The card does come with an element of caution, however: There is a real need for attention to detail now and for diligence in all practical affairs, so double-check all arrangements and agreements. Also, check through your personal schedule to ensure everything you plan is realistic. The Page of Pentacles can also be a sign that it's time to attend to finances; he comes up in readings to nudge us to do our taxes and renew outstanding insurance policies.

As a person: Hardworking and methodical, reliable and dedicated—this Page is practical and trustworthy. As a Page he is a younger person, or someone with youthful vigor. He may be starting out in the world,

or in a new line of business. He may not have money now, but he has the potential to achieve great things in future, so you can believe in him and his plans; he will succeed, and he will not give up.

The card can also show a young person's achievement and reward for his or her efforts in sport or education.

As the "you" card in a reading: Money and opportunities beckon—you have an opportunity to establish a new venture.

If two or more Pages fall close together in a reading, the meanings are as follows:

- **Two Pages:** Friendship if upright; rivalry if one or both cards are reversed
- **Three Pages:** Lots of social activities
- **Four Pages:** A social group of young people

REVERSED MEANING

When the Page of Pentacles is reversed, there may be unwelcome news regarding finances or property. Unlike the responsible upright Page, the card in this position means extravagance and irresponsibility rule. You may suffer due to someone else's selfish actions. This may apply to young people you live with or to friends with immature tendencies.

The card can also apply to a person with a sense of entitlement who helps himself to what is yours; while this is not necessarily theft, it is underhanded. Observe and take note for future reference.

KNIGHT OF PENTACLES

KNIGHT *of* PENTACLES.

Element: Fire of the suit of Earth

Astrological Associations: Leo and Virgo

Key Meaning: Improving prosperity

UNDERSTANDING THE KNIGHT OF PENTACLES

This is the only Knight of the tarot's four minor suits whose horse is at rest, which seems at odds with the usual mission of a Knight, galloping boldly onward to fulfill a quest. The steed of the Knight of Pentacles—built more for pulling a plough than raging into battle—symbolizes a measured approach, very unlike that of the dashing Knight of Swords, who rushes headlong toward his goal. This Knight's mission is long term; he has no interest in hasty action and will work hard and long to ensure his success.

The plumes on the horse bridle and the Knight's helmet are green, the color of nature. They resemble a cluster of oak leaves, a reminder of the idiom "From acorns great oaks come." This gives us the meaning of investment for the future, a concept supported by the fields of rich terracotta soil; the time is right for sowing, and we might even imagine the Knight planting his coin in those furrows and waiting for money trees to grow.

The Knight of Pentacles is methodical and thinks ahead; he is fully prepared for his journey. The blanket under the saddle shows that he has equipped his horse for the discomfort of a long day's ride, and behind the saddle is a black book; he's brought something to read during rest periods or perhaps it is a notebook in which to record his progress. The card's element is Fire of the suit of Earth, and for this reason, the Knight of Pentacles has the ingredients of steady purpose—Fire energy to drive him forwards and Earth energy to help him plan and rationalize his ideas.

The Knight holds his coin in his right hand, which is the same color yellow as the sky. Like the Page of Pentacles, he sees potential prosperity all around him. His coin is not hidden, and he is clear that financial security is his central concern. The red of his tunic and the horse's bridles show he has energy, and like the other minor Knights, his blue armor shows he is true to his purpose.

Knights and Pages in tarot are generally regarded as people or influences, whereas the other court cards (the Queens and Kings) are assumed to be people. Let your intuition guide you toward the most appropriate meaning for the Knight in a reading by working with the card's imagery first, then the written interpretations here (see also the Introduction, page 8).

UPRIGHT MEANING

As an influence: Showing financial growth and good investment, this card means plans concerning property progress. With strategizing and setting a realistic goal, you will succeed. Pay attention to the practical details now, and future benefits are assured. Day to day, this Knight asks you to get through boring and routine, but essential, tasks. In work, the card can indicate more money coming to you due to a raise, bonus, or promotion, but you may need to work harder in return.

An additional meaning of the card is finding a secure home, potentially with a partner.

As a person: This Knight is loyal and dependable. He is a natural protector, and security is very important to him. He may work in property or finance.

As a potential partner, he has much to offer and is genuine. For some, he may lack excitement, as he plans rather than reacts; he can be slow to judge and to express his feelings, and keeps on safe subjects. Depending on what you need from a relationship, he could be a gift—your rock through thick and thin. If you crave excitement, he won't be entertaining enough to capture your heart.

As the "you" card in a reading: Invest your time wisely. Be consistent in your efforts.

If two or more Knights fall close together in a reading, the meanings are as follows:

- **Two Knights:** Friendship if upright; rivalry if one or both cards are reversed

- **Three Knights:** Men meeting up

- **Four Knights:** Lots of action; events speed up

REVERSED MEANING

When reversed, the card advises that you avoid complacency and check out all financial arrangements. The most negative interpretation of the card is financial mismanagement and misleading advice.

As a person, the reversed knight is stubborn and cannot see others' viewpoints. He is plodding and pessimistic, reluctant to take action and unwilling to go beyond his comfort zone. He may tend to be materialistic and secretive and, in extremis, dishonest.

QUEEN OF PENTACLES

QUEEN *of* PENTACLES.

Element: Water of the suit of Earth

Astrological Associations:
Sagittarius and Capricorn

Chakras: Base and solar plexus, for security (earthiness) and wisdom

Key Meaning: A reliable woman

UNDERSTANDING THE QUEEN OF PENTACLES

The Queen of Pentacles is an aspect of card III, The Empress, or mother archetype. The Queen of Cups is the heart, the Queen of Swords, the mind, and the Queen of Wands, the soul (see pages 144, 200, 228, and III, The Empress, page 42). Our Queen of Pentacles is the physical, or material, side of the mother—the aspect that deals with money, property, and practical concerns to make our lives secure.

This Queen looks down upon her golden coin and to the earth itself, Earth being her suit element. All around her are symbols of spring and fertility—the hare, lush vegetation, flowing water, and flowers. The rose briar is also seen on card VIII, Strength, and I, The Magician—which also shares the dominant colors of red and yellow for practicality and clear sightedness. The land is part cultivated and part wild, giving the sense that work is ongoing and that the Queen is comfortable in nature and in the domain of her own garden or yard. She is pragmatic, cares for her environment, and above all, works hard to achieve long-term success. She is patient and will wait to see the fruit of her labor.

Engraved on the Queen's throne are pears. Symbols of fertility and long life, pears were sacred to the Italian deity Pomona, goddess of fruit trees and the orchard. According to Ovid, Pomona was a wood nymph—which the Rider-Waite deck's artist, Pamela Colman Smith, may well have referenced in the carving of a nymph on the right of the throne. The goat's head is the symbol for Capricorn, one of the Queen's zodiac signs, mirrored as a winged goat on the crest of her crown. The goat also appears on card XV, The Devil, and is a symbol of excess that, in the case of the Queen of Pentacles, translates as sensuality.

The card's element combination is Water of Earth. As water feeds earth and makes crops grow, this underlines the Queen's association with fertility and plenty.

Queens and Kings in tarot are traditionally regarded as people in your life or people about to come into your orbit. However, you can also read the Queen as a general influence, so this interpretation is included last.

UPRIGHT MEANING

As a person: The Queen of Pentacles is usually well off, generous, and supportive. She has a strong maternal instinct, is affectionate and wise—and she may be an older woman, or a younger female with wisdom beyond her years.

Her vocations include public office, ecology, agriculture, politics, sports coaching, food and catering, and business—any work that benefits large numbers of people. She may be a homemaker, as she loves caring for her home and garden. She likes the good things in life and knows how to spend money well—on beautiful objects, on gifts for loved ones, and of course, on herself. She is physically affectionate and hands-on in her projects; rather than dictating from the sidelines, she will lend practical help. In readings, she commonly shows up as a benefactor.

As the "you" card in a reading: Care for your body and your finances.

As an influence: In addition to practical support, wisdom, good financial management, and financial help, the Queen of Pentacles can show marriage and money coming to a couple. It is also a positive card for good health, a sensual sex life, fertility, and children.

If two or more Queens fall close together in a reading, the meanings are as follows:

- **Two Queens:** Rivalry

- **Three Queens:** Helpful friends

- **Four Queens:** Women meeting up

REVERSED MEANING

When this card is reversed, finances can suffer. Money you relied upon doesn't roll in or funds are misappropriated. You may have to deal with the impact of someone's financial mishaps. This is temporary, however. An additional meaning is your home is neglected while other concerns take over.

As a person, the reversed Queen can be stubborn and unimaginative. She can be mean with money, or at the other extreme, an emotional spender. Her erratic behavior is for self-comfort, or she uses money to buy other people's affection.

KING OF PENTACLES

KING *of* PENTACLES.

Element: Air of the suit of Earth

Astrological Associations: Aries and Taurus

Chakras: Solar plexus and base, for wisdom and security

Key Meaning: A generous man

UNDERSTANDING THE KING OF PENTACLES

The King of Pentacles is an aspect of card IV, The Emperor, or father archetype, who brings structure, order, and authority. The King of Pentacles is the father-aspect that deals with money, property, and practical concerns to make our lives secure.

The four bulls' heads on the King's throne stand for Aries, one of his zodiac signs, and the number four relates to his ancestor card, IV, The Emperor (see page 46), and also symbolizes the four elements. The King has his right foot on the head of a boar to show his mastery over base instincts. His foot and leg are armored, to symbolize he has fought hard for his position. This is echoed in the victory wreath under his crown, which is decorated with red flowers and fleurs-de-lis, three-petaled lilies or irises, ancient Egyptian fertility symbols. In this way, the King presides over the fruits of the Earth—the element of his suit.

The grapes and bull imagery also invite a comparison with the ancient legend of Ampelos, a young satyr loved by the Greek god of wine, Dionysus. Ampelos was savaged by a wild bull and died. Then Dionysus turned Ampelos's corpse into a grapevine and his blood into wine. On the card, vines grow plentifully around the bulls on the throne of the King of Pentacles and creep onto his robes as a pattern of leaves and red grapes—symbols of fruitfulness and success. From this, we deduce that the King plans carefully and expects results from long-term investments.

He holds a scepter in his right hand and his precious coin in his left, which rests on his knee. He is protected by a stone wall, and it seems he is stationed within castle battlements, as we can see the castle keep and towers on the right of the card. We sense he is secure and protected. The background is golden and orange, like his coin, reminiscent of late summer sky and harvest time, a symbol of abundance. The King's cowl is red, for energy and the material world; he does not rest on his laurels.

The card's element is Air of Earth, which can be interpreted as grounded ideas—the King sees through the projects he begins. Air and Earth can also be thought of as seeds borne on the wind to impregnate the earth, relating to the King's meaning of fertility and foundation for future growth.

Kings and Queens in tarot are traditionally regarded as people in your life or people about to come into your orbit. However, you can also read the King as a general influence, so this interpretation is included last.

UPRIGHT MEANING

As a person: A visionary man with a plan, the King will work hard for rewards and is usually well off. He is reliable and generous and offers practical support. Security is important to him, and he is happiest in a settled relationship. He needs to be a protector, and he has firm boundaries—he will not tolerate those looking to take what is his. His ideal vocations include property and building, business, accounting or any work that is number-based as well as agriculture or land management. An additional meaning is a generous benefactor.

As the "you" card in a reading: Make the most of your assets.

As an influence: Financial and property matters improve, and you enjoy success and comfort. The King of Pentacles also predicts conflicts that will be resolved. In relationships, he offers security and loyalty.

If two or more Kings fall close together in a reading, the meanings are as follows:

- **Two Kings:** A good partnership

- **Three Kings:** Influential men

- **Four Kings:** A power battle

REVERSED MEANING

When reversed, the King is greedy and untrustworthy, so double-check all financial agreements to ensure that there are no hidden catches. Debt is an interpretation of the reversed King, so turn the spotlight on your finances now to limit the damage of overspending.

As a person, the reversed King is corrupt and may be involved in fraud or gambling. He is determined to win at any cost.

ACE OF SWORDS

Element: Air

Astrological Association: The Air signs—Gemini, Libra, and Aquarius

Number: 1

Tree of Life Position: Kether, the sphere of divine light

Key Meanings: Success, decisions, and beginnings

UNDERSTANDING THE ACE OF SWORDS

A hand appears from a cloud, offering an upright sword. Circled with a crown, the image is a symbol for the card's Tree of Life sphere, Kether, for divine light, also traditionally titled as "the crown." Hanging from the crown are a frond of fern and a sprig of mistletoe and berries. As both plants can attach themselves to trees, the sword here becomes the tree, a symbol of everlasting strength. Above the sword hilt are six golden leaves, similar to those on the Ace of Wands (see page 204). The number six corresponds to *Zain*, the sixth letter of the Hebrew alphabet; its symbol is the sword. The six also links with card VI, The Lovers, for decisions—the sword's action is nothing other than decisive.

The scene beneath the sword shows blue-and-purple mountains, symbols of spiritual truths and goals. While there are no dwellings or green pastures to muse upon, growth is symbolized on the crown itself, with the mistletoe and fern, signifying the fertility of the mind; the sword therefore offers us the gift of intelligence (linking with the card's element of Air, for the mental realm) and because it is held upright in victory, a second gift of success. As with the other Ace cards and their symbols, in the Ace of Swords, the sword is offered with the right hand, the hand of giving (as opposed to the left hand, which is the receiving hand).

Aces offer the pure energy of their suits. As number ones, they represent oneness with the divine spirit or God. Indivisible, their energy is singular, strong, and purposeful. They all represent beginnings, impulses, and new possibilities, in the most pure and obvious form. In this Ace, the sword we see is double-edged—in cutting to the truth, it can defend us or turn against us. The sword is certain and strong; A. E. Waite, the creator of the Rider-Waite deck, describes the Ace of Swords as "the triumph of force." As the swords are part of battle, the Ace does not come without potential conflict.

UPRIGHT MEANING

The upright meaning of the Ace is auspicious for every aspect of your life. In a spread, it overrules any negative minor arcana cards close by (just like the major arcana card XIX, The Sun). The Ace of Swords predicts new beginnings, decisions, and clear thinking and usually relates to work and love. It heralds action, drama, and sometimes confrontation. However the Ace of Swords manifests in your life, it will bring an immediate change to your circumstances—for the better.

As a prediction card, it shows that mental agility and assertiveness will bring success. The other cards around the Ace in a reading will guide you to nature of this conquest. Be cautious, though, not to be too zealous—judge the situation and be direct, rather than abrasive, mindful of how you would want to be treated if you were on the receiving end.

In relationships, it reveals triumph over past obstacles—you win through to your heart's desire.

In a reading, one Ace brings a focus on the life area according to the suit, which can set the theme of the reading. If two or more Aces appear near each other in a reading, it means the following:

- **Two Aces:** An important partnership
- **Three Aces:** Good news
- **Four Aces:** Excitement, beginnings, and potential

REVERSED MEANING

When the Ace reverses, the card can predict conflict and arguments, and you may become involved in a hurtful battle of wills. The card can also predict a contest that you cannot win, at least at present. The message is to withdraw, tend your wounds, and turn your attentions elsewhere.

You may also lack confidence in your intellectual abilities just now and not feel equal to others—which is your perception, not the reality.

Another common meaning of the reversed Ace in readings is a decision going against you, such as failing a test or interview and, in more general terms, not being able to hold your ground under fire from more dominant personalities.

TWO OF SWORDS

Element: Air

Astrological Association: Moon in Libra

Number: 2

Tree of Life Position: Chockmah, the sphere of wisdom

Key Meanings: Time to think and a stalemate

UNDERSTANDING THE TWO OF SWORDS

A lone woman holds two swords across her chest in a pose of self-defense. She appears to be resting from a duel and protects her heart with her weapons, as if fearful that the pain of the Three of Swords, with its pierced heart, may come. Although blindfolded like the maiden on the Eight of Swords, unlike that woman, she has taken herself to a safe space. Seated on high ground, this is her place of contemplation. Her pale robe is monastic in style, which tell us she is taking time out from the world and keeping her thoughts to herself. The rocks, partly submerged, symbolize issues yet to surface fully; but they do exist—they are part of her landscape and will not go away. Her hair is parted so that the third eye, between the brows, is visible. Temporarily deprived of sight, she "sees" with her intuition. The sky, graduating from gray to twilight blue, reflects a changing emotional landscape: She is in two minds, also signified by the two swords.

The figure's position—facing us, sitting squarely on a stone plinth, and holding swords—reminds us of card XI, Justice. Traditional representations of Justice in art and sculpture show this virtue personified as a blindfolded female holding the sword of justice in one hand and the scales of mercy in the other. Similarly, our Two of Swords woman must also adjudicate, but in the sphere of her own affairs.

The card's Tree of Life sphere is Chockmah, which means wisdom and links with the figure's exposed third eye. She must use her knowledge and experience to make the right decision, to choose between two possibilities. There's a further duality in the Tree of Life and the card's astrological associations. Chockmah represents the male principle, or yang, as opposed to the yin, or feminine qualities of the Moon in the card's astrological profile of the Moon in Libra. The moon, celestial body of the subconscious, joins balanced Libra. This combination reveals a tendency to keep the peace rather than act. We see a crescent moon on this Two of Swords, which echoes the moon on card II, The High Priestess, the psychic who symbolizes the divine feminine.

The waxing moon we see on the top right of the card is in its growth phase and will change shape throughout its cycle, just as our blindfolded woman goes through the process of decision-making, weighing up alternative outcomes.

UPRIGHT MEANING

The Two of Swords shows thinking time before a decision. A situation has reached a stalemate, so you can view this period as a truce or a rest before further negotiation. The tendency is to protect yourself, have a little peace, and not take action. Unfortunately, this upcoming battle may not go away; resolve it now and it's done. Otherwise, the situation festers and may return.

As there are two swords on the card, this Two can reveal a person you cross swords with. It's likely that your difficult person is sharp-tongued, but don't be afraid of a lashing: Stand your ground and say what you think.

The card commonly comes up in readings to show employment issues and also time out in relationships. This may be circumstantial, due to partners living in different places; if negative cards such as the Three of Swords or Lovers reversed appears with the Two of Swords, it shows making a decision about the future of a relationship.

Whatever your experience of the Two of Swords, help is at hand in the form of supportive friends and colleagues. Listen to advice and then take the best practical steps forward.

REVERSED MEANING

When reversed, the traditional meaning of the Two of Swords is deception and being blind to someone's manipulation. This card applies particularly to partnerships—love, friendships, and in business and your career. If you intuition is telling you that someone is dishonest, pay attention and carry out your own detailed investigation to get to the heart of the matter. There is an opportunity here to act, but the timing is sensitive; the message is not to delay.

THREE OF SWORDS

Element: Air

Astrological Association: Saturn in Libra

Number: 3

Tree of Life Position: Binah, the sphere of understanding

Key Meanings: Sorrow, heartbreak, and pain

UNDERSTANDING THE THREE OF SWORDS

The Three of Swords shows clouds, rain, and three swords plunged into a heart—to the left, to the right, and through the center. The heart is large and the swords smaller, and the effect is that of a heraldic shield, a defensive device that has been penetrated. The rain echoes the action of the swords, like headless arrows striking through the gray sky. What is unexpected in this sad card is the subtle blue sheen on the lower parts of the sword shafts, which appear at the bottom of the heart motif. Blue stands for truth—and the swords pierce to the truth, whatever the situation; in cruelty lies some kindness. Perhaps, after all is said and done, a blue sky awaits, a brighter outlook for the future.

This is one of two minor arcana cards without people (the other is the Eight of Wands), so there is no obvious action to interpret. This is intentional, in that the sole focus is the impact of the swords, giving the cards its primary meaning of pain. As creator of this deck A. E. Waite says, the card represents "all that the design signifies naturally, being too simple and obvious to call for specific enumeration."

Swords are of the suit of Air, but here we are dealing with emotional pain, so there is an element of Cups or Water for emotions here too. The swords lend drama to the situation, but the pain is very much in the heart rather than the head. The card's Tree of Life sphere, Binah, means understanding and compassion and represents the female principle of reception. In this sense, there is little we can do but accept the pain and surrender to it.

In numerology, three is a dynamic number (see also card III, The Empress, page 42). It symbolizes the trinity of mind, body, and soul—which, unfortunately, may all be affected when we experience deep disappointment or betrayal. The three can also be interpreted as three people in a relationship, which gives the card one of its meanings of affairs. This reflects old versions of major arcana card III, The Lovers (see The Historical Lovers, page 56), in which three people were shown on the card; a man had to choose between two lovers, hence once of its meanings of decisions and affairs of the heart.

The Three of Swords has an astrological association with Saturn in Libra. Saturn's influence is harsh and demands the truth, whereas Libra likes balance, like the sign's symbols of the scales. However, Saturn is more powerful in this combination, so the truth will come out—no matter how much it hurts. In the card's image, the swords cut right through to the heart of the matter.

UPRIGHT MEANING

The upright meaning of the Three of Swords is direct in its meaning and reveals the pain of truth. The clouds of doubt are cleared, and you can do nothing but face reality. This is a common card for relationship betrayal and can denote affairs or disloyalty in other life areas, such as work relationships and business dealings. On a more positive note, you do get right to the heart of the matter—any confusion is banished, and you are now in a position to begin to move on from shock, to begin the healing process and move forward.

In health, this Three can relate to heart issues that may need attention—such as blood pressure issues, circulatory problems, conditions such as angina, and very occasionally, the need for surgery. Please note that this is a message to take care of the heart and safeguard health; it is not a prediction of serious illness.

REVERSED MEANING

When the Three of Swords reverses, the upset of the upright card is accompanied by quarrels and drama. In a sense, despite the upheaval, this gives a more positive meaning than that of the upright card, as at least feelings are expressed and some of the confusion and pain is shared and released. Those around you will understand your need to vent.

FOUR OF SWORDS

Element: Air

Astrological Association: Jupiter in Libra

Number: 4

Tree of Life Position: Chesed, the sphere of love

Key Meanings: Rest, passivity, and quiet time

UNDERSTANDING THE FOUR OF SWORDS

Existing as it does between the Three, the card of strife, and the Five, the "battle" card, the Four of Swords offers welcome rest: an opportunity to recover from the stress and betrayal of the Three before the onslaught of the Five. The knight shown in this card has temporarily laid down his tools; one sword is displayed lengthwise, the hilt aligning with his head, in the sculpture as part of the tomb, to signify his identity as a warrior. The other three swords hang above him, secured on the wall, ready for him to take up when he rises. But for now, the knight is at rest, safe from attack and the demands of assault.

The stained-glass window symbolizes the world being held at a distance during the knight's period of withdrawal. The figures in the stained glass suggest a monk helping a child or devotee, embodying the medieval knight's commitment to charity. This is echoed in the knight's code of chivalry, which commits "to give succor to widows and orphans," and hints at the two beggars on the Five of Pentacles (see page 156) who are also depicted below a stained-glass window, another world they cannot see and are not part of.

The stone knight is similar to those in the twelfth-century Templar Church in London, which was built by the Knights Templar, an order of charitable knights in the Middle Ages who were powerful protectors of Christianity. The knight on the card could be Baron Robert de Roos (1177–1226/27), as the hands of his effigy at Templar Church, unlike the other eight effigies displayed there, are placed in prayer position like those of the knight on the Four of Swords. De Roos took a year out to become a monk and relinquished his lands, so the monk depicted in the stained-glass window may also in fact be De Roos himself.

Number four is the number of stability and balance. In the warring suit of Swords, it denotes ceasefire; there is no need to continue a conflict. In the kabbalistic Tree of Life, the card links with Chesed, the sphere of love. This is love in the broadest sense, encompassing gentleness, harmony, and peace—just what the resting knight needs.

Astrologically, the Four of Swords is linked to the planet Jupiter in the sign of Libra. Jupiter indicates philosophy and possible solitude. Libra, however, is a sociable sign, so we have the conflicting qualities of the lone thinker with the socialite. In this way, perhaps the astrological association tells a story of the knight stepping away from his comrades to spend time at rest in contemplation, taking on the life of a monk in the church in which he takes sanctuary.

UPRIGHT MEANING

The Four of Swords has the meaning of time out, so you may be taking a rest from work, a personal project, or a relationship. The card often comes up in readings in the past or present position to show taking a break from a relationship and also the need for recovery from illness or an operation. Commonly, as a prediction card, the Four of Swords shows recovery from stress, so the message is to conserve your energy and take quiet time if you can.

The solitude of the Four of Swords can also apply to meditators and lightworkers and any individual following a spiritual path. You may need more mental space and private time than usual, so in this sense, the card is a nudge to take some alone to recharge.

An additional meaning of the card is counseling or therapy and, rarely, attending a memorial service.

REVERSED MEANING

When the Four of Swords reverses, the time-out message is enforced—so you may have to take time away from work or other responsibilities due to influences out of your control. Unfortunately, there is little you can do to alter this situation, so you must surrender to events. This is a phase, and the message is to find peace. Use the time positively. You may need to rethink your working arrangements or come to terms with changes in a relationship, particularly if you live apart from a partner or potential love.

FIVE OF SWORDS

Element: Air

Astrological Association: Venus in Aquarius

Number: 5

Tree of Life Position: Geburah, the sphere of power

Key Meanings: Upheaval, conflict, and loss

UNDERSTANDING THE FIVE OF SWORDS

The Five of Swords shows a young man holding three swords, two hoisted proudly at his shoulder and one held downward, by the hilt, as if to stake his territory. Two swords are cast down on the beach, surrendered by the retreating figures. Rather than having dignity in victory, however, the young man appears to be grinning, perhaps taking sadistic pleasure in his opponents' defeat. The defeated figures have their backs to us, unable to face their challenger again, and the one on the right has his hands to his face in shame. The clouds tell the story of the conflict that has just ended—they are gray and slashed, like torn fabric.

The youth wears red, for energy and vitality, and green, the color of nature. First, this tells us about his personality: Red reflects his energy and ego, and green, his sense of natural entitlement—not just to take his challengers' weapons, but to enjoy their humiliation. The green can also symbolize his greenness in the ways of the world. He is yet to learn the karmic lesson of "what goes around, comes around." Second, if we see ourselves as the victims, we can interpret the red and green as symbols of growth and the wisdom gained from the experience of conflict. This also links with the card's number, five, the number of mankind and our physical experience on the earth plane. Five is also the quintessence, or fifth element in alchemy. In the Five of Swords, the quintessence is experience or what we gain from the aftermath of battle. This is symbolized on the card by the blue sky behind the slashed clouds and the calm waters of the sea: The storm is abating.

On the kabbalistic Tree of Life, the sphere associated with this card is Geburah, or power, which means conflict and judgement—in this Five of Swords, it reveals the need for power and control, the impetus behind the battle. Geburah is ruled by the planet Mars, known as the war-bringer.

The astrological association of Venus in Aquarius gives the meaning of idealism, one of Aquarius's attributes, with sensitive, romantic Venus; one interpretation is unconventional choices; it may also reveal a clash of fantasy and pragmatism. This is reflected in the card's upright meaning to retreat when battle is done, rather than continue to fight in a war that cannot be won.

UPRIGHT MEANING

The traditional meaning of this Five of Swords is battle and loss. It often shows family disputes, conflicts with managers, and also being the victim of "the system"—specifically, educational boards and government and educational bodies. In relationships, the card predicts tension and conflict. Overall, the Five of Swords reveals ongoing stress, continual challenges to your position—and, often, defeat.

However this disruptive Five of Swords manifests for you, the overriding message is that all is not lost. You may not win the battle, but you can recover and walk away with your self-respect—provided you make a gracious exit at the right time. There's a danger here that you continue the fight even when the battle is over. Regardless of the provocation, deal with your anger and disappointment. There's a saying, "It's all

over, bar the shouting." Don't keep shouting too much longer or hope to revisit the situation or relationship. It's done.

REVERSED MEANING

The Five of Swords reversed shows unnecessary conflict; you could become caught in the middle of another person's fight, and you may be the injured party through no fault of your own. This battle is not for good reason. Whoever initiates it has a selfish agenda; this person may be trying to cover up his or her incompetence at work, blaming others to deflect attention; equally, the drama may be due to ego and a need to make a show of power. In this sense, it can be easier to extricate yourself because you know the battle is less personal.

An additional meaning of the card is bullying and oppression. There is no shame in this—rather, the card suggests finding an opportunity to expose the unfairness and to shift the balance of power.

SIX OF SWORDS

Element: Air

Astrological Association: Mercury in Aquarius

Number: 6

Tree of Life Sphere: Tiphareth, the sphere of beauty and rebirth

Key Meaning: Moving on

UNDERSTANDING THE SIX OF SWORDS

The Six of Swords is one of the more positive Swords cards, along with the winning Ace (see page 176) and the peaceful Four (see page 182). In this card, there are battles, blindfolds, or stress: A ferryman is steering a boat to a promising destination with gentle hills and trees. We see the water on the right of the boat is choppy, whereas the water before him is calm. The troubled water symbolizes a rough situation he is moving away from and the still waters ahead, a period of serenity away from strife.

He is accompanied by two passengers, a child and a shrouded figure, perhaps the child's mother. All three figures face away from us, suggesting they are fixed on their destination; the decision to leave has been made, and the journey has begun. This determined focus is a feature of the card's astrological association, Mercury in Aquarius, which also suggests a rational approach that is in keeping with Swords, the suit of the mind. The card's gray sky is neutral, so there is no emotion here; the ferryman is a neutral actor, too, paid for his services without any attachment to the outcome. The card's Tree of Life sphere, Tiphareth, means beauty and rebirth, offering a happy new beginning for the ferryman's passengers. One further aspect to note is the traditional role of the male ferryman as active and the female passenger as passive. The presence of male yang and female yin energy in balance suggests peace and harmony, which chimes with the card's numerological association.

The number six stands for serenity and peace. The six-pointed Star of David comprises two triangles, representing the concept of heaven on earth—a reminder that we can realize the heavenly and spiritual aspects of ourselves in our daily lives to enjoy harmony in mind, body, and spirit. In the Six of Swords, the two themes are the present and the future. The challenge is to integrate our experiences and move forward.

UPRIGHT MEANING

The Six of Swords shows you moving on from a situation or relationship and enjoying a period of peace and harmony. This may manifest mentally rather than physically, as you take a more detached approach, distancing yourself from drama and complication. This gives you an opportunity to rest and recharge; it may lead you to explore a new environment or make a spiritual discovery.

In work, the card can show travel as part of your role (and respite from the office or other workplace), and in relationships, the card commonly shows two people spending time apart. More negatively, the interpretation is a relationship ending (look for accompanying cards such as the Three of Swords or the revised VI, The Lovers, for validation). This ending may be positive or negative, depending on your situation.

On a more literal note, the card can simply show taking a break from work or your usual environment, and you may travel, possibly on a trip overseas. When the Six of Swords appears with major arcana cards VII, The Chariot, for progress and XIII, Death, for transition,

a more permanent move is suggested, so the combination can be interpreted as emigration or a long period of travel. If we see the three figures on the card as a family rather than ferryman and passengers, the card suggests a major move for two or more people.

REVERSED MEANING

When reversed, the Six of Swords has a meaning that is similar to that of the upright card. It reveals a need to escape, but your plans are delayed. It may not be the right time for you to travel or leave an unsatisfying situation, as certain problems need to be addressed and resolved before you can be free. However, check that your intentions are sound and that you're looking in the right direction; rather than fixating on a particular outcome, which may blind you to other possibilities, keep your plans realistic. You may feel frustrated now by lack of progress, but stay focused and grounded and your time will come.

SEVEN OF SWORDS

Element: Air

Astrological Association: Moon in Aquarius

Number: 7

Tree of Life Position: Netzach, the sphere of endurance, instinct, and desire

Key Meanings: Theft and dishonesty

UNDERSTANDING THE SEVEN OF SWORDS

A smug thief makes off with five of seven swords while an encampment is unguarded. The inhabitants are silhouettes, engrossed elsewhere while their weapons are stolen. This seems an easy take—the tent doors are open, and their bright colors make them attractive to the passerby. The thief knows he is safe with his hoard and gives a sarcastic smile as he looks back at the site, knowing full well he will not be discovered. The card's bright yellow background symbolizes consciousness, so this thief does not operate in secret under cover of night. He commits daylight robbery.

His dress is ostentatious. His red, fur-trimmed boots and matching hat give the impression of someone with a sense of entitlement to the best things life has to offer—except, he is willing to possess them by illegal means. The red symbolizes energy, ego, and the material world. Red on his feet suggests he will act on his ego to get what he wants. Note how his boots and hat don't fit with the rest of his outfit; perhaps they are stolen, too, as they make a sharp contrast with his everyday leggings and basic drawstring shirt, the clothes of the common man—or common thief.

One question remains, however. Why does the thief leave two swords behind? The two remaining swords highlight one of the positive meanings of the card, in that the victims may still defend themselves, even when their opponent has the advantage. The thief takes with him just five swords. Five in the minor arcana is also the number of upheaval—the Five of Swords, conflict; the Five of Pentacles, money issues; the Five of Wands, challenges; and the Five of Cups, loss.

The card's Tree of Life sphere is Netzach, which means endurance and instinct. These are the qualities the potential victim will need to uncover the identity of the thief; they are also the personality of the thief himself, in his willingness to take risks. He is also able to wait patiently for the right moment to strike. Further qualities are revealed by the astrological association of the Seven of Swords with the Moon in Aquarius, which blends the Moon's intuition with Aquarius's idealism and detachment.

The number seven is a mystical number. It was sacred to the god Apollo, founder of the famous Delphic oracle, and is the number of the days of the week, the deadly sins, and the wonders of the world (see Understanding The Chariot, page 58). Seven represents possibilities, as it comprises three, the number of heaven, and four, the number of earth, and so shows the potential to bring heaven down to earth—to manifest an ideal. However, in the Seven of Swords, the thief's idea of heaven on earth has moral implications.

UPRIGHT MEANING

The common name for this Seven of Swords is "the thief." Traditionally, the message is to protect your belongings and property. In general, we can think of this as a potential transgression—you may encounter a challenge to your position, an individual invading your space, or in relationships, a selfish partner who takes too much emotionally, or at worst, defrauds you. As the suit of Swords relates to intellect, you'll need your instincts and your wits to discover the truth. You

may need to be devious and play this person at his or her own game, too, to find out what you need to know. Your opponent may be strong, but you still have valuable resources on your side.

The card can also show legal problems and unfair or fraudulent business dealings.

REVERSED MEANING

The reversed Seven of Swords shows a tendency to give up rather than take a stand. It may feel unnatural to you to think like your opponent to anticipate their next moves, but this attitude will help you defend what is yours. Otherwise, you may surrender too soon. This particularly applies to work, when a colleague tries to disempower you. It's important to stand your ground.

As with the upright card, the reversed Seven of Swords can show legal problems of and in business dealings, beware of unscrupulous people.

EIGHT OF SWORDS

Element: Air

Astrological Association: Jupiter in Gemini

Number: 8

Tree of Life Position: Hod, the sphere of majesty and the mind

Key Meaning: Restriction

UNDERSTANDING THE EIGHT OF SWORDS

The Eight of Swords shows a fairytale gone bad: A maiden is outcast from a castle, and her hands are bound. She stands alone within a semicircle of planted swords, with her back turned to her home. A hostage, she is a symbol of otherness, separated from the castle, which stands for civilization and inclusion. Her red robes symbolize energy, but she is tied, so her movements are restricted. The rock pools look pretty and innocuous, but if she cannot shift her position soon, she may be in danger when the water rises with the high tide. Her eyes are blindfolded, symbolizing an inability to see a way ahead. A blindfolded woman also features on the Two of Swords, the "stalemate" card—so perhaps the hostage of the Eight of Swords was once the Two, but now her bonds are tighter and her situation more precarious.

Thankfully, this bondage will not last: A. E. Waite, the Rider-Waite tarot's creator, says, "it is rather a card of temporary durance than of irretrievable bondage." At some point, our maiden will muster the determination to save herself; no prince on a white charger will come.

The astrological association of this Eight of Swords is expansive Jupiter in sociable Gemini, a highly creative and intellectual combination. The challenge is to manage information overload, as ideas can go too far, leading to potential failure due to a lack of perspective and focus—a link with the blindfolded hostage, the card's central image.

The card's number is eight, and one of its meanings is change, renewal, and stability. This reflects the hostage's need to extricate herself from thoughts that are keeping her trapped and to find new ground. As Swords are the suit of Air, which rules the mind, this also links with card's Tree of Life sphere, Hod. Its common meaning is majesty, and in this Eight of Swords, refers to the mastery of the mind.

UPRIGHT MEANING

The upright card shows feeling trapped. This may be due to a series of bad experiences and poor luck, and you begin to wonder if things can ever improve. You may be anxious due to an unsatisfactory bond with an individual or an organization; specifically, you may be trapped by a credit agreement that leaves you little money for yourself.

This unfortunate Eight of Swords commonly reveals problems in careers and the intellectual or mental realm, showing frustration and, at its most extreme, panic. Hemmed in and unhappy, you may be finding it impossible to do your work to your satisfaction due to unreasonable demands or disorganized management. Also, there may be a sense of conversations going on behind closed doors that you are not party to, so you feel isolated and even vulnerable. The card commonly arises in readings to show someone who is in a role that doesn't suit them, but they are under pressure to conform—such as working in the family business

or taking a course because it will lead to a profession, although it isn't what they love doing at all. Many creatives and lightworkers go through this experience of not fitting in, but it takes time and confidence to find your path. You can release yourself from these bonds, but it will take determination, and you may need to swallow your pride and ask others for support and advice. On a social level, the Eight of Swords can show you feeling humiliated or ignored, and you fear others' attitudes toward you.

An additional meaning of the card is illness and incapacity. Again, this does not imply permanent disability, but a phase of physical restriction.

REVERSED MEANING

In the reversed position, much of the upright meaning applies, except that it is often accompanied by strong emotions such as guilt, anger, and regret. It's likely you'll express these feelings in negative ways, however, because you are so frustrated; try not to lash out on whoever is closest. As with all the minor arcana cards, the Eight of Swords shows a phase that will not last.

NINE OF SWORDS

Element: Air

Astrological Association: Mars in Gemini

Number: 9

Tree of Life Position: Yesod, the sphere of foundation and the unconscious mind

Key Meaning: Anxiety

UNDERSTANDING THE NINE OF SWORDS

The meaning of the Nine of Swords, like many of the cards of the suit, is obvious at first glance. An anguished figure sits upright in bed, awake in the night in clear distress. Nine horizontal swords appear behind and above the figure, like bars at a window. Swords represent the intellect and thoughts, here en masse as a symbol of restriction; their hilts are crossing, crowding the space like unwanted thoughts. The third sword from the bottom crosses the crown of his head, oppressing him; the second sword from bottom strikes through his head; and the lowest sword appears to cut through the area of his heart. What began in the mind now hurts him at a deep level, and he is cut off from usual sources of comfort in a painful internal struggle.

The mattress is a pale purple color, the color of intuition, linking with the card's Tree of Life sphere Yesod, which is ruled by the Moon, ruler of the unconscious mind. The pastoral scene carved on the side of the bed or couch is suggestive of dreams, but the two figures depicted are not at peace; there is an aggressive current to the image. A figure is brandishing an implement at a prone figure, indicating that the dreamer is a victim of his thoughts.

In contrast to the dark feel of the card, the quilt is bright and beautiful, showing the twelve glyphs of the zodiac signs with alternating patches of red roses. The glyphs represent multitude—rather than having any individual significance, they tell us that the person's worry may encompass lots of life aspects. The red roses are a symbol of love and hope. The dreamer cannot see this just now, as his hands are covering his eyes, much like the two beggars on the Five of Pentacles, who cannot see the money tree depicted in the beautiful stained-glass window about them.

The card's number is nine, or three sets of three. Three is a dynamic number, and when multiplied by itself, symbolizes intense productivity—however, in the suit of Swords, the mind is overproductive, awash with worries and negative thoughts.

The astrological association, Mars and Gemini, is a forceful combination. Free-spirited Gemini is controlled by Mars, an unstoppable, aggressive force, bringing frustration and a sense of entrapment.

UPRIGHT MEANING

I call this Nine "the 3 a.m. card" because it describes the meaning so accurately: It's what you wake up worrying about in the small hours of the night, showing you are dealing with high levels of anxiety. You may have suffered an illness and the resulting low energy or a shock or a buildup of minor stresses that begin to disrupt your sleep patterns and peace of mind. External events such as these may have triggered the initial stress, but the issue now is how you are responding to it.

Look to the surrounding cards to see the life area that this relates to, although the anxiety in the Nine of Swords can reflect unhappiness in key areas, from work to relationships, coloring your usually positive attitude. The card also indicates the habit of worry—so you may be worrying about inconsequential things that usually don't warrant your attention. Thankfully, as this is a minor card, this pattern is temporary.

In work, the Nine of Swords can show feeling overwhelmed. You simply have too much to do, particularly if the card appears with the Ten of Wands, known as the burden card.

The Nine of Swords occasionally comes up in a reading to show mental health issues associated with anxiety, such as panic disorder or anxiety and depression. Insomnia and nightmares are additional interpretations.

REVERSED MEANING

Unfortunately, as you might expect, the reversed Nine's meaning is more extreme than that of its upright counterpart and traditionally means despair, guilt, or feeling trapped. However, this is the lowest point of the cycle, and these feeling will begin to shift. As you gradually move out of this difficult phase, you will feel more able to turn these feelings of powerlessness around. Be patient and compassionate with yourself and turn to others for support rather than suffering alone.

TEN OF SWORDS

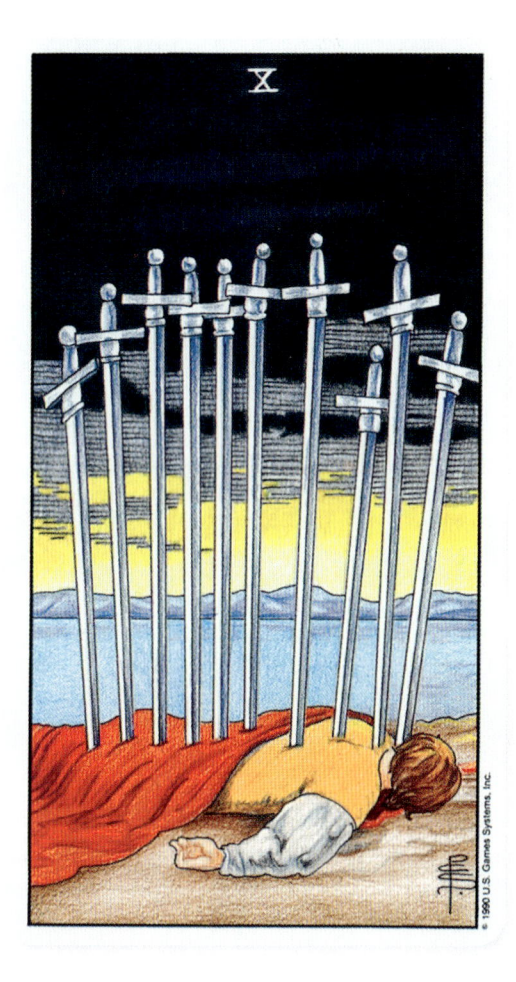

Element: Air

Astrological Association: Sun in Gemini

Number: 10

Tree of Life Position: Malkuth, the Kingdom, the sphere of experience

Key Meaning: Endings

UNDERSTANDING THE TEN OF SWORDS

The Ten of Swords has a black background that appears on the Nine of Swords (known as the stress card) and card XV, The Devil. We are indeed in a dark place again here, as we see a young man pinned to the ground by ten swords embedded along the length of his back. There's also a sense of shock in the card, symbolized by the blue water, purple mountains, and yellow sky set against charcoal-gray clouds, heavy with rain, in a black sky. This dual skyscape represents two worlds: the bright outlook of the "before-world" prior to the conflict and the "after-world," in which everything is changed and a sudden darkness descends like a shroud, to eventually cover the body. The victim is facedown and does not show his face, as if he is no longer relevant; the focus of the card is the points of the swords.

The victim's right hand is slightly twisted, and if we look closely, we see it makes the sign of blessing, with the first two fingers straight as in card V, The Hierophant (see page 50). In this sense, we may interpret the figure as a fallen master or guru; or this pose may be a sign of the man's acceptance of this ending—that what has befallen him is in fact a blessing. A red cloth is draped over him, and the fabric flows like blood from his body. Red symbolizes love, vitality, and, here, the life force, or blood.

In numerology, ten represents completeness and perfection. In the Ten of Swords, the completeness is an ending. The individual sphere associated with this card is Malkuth, for kingdom—so the Ten of Swords reveals an end to our personal kingdom or one aspect of our material world.

This card's astrological association of the Sun in Gemini brings a bright, sociable influence that is at odds with the card's meaning and can only highlight newfound happiness after the influence of this dark card has passed. As the sun goes down on a life phase, the Sun in Gemini offers light at the end of the tunnel.

UPRIGHT MEANING

The traditional meaning of the upright card is ruin. While this sounds frightening, it does not, however, mean death or destruction; it is also worth bearing in mind that this event, although sudden, has a history. This is not an act of God, like the lightning strike of card XVI, The Tower, but the natural outcome of a culmination of events that leads to inevitable change. This ending clears the way for new possibilities, and you may find the finality of it releases you from frustration and stress, as is expressed in the preceding card, the Nine of Swords (see page 192). In this sense, the Ten of Swords is an aspect of card XIII, Death, in its meaning of endings, transition, and new beginnings.

In your personal life, bonds of friendship may break, and there may be no turning back; this, unfortunately, is unavoidable, but with hindsight, you may see that certain people in a group were causing discord and stress. In love relationships, the card signifies a dramatic ending (particularly if it appears close to the Three of Swords, the "sorrow" card). However, the Ten of Swords often applies to a group of people, rather than individuals. In work, this may manifest as the closure of a department accompanied by job loss or a failing business.

On a more positive note, this is the end of an era; soon the strife and upset will be over. Health issues, such as low energy and exhaustion, will improve.

REVERSED MEANING

When reversed, the Ten of Swords holds the meaning of the upright card, but indicates there may be more repercussions. You may examine your past actions and feel guilty or angry and react more deeply to the fallout; try not to hold on to the stress. Accept the situation and let go.

The reversed Ten of Swords can also show feeling helpless, particularly if you have been ill or overwhelmed emotionally. Soon you will feel able to pick yourself up and start over.

PAGE OF SWORDS

PAGE *of* SWORDS.

© 1990 U.S. Games Systems, Inc.

Element: Earth of the suit of Air

Key Meanings: Intelligence and contracts

UNDERSTANDING THE PAGE OF SWORDS

A young man stands strong, sword raised in both hands and alert to the signs of trouble. The landscape is blown with clouds, and we see a lone tree almost doubled over by the wind. A circling flock of black birds suggests something is about to take flight or take form. Whatever happens, though, our hero is poised for action in unsettled times. On high ground, he has chosen the best position to fend off any enemy. He stands tall for all to see and brandishes his sword. The weapon is a symbol of his intention and his mind, which extends beyond the edge of the card itself. He is willing to deal with known and unknown threats, to plan his response and ultimately to win. While not dressed for battle—he has no armor and possibly no experience of conflict—his pose suggests he is ready to attack or defend; looking over his right shoulder away from his sword, he is alert to attack. He minds his position on both sides, a knight in training—his tunic is dark red, a regal color, symbolizing his ambition to rise through the ranks. His boots are red, for energy and matter, while his hose and sleeves are yellow, a symbol of the intellect.

The mountains beyond are blue, a color commonly used in this tarot to denote truth and spirituality (think card II, The High Priestess, and her robes, or VII, The Chariot, and its heavenly canopy of stars). Like card XI, Justice, this Page with his sword cuts to the truth, bringing clarity: The clouds disappear.

Young, feisty, and confident, the Page of Swords is clear-thinking and dedicated to his cause. His element is Earth of Air. His foremost skill is his intellect and wit, so when combined with practical Earth, he is a strategist, planning the most effective action to take. The negative aspect of this Earth-Air pairing is conflict between Air's need to show off and Earth's pragmatism. If Air dominates, the Page of Swords can be precocious and superficial, losing sight of the bigger picture.

Pages and Knights in tarot are generally regarded as people or influences, whereas the other court cards (the Queens and Kings) are assumed to be people. Let your intuition guide you toward the most appropriate meaning for the Page in a reading by working with the card's imagery first, then the written interpretations (see also the Introduction, page 8).

UPRIGHT MEANING

As an influence: This card denotes useful information. Your hard work pays off in business and other work dealings. The Page of Swords also suggests people around you will be helpful, furthering your ambitions. This is a time to be alert and observe carefully what others say. Be ready to take action as you see the right opportunity and consult others who can act as advocates on your behalf.

This card often comes up in readings to say that a contract will be coming your way—regarding property, careers, travel documents, and other agreements.

As a person: The Page of Swords suggests an individual who is charming, clever, and very good company. As he's a Page, this is often a younger person or someone with a youthful, quick-fire brain. He may be forthright with his words, but he is ultimately a good ally who can turn challenges into opportunities. Quick

to learn, he is curious and open, but the downside is that he can be mischievous and so set on achieving his aims he forgets to treat others with sensitivity.

As the "you" card in a reading: Rely on your intelligence.

If two or more Pages fall close together in a reading, the meanings are as follows:

- **Two Pages:** Friendship if upright; rivalry if one or both cards are reversed

- **Three Pages:** Lots of social activities

- **Four Pages:** A social group of young people

REVERSED MEANING

When reversed, this clever Page of Swords becomes manipulative and cunning. Be cautious about information you receive now, as it may not be reliable, and be discerning about what you hear about other people, as it may be unjust and even slanderous. As a person, the reversed Page of Swords can be a gossip who seems to care little about the misconceptions he spreads. At his worst, he can be devious and unscrupulous. Ignore his needs for constant attention; don't fuel his fire.

KNIGHT OF SWORDS

KNIGHT *of* SWORDS.

Element: Fire of the suit of Air

Astrological Associations: Taurus and Gemini

Key Meanings: Stress and truth

UNDERSTANDING THE KNIGHT OF SWORDS

Such is the force of the Knight of Swords that even his horse seems on the brink of terror as they leap toward an unseen enemy. The Knight, in full battle armor, is on the brink of war, his sword brandished, horse's reins held high, and feet forced down into the stirrups to urge the animal to keep pace. His visor is up, showing us that he is more than ready to look his enemy in the eye.

The wind is against him—the trees to the left of the card bend to the right while our rider gallops to the left—a sign that he is not afraid to ride toward, not from, whatever opposes him. The desert landscape is rather bleak, a symbol for the need to survive, and the clouds are ragged, as if the Knight had sliced them to pieces. His sword extends beyond the card, like that of the Page of Swords, to suggest that this Knight's intention goes far beyond the limited landscape we see. Fixated on his mission, it feels as if nothing can stop him. The "true blue" of his armor and horse bridle and collar show he is prepared to cut to the heart of the enemy—or matter—at hand.

The card's element is Fire of the suit of Air. Fire, or passionate energy, is symbolized by his red cape and plume, and Air is denoted by the birds and butterflies decorating the horse's collar. The mix of air, or wind, with fire, or lightning, suggests thunderstorms and hurricanes—a surge of power that erupts then dissipates. This is the Knight's modus operandi. He charges, confronts the enemy, and then departs in a flash.

Knights and Pages in tarot are generally regarded as people or influences, whereas the other court cards (the Queens and Kings) are assumed to be people. Let your intuition guide you toward the most appropriate meaning for the Knight in a reading by working with the card's imagery first, then the written interpretations here (see also the Introduction, page 8).

UPRIGHT MEANING

As a person: The Knight of Swords is determined and driven, and he has a strong sense of himself and his mission. He may be quirky and entertaining with an offbeat sense of humor, and he may even dress in a distinctive way. Incisive, forthright, and intelligent, he makes a strong advocate and is prepared to fight for his beliefs. The downside is that he often makes his mark, gets bored, and moves on. In relationships, he may cause drama, but takes no responsibility for reconciliation, leaving others to make peace while he's charging ahead with his next obsession. In work, he can show up in readings to represent auditors and other assessors, such as doctors and lawyers, or consultants who are hired to fire, not fix—in short, professionals who are adept at diagnoses and whose opinions matter. Ultimately, though, you are the one who will have to deal with the outcomes.

As the "you" card in a reading: Expect the unexpected.

As an influence: Unpredictable, tempestuous times are ahead—you're in for a roller coaster drama of highs and lows. Sudden truths may come to light or underlying conflicts are exposed. This may be illuminating, stressful, or bewildering, depending on your position.

The card often comes up to show disputes at work and tension within families and in romantic relationships. While you may not be responsible for the cause of the trouble, what counts now is how you recover. There is a way forward, but you may need to wait until the situation is calmer before you can make a move.

If two or more Knights fall close together in a reading, the meanings are as follows:

- **Two Knights:** Friendship if upright; rivalry if one or both cards are reversed

- **Three Knights:** Men meeting up

- **Four Knights:** Lots of action; events speed up

REVERSED MEANING

When reversed, the Knight of Swords means stressful situations are blown out of proportion as an individual thrives on drama but lacks the courage to take control. The card also advises that you may be let down by someone you thought was reliable and steadfast. A person with a big personality may have lots to say but have little substance. However, this individual's high intelligence means he usually talks his way out of trouble, denying any involvement.

QUEEN OF SWORDS

QUEEN *of* **SWORDS.**

Element: Water of the suit of Air

Astrological Associations: Virgo and Libra

Chakras: Crown and third eye, for openness and intuition

Key Meaning: An incisive woman

UNDERSTANDING THE QUEEN OF SWORDS

The Queen of Swords is an aspect of card III, The Empress, or mother archetype. This Queen is the "mind" aspect of the mother, just as the Queen of Cups is the heart (see page 144 and The Empress, page 42).

Our Swords Queen has a sense of sovereignty like no other—she is the only female monarch shown in profile, like a head on a coin. One hand is raised, as if to greet a visitor, and like the Queen of Wands, her pose is alert. This is a woman in charge: She holds her sword at a perfect right angle to her throne arm and sits on high ground, giving a sense of authority over her domain.

The card's element is Water of Air. We see the Water element in the river below four trees; it extends from the Queen's red veil, which flows down behind her throne. This creates the effect of a river of blood, a reminder that this Queen, unlike her jewelry, is not for show. If necessary, she will fight, and it won't be pretty.

The Air element, for the mind, is expressed through motifs of winged creatures—the single bird, the cherub, and the butterflies on her throne and crown. Her butterfly crown is open, a sign that she welcomes ideas and opinions. She is very much part of her airy landscape, wearing clouds on her cloak and white, billowing robes. The blue-sky background symbolizes her motivation to find the truth.

On her throne are two crescents: either two crescent moons or two sickles, or curved blades. As moons, they link her to the crescents on card II, The High Priestess, who deals with the hidden world of the subconscious and the sixth sense: The Queen of Swords also has sharp instincts and is not afraid to follow them. As sickles, they echo the purpose of her magical object, the sword, again linking with her element of Air.

Queens and Kings in tarot are traditionally regarded as people in your life or people about to come into your orbit. However, you can also read the Queen as a general influence, so this interpretation is included last.

UPRIGHT MEANING

As a person: An astute strategist, the Queen of Swords is single-minded and highly ambitious. Like her sign of Libra, she can quickly assess all aspects of a situation to get to the truth, including the underlying psychological motivation for others' attitudes and actions. Adept at numbers, she may be an administrator, IT specialist, researcher, or financial executive—the need for attention to detail relates to her associated sign of Virgo. Sword Queens also make successful businesswomen or bosses. She has much life experience and may have had hurdles to overcome in her early years. This makes her the strong woman she is. For all this, she is still willing to take risks on new experiences and relationships. She does not suffer fools gladly, but if she likes you, she will reward and trust you implicitly.

Traditionally, this card is known as the widow, but means in general a single woman or a woman who has to make her own way in the world. It's also a common card for single parents.

As the "you" card in a reading: Be determined and stand strong.

As an influence: The Queen of Swords offers wisdom and intelligence, perspective, and the ability to see the bigger picture. When placed closed to negative cards in a reading, the Queen shows strength in adversity.

If two or more Queens fall close together in a reading, the meanings are as follows:

- **Two Queens:** Rivalry

- **Three Queens:** Helpful friends

- **Four Queens:** Women meeting up

REVERSED MEANING

Reversed, the Queen of Swords suggests excuses for bad behavior or a situation in which you are unjustly attacked. As a person, this individual can be an opponent or someone who has suddenly turned bitter and vengeful. However, a common reason for the Queen to invert can be extreme stress—this woman lacks awareness of just how unreasonable her demands have become. If this is the case, back away; she must help herself.

KING OF SWORDS

Element: Air of the suit of Air

Astrological Association: Capricorn and Aquarius

Chakras: Crown and third eye, for openness and intuition

Key Meaning: An ambitious man

UNDERSTANDING THE KING OF SWORDS

The King of Swords can be considered as an aspect of card IV, The Emperor, or a father archetype who brings structure, order, and authority. The realm of the King of Swords is the mind, just as the King of Cups rules the heart, the King of Pentacles, the physical body, and the King of Wands, the soul (see pages 146, 174, 230, and The Emperor, page 46).

The King is comfortable in his regal position and resembles card XI, Justice, in his pose with Justice's sword (see page 74). Like his partner, the Queen of Swords, the King's throne is engraved with butterfly motifs, for his element of Air. On the right—almost perching on the King's shoulder—is a female fairy. The two crescents forming a crest with the butterflies at the top of the throne may be sickles, another implement that cuts like his sword. Equally, they could be two moons. One of the moons of Uranus, the planet of awakening that rules the King's sign of Aquarius, is named Titania, after the legendary queen of the fairies. If the fairy on the throne is intended to be the beautiful but cruel Titania, she embodies the dark and light sides of the King's mighty sword: This charming sovereign can be ruthless.

The card's element is Air of Air, so this King is idealistic and ambitious. His throne is placed above the base of the trees, suggesting perspective from a high position. His sword is held at an angle, rather than in upright, ceremonial pose, so we sense he is familiar with the feel of its swipe. The clouds, symbols of doubt or confusion, seem banished to the mid- and lower parts of the card, as if the King had just cut through the clouds above him, revealing a soft bluish sky. Blue is the color of truth and clarity, echoed in the color of his robes.

The King's purple cloak stands for intuition, and the red cap and orange sleeves are for passion and the material world. He focuses his sharp mind on what needs to be done.

Kings and Queens in tarot are traditionally regarded as people in your life, or people about to come into your orbit. However, you can also read the King as a general influence, so this interpretation is included last.

UPRIGHT MEANING

As a person: The King of Swords can be an intellectual or a man who relies on logic to help him win. He is also open to ideas, although he can be impatient if he has to wait for a consensus before taking action. However, he is outwardly calm and makes good judgements. He often has a dry sense of humor and is very charming. In readings, he can appear as a seductive man you meet at work or through other professional connections.

His ideal vocations include traditional professions, and you will often find him in powerful roles: doctor, judge, solicitor, or member of the armed forces or law enforcement; academic, IT, and research work may appeal, and in business, he is often a manager or director. Whatever profession he chooses, he must be able to make decisions that make a difference, and preferably, have hands-on involvement.

As the "you" card in a reading: Take charge.

As an influence: When the King of Swords arrives in a reading, the focus is on the mind rather than the heart. You may be going through an intensive time of work or study. In relationships and domestic affairs, it's time to take the initiative.

If two or more Kings fall close together in a reading, the meanings are as follows:

- **Two Kings:** A good partnership

- **Three Kings:** Influential men

- **Four Kings:** A power battle

REVERSED MEANING

When reversed, the influence of the usually balanced King of Swords can be destructive. You may be put under unreasonable pressure to produce results. Unfortunately, there's no room for argument or personal interpretations, so you may feel oppressed. Thankfully, this is a temporary situation. As a person, you may be dealing with someone who plays mind games and who will do almost anything to win.

THE SUIT OF WANDS
ACE OF WANDS

Element: Fire

Astrological Associations: The Fire signs—Aries, Leo, and Sagittarius

Number: 1

Tree of Life Position: Kether, the sphere of divine light

Key Meanings: Enterprise, career, travel, and beginnings

UNDERSTANDING THE ACE OF WANDS

A hand, offering a single wand, appears from a cloud. The Ace of Wands is the only card of the suit to show multiple buds, symbolizing new ventures. There are four leaves on one stem, and the two lower stems each have three leaves. A further eight leaves float around the wand, giving a total of eighteen. This may relate to the eighteenth letter of the Hebrew alphabet, *Tzaddi*, meaning hope. The leaves are similar in appearance to the droplets on the Ace of Cups; the Ace of Swords; XVI, The Tower; and XVIII, The Moon (see pages 120, 176, 94, and 102).

The scene below shows purple mountains, symbols of spiritual goals. A building, a fairytale castle or a monastery, is perched on a hill—signifying the ambition to attain a dream or spiritual aspiration. The castle is isolated and protected by high walls and a tower. Seeing the strong wand grasped before us, we may view it as a club, held high in a gesture of protection and ownership of the land. In the valley, pure water flows, the blue a color for true purpose. Three trees grow on the right bank, symbols of growth and fertility.

Unlike the cultivated garden of the Ace of Pentacles, the landscape of the Ace of Wands is natural and untamed: This Ace is a true pioneer, venturing into wild new territory. In this sense, the card presents the gift of enterprise and adventure. As with the other Ace cards and their symbols, the offering is made with the right hand, the wand held with the hand of giving (as opposed to the left hand, which is the receiving hand).

The second gift of the Ace of Wands is the drive to succeed. We may have an enticing vision or prospect, but need the energy to make it happen. The card's element is Fire, full of burning purpose—just as the wand, if planted, will determinedly grow into a tall, strong tree. The card's Tree of Life sphere is Kether, for the divine light of God, or great spirit. In the Ace of Wands, this stands for the spirit of adventure.

The Aces offer the pure energy of their suits. As number ones, they represent oneness with the divine spirit or God. Indivisible, their energy is singular, strong, and purposeful. They all represent beginnings, impulses, and new possibilities, in the most pure and obvious form.

UPRIGHT MEANING

The upright meaning of the Ace of Wands is auspicious for every aspect of your life. In a spread, it overrules any negative minor arcana cards close by (just like the major arcana card XIX, The Sun). The Ace predicts new beginnings, enterprise, and invention and often relates to work issues and projects. It's a happy card for creative work, too. With this Ace, you experience a flash of inspiration and know what do next to give form to your concept.

As you conceive ideas, so the card works at a literal level as a phallic symbol, for male virility and starting a family.

An additional meaning of the card is travel and adventure, particularly when it appears in a reading with the Three or Eight of Wands (see pages 208 and 218).

In a reading, one Ace brings a focus on the life area according to the suit, which can set the theme of the reading. If two or more Aces appear near each other in a reading, it means the following:

- **Two Aces:** An important partnership
- **Three Aces:** Good news
- **Four Aces:** Excitement, beginnings, and potential

REVERSED MEANING

When the Ace of Wands reverses, it can show blocks to creative projects and delays to travel. In work, a project may be abandoned or postponed due to poor management. In general, the card reveals false starts; plans need a rethink.

In relationships, this Ace can reveal a lack of commitment from a man or time apart for a couple, usually due to work, and the woman finds herself waiting for the man.

Another common meaning of the reversed Ace of Wands in readings is difficulty conceiving a child, particularly if the card appears close to the Three of Swords, the card for sorrow (see page 180).

TWO OF WANDS

Element: Fire

Astrological Association: Mars in Aries

Number: 2

Tree of Life Position: Chockmah, the sphere of wisdom

Key Meanings: Plans, partnership, and influence

UNDERSTANDING THE TWO OF WANDS

In the Two of Wands, a young man holds a globe in his right hand and a wand in his left hand. The wand is held toward its base, and the man rests it on a raised section of wall so that it stands taller than his head. Altogether, these symbols offer us the meaning of extension, of looking beyond the immediate vicinity and into the future. Positioned at the top of a castle, this is a man with a view: purple mountains for goals and intuition, a peaceful lake and sandy shore, and, rising into the hills, modest dwellings, forests, and fields. This feels like fertile land, where ideas and dreams are nurtured. Our hero has plans, and they are beginning to grow, just like the leaves budding from the two wands. He stands partly in profile, rather than facing us, gazing into his globe. The two wands on each side of our hero and the card's Roman number, II, create a portal, a doorway to another realm of experience, and soon the man will be ready to step into it. This links with his Tree of Life sphere, Chockmah, for wisdom. His red robe and hat signify vitality and the material world.

The man on the Two of Wands already knows he is partway toward his dream, and he has gained confidence through the work he has already done. This is shown by the wand on the right on the card, which stands on the ground, lower than the wand he holds. A small ribbon is tied at the base, perhaps as a seal, to signify that this wand, or part of his project, is complete.

On the plinth at the left is the intriguing emblem of a black cross with red-and-white flowers: roses for passion, lilies for purity, and the cross for faith. (The saltire, or St. Andrew's cross, is also depicted on the Six of Cups.) Roses on a cross can signify the Rosicrucian order, a secret esoteric brotherhood that took the Rosy Cross as its symbol. A principal text of Rosicrucianism is the fifteenth-century allegory *The Chymical Marriage of Christian Rosenkreutz*, which features a rose cross and a magical castle. On our Two of Wands, both the castle wall and cross may be an intentional reference to Rosicrucianism, as this order also influenced Freemasonry; the Rider-Waite's creator, A. E. Waite, was a mason, and so familiar with this alchemical image. Note, too, the cross and roses design in stone on the Three of Pentacles (see page 152).

Astrologically, this card is linked with Mars in Aries, a fiery pairing that signifies willpower and energy. The challenge is to temper the fire when necessary and resist impatience.

UPRIGHT MEANING

The Two of Wands shows you making plans and moving forward, so travel arrangements are one meaning of the card. In your work, you are gaining influence and proving your worth. In return, you receive good support and advice. The card can also show new creative partnerships and beginning a new project or enterprise.

As there are two wands on the card, there are also two aspects to your situation. Consider what helps you on your path and any issues that hold you back. Make a plan that maximizes your strengths so your talent continues to shine.

An additional meaning of the Two of Wands is a new romantic partnership, and it often comes up in a reading to reveal that the relationship begins at work or through a mutual friendship or leisure interests. Spiritually, too, you are feeling more connected within yourself and the world at large, so you may feel drawn to development courses or simply spending time connecting with nature.

Overall, great opportunities are on the way, allowing you to move up a level. Make the most of these offers—your star is rising.

REVERSED MEANING

When reversed, your talent may be wasted because those who can help you progress are not listening. If this is the case, consider a change of scenery. You need to be with people who understand your views and appreciate your skills. The card can also show misplaced trust and an unreliable partner. Check if those close to you are pulling their weight—or you could be the one doing all the work. In relationships, a partner may be irresponsible.

THREE OF WANDS

Element: Fire

Astrological Association: Sun in Aries

Number: 3

Tree of Life Position: Binah, the sphere of understanding

Key Meanings: Action and adventure

UNDERSTANDING THE THREE OF WANDS

For one time only in the tarot sequence, we see a figure with no visible face. Whereas on the Two of Wands the man is in part profile, in the Three he has turned his back on us entirely. He has stepped down from the protection of his castle and now stands on higher ground right above a bay, where he has planted three wands firmly in the land, one of which he also holds. The two wands behind him offer protection; the third one he leans on, giving him support. He has passed through the portal of two wands and taken a step closer into the scene we saw at a distance in card Two. Now, our adventurer's cloak is a more vibrant red, for energy; he sports green, the color of nature and fertility, and wears a thin headband like card I, The Magician (page 34), symbolizing the mind—and his willpower to succeed. In this card, the man's headband looks as if it is waiting for a Roman victory wreath, the honor given to a homecoming hero. This theme continues with the checkered throw that sits over his left shoulder, Roman style; the pattern is reminiscent of flags used to signal the start and end of races, traditionally taken as a trophy by the champion. With headband and throw, the figure on the Three is already signaling that he is one of life's winners.

Astrologically, the Three of Wands is linked with the Sun in the sign of Aries. This indicates passion, strong communication, and clear goals. The potential issue with super-solar Aries is impatience, but that's because Ariens simply want results. This action-driven influence is softened by the meaning of the card's Tree of Life sphere, Binah, for understanding and the receptive feminine principle.

Dynamic number three, number of growth and change, is shown in three boats, three wands, and three buds on each wand, reinforcing the card's meaning of productivity—this is work in progress. The boats are pointing away from the shore, so we sense that this young man is an entrepreneur who has just launched his first fleet of three, carrying valuable cargo to a new destination. The vessels are symbols of the beginning of his journey toward distant shores and his future goals.

UPRIGHT MEANING

The Three of Wands is one of the tarot's good-fortune cards. It reveals successful enterprise and seeing your projects and relationships thrive; it is also a great indicator for weddings and a new, important relationship. It predicts a busy, intense period of activity so be prepared to be inundated with texts, emails, calls, and visitors.

This card is often an indicator of an imminent trip away and seeing your plans realized—whether those are travel plans, business plans, a wedding, or other projects you have nurtured. This is also a time for great communication and self-expression through chosen interests such as art, music, crafts, and sport. The Three of Wands also favors individuality and nonconformism, so you may feel drawn to unconventional people and projects now. Also, pride yourself on your quirks and eccentricities, and let others see all you have to offer rather than the aspects of you with which you assume

they are most comfortable. From this, you can gain even more confidence and even admiration. You are unique, after all.

The Three's challenge is to keep the balance between staying focused on the prize while remaining patient, calm, and in the now. Appreciate, too, those people who are around you now; try to make time for friends who don't immediately fit into your future plans.

REVERSED MEANING

When reversed, the Three of Wands shows communication problems. Plans are delayed and it may be difficult to make progress in your projects. Relationships can suffer under this influence, as you find it hard to express yourself and understand what others are saying. Misunderstandings may make you feel needlessly isolated. If this applies to you, resist the frustration that this influence brings and go with a slower pace for a while. Overall, however, these are minor negatives; this is still a card of good fortune, even when reversed, so don't let glitches become a distraction. You can still succeed.

FOUR OF WANDS

Element: Fire

Astrological Association: Venus in Aries

Number: 4

Tree of Life Position: Chesed, the sphere of love

Key Meanings: Freedom, creativity, and domestic happiness

UNDERSTANDING THE FOUR OF WANDS

One of the happiest cards of the tarot's minor arcana, the Four of Wands shows celebration. A couple stands triumphant, holding up bouquets of flowers. Four wands make an arbor hanging with garlands of ripe fruit—lemons, apples, plums, purple grapevines, and pink blooms. Three tiny figures are dancing, outside the walls of a city. This scene might depict harvest time, a public holiday, or even a wedding. The inspiration for the card may draw upon two pagan festivals—Beltane, or May Day, if we see the wands as maypoles, and Lammas, the Celtic celebration of the first day of the harvest.

May Day, held on May 1, has its origins in the Celtic festival of Beltane, which celebrated the coming of spring and the end of seed-planting. Maypoles—tall wands—were raised in villages, where the people danced around them to honor fertility. A May Queen and King were crowned with flowers—much like the couple on the Four of Wands, who, dressed in Roman-style robes, echo the origins of the celebration as the Roman holiday of Florlia, or festival of flowers.

The bright-yellow background of the card signifies solar energy, the power of the sun to make all life grow. It also symbolizes consciousness, in that the couple present themselves for all to see in public celebration. They wear blue and red robes, for truth and passion and the material world, respectively. The dominant red and yellow are similar to the colors of card I, The Magician, with his luminous yellow background, rose briars, and red robes, for the energy to manifest his desires. Strength, card VIII, has a similar palette, again for vitality and also, acting with conscious awareness.

Number four is the number of stability and balance. In the passionate suit of wands, it denotes security, shown by the protective walls of the castle, and celebration. In the kabbalistic Tree of Life (see page 328), the card links with Chesed, the sphere of love—which is why this card is often referred to as "the honeymoon."

Astrologically, the Four of Wands is linked to the planet Venus in the sign of Aries. This indicates passion, spontaneity, and joie de vivre. Aries, however, can be dominating at times, which can make love too intense or driven.

UPRIGHT MEANING

This lovely card reveals success after completion—a time for reward. Socially, you will have the opportunity to celebrate and really enjoy yourself; the card predicts you will be brimming with confidence and full of vitality. You also establish yourself in your work and at home, completing a building or remodeling project or moving to a larger property. The vibe of the card is putting down roots, just like the wands. People around you note your willingness to be a pillar of the community and involve yourself in local issues and social events. In work, your talent is appreciated, and you are full of ideas and enthusiasm. Spiritually, the card shows that you share your light with others.

This often comes up in readings to predict that a new partner or love interest will open their hearts and express love and affection. It is also known as the honeymoon card—literally, or as a time to celebrate, run free, and enjoy what life has to offer. It is auspicious for creativity, and artistic projects flourish under the uplifting influence of the Four of Wands.

REVERSED MEANING

When reversed, this is one of the few minor arcana cards that retains its positive meaning, albeit with minor irritations. You don't get all the time you need to focus on doing what you love—from traveling to creative projects and socializing—and you may experience some disruption to plans. In this position, you might just be feeling invisible and not heard. However, if you are feeling too much like the outsider, consider if your environment is right—it's likely that it's them, not you. Overall, however, this unsettled phase will soon pass as the sunny aspect of the upright card prevails.

FIVE OF WANDS

Element: Fire

Astrological Association: Saturn in Leo

Number: 5

Tree of Life Position: Geburah, the sphere of power

Key Meanings: Competition and debates

UNDERSTANDING THE FIVE OF WANDS

The Five of Wands shows five young men at odds with one another, holding a wand, a symbol of the ego and passion, which links with the card's element of Fire. They all have their own take on a situation, and because they are not acting in harmony as a group, they appear to be getting nowhere. Each is absorbed in his own game: one stands victorious, holding up his wand in triumph; a group of three crosses wands; and a fifth holds his wand over his shoulder, trying to keep it for himself.

These individuals can be seen as the pages of the four minor arcana suits, which approach this contest of strength in different ways. The victorious youth in brown and the youth in green, right in the center of the fight, are fiery Pages of Wands; the youth in blue, holding tight to his prize and showing he can lift its weight, the Page of Pentacles; the aggressor in red, the Page of Swords; and the passive youth in blue and white, defending himself, the Page of Cups. On the kabbalistic Tree of Life, the sphere associated with this card is Geburah, or power—here, the youths make a show of their power, but to no great effect. No one will get hurt; as the Rider-Waite's creator, A. E. Waite, says, "This is mimic warfare" and "a sham fight."

The twelve total buds growing from the wands symbolize budding ideas. The number twelve relates to *Lamed*, the twelfth letter of the Hebrew alphabet, which originally meant to goad—its pictogram represents a staff, or wand.

Five is the number of mankind as well as of the quintessence, or fifth element in alchemy. In the Five of Wands, this suggests that despite ongoing disorder, order can at some point be restored. Like the quintessence, the solution may be invisible now, but it is possible. The chaos will calm, as the next card in the suit sequence is the six, the number of harmony, and the meaning of that card is victory (see page 214).

The card's astrological association of Saturn in Leo presents a conflict—Leo's heady highs and need to show off do not sit easily with the disciplinarian planet Saturn. In the Five of Wands, this brings a sense of frustration, like a fire trying to stay alight despite lashings of rain.

UPRIGHT MEANING

The traditional meaning of this Five of Wands is competition, and the message is to hold your position, rather than compromise. Unlike the Five of Swords, this card does not predict outright battle, but there will be fiery opinions and a lack of agreement, at least for now. Misunderstandings abound, particularly in work matters. You may find yourself in meetings during which everyone is talking at once, defending their position rather than reaching a consensus; it's a fight just to be heard.

Scheduling problems and delays to travel plans are an additional meaning, so double-check travel documents and emails, appointments, accounts, and agendas; pay close attention to any written documents.

The Five of Wands often comes up in readings to show being surrounded by people with strong opinions, particularly in families; in education, it predicts that you will need to compete hard in tests or examinations—but you can succeed. On a lighter note, the card can also show competitions that are important to you, such as sporting events.

REVERSED MEANING

The reversed meaning of the Five of Wands is deception and misinformation. You may be mislead, so carefully consider the source of messages before you make assumptions; what you hear may be exaggerated or untrue. In its most negative aspect, the card can show dishonesty.

In general, the Five of Wands can show you feeling stressed and in a weak position, and if so, it is better to keep your own counsel just for now, or at least be highly selective about the people you choose to trust.

An additional meaning of the card is litigation.

SIX OF WANDS

Element: Fire

Astrological Association:
Jupiter in Leo

Number: 6

Tree of Life Position: Tiphareth, the
sphere of beauty and rebirth

Key Meaning: Victory

UNDERSTANDING THE SIX OF WANDS

A young man on a white charger parades in triumph, wearing a laurel wreath, the Roman symbol of victory and power, echoed by the wreath tied to his wand. The wand through the wreath is a symbol of fertility, of hopes coming to fruition, echoed in the horse's green caparison, the color of nature and new life. The steed is white, for purity of intention. The spectators carry five wands; they might be the five sparring youths from the Five of Wands, now holding their wands upright and orderly, focusing on celebrating the homecoming hero. One of the youths is facing away from us, as if standing guard over the procession, to show that the rider's victory is protected and cannot be challenged.

The horseman can also be seen as an important messenger, bringing great news. The youths may be footmen, making way for the rider on his course to deliver his message to royals or other dignitaries. He has his horse on a tight rein, to show that he has his element, Fire, under control. He may be exuberant, but there is a calmness in his victory that is gracious and stately. This attitude of dignity links with the card's number, six, which stands for harmony and passivity. Six also has the meaning of the past creating the present and future, so we might also assume that the rider's past efforts have been rewarded, which makes for a glowing future.

The Tree of Life sphere associated with this card is Tiphareth, which means beauty and rebirth, which can be interpreted as relating to beauty, or grace, in victory. The card's astrological association of Jupiter in Leo highlights leadership and innovation, and reveals resilience—the ability to overcome minor obstacles and develop a bigger and higher perspective, which is symbolized by the laurel wreath set high on the rider's tall wand.

UPRIGHT MEANING

This card signifies deserved success. The Six of Wands is a very welcome card if you have been struggling recently and feeling unsure if your hard work will finally pay off. The card often relates to work, career, and projects and can show promotion and a new contract or bid; it can also reveal that an outstanding legal matter will go in your favor. Enjoy this happy time and don't be afraid to share your accomplishment; others will support and applaud you. It's time to bask in glory, be self-satisfied, and make space to celebrate, regardless of how busy you may be.

In personal relationships, the card shows that feelings are declared—and will be well received. The card can also indicate a proposal when it appears close to emotion cards such as the Ace of Cups, Two of Cups, Ten of Cups, and the major arcana card VI, The Lovers (see pages 120, 122, 138, and 54). This explains the additional meaning of the Six of Wands for celebrations, such weddings or attending parties and degree ceremonies.

A traditional meaning of the card is good news, which can relate to any life aspect—love, property, education and work, and decision-making. Look to the other cards that appear close to the Six of Wands in a reading to determine the nature of the news on the way.

REVERSED MEANING

Unfortunately, when the Six of Wands reverses, the reward you have hoped for doesn't materialize when you need it to. But all is not lost—this is a card of delay rather than cancellation, so hold fast to your goals. The wait for news may be frustrating, but this is due to circumstances beyond your control rather than a reflection on your abilities. The message is to be as patient as you can, and distract yourself with other tasks (rather than check your emails and text messages every five minutes).

The card can also show you being let down by others, which dints your confidence. However, as with all the tarot's minor arcana cards, this is a passing phase, so try not to take such disappointments to heart.

An additional interpretation is pride, which in the reversed position can reveal an arrogant, self-important individual.

SEVEN OF WANDS

Element: Fire

Astrological Association: Mars in Leo

Number: 7

Tree of Life Position: Netzach, the sphere of endurance, instinct, and desire

Key Meanings: Courage, effort, and challenges

UNDERSTANDING THE SEVEN OF WANDS

The scale of this card is curious—a singular young man dwarfs the landscape at his feet. He is giant-sized, rather like Jonathan Swift's Gulliver in Lilliput, the island of tiny people who ask for Gulliver's help and then seek to punish him when he will not obey their immoral commands. Towering over the small land of hills and the river below, the youth of this Seven of Wands is certainly out of place.

With both hands on the wand, he uses everything in his power to defend his position. Due to his size, he sees the bigger picture, and he has great ideas, symbolized by the five buds on his wand compared with the groups of two and three buds on the six wands before him. His effort is all for a good purpose—he is dressed in green, the color of nature, to symbolize growth, and his hose is orange, the color of his suit element, Fire. He is very sure of his territory, standing astride a river; his position and intentions are clear. Six other wands rise up toward him, but he is ready for the challenge.

The card's astrological association, Mars in Leo, brings together the warlike planet, Mars, with exuberant Leo, creating an unstoppable force. Leo the lion is also depicted in major arcana card VIII, Strength, one of the ancestor cards of the Seven of Wands (see Strength's Reflections at VIII, Strength, on page 62). Netzach, the card's Tree of Life sphere, stands for endurance, which the youth needs to avoid letting his fiery ambition burn out. The twenty total buds on the seven wands can be linked with the Hebrew letter *Resh*, which means success. Victory is within his grasp.

The card's number is the mystical number seven. Seven comprises three, the number of heaven, and four, the number of earth, so the challenge is to bring heaven down to earth—to make your dreams reality (see VII, The Chariot, page 58). In the Seven of Wands, this reward comes from negotiation and courage—standing your ground.

UPRIGHT MEANING

The Seven of Wands reveals obstacles in your path, but you will keep going and overcome them. Success is in reach. The card is particularly relevant to work and career matters and highlights all negotiations; regardless of how difficult the conversation becomes, there's a need to keep talking and stay in conversation until you are satisfied with the outcome. You will need to stand tall, and by being very clear on your position, you can win.

There's a noble aspect, too, about this card, and it often comes up in a reading to show you may be defending others, not just your own interests. In this sense, the Seven of Wands is the card of the advocate, and you may find you need to stand up for those who are not able to speak for themselves. Morality is important to you now, so the Seven of Wands shows you may become the spokesperson for a group—such as a committee or jury. The task isn't an easy one, but you will persist.

In relationships, there are hurdles, and you may need to fight for love. This can be only temporary, however, so by all means stand up for your relationship in the short-term, provided you are sure your partner will return your loyalty.

REVERSED MEANING

When reversed, the Seven of Wands can indicate that you doubt your purpose. You may struggle to be heard and may have to overcome constant obstacles—but now it's unclear if it's all going to be worthwhile. As a result, the card can show anxiety and hesitation. An additional meaning is feeling overwhelmed with continual problems, particularly if this Seven appears with the "burden" card, the Ten of Wands. If so, the message here is to focus on the areas where you can still make a difference, while accepting the things you cannot change. This applies to relationships, too, so ask which imperfections you can live with and which aspects—such as your partner's attitude or circumstances—are nonnegotiable.

EIGHT OF WANDS

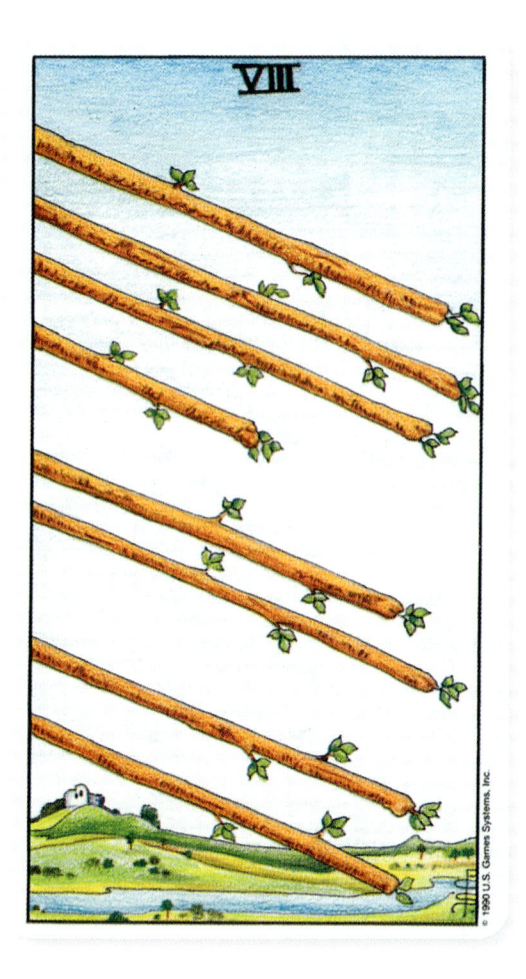

Element: Fire

Astrological Association: Mercury in Sagittarius

Number: 8

Tree of Life Position: Hod, the sphere of majesty and the mind

Key Meanings: News and travel

UNDERSTANDING THE EIGHT OF WANDS

The Eight of Wands shows eight wands, all with green buds, flying through a gray and blue sky. The scene below is very similar to that in the Ace of Wands—a small white dwelling on a hill with green hills and a river below. This is one of two minor arcana cards without people (the other is the Three of Swords), so there is no obvious action to interpret. This is intentional, in that the sole focus is the flight of the wands, giving the card its primary meaning of movement. Simply, we see a flight of wands, ripe with green leaves of potential, over a calm landscape. They may be carrying messages, like carrier pigeons, perhaps fixed to the lower part of the wands that are not visible in the image; perhaps they are spears or love's arrows about to land. However we view these magical wands, all events are about to speed up. The wand motifs take up most of the card's space, dominating everything below.

The card's astrological association is Mercury in Sagittarius. Sagittarius, the sign of exploration, combines with Mercury, the winged messenger, to give the meaning of dynamic movement and travel. An additional quality is perspective and insight—just what we need if we are to effectively deal with this Eight's fast and varied demands. The card's Tree of Life sphere is Hod, which relates to the power of the mind: Creative thinking, logic, and a sharp wit are called for.

The card's number is eight, which stands for both stability and renewal (see also card VIII, Strength, page 62). The eights in the minor arcana, as they are near the end of the numbered sequences, hold all our experiences up to that point. We have past knowledge to draw upon, which gives us wisdom and enables new choices—to make new contacts and find a fresh direction.

UPRIGHT MEANING

Along with the Ace, the Eight of Wands is one of the most positive cards of the suit. It brings lots of communication, so you may be inundated with emails, calls, and exciting offers. If you have felt held back, or stuck waiting for decisions, you will soon have positive news. All your projects grow wings, moving swiftly forward. Just be prepared for the shift; fast, frantic events will energize you, but you will also need to prioritize any offers. Don't feel you have to say yes to everything. Choose wisely and enjoy this frenetic, exciting influence.

In relationships, the Eight of Wands can bring great news about love, particularly if you have been separated from a partner recently or are waiting to hear from a potential partner. You may be traveling soon to see one another.

Additionally, the card has often come up in readings to show the professions of carpentry and scaffolding— work that involves using or building a framework.

REVERSED MEANING

When reversed, the simple meaning of the card is delay. You may have lots of pending work to finish and may be waiting for a particular decision that will unblock other ambitions, but just for now, you'll need to be patient. It's also important to be discreet about any grievances you have just now.

In relationships, you may be finding it hard to communicate and as a result be drawn into petty arguments. If you have hopes for a new love, you may be feeling disappointed by the person's lack of contact. Look to the surrounding cards for indictors as to what this means; negative cards such as the Three or Ten of Swords or The Lovers reversed (see pages 180, 194, and 54) suggest that this potential relationship may not get off the ground. More positive cards, such as the upright Lovers or the Ace, Two, Six, Nine, or Ten of Cups (see pages 54, 120, 122, 130, 136, and 138), say that there is still hope you'll connect again. An additional meaning of the reversed card is jealousy.

NINE OF WANDS

Element: Fire

Astrological Association: Moon in Sagittarius

Number: 9

Tree of Life Position: Yesod, the sphere of foundation and the unconscious mind

Key Meanings: Defense and strength

UNDERSTANDING THE NINE OF WANDS

A wounded man is on the lookout. Among eight protective wands, symbols of his resources and responsibilities, he holds a ninth tightly with both hands, like a weapon. The other eight wands are orderly, as if standing at attention, ready for any eventuality.

He has positioned himself on a man-made platform, which relates to his Tree of Life sphere, Yesod, or foundation. He has a solid base from which to operate. The platform also sets our would-be warrior away from the green hills behind him; he needs to be a little detached from society so he can better see the approach of potential opponents. And physically, this defender is not to be taken lightly. With his powerful build, he symbolizes strength and endurance; from experience, he has learned to expect challenges to his position, and his past battles are symbolized by the bandage worn around his head. This injury doesn't deter him, and he almost wears it like a bandana, with pride.

The card's astrological association, Moon in Sagittarius, shows great resilience and strength of character—it combines the sensitive mind, the Moon, with the Sagittarian qualities of directness, perception, and the willingness to take risks. This combination may also reveal a need to explore hidden factors, to dig deep to get to the truth.

The card's number is nine, comprising three sets of three. Three is a dynamic number, and when multiplied by itself, symbolizes intense productivity. It also holds the threes as a symbol of the integration of mind, body, and spirit. In the Nine of Wands, all the wands of the previous suit cards accumulate. This reflects the wisdom of experience, but also the responsibility of accrued demands and pressure that is expressed in card Ten, "the burden." By keeping his wands in order in the Nine, the inevitable buildup of untenable demands expressed in the Ten can be avoided.

UPRIGHT MEANING

The upright Nine of Wands shows that you are in a very strong position. You have fought long and hard to get where you are, and have endured heavy challenges, particularly in work. Being constantly vigilant and ingenious can be exhausting, however, so use your energy wisely; plan all activities meticulously and don't overexert yourself, and you will have all the resources you need to see you through. Thankfully, as with all minor arcana cards, this influence will not last forever. You won't always need to defend yourself to this degree, or make so many sacrifices.

This card also highlights the fine balance between being adequately defended and being defensive. While it's appropriate to establish and protect your boundaries, defensiveness keeps you in a negative mind-set; the Nine often comes up in a reading to show a person who is fearful that his or her idea or other work will be stolen—but this is just a perception rather than reality. It can also show an unwillingness to hand in an assignment or to make your work public in some other way due to fear of rejection or criticism. If so, it's time to let go—you have worked hard, and your efforts will meet with appreciation and support.

REVERSED MEANING

When the Nine of Wands is reversed, you endure strong opposition, which seems unfair. You put in hard work—but receive little thanks in return. You give your all, but it still doesn't seem to be enough, so you may be at the mercy of an unreasonable boss or demanding children, friends, or clients. This situation is demotivating, so you become fixed on getting through tasks without enjoying the aspects of your work that used to be satisfying. Equally, you could be the one who is obstinate and inflexible in your attitude.

The reversed card can also show issues with boundaries. Someone may be invading your territory. In relationships, you may be dealing with an individual who is acting defensively because you are veering into uncomfortable territory for them.

TEN OF WANDS

Element: Fire

Astrological Association:
Saturn in Sagittarius

Number: 10

Tree of Life Position: Malkuth, the
Kingdom, the sphere of experience

Key Meanings: Responsibilities and
a burden

UNDERSTANDING THE TEN OF WANDS

A blond man is striding toward a house he can't see. He knows it is there—perhaps he has visited before, which might explain his confident step. There's an element of desperation here, too: Why would he choose to be so uncomfortable and sightless on his journey? He even chooses to hold his wands so his right hand is in front of his eyes, further blocking the view. Perhaps he sees himself as less than human, a blind beast desperate to release its burden.

The man's determination to arrive at his destination is symbolized by his orange tunic, representing his suit's element of Fire, for passion and energy. And the destination looks worthwhile: We see fertile lands, with rolling hills, trees, and a field ploughed and ready for planting—maybe his ten wands will grow there into strong trees. To the right is a manor house, symbolizing that hard work now will pay off in the future if our laborer can endure the load and keep going. This links with the card's astrological association of Saturn in Sagittarius; Sagittarius's need for freedom and travel is eclipsed by the dour taskmaster planet, Saturn. In this sense, the Ten of Wands suggests the struggle between grinding work and keeping our dreams alive.

In numerology, the number ten represents completeness and perfection. In the Ten of Wands, however, the impact of ten wands of Fire is exhausting, both emotionally and financially. The individual sphere associated with this card is Malkuth, for kingdom—so the Ten of Wands in this sense suggests taking on the whole kingdom, or world, which can be both a burden and a burning ambition.

UPRIGHT MEANING

The upright Ten of Wands reveals that you are carrying too much on your shoulders just now. You may have become so used to being overloaded that you've lost sight of the reason you're doing the work. It's a common card for homemakers and entrepreneurs, those of you who must multitask and constantly respond to a wide range of demands. Consider saying no to any future requests and decide which projects or jobs you can stop or hand over to someone else. There's a real need here for delegation and support from others. No one expects you to carry this on your own, and this goes for emotional burdens, too—they need to be shared. The card can also suggest that you may be carrying issues from the past. On a more positive note, the card reveals that you can be successful, albeit with careful management of time and resources.

This card can show up in a reading to reveal that you may need to look for less demanding work, but you feel too drained by your present job to spend time searching. This puts you in a catch-22: The situation can't change until you pull back from current responsibilities and invest what energy you possess into changing your circumstances. The Ten of Wands can also show that relationships are neglected because all your attention is on work.

Also note that if the Ten of Wands comes up as the you/situation card in a reading, you or the person you are reading for may not be receptive to the reading simply because too much is going on. Lay the cards again or wait three days.

REVERSED MEANING

When reversed, the card's meaning is very similar to that of the upright card, except that some of the burdens may be more perceived than real. This may be a sign of ongoing stress, where every task gets framed as a potential problem. The message here is to try to lighten up a little and take some of the pressure off yourself—you don't need to be perfect. Obstinacy is one of the card's meanings, so do ask yourself if you have created too much self-pressure, fixating on impossible goals.

The reversed card can also show you being caught in an exhausting grind between work and domestic commitments because you are trying to keep everyone happy. Make a vow to make some space for your own needs—you need to please yourself, too. When you can do this, you'll see the way ahead more clearly.

PAGE OF WANDS

Element: Earth of the suit of Fire

Key Meanings: Good news and communication

UNDERSTANDING THE PAGE OF WANDS

The Page of Wands is looking upward toward the top of his wand, out of which are growing tiny leaf buds. The red plume on his hat looks like a flame, linking with the element of his suit—he is burning with ambition. The Page's tall wand is higher than him, showing that his ideas are greater than his experience, but he is inspired to overcome any shortfall in his knowledge with enthusiasm. His passion will propel him forward as he sees the potential in everything.

The card's element is Earth of Fire, which is the most grounded aspect of the passionate Fire element of this suit. The Earth and Fire elements combine in the pyramids, to the right of the picture—they comprise a square base (the square is an Earth symbol) and triangular sides (the triangle is a symbol of Fire). The pyramids also signify grand design, establishment, and wisdom—to which our ingénue Page aspires. He wears orange hose, the color of his Fire element, and a tunic decorated with black salamanders, creatures with legendary fireproof skin. The yellow background of the tunic fabric and the trim of the Page's boots echo the yellow tunic of the Fool (see page 30), who too aims to set the world alight.

The Page's wand, with its five buds, echoes nature and growth. He may be in an arid desert land, but he has the resources to succeed.

Pages and Knights in tarot are generally regarded as people or influences, whereas the other court cards (the Queens and Kings) are assumed to be people. Let your intuition guide you toward the most appropriate meaning for the Page in a reading by working with the card's imagery first, then the written interpretations here (see also the Introduction, page 8).

UPRIGHT MEANING

As an influence: The Page of Wands in a reading brings good news about projects and any situation that requires negotiation. Messages, urgent emails, and phone calls keep you busy and may be demanding, but cool the fire a little and take a measured view before you react and assess just how much work you need to do. The atmosphere overall, however, is one of trust, and you can rely upon information you receive. Pages, with their youth, suggest young, or new, situations, from relationships to work.

The Page of Wands can bring a creative enterprise or job offer—and, while the status of the job may not be as high as you might expect, the overall package may appeal, at least in theory. Do, however, check the details and practicalities before you agree to anything.

As a person: A talkative, entertaining individual, the Page of Wands often turns up in reading to denote a writer. His wand is his pen, his way to express himself in the world at large. Equally, he may be a marketing executive, salesperson, actor, or team manager—any role that relies on personality and great communication skills. This Page is a hard worker, dedicated and enthusiastic, and charming company. He can influence others—just be aware that he can get bored easily and move on to whatever attracts him next (so if you see

him as a potential lover, note his actions as well as his words). An additional interpretation of the Page is a reunion with a friend or old colleague with whom you will enjoy chatting and reminiscing.

As the "you" card in a reading: Express yourself.

If two or more Pages fall close together in a reading, the meanings are as follows:

- **Two Pages:** Friendship if upright; rivalry if one or both cards are reversed

- **Three Pages:** Lots of social activities

- **Four Pages:** A social group of young people

REVERSED MEANING

When reversed, the Page of Wands brings delays. Emails and other messages go astray and communication gets complicated. As a person, the Page reversed talks much like his upright counterpart, but the theme of the conversation is negative and rather relentless. As the upright Page holds fast to his goals, so the reversed Page won't let a morose subject drop. The card can also show stubbornness and an inability to listen to others' opinions.

This Page is fickle and does not follow through what he initiates. Eventually, his enthusiasm or obsessions burn out, he becomes easily bored or distracted, and he leaves you to deal with any fallout.

An additional meaning is problems with literacy and can apply to a child or young person struggling with written communication or speech.

KNIGHT OF WANDS

KNIGHT *of* WANDS.

Element: Fire of Fire

Astrological Associations: Scorpio and Sagittarius

Key Meaning: Speed and action

UNDERSTANDING THE KNIGHT OF WANDS

A horse appears to be dancing in the desert, near some pyramids. There's a flamboyant rider, full of verve and vigor; holding a wand, this Knight is on a mission to deliver a message.

The card's element is Fire of the suit of Fire. Fire doubled is a hot mix of passion, ambition, and desire, expressed in many of the card's motifs. The horse's mane and the Knight's red plume, sleeve, and saddle resemble flames; the three pyramids on the left of the card, with their triangular sides, link with the Fire element; and the Knight's tunic has a pattern of black salamanders, the creatures with legendary fireproof skin (see the Page of Wands, page 224). The wand itself can be seen as a torch, the carrier of a flame. The yellow tunic stands for the light of the sun, or the mind and conscious illumination.

Although the card's imagery speaks of fiery ambition and desire, there's no sense of chaos, danger, or imminent battle. The horse's reins are short and tight, which at first glance gives the impression that the horse is dancing or performing dressage. The Knight has control over the primal urges of the animal and knows when to give free rein and when to hold back.

The wand has no flame, but it is living wood, sprouting five buds, symbols of news and ideas. The number five in the tarot's minor arcana suits also indicates tests—with the Knight of Wands, the test is to control fiery impulses and manage our energy and talent to achieve success, much like the charioteer of card VII, The Chariot (see page 58). The three, the number of pyramids on the card, is a dynamic number, for creativity and production (see also card III, The Empress, page 42).

Knights and Pages in tarot are generally regarded as people or influences, whereas the other court cards (the Queens and Kings) are assumed to be people. Let your intuition guide you toward the most appropriate meaning for the Knight in a reading by working with the card's imagery first, then the written interpretations here (see also the Introduction, page 8).

UPRIGHT MEANING

As an influence: Events speed up. Any blocks to progress will be lifted, so this is a welcome card if you have been waiting for decisions or have generally been feeling stuck. You can now have the conversations and action you need to move your projects on; follow your intuition and push forward. This card is particularly auspicious for moving house, finding new work, and making progress on personal and professional projects.

In readings, this Knight often appears to predict a successful writing project. In other creative pursuits, you attract acknowledgment and support, both emotionally and financially.

An additional meaning of the card is travel and emigration.

As a person: Creative and dynamic, the Knight of Wands is an innovator and likes to do things his way. He inspires those around him and is excellent at networking to promote his ideas. He may be a traveler or visitor, and he will have had many experiences and stories to tell. He is, however, impatient to get things done and can make snap judgements about people

based on first impressions. As a potential partner, he can show a charismatic, talkative individual who may take things a little too fast at first.

As the "you" card in a reading: Fire up your ambition.

If two or more Knights fall close together in a reading, the meanings are as follows:

- **Two Knights:** Friendship if upright; rivalry if one or both cards are reversed

- **Three Knights:** Men meeting up

- **Four Knights:** Lots of action; events speed up

REVERSED MEANING

In general, the reversed Knight of Wands reveals a creative block or miscommunication—so emails go astray and other messages are not delivered. The reversed Knight also indicates delays and deferred decisions; you may feel frustrated at the lack of progress. Know that this influence is temporary and will pass. In the meantime, hold fast to your plans and your self-belief.

As a person, the reversed Knight is egotistical. He thrives on status but is generally unwilling to do any hard work to deserve it; regardless, he will step up to take the credit. Insincere and attention-seeking, he acts out of self-interest.

QUEEN OF WANDS

QUEEN *of* WANDS.

Element: Water of the suit of Fire

Astrological Associations: Pisces and Aries

Chakras: Sacral, throat, and third eye, for creativity, communication and insight

Key Meanings: Creativity and focus

UNDERSTANDING THE QUEEN OF WANDS

The Queen of Wands is an aspect of card III, The Empress, or mother archetype. She is the soul aspect of the mother, just as The Queen of Cups is the heart aspect and the Queen of Swords, the mind (see pages 144, 200, and The Empress, page 42).

The most vital of the four Queens, the Queen of Wands sits directly facing us, holding a tall wand, her suit symbol of creativity and purpose. Like the Magician (see page 34), she manifests her ideas to follow her soul's path. The wood of the wand is alive with green shoots; it is the Queen's job to see them thrive. In her left hand is a sunflower, a solar symbol for energy, growth, and illumination. Three tiny buds shoot from the upper part of the wand. Three is a dynamic number of creation, and also the number of her ancestor card, the Empress.

The red-haired Queen's suit element is Fire, shown in many motifs on her card. Robed in gold, her throne is decorated with sunflowers and heraldic lions in orange, the color of flames. Low pyramids appear to her left. The triangle shape of the pyramids is a symbol for Fire in alchemy, and these ancient structures also offer a metaphor for this Queen's strong foundation in the world.

Along with Fire, her suit element, the Queen also takes Water, the element of all the Queens. The combination of Fire and Water reveals the careful balancing of emotion and ideas to create conditions for success. Both practical and cerebral, she is highly resourceful, knowing when to draw upon her Fire energy to take action or attune to her Water emotions to show sensitivity to her environment and others' needs.

In esoteric tarot, the Queen of Wands is associated with the leopard, but in the Rider-Waite deck, she is shown with a black cat, a sign of magic—the witch's familiar. The statuary lions on each side of her throne symbolize Sekhmet, an ancient Egyptian lioness deity associated with Bastet, depicted originally as a lioness and later as a cat. The Queen of Wands wears a red cat brooch at her heart, a Bastet amulet, which symbolizes power, protection, and pleasure.

Queens and Kings in tarot are traditionally regarded as people in your life or people about to come into your orbit. However, you can also read the Queen as a general influence, so this interpretation is included last.

UPRIGHT MEANING

As a person: This Queen is often the card of the artisan, entrepreneur, counselor, organizer, or leader—the writer, producer, marketer, or business administrator: whatever relies upon spark and communication for success. Sociable and supportive, she is intensely loyal, just like her associated sign of Aries. This self-aware Queen is also in touch with her intuition, so she makes good choices in relationships. The Queen of Wands often loves nature and animals, too.

As an influence: Ideas flourish, and you can now show others what you can do. This is no time for reticence; fire up your enthusiasm and express yourself.

Reflect, also, on how you are managing your life just now, to make sure you have the time to make space for the opportunities coming your way. Overall, though, the Queen of Wands shows you will have the strength you need, and your relationships, too, are energized—romance, friendships, family ties, and professional contacts.

As the "you" card in a reading: Step in to your power.

If two or more Queens fall close together in a reading, the meanings are as follows:

- **Two Queens:** Rivalry

- **Three Queens:** Helpful friends

- **Four Queens:** Women meeting up

REVERSED MEANING

You may feel controlled when the Queen of Wands reverses due to others' pointless interference. There is a great need for organization—but disorder rules. This may be because you, or someone close, has taken on too much and cannot admit it. Consider if this is a pattern—a way of avoiding being who you are, due to fear of rejection.

As a person, the reversed Queen of Wands breaks promises. She can be envious and does not want anyone around her to shine more brightly.

KING OF WANDS

KING *of* WANDS.

© 1990 U.S. Games Systems, Inc.

Element: Air of the suit of Fire

Astrological Associations: Cancer and Leo

Chakras: The sacral, throat, and third eye, for creativity, communication, and insight

Key Meaning: An honorable man

UNDERSTANDING THE KING OF WANDS

The King of Wands is an aspect of card IV, The Emperor, or father archetype, who brings structure, order, and authority. The King of Wands is the father-aspect of the Emperor who offers inspiration and communication.

The King's robe and the back of his throne are decorated with black salamanders, the creatures who have legendary fireproof skin (see also the Knight and Page of Wands, pages 226 and 224). A live salamander appears to the right of the card to reinforce its importance as a symbol of the King's suit element of Fire. Lions also decorate the throne, and the King wears a lion-head amulet around his neck, a symbol of strength and protection linking with one of his zodiac signs, Leo the Lion.

His wand has four buds, which relate to the number of his ancestor card IV, The Emperor, and also symbolizes the four elements. His crown, cuffs, and cape have flame motifs, and he wears a fiery orange robe and cloak. His cap is red—at first glance, it would appear he has red hair, but this is actually called a "cap of maintenance," worn by nobility and the other three minor arcana Kings (see pages 146, 174, and 202), that fits under a crown. Red and orange denote passion in the real world—or fiery ambition.

The card's element is Air of Fire, which can be interpreted as fire that breathes. The more air a fire has to burn, the brighter the fire and higher the flames. This also reveals the King's challenge: to keep feeding his desires without burning himself out. The green of his cowl and shoes symbolizes nature and wood, which feeds a fire, so he is mindful that to thrive, he needs to be in a productive, supportive environment.

Kings and Queens in tarot are traditionally regarded as people in your life or people about to come into your orbit. However, you can also read the King as a general influence, so this interpretation is included last.

UPRIGHT MEANING

As a person: This King of Wands is a man of the world, and it's likely that he has traveled widely, experiencing many cultures and countries. Talkative and energetic, his ideal vocations include business and management, communications and marketing, the travel industry, acting, and other roles that depend on self-motivation and individuality. He may be self-employed, running a business or acting as a freelance consultant.

His has wisdom, very high standards that he applies to himself and those around him, and strong integrity. Courteous and considerate, he stays true to his values and acts according to his moral code. He is open and self-aware and does not judge other people on their backgrounds or beliefs; he often learns by listening to people talk about their experiences. As a free spirit, he respects others who don't conform. As a potential partner, he is passionate and communicative.

As an influence: This is the right time to express your ideas and be the individual you are. Summon your entrepreneurial spirit, make a plan, and what you propose will be well received. The practical support you need will be there, but you need to be the initiator. What you do now reflects your truth. Don't let perfectionism get in the way of your creativity—what you do is more than good enough.

As the "you" card in a reading: Be a free spirit.

If two or more Kings fall close together in a reading, the meanings are as follows:

- **Two Kings:** A good partnership

- **Three Kings:** Influential men

- **Four Kings:** A power battle

REVERSED MEANING

This card reversed indicates a time of restriction when you can't get others to see your point of view. Equally, check that you're not going against your intuition if you feel you're not following the right path—drop the self-pressure and be open to alternative routes.

Bullying, selfish, and opinionated, the reversed King as a person is narrow-minded and obsessive about rules. He can be an overbearing manager or a strict parental figure. He does not want to listen to anyone who doesn't agree with him, and full of self-interest, he is determined to get his own way.

6

LOVE AND ROMANCE SPREADS

THESE LOVE LAYOUTS ARE PERFECT FOR EVERY STAGE in a relationship or potential partnership. Whether you're enchanted by a brand-new partner or caught in a love dilemma, overwhelmed by the affections of two people (if so, lucky you!), this selection of spreads helps you view your situation in the light of a love that lasts or a passion that ignites, burns bright—and then disappears. Two of the most frequent love questions asked in readings are, "When will I meet a partner?" and "Will they come back into my life—or is it really over?" That's why this chapter includes spreads that offer insight into each and every one of these affairs of the heart. And to finish on a lighthearted note, take a look at Solitaire's Oracle, the spread used in the famous Bond movie *Live and Let Die*, and discover what your Bond, or Bondette, is really up to.

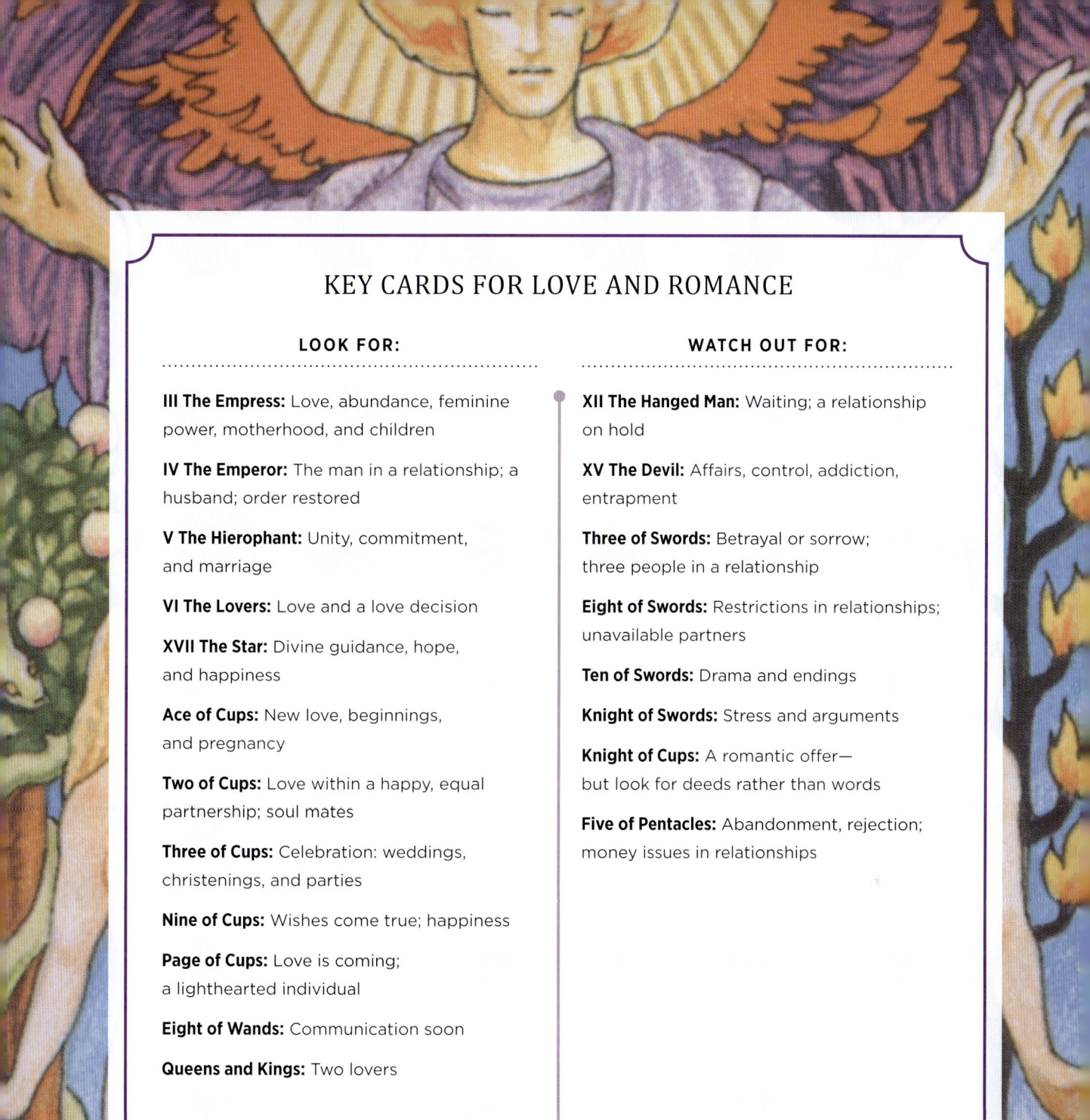

KEY CARDS FOR LOVE AND ROMANCE

LOOK FOR:

III The Empress: Love, abundance, feminine power, motherhood, and children

IV The Emperor: The man in a relationship; a husband; order restored

V The Hierophant: Unity, commitment, and marriage

VI The Lovers: Love and a love decision

XVII The Star: Divine guidance, hope, and happiness

Ace of Cups: New love, beginnings, and pregnancy

Two of Cups: Love within a happy, equal partnership; soul mates

Three of Cups: Celebration: weddings, christenings, and parties

Nine of Cups: Wishes come true; happiness

Page of Cups: Love is coming; a lighthearted individual

Eight of Wands: Communication soon

Queens and Kings: Two lovers

WATCH OUT FOR:

XII The Hanged Man: Waiting; a relationship on hold

XV The Devil: Affairs, control, addiction, entrapment

Three of Swords: Betrayal or sorrow; three people in a relationship

Eight of Swords: Restrictions in relationships; unavailable partners

Ten of Swords: Drama and endings

Knight of Swords: Stress and arguments

Knight of Cups: A romantic offer— but look for deeds rather than words

Five of Pentacles: Abandonment, rejection; money issues in relationships

SPREADS FOR NEW LOVE

THE HEART: HAVE I MET "THE ONE?"

We've all asked ourselves this essential question at some point in our romantic lives. Is it time to invest emotionally in this relationship? Will it last, and will it be worthwhile? To give you the insight you need, this reading really helps you connect with your intuition and emotions—the only true sources of guidance when it comes to matters of the heart.

First, shuffle and choose your cards (see page 16), laying them all face down before you in the order shown below. Then turn all the cards face up, and interpret them according to their position.

Now look at the suits of any minor arcana cards you have. The suit of a card reveals at a glance the way in which you relate to one another.

- **Swords:** A relationship based on the mind and a strong physical attraction

- **Wands:** Soulful passion: speed and intensity

- **Cups:** A deep emotional bond

- **Pentacles:** Shared values and a slow-burn love that lasts

Interpret the cards in order (see chapters 4 and 5). If your outcome card doesn't give you an instant yes or no—in that its meaning is not overtly positive or negative—see page 23 for the full list of "yes," "no," and "neutral" cards. Your answer lies therein.

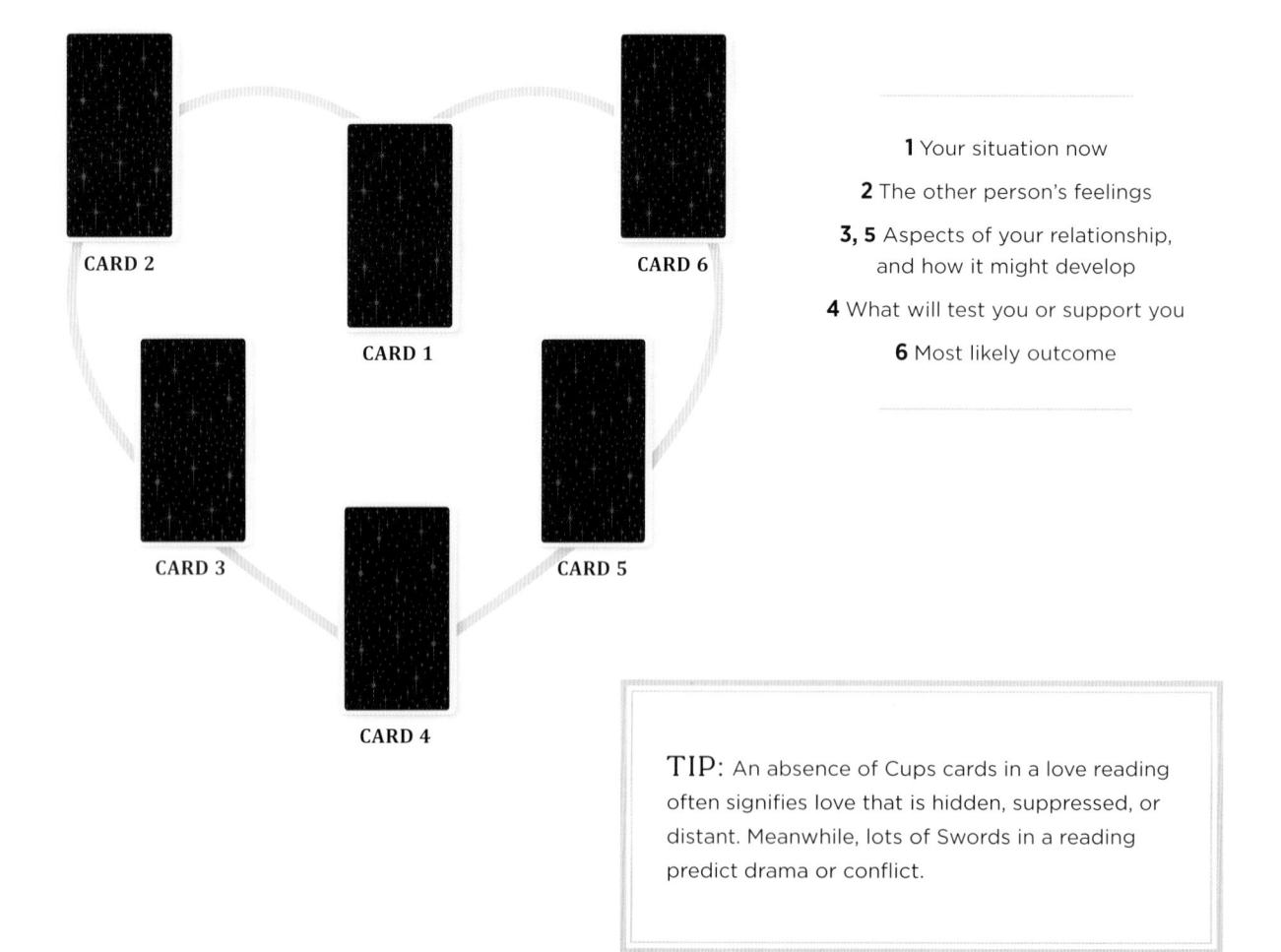

CARD 2

CARD 6

CARD 1

CARD 3

CARD 5

CARD 4

1 Your situation now

2 The other person's feelings

3, 5 Aspects of your relationship, and how it might develop

4 What will test you or support you

6 Most likely outcome

TIP: An absence of Cups cards in a love reading often signifies love that is hidden, suppressed, or distant. Meanwhile, lots of Swords in a reading predict drama or conflict.

LOVE'S TRUTH:
DO THEY FEEL THE SAME?

This layout can give insight into your relationship, because it shows both your perspective (the cards on the left) and your current, former, or prospective partner's attitudes and feelings (the cards on the right).

To begin this reading, take card VI The Lovers, from the deck and lay it in the center, as shown. This card is the Significator: It stands for love and future choices. Then shuffle and cut the remaining cards (see page 16), and lay them out, face down, in the order shown below.

First, turn over cards 1 to 6, face up, leaving cards 7, 8, and 9 face down. To interpret the cards, read your perspective first (1, 3, and 5), then the other person's perspective (2, 4, and 6). Then look at card 3, The Lovers, and card 4 together: This reveals your position now, this moment, as lovers or potential lovers. Next, turn over cards 7, 8, and 9 to see the outcome, and to discover where your relationship might go.

S Significator: VI The Lovers

1, 3, 5 How you see the relationship

2, 4, 6 How they see the relationship

7, 8, 9 The outcome

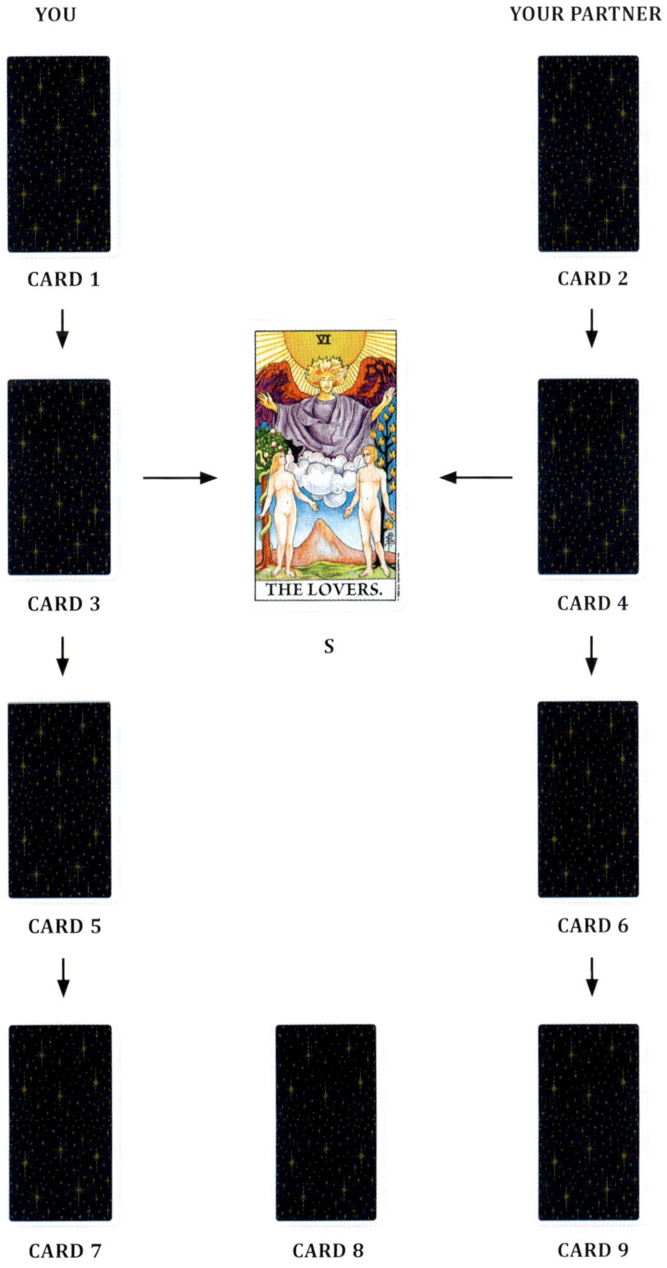

YOU

YOUR PARTNER

CARD 1

CARD 2

CARD 3

THE LOVERS.

CARD 4

S

CARD 5

CARD 6

CARD 7

CARD 8

CARD 9

Example: Sasha's Reading

Sasha, whose four-year relationship with Amelia had ended, wanted to see whether there might be any chance that they'd get back together. Did she still have feelings for her?

The Sun reveals the happiness that was present in the relationship before their issues arose. Justice reversed shows that Sasha feels she'd been unfairly treated, while the Four of Swords shows Sasha's retreat from the relationship. The Four also reveals that she'd found the problems and process of separating very stressful. Amelia's cards—2, 4, and 6, on the right—showed two women, the Queen of Wands and the Queen of Pentacles. Sasha felt the Queen of Pentacles represented herself, while the Queen of Wands represented another woman Amelia had begun seeing after the split. The Two of Pentacles showed that Amelia was unsure where her future lay, and she needed to make a choice.

Sasha viewed the outcome cards— the Three of Pentacles, for acknowledgment, and the Six for generosity—as a sign that their relationship still had value. She also noted that the Six could show that she'd need to be generous in forgiving Amelia for seeing another woman so soon after their separation, while Amelia needed to be honest about her past actions (implicit in Judgement). Judgement, as the major arcana card of the last trio, spoke loudest to Sasha, and she reflected on its meaning, which includes reviewing the past, second chances, and renewal.

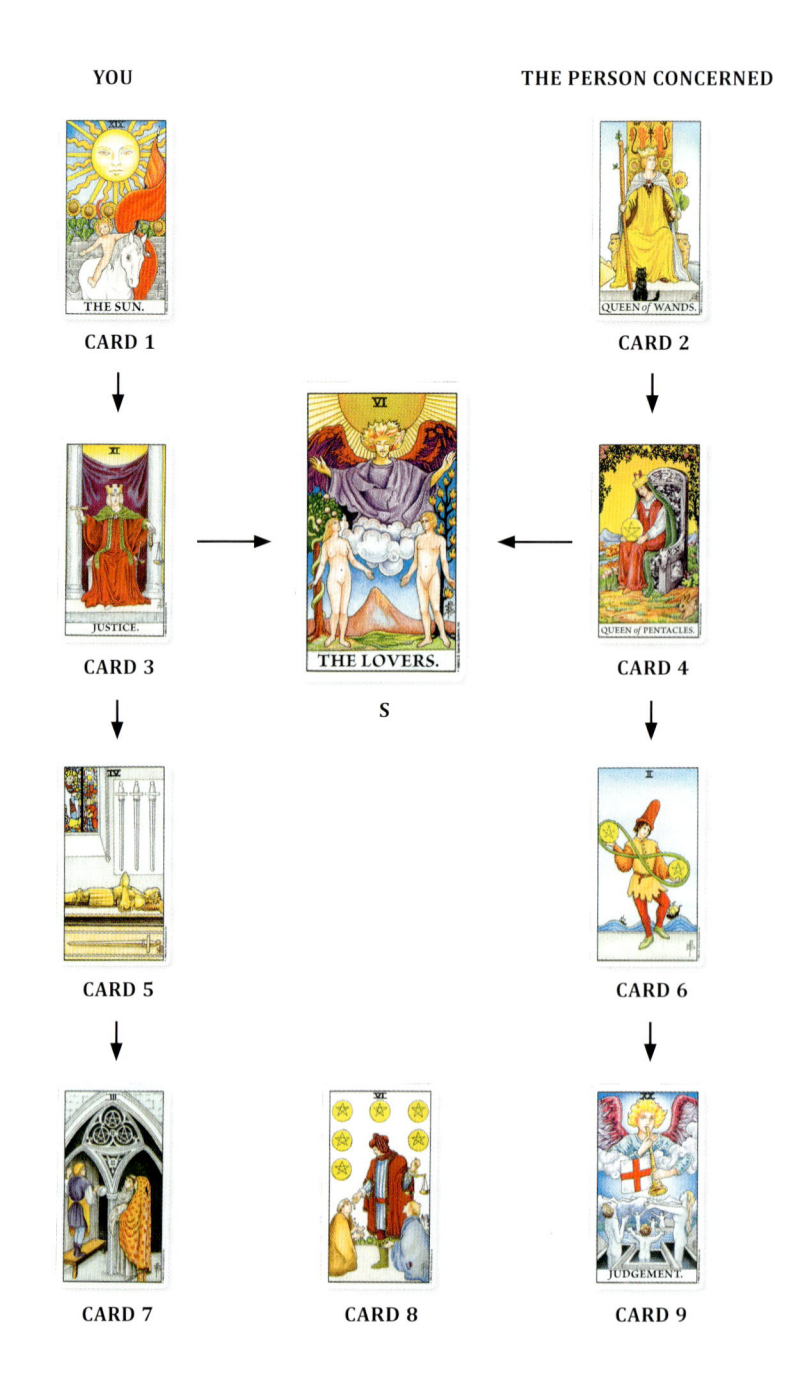

YOU   THE PERSON CONCERNED

CARD 1   CARD 2

CARD 3   CARD 4

S

CARD 5   CARD 6

CARD 7   CARD 8   CARD 9

THE LILY: WILL LOVE GROW?

The fleur-de-lis is a trifold symbol of mind, body, and soul; when we are in love, we love with the heart, the body, and the spirit—all three at once.

In this layout, the cards form the shape of the lily to divine how your relationship might flourish. Cards 1 and 2 reveal your situation and what you show the world: They form the shape of the lily's stem and protective cup. Cards 3, 4, and 5 are the three petals, which show inner, or secret, values at work, and which reveal the most likely outcome.

1 You

2 The nature of the relationship

3 Emotions

4 Hidden factors

5 The outcome

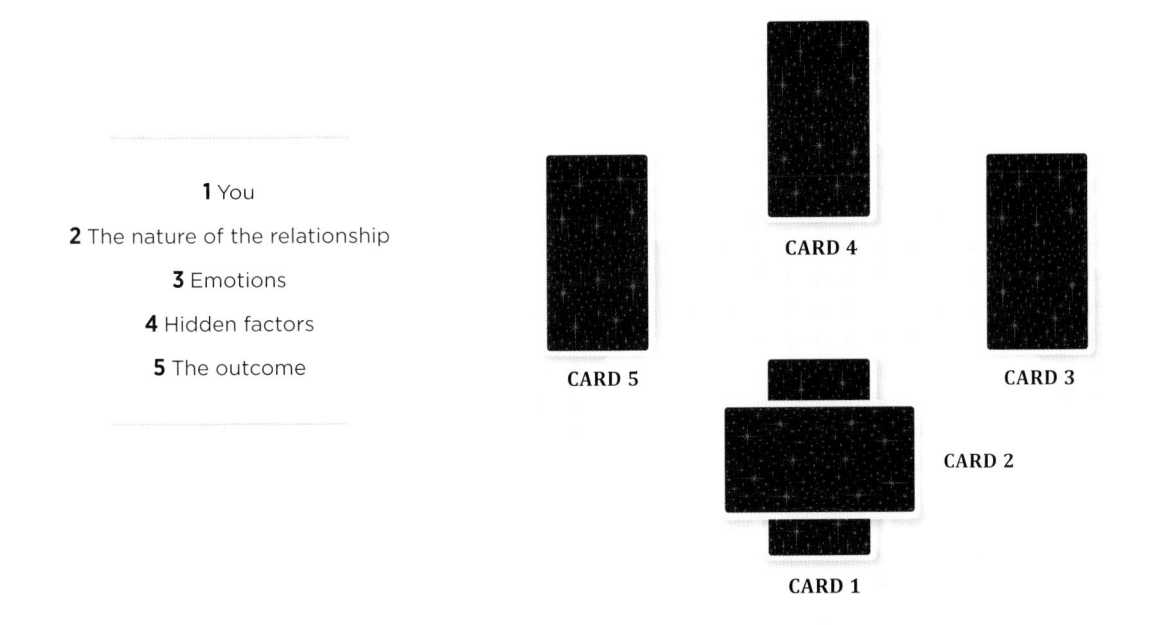

Shuffle and choose your cards (see page 16) and lay them face down in the layout shown above. Then turn all the cards face up, and interpret them in order to reveal your relationship story.

SPREADS FOR FUTURE LOVE

DIVINE YOUR LOVER:
WHEN WILL I MEET A NEW PARTNER?

Take out The Lovers card and place it face up as shown. Then shuffle the remaining deck and choose your cards (see page 16), placing them face down, following the layout above. Now turn over cards 1 to 4 face up and begin your interpretation.

Example: Rhianne's Reading

Rhianne's card 1 was The Queen of Cups—a loving, nurturing woman. This indicated to Rhianne that she was ready for a new relationship now. Her card 2, for the present month of March, was The Hermit—a time for introspection instead of forging new connections. April's card, 3, was The Fool, indicating new adventures and risks, while card 4 for May was The Ace of Cups, which suggests new beginnings—including falling in love.

CARD 2

CARD 2

S   CARD 1   CARD 3

S   CARD 1   CARD 3

1 Are you ready for love now?

   2 This month

   3 Next month

   4 Month after

CARD 4

CARD 4

TIP: Don't be concerned if you don't see positive love cards the first time you try this spread. We all have free will, and our lives change from day to day depending on our decisions. The more open and positive you feel about meeting someone, the more likely it is to happen. Repeat the reading every week and you'll see, hopefully, that love is beginning to come closer. You can use your own thoughts to bring the future forward.

SPREADS FOR LOVE COMPLICATIONS

THE LOVE STAR: COSMIC LOVE OR CATASTROPHE?

This is a great spread, and it illuminates those really intense connections we experience from time to time—when the bond between you and your partner is so powerful that it's almost overwhelming. Need to know whether your high-octane love will last or burn out in a fiery blaze? Read on!

CARD 5

CARD 7

CARD 1

CARD 2

CARD 3

CARD 6

CARD 4

1, 2 You and the person in question

3 Positive aspect of your relationship (the past)*

4 Challenging aspect of your relationship (the past)*

5 Positive future aspect

6 Challenging future aspect

7 Outcome

* If your relationship is very new, interpret cards 3 and 4 as what you're bringing to the relationship—both the positive aspects and the challenges.

Shuffle and choose your cards (see page 16), and lay them out as shown above, placing card 1 face up and card 2 on top of it, face down. Then lay out the other cards, from 3 to 7, all face down.

Open up cards 1 and 2 so that they're side by side. One card represents you, and the other represents your partner. Turn over all the remaining cards and interpret them in the usual way.

VENUS'S LOVE TRIANGLE: LOVE OR WAR?

Venus, the Roman goddess of love, had an ugly husband called Hephaestus and a hot lover, Mars, the god of war. This spread reveals the choice you might make between two potential lovers. Will passion mature into love—or will it turn into a full-blown battle?

S Significator: overall theme of the reading

1 Person or situation

2 Person or situation

3 Guidance: solution or outcome

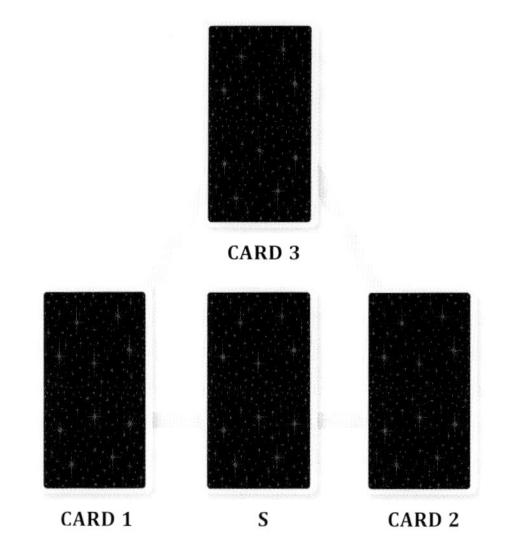

CARD 3

CARD 1   S   CARD 2

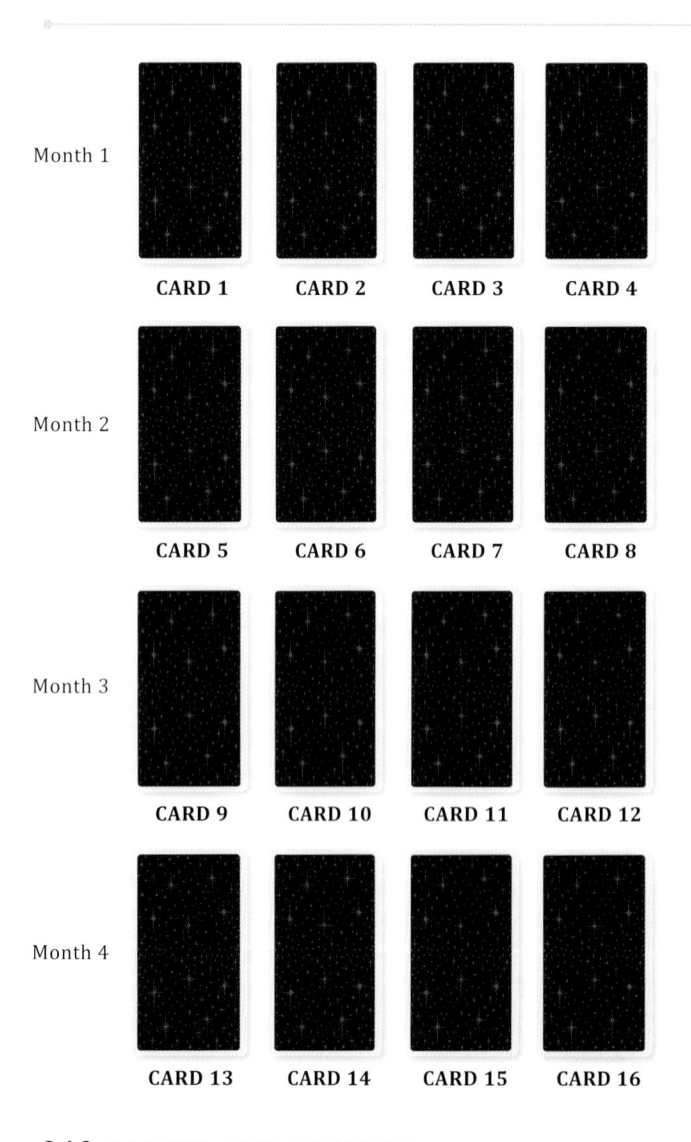

Month 1

CARD 1   CARD 2   CARD 3   CARD 4

Month 2

CARD 5   CARD 6   CARD 7   CARD 8

Month 3

CARD 9   CARD 10   CARD 11   CARD 12

Month 4

CARD 13   CARD 14   CARD 15   CARD 16

LOVE'S RENEWAL: WILL THEY COME BACK?

This is one of the most frequently asked questions in tarot readings. Uncertainty after a breakup or confusion in a new relationship often guides people to their first tarot readings. That's because they can't move on with their lives without knowing whether or not their relationship will reignite.

Take a card that represents your person. Choose from the Court cards: Pick a Page, Knight, King, or Queen of any suit. Now shuffle that card back into the deck. Focus on your question as you shuffle. Then lay down the cards in four groups of four.

Each card represents one week, beginning with the present week and moving into the next four months. Turn over all the cards. Is your chosen card there? If not, say to the cards, "Tell me more," and lay down three more cards from the top of the pile. See these as advice cards: They'll indicate whether or not it's worthwhile to be proactive and make contact.

This spread, which is intended to divine the outcome of a love dilemma, comes from the Bond movie *Live and Let Die*. In it, Solitaire, psychic to crime lord Kananga, gives the reading at the right to predict Bond's arrival and his intentions.

CARD 1
"A man comes"

CARD 2
"He travels quickly.
He comes over water.
He travels with others."

CARD 5
"He brings violence and
destruction."

CARD 4
"He will oppose."

CARD 3
"He has purpose."

CARD 1

CARD 5

CARD 3

CARD 2

CARD 4

From these card positions, the spread questions look like this:

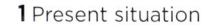

1 Present situation

2 What is this person doing now?

3 What's the reason
for the situation?

4 Most likely thing to happen next

5 Outcome

Shuffle and choose your cards (see page 16), then lay them all face down in the sequence shown at the left. Turn all the cards face up, and begin your interpretation.

7

MONEY, HOME, AND SECURITY SPREADS

NEED TO EXAMINE YOUR FINANCES OR YOUR HOME SITUATION? The nine readings in this chapter will help you do just that. And here's a hint before we get started: Be open to a broader interpretation of Pentacles. Sure, they may be the "money" cards of the tarot, commenting on material wealth and possessions, but they can also reveal our own beliefs to us. For instance, do we attract abundance thanks to a positive outlook, or are we stuck in a poverty mentality? By making us aware of our patterns—and of the future we think we deserve—these spreads can help us create change in our lives. As for the "home" spreads, take a look at them when you might move, or try the House of the Psyche to excavate buried issues that might be lurking around your sense of security. And the Feng Shui spread, based on compass directions, will show you how to divine whether or not your home supports your life goals.

KEY CARDS FOR MONEY, HOME, AND SECURITY

LOOK FOR:

III The Empress: Abundance, resourcefulness

IV The Emperor: Order and financial security

VII The Chariot: A major step forward

X The Wheel of Fortune: A turn for the better; money coming

XI Justice: A fair decision; legal matters are resolved in your favor

XXI The World: Success and rewards

Ace of Pentacles: New home, new beginning

Two of Pentacles: Cash flow; deciding between properties or locations

Nine of Pentacles: Material security and luxury; a comfortable home

Ten of Pentacles: Money coming; legacies and inheritance

Eight of Cups: Leaving an old situation behind

Nine of Cups: Wishes come true

Ten of Cups: A happy home and family

Four of Wands: Freedom, new home, protection

Knight of Wands: Moving home

Six of Swords: Moving away from problems

WATCH OUT FOR:

XV The Devil: Being controlled financially

XVI The Tower: Property issues; unexpected expenses; drama or conflict

Five of Pentacles: Poverty, fear of poverty, and isolation

Knight of Pentacles reversed: Financial delay, stubbornness

Seven of Swords: Theft

Eight of Swords: Restriction in your affairs

King of Swords: Legal conflict; opposition

Ten of Wands: Too much going on; finances get neglected

SPREADS FOR MONEY MATTERS

HOW CAN I BECOME MORE AFFLUENT?

This spread shows you what you can focus on to help you move toward a more abundant lifestyle—and it can also shed light on the blocks that might be standing in your way.

1 What to consider now

2 What or who can help you

3 A challenge you need to deal with

4 Outcome

Shuffle and choose your cards (see page 16). Lay them all face down in the order shown here. Turn them face up, and interpret them in turn.

TIP: If you see one or more Aces in your spread, it's a sign that new ventures will go well and will bring you money.

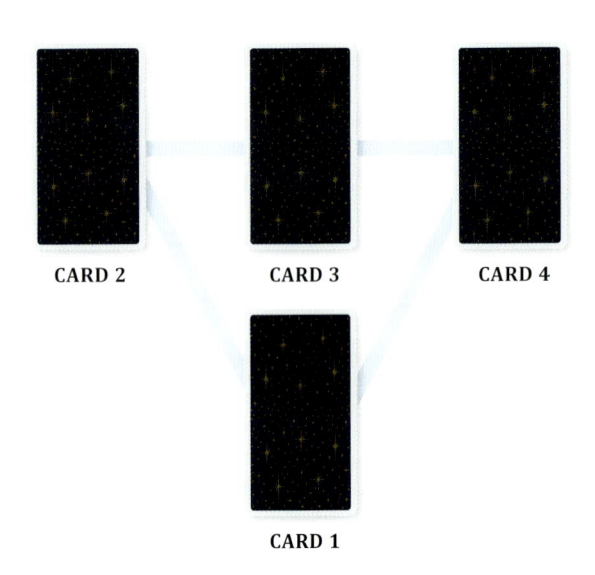

CARD 2   CARD 3   CARD 4

CARD 1

RUNNING THE NUMBERS: HOW CAN MY FINANCIAL CIRCUMSTANCES IMPROVE?

I call this spread "running the numbers" because all you need to do is add up the card numbers, then reduce them to a single digit. Apply this number to its corresponding major arcana card; this card will yield a meaning that relates to your finances, as shown in the table on the following page.

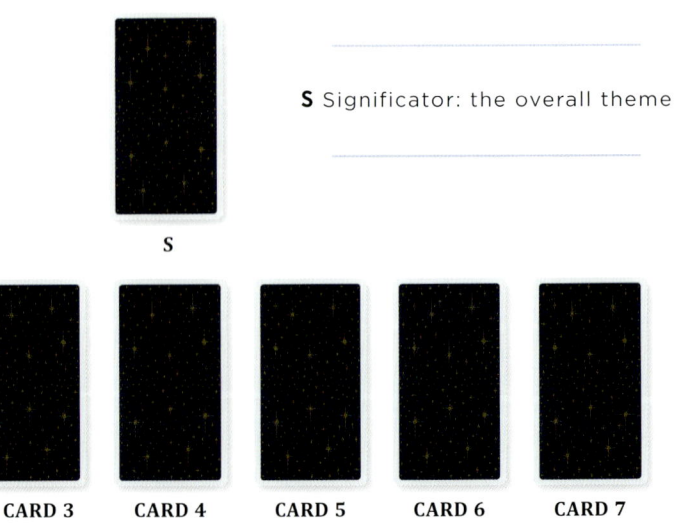

S

S Significator: the overall theme

CARD 1   CARD 2   CARD 3   CARD 4   CARD 5   CARD 6   CARD 7

Shuffle and choose your cards (see page 16), then lay them out as shown on the bottom of the previous page, placing the Significator (S) first, then cards 1 through 7.

Add up the numbers of cards 1 through 7: Aces count as 1, and each Court card counts as 10. Add all the numbers together (but don't include the Significator): For example, major arcana card XI equals 11, plus the Two of Cups, which equals 2, and so on. When you have a final number, add it together so that it results in a number between 2 and 10. For example, if your final number were 88, you'd add 8 plus 8, which gives 16; then, 1 plus 6 gives 7. This is known as the "quintessence," the hidden number of a spread (see page 27). Then you'd relate that 7 to its corresponding major arcana card—VII The Chariot—and look up its meaning in the table below.

MAJOR ARCANA FINANCIAL MEANINGS

MAJOR ARCANA CARD	ADVICE IN A MONEY/HOME READING
II The High Priestess	Patience. Money is coming, but it will take time.
III The Empress	Look at what you own and what you owe. You may have more resources than you think.
IV The Emperor	Get your accounts in order; focus on saving.
V The Hierophant	Ask for help from an advisor.
VI The Lovers	Look for value rather than money.
VII The Chariot	Your determination can bring in money and success.
VIII Strength	Hold on. Don't spend more until you're sure of your position.
IX The Hermit	Get information: You need to know more before you make financial decisions.
X The Wheel of Fortune	Your fortunes improve quickly.

WHY AM I FACED WITH SO MANY FINANCIAL CHALLENGES?

Card X The Wheel of Fortune stands for destiny and a change in our fortunes. In this spread, we derive meaning from the symbols in each corner of the card, which represent the four Evangelists of the Gospel: Matthew, Mark, Luke, and John. Take the Wheel from your deck and place it in the center, face up. Now take a look at the symbols:

Top left: Matthew, the winged man; Aquarius and the element of Air

Top right: John, the eagle; Scorpio and the element of Water

Bottom left: Luke, the ox; Taurus and the element of Earth

Bottom right: Mark the lion; Leo and the element of Fire

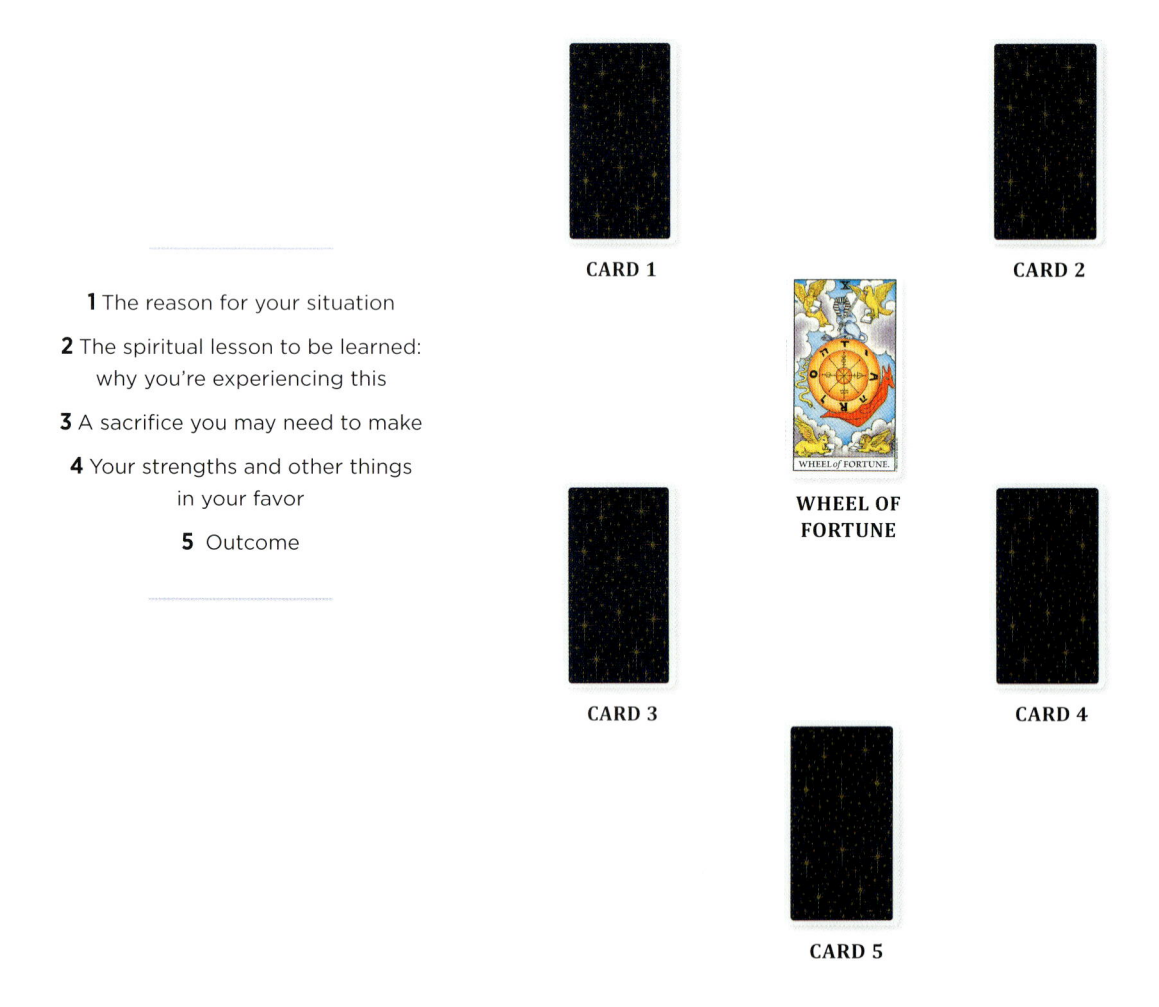

CARD 1

CARD 2

WHEEL OF FORTUNE

CARD 3

CARD 4

CARD 5

1 The reason for your situation

2 The spiritual lesson to be learned: why you're experiencing this

3 A sacrifice you may need to make

4 Your strengths and other things in your favor

5 Outcome

Shuffle the remaining deck, choose your cards (see page 16), and lay them out face down, as shown below. Turn over cards 1 to 4: Interpret them first, then turn over card 5, the outcome.

You can extend the reading by asking, "If I can follow the advice of the previous cards, what might change for the better?" Then lay another five cards on top of those you've already turned over. This time, lay them face up as you deal them from the deck, as shown below.

Compare the first layout and the overlaid cards to see how you might move forward.

DO I HAVE AN ABUNDANCE ATTITUDE?

Sometimes when cash seems elusive, you may notice this pattern emerging in your relationship toward money: As soon as you get it, it's gone. Investigating our attitudes towards money and abundance can help us discover why it's so hard to hold on to the pennies. The Significator question, "Should I have money?" may seem more obvious that it actually is. You may agree in principle—but do you feel you deserve it?

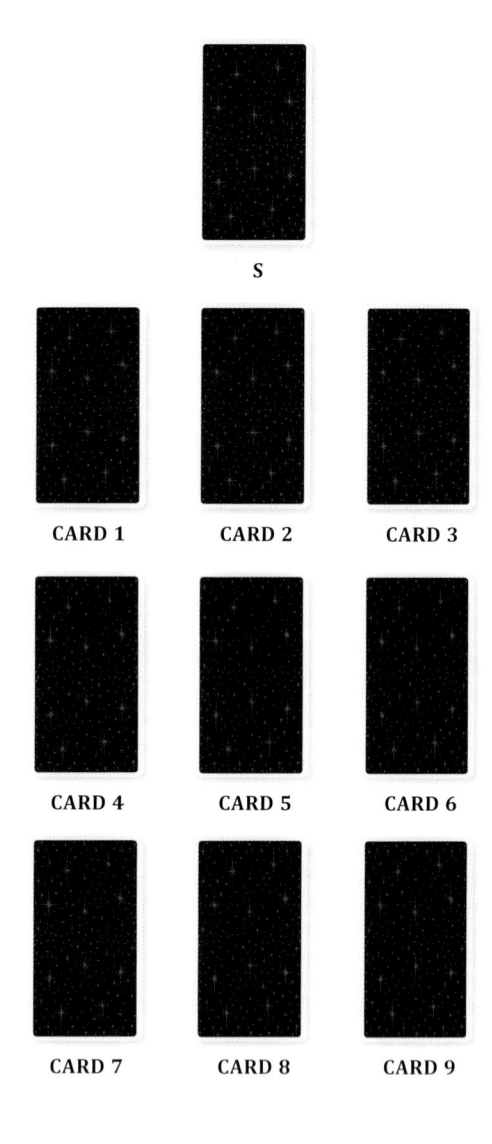

S Significator: Should I have money?

1, 2, 3 What does money mean to me?

4, 5, 6 What do I think about people who don't have money?

7, 8, 9 What do I think about people that have money?

Shuffle the cards. Choose a Significator card and lay it face down at the top of the spread as shown. Then choose three cards for each question and place them face down in the order given. Now turn all the cards face up. The cards' interpretations reveal the value you place on money: This, in turn, helps you understand what motivates you to make it—or what blocks you from having it.

> **TIP:** Look at cards 4, 5, and 6, which represent your feelings toward people who don't have money. Do you do any of these things yourself? Could these habits be blocking an abundance attitude?

Example: Simon's Reading

Simon's reading went like this:

Significator: Should I have money?

To Simon, the Two of Pentacles means money is something that requires juggling; was he, perhaps, even ambivalent about having wealth?

What does money mean to me?

Having money is a trial (Five of Wands); it causes anxiety (Nine of Swords); I get disillusioned about having enough (Four of Cups).

What I think about people who don't have money: They're in crisis (The Moon); they procrastinate (The Hanged Man); and they make bad decisions (Ace of Swords reversed).

What I think about people who have money: They're always having a good time at parties (Three of Cups); they are powerful, creative, and busy (Knight of Wands); they are entrepreneurs and self-starters (Ace of Wands).

S

Should I have money?

CARD 1 **CARD 2** **CARD 3**

What does money mean to me?

CARD 4 **CARD 5** **CARD 6**

What do I think about people who don't have money?

CARD 7 **CARD 8** **CARD 9**

What do I think about people who have money?

SPREADS FOR THE HOME AND SECURITY

HOUSE OF THE PSYCHE: WHAT'S GOING ON IN MY LIFE?

In psychology, the house can be viewed as a metaphor for the psyche. Dreaming of houses and rooms often shows us how we feel about different aspects of our lives, and the condition and position of these rooms can indicate hidden conflicts or memories that are finally surfacing. In this spread, we use the structure of a house to examine what's going on both consciously and subconsciously. Try this spread if home and security are issues for you at present.

1 What's coming through the front door: your immediate situation

2 What's below: Do your plans have a solid foundation? Is anything hidden?

3, 4, 5, 6: Windows:

3 Window to the past: hidden past issues

4 Window to the past: conscious past experiences or memories

5 Window on the future: what you are subconsciously manifesting; your attitudes

6 Window on the future: what you are consciously manifesting; your plans

7, 8: What's in the attic?

7 Secret hopes and dreams

8 Known hopes and dreams

9 The roof: Are you protected?

10 The outcome

Shuffle and choose your cards (see page 16), then lay them down as shown here. Turn over all the cards and begin your interpretation of each one. When you've done this, look at the "subconscious" cards—cards 2, 3, 5, and 7—as a group. These are feelings or issues that may require more attention. Then look at the "conscious" cards as a group: These are cards 1, 4, 6, and 8. They reveal your current plans and expectations—the things you show to the outside world.

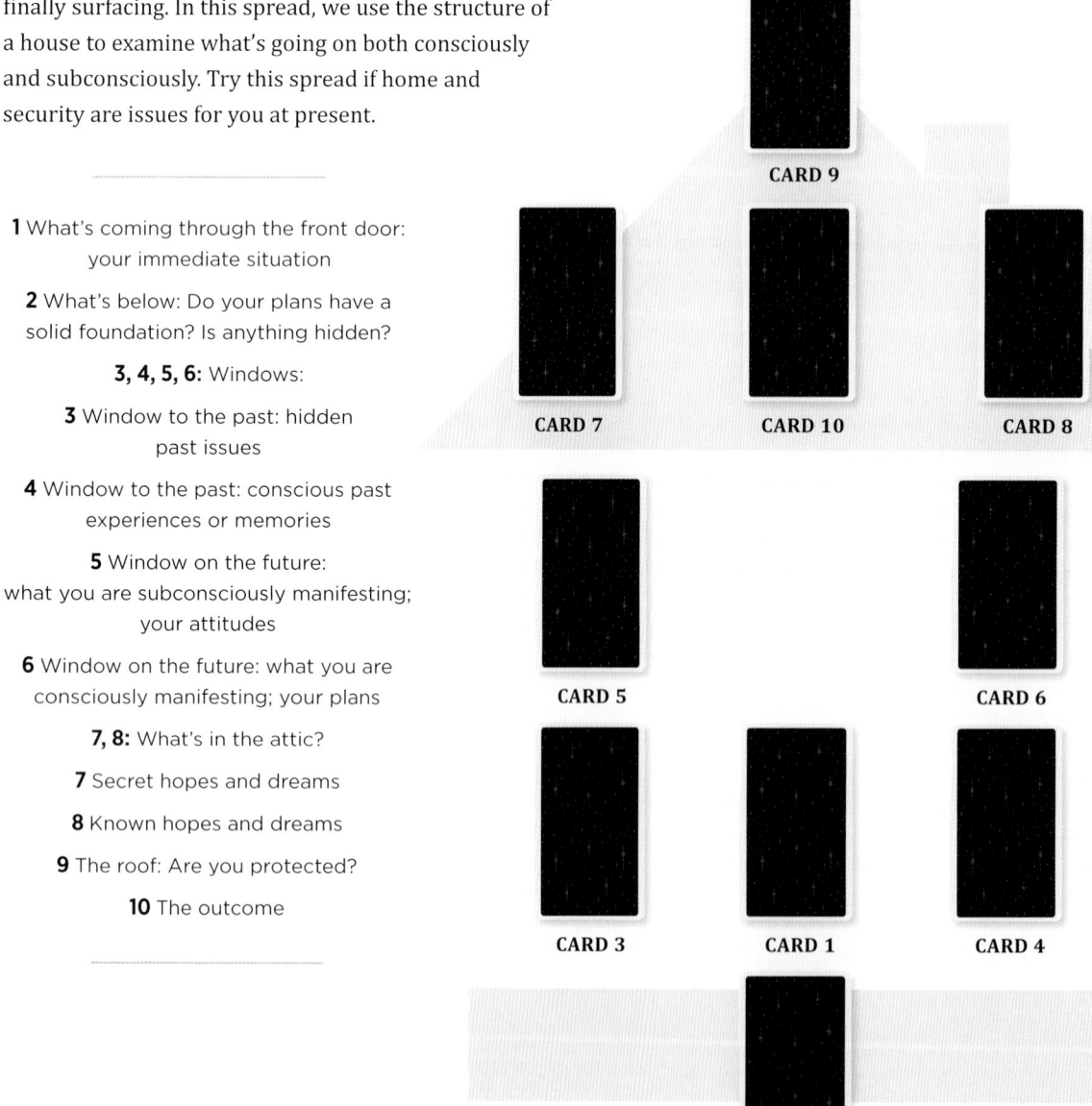

CARD 9

CARD 7   CARD 10   CARD 8

CARD 5   CARD 6

CARD 3   CARD 1   CARD 4

CARD 2

Example: Michael's Reading

Michael tried this spread to assess the impact of a recent house move.

1 **Ten of Pentacles (present situation):** He and his partner had moved away from the city for his new job, which meant more money and career progress.

2 **Six of Wands (foundation):** He had been successful in his career to date.

3 **Knight of Swords (hidden past):** The Knight showed how stressful the move had been.

4 **0 The Fool (conscious past):** The Fool is Michael's new journey. Leaving his old job was a huge risk. Plus, he felt like the new kid on the block: He'd have to prove himself all over again.

5 **King of Wands (subconscious future):** Michael saw the King as his new manager, someone he wanted to emulate, a possible mentor.

6 **Four of Pentacles (conscious future):** The Four revealed the stability he and his partner hoped to enjoy in their new place in the country. In fact, the only downside he could see was the possibility of getting too parochial!

7 **Three of Cups (secret future hopes):** The Three predicts sociability and joy. Michael and his partner were looking to adopt, so he also hoped this card could mean celebrating the arrival of a child.

8 **Seven of Pentacles (known hopes):** Financial potential; hard work could bring reward. The Seven also felt like a message to Michael and his partner, telling them to appreciate what they have.

9 **Ace of Swords (protection):** Michael's decision to move for work was a positive one. It would bring success and protect their long-term future.

10 **Nine of Cups (outcome):** The outcome card. As the "wish" card of the tarot, the Nine told Michael that he and his partner would be happy with their decision and their new home.

Michael's subconscious cards are the Six of Wands, Knight of Swords, King of Wands, and Three of Cups. He noted that there were no Pentacles cards, which indicates that his true needs didn't have to do with money, but with communication, exploration, and

CARD 9

CARD 7   **CARD 10**   **CARD 8**

CARD 5   **CARD 6**

CARD 3   **CARD 1**   **CARD 4**

CARD 2

relationships. The Knight of Swords represented his decision to leave the stressful world of city living behind him.

Michael's conscious cards, the Ten of Pentacles, The Fool, the Four of Pentacles, and the Seven of Pentacles show that he wanted a new challenge and financial success—but to support his family and their security (the Ten of Pentacles) rather than to increase his status.

How Can We Move to Our New Home More Quickly?

Try this simple four-card reading if you're trying to move but finding that the way ahead seems blocked. If there's something you can do to speed up the process, this little spread will show you how.

CARD 1

CARD 2

CARD 3

CARD 4

1 Present situation

2 What to do

3 What to avoid

4 Outcome

Shuffle and choose your cards (see page 16). Lay them out as shown above, face down, then turn them all face up and begin your interpretation.

You can use this two-card reading on its own, or you can add it to another spread of your choice. Use only the major arcana: You can use the minor arcana cards alone to try the "Where's the ideal place to live?" spread that follows this one.

1 When not to move or renovate

2 When to move or renovate

CARD 1 **CARD 2**

Shuffle the major arcana cards only, and choose two cards (see page 16). Place them face down in front of you, then turn them over and interpret each one according to the dates listed below. If you get a card that's not listed, try your reading again in a few days: The answer may be clearer then.

MAJOR ARCANA AND RELATED DATES

MAJOR ARCANA	DATES
IV The Emperor	March 21–April 20 (Aries)
V The Hierophant	April 21–May 21 (Taurus)
VI The Lovers	May 22–June 21 (Gemini)
VII The Chariot	June 22–July 23 (Cancer)
VIII Strength	July 24–Aug 23 (Leo)
IX The Hermit	Aug 24–Sept 23 (Virgo)
XI Justice	Sept 24–Oct 23 (Libra)
XIII Death	Oct 24–Nov 22 (Scorpio)
XIV Temperance	Nov 23–Dec 21 (Sagittarius)
XV The Devil	Dec 22–Jan 20 (Capricorn)
XVII The Star	Jan 21–Feb 19 (Aquarius)
XVIII The Moon	Feb 20–March 20 (Pisces)

WHERE'S THE IDEAL PLACE TO LIVE?

This spread uses only the four suits of the minor arcana: Cups, Wands, Swords, and Pentacles. The suit's element guides you toward your ideal location. Try this spread when you're checking out a number of properties and locations to divine which one may be best for you.

Take the minor arcana cards from the deck and shuffle them. Choose your cards (see page 16), then lay them out in front of you, face down, as shown below. Turn them all over together, and see which suit or suits dominate your spread. Then interpret them according to the table below to see whether country or urban living is best for you. Remember, we're only looking at the suit elements here, not the card meanings, so hold back from interpreting the individual card meanings this time.

| CARD 1 | CARD 2 | CARD 3 | CARD 4 | CARD 5 | CARD 6 | CARD 7 |

WHERE SHOULD YOU LIVE?

SUIT	ELEMENT	PROPERTY LOCATION AND TYPE
Cups	Water	Near sea, river, lake, stream, or canal Blue or black colors inside or outside The place that feels most comfortable
Swords	Air	Mountains, high terrain, views High-rise, balconies Metallic colors The logical option
Wands	Fire	Desert, other warm climates Hot colors: oranges, yellows, reds A creative, inspiring location
Pentacles	Earth	Close to the land, agricultural areas Nature colors: greens and browns Ground or lower-floor properties; close to where you work, or with possibilities to work at home

> **TIP:** If no suit dominates your spread the first time, repeat the reading.

This spread layout represents the Pa Kua, or Ba Gua, the eight-sided feng shui symbol that relates compass directions to life areas. The order of cards laid follows the number order of the ancient Chinese Lo Shu, or "magic" square, which is part of feng shui teachings. In this square, all rows of numbers add up to 15.

Unusually, card 5 becomes the Significator in this reading. You'll also notice that the card's associated compass directions begin with card 1, North, at the bottom, while 9, South, is at the top. That's because this is how the feng shui Pa Kua is traditionally shown.

Shuffle and choose your cards (see page 16), laying them all face down in the order shown. Turn over all the cards, interpreting the central Significator (card 5) first, then the others, starting with 1 and ending with 9.

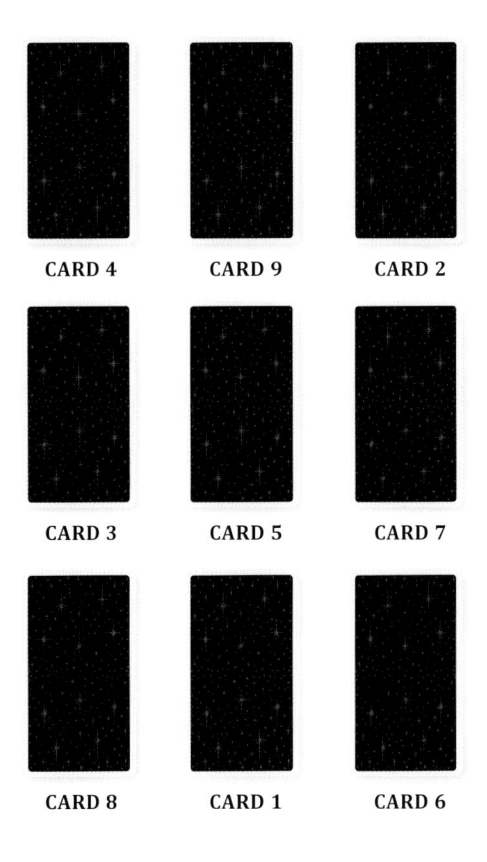

CARD 4	CARD 9	CARD 2
CARD 3	CARD 5	CARD 7
CARD 8	CARD 1	CARD 6

FENG SHUI CARD INTERPRETATIONS

CARD	DIRECTION	INTERPRETATION
5	Significator	The theme of the reading
1	North	Career
9	South	Fame, reputation, and success
3	East	Health and family
7	West	Children and projects
8	Northeast	Education and personal development
6	Northwest	Helpful people and mentors
2	Southwest	Love and relationships
4	Southeast	Money and prosperity

DEVELOPING THE READING:
GETTING THE CHI FLOWING FOR ABUNDANCE

Your tarot reading can help you pinpoint which rooms in your home have stagnant energy: They can slow down the flow of positive energy, or *chi*, which is thought to invite abundance into your home. Here's how to do it: Stand at your front door and look out. Take a compass reading: This shows you the facing direction of your property. Make a sketch of each floor and apply the card layout as a nine-square grid over your sketch, allocating a compass direction to each sector (excluding the central square, which isn't given a direction).

Now place your tarot cards from your reading on your sketch, so that you're connecting different rooms or areas of your home with your tarot cards. Watch where any negative or "flat" cards fall (such as the Four of Cups or Swords) and pay attention to these areas in your home. Declutter and tidy them, and clean and air them; remove any negative artwork (representing battle scenes or sad characters, for example) and cleanse the space with a smudge stick or incense.

Example: One Family's Home
The property faces west, and the family room is located in the northwest, in position 6. Card 6 is the Four of Cups, meaning boredom and stagnation. This card suggests that the energy in this space is flat and needs revitalizing. According to the principles of feng shui, energy needs to flow in order to bring abundance into the home.

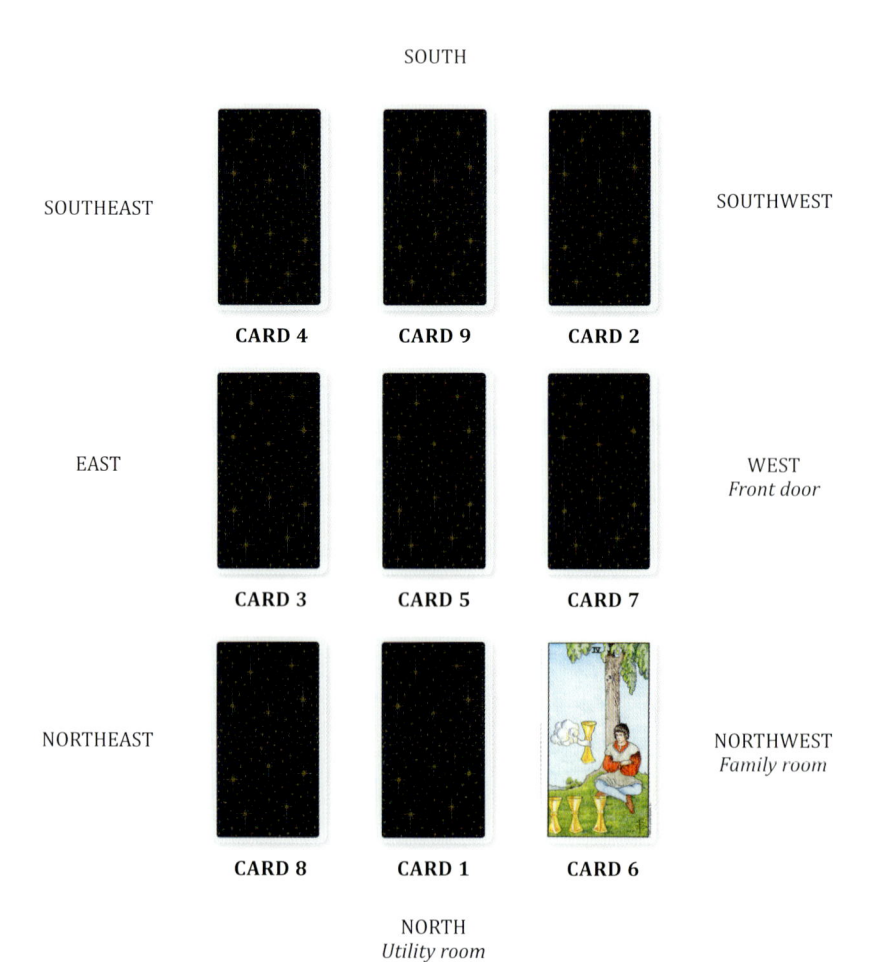

SOUTH

SOUTHEAST

CARD 4   CARD 9   CARD 2

SOUTHWEST

EAST

CARD 3   CARD 5   CARD 7

WEST
Front door

NORTHEAST

CARD 8   CARD 1   CARD 6

NORTHWEST
Family room

NORTH
Utility room

8

HEALTH, HEALING, AND SELF-EMPOWERMENT SPREADS

TAROT CAN HELP GUIDE US TOWARD AN ENHANCED AWARENESS OF our spiritual, emotional, and physical health. In these ten spreads in this chapter, we'll explore our characters through palmistry and astrology readings, uncovering our personal strengths, and we'll experience the interconnection between mind, body, and spirit, taking inspiration from the chakra points (energy centers located in the body and the aura), The Four Aspects of the Self, and the practice of loving-kindness, or self-compassion—perhaps the most powerful self-healing tool of all. While tarot is not designed to diagnose an ailment, it may lead us toward any emotional block that can be diffused—and without the blocks, we have more energy and confidence. In this way, tarot offers a whole-person approach to health and healing.

KEY CARDS
FOR HEALTH, HEALING, AND SELF-EMPOWERMENT

LOOK FOR:

I The Magician: Action and vitality

III The Empress: Fertility, motherhood, nurturing, protection

IX The Hermit: Reflection and meditation

VIII Strength: Strength and calmness

XVII The Star: Healing and guidance

XIX The Sun: Well-being, recovery, relaxation, happiness

XX Judgement: Dealing with past issues

Four of Swords: Inaction; recovery after illness; stress, depression

Ace of Wands: Male fertility

Four of Wands: Freedom, playfulness

Ace of Cups: Female fertility; pregnancy

Six of Cups: Peace

Six of Pentacles: Kindness and compassion

WATCH OUT FOR:

XV The Devil: Addiction; irrational thinking

XVI The Tower: Shock, traumatic change; also, migraine headaches

Three of Swords: General ill health; can be associated with heart issues

Five of Swords: Stress, conflict

Nine of Swords: Anxiety and insomnia

Ten of Wands: Exhaustion, feeling overwhelmed

Five of Pentacles: Isolation, loneliness

SPREADS FOR HEALTH AND HEALING

CHAKRA WISDOM

There are seven principal chakras, or energy centers, in the body, running from the base of the spine up to the crown of the head. In this spread, we lay a card to represent each chakra; through the interpretation of the chakra points given below in the key, you'll be able to view the body as a messenger or medium for the mind and spirit.

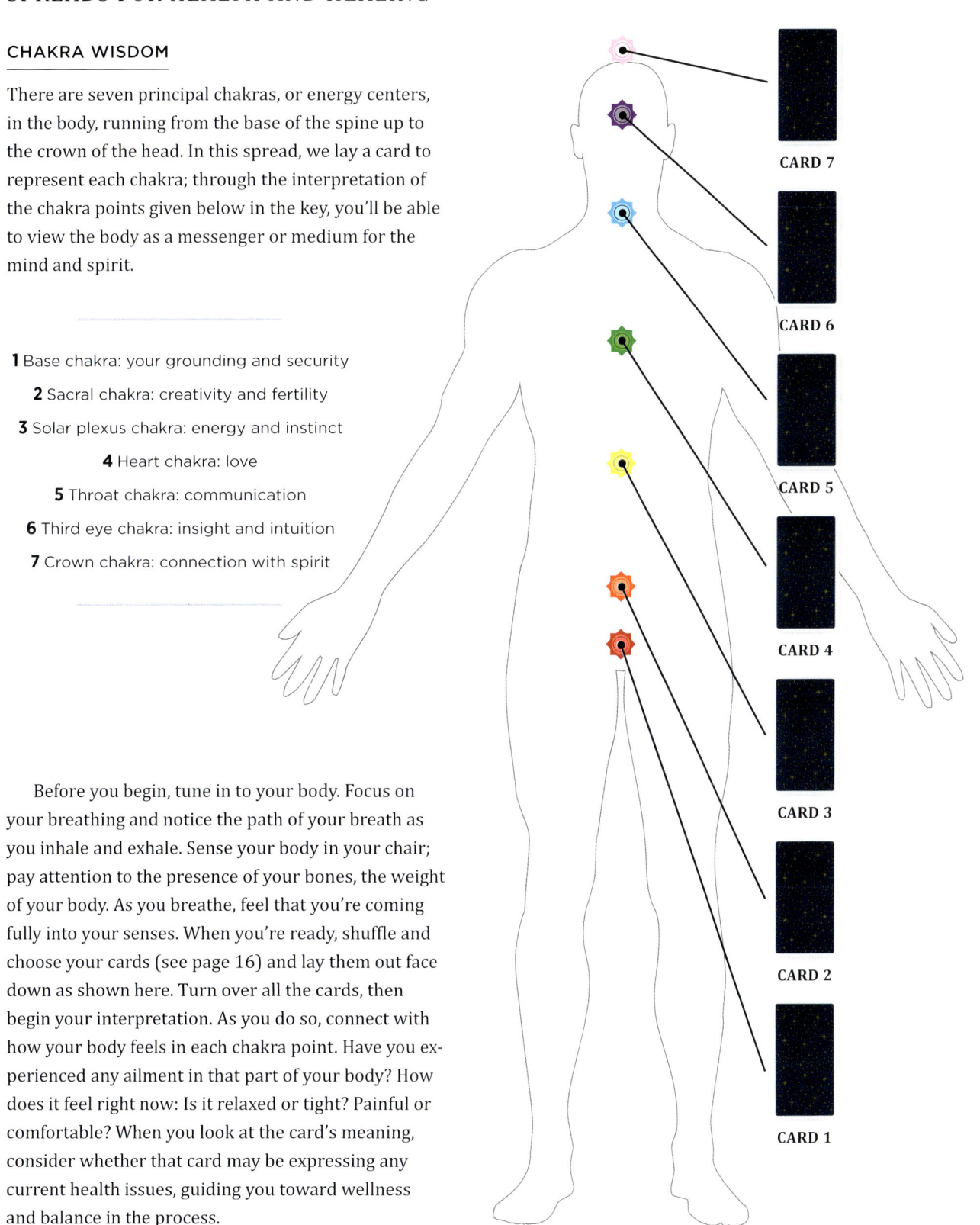

1 Base chakra: your grounding and security

2 Sacral chakra: creativity and fertility

3 Solar plexus chakra: energy and instinct

4 Heart chakra: love

5 Throat chakra: communication

6 Third eye chakra: insight and intuition

7 Crown chakra: connection with spirit

CARD 7

CARD 6

CARD 5

CARD 4

CARD 3

CARD 2

CARD 1

Before you begin, tune in to your body. Focus on your breathing and notice the path of your breath as you inhale and exhale. Sense your body in your chair; pay attention to the presence of your bones, the weight of your body. As you breathe, feel that you're coming fully into your senses. When you're ready, shuffle and choose your cards (see page 16) and lay them out face down as shown here. Turn over all the cards, then begin your interpretation. As you do so, connect with how your body feels in each chakra point. Have you experienced any ailment in that part of your body? How does it feel right now: Is it relaxed or tight? Painful or comfortable? When you look at the card's meaning, consider whether that card may be expressing any current health issues, guiding you toward wellness and balance in the process.

Developing the Reading:

Adding Three Magnifier Cards

You may like to place three additional cards (see page 21) around any chakra point you'd like to know more about. These three extra cards examine the past, present, and future. For example:

CARD 1
Base chakra: security

a Past issues affecting me now; what happened?

b Present issues

c What can I do to feel more secure in my life? What do I need?

a   b   c

TIP: Try any of the three-card readings in this book to expand this reading, such as "What Shall I Do?" (chapter 3, page 22) or the "Simple Layouts of Three" (chapter 11, page 318).

ADVANCED CHAKRA READING

This spread calls upon some of our developing, or higher, chakras. These energy centers open within us as our consciousness shifts to embrace an awareness of higher spiritual realms.

Lay out the cards as for the basic chakra spread, as shown on page 259. This time, add the five cards listed below.

8 Left palm chakra: what you have manifested for yourself in the past

9 Right palm chakra: what you can manifest now for the future

10 Earth star: how you can ground yourself further to advance your spiritual journey

11 Soul star: guidance from your higher self

12 Stellar gateway: divine; connection with other realms

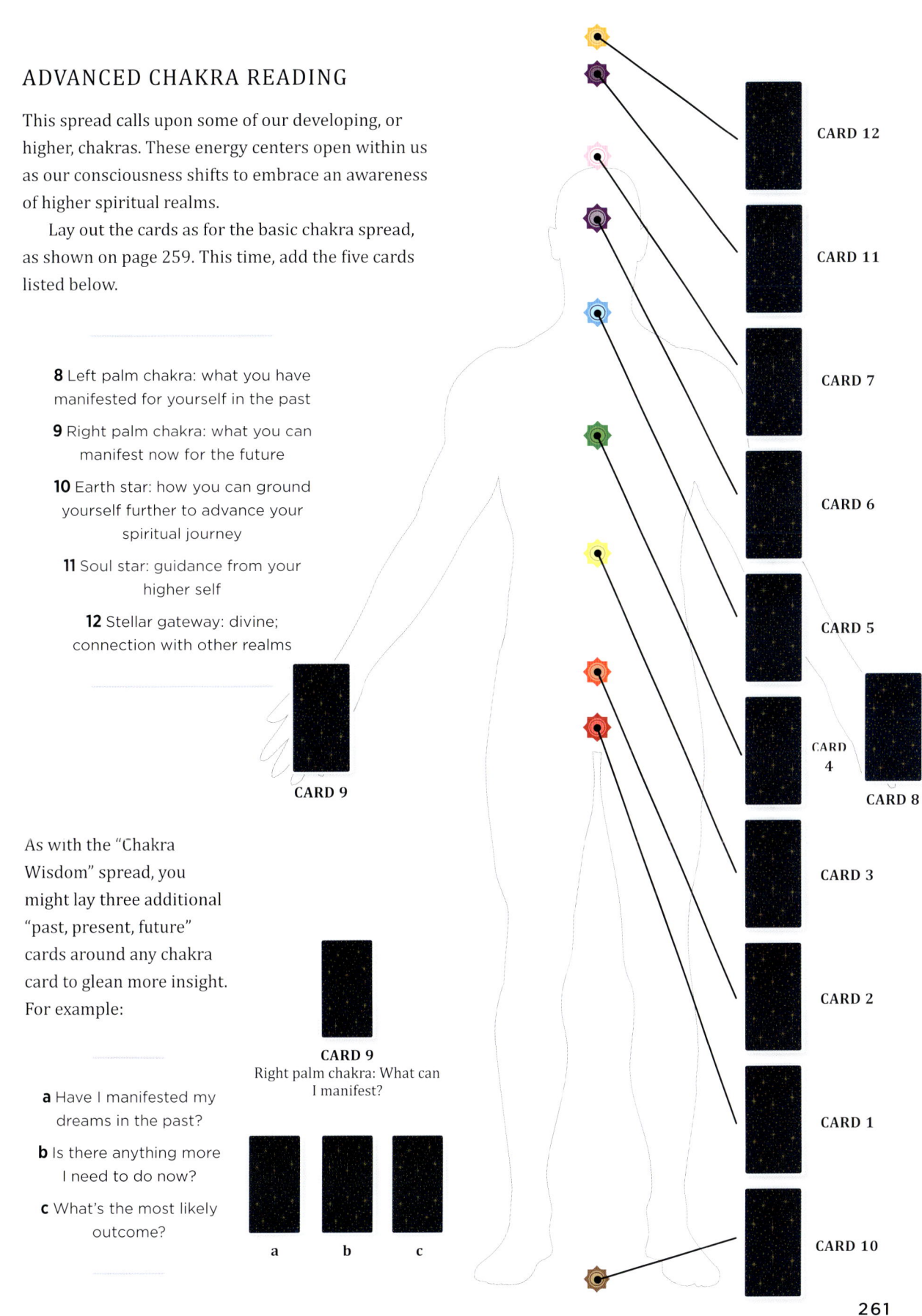

As with the "Chakra Wisdom" spread, you might lay three additional "past, present, future" cards around any chakra card to glean more insight. For example:

a Have I manifested my dreams in the past?

b Is there anything more I need to do now?

c What's the most likely outcome?

CARD 9
CARD 9
Right palm chakra: What can I manifest?

a   b   c

CARD 12

CARD 11

CARD 7

CARD 6

CARD 5

CARD 4

CARD 8

CARD 3

CARD 2

CARD 1

CARD 10

Here's a fast way to connect with your solar plexus chakra, the seat of your soul's wisdom and of your deepest instincts.

1, 2 Your situation now

3 Instinct revealed

CARD 1

CARD 2

CARD 3

Shuffle and choose your cards. While you're doing this, focus your attention on your solar plexus chakra. How does it feel? This chakra's color is yellow, so you might like to visualize this color as you shuffle. Then lay out the cards, face up, as shown above. Use the first two cards to reflect on the present: These cards reveal two aspects of your situation. The third card guides you toward your inner awareness, helping you make a decision and move forward.

SIMPLE CHAKRA CHECK-IN 2: WHAT IS MY TRUE SELF TELLING ME?

Your true self is your higher consciousness, the part of you that sees the bigger picture and knows which way to go on life's path. The higher self acts only for your good. By connecting to this self-aspect, we can avoid being distracted by feelings of confusion or other difficult emotions, and we can clearly see what we need to do next.

1, 2 Your situation now

3 Soul star:
guidance from your higher self

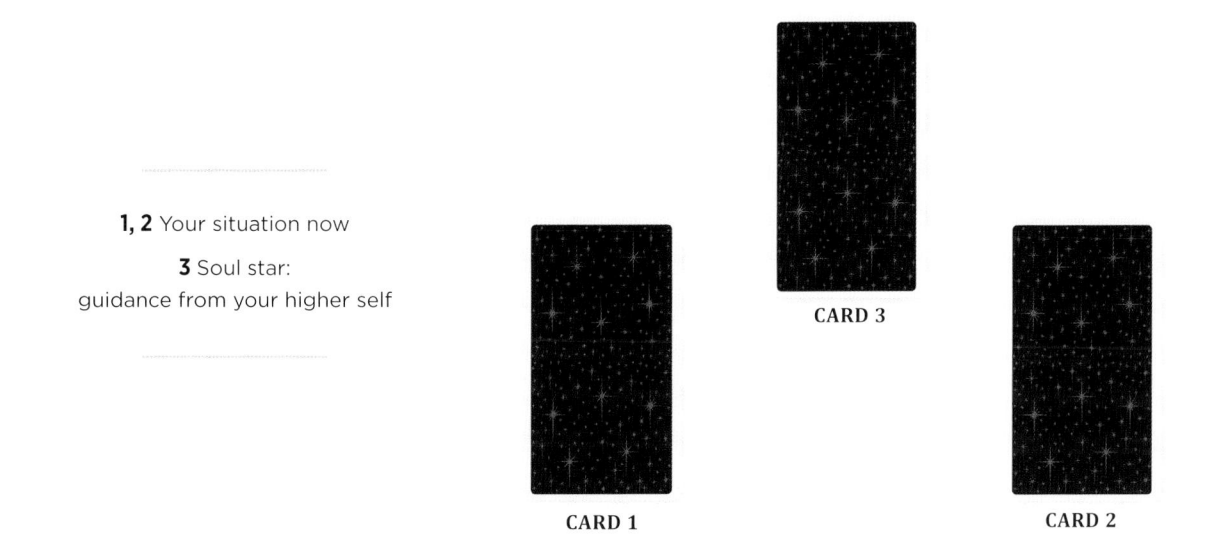

CARD 3

CARD 1

CARD 2

Shuffle and choose your cards. While you're doing this, focus your attention on your soul star chakra. This is located about 5 inches above the crown of your head; it is linked with divinity and with your higher self. Then lay out the cards as above. Use the first two cards to reflect on the present: These cards reveal two aspects of your situation. The third card suggests your true purpose.

> TIP: You might like to adapt the simple chakra spreads to consider any other chakra point. For example, you might ask, "What do I need to know about communication and truth now?" and focus on the throat chakra as you shuffle, laying one card for the throat as for the solar plexus or soul star chakras.

THE FOUR ASPECTS OF THE SELF

This spread explores four aspects of our being: mind, emotions, spirit and intuition, and body. The mind relates to our knowledge, intellect, attitudes, and beliefs. The body is our physical structure but has its own wisdom too: Our gut tells us what is safe and what is to be avoided. The category of emotions naturally encompasses our feelings, relationships, and compassion for ourselves and others. Spirit and intuition expresses our affinity with the spiritual realm and with our higher self—a connection that may also inspire us to create. In this reading, we lay our cards on the quartered wheel below, a symbol for the four aspects of the self.

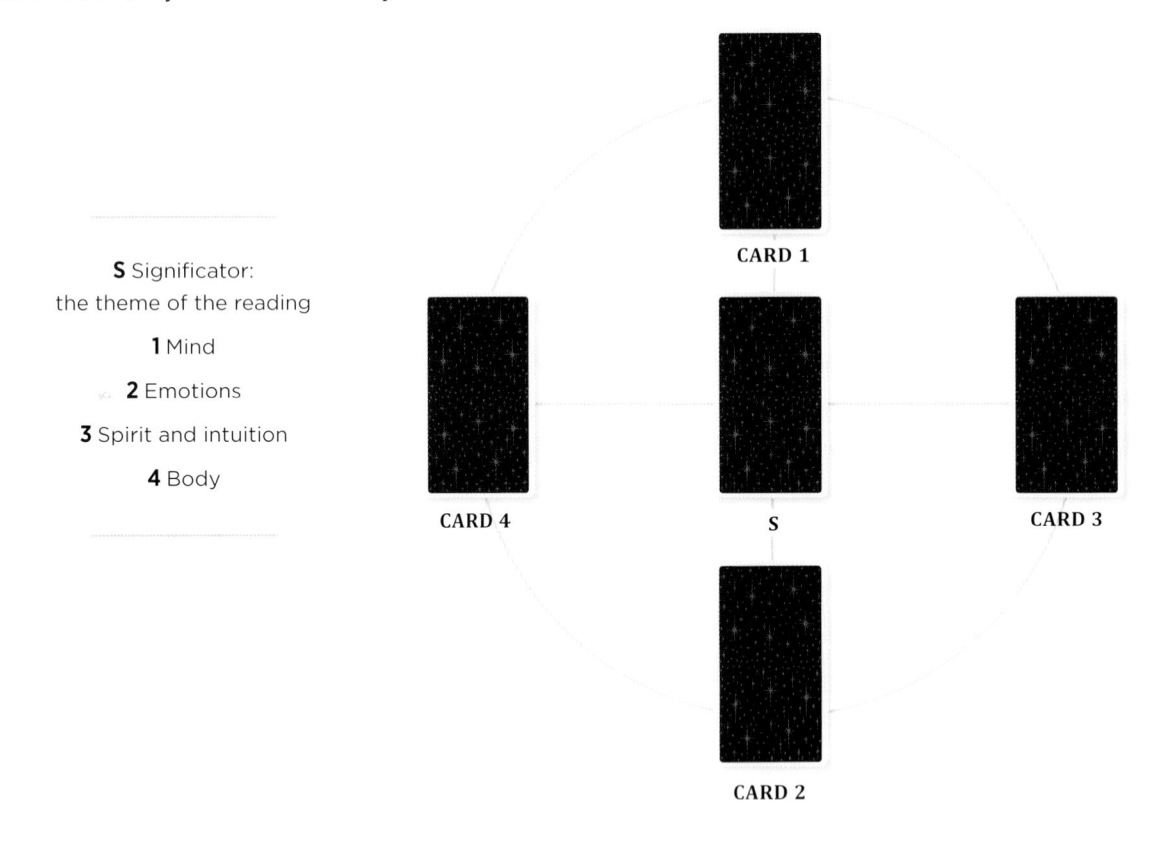

S Significator:
the theme of the reading

1 Mind

2 Emotions

3 Spirit and intuition

4 Body

CARD 1

CARD 4

S

CARD 3

CARD 2

Shuffle and choose your cards (see page 16). Lay the Significator card first, then cards 1 through 4, all face down. Turn them all face up. Now ask yourself these key questions:

Which of the cards feels most positive?
Which do you like the best?

The card you feel most positive about reveals your dominant aspect just now. The card opposite your favorite card reveals an aspect that may be suppressed and needs attention.

Example: Favorite Cards and Opposite Cards

For example, if you had chosen card XIX The Sun as your favorite, it'd be your "mind" card, and would reveal that your current focus is on thinking and analyzing. Opposite the Sun is the Five of Cups in the emotions position, which indicates loss and sadness. You might ask yourself whether healing is necessary in this area of your life.

CARD 1
Mind: the card I like most

CARD 4
Body

S

CARD 3
Spirit
and
intuition

CARD 2
Emotions:
the suppressed aspect

> TIP: The Four Aspects of the Self is a great spread to record regularly in your tarot journal, because it provides insight into where you're putting your energy—and it'll help you find out whether you need to shift your priorities in order to create more balance.

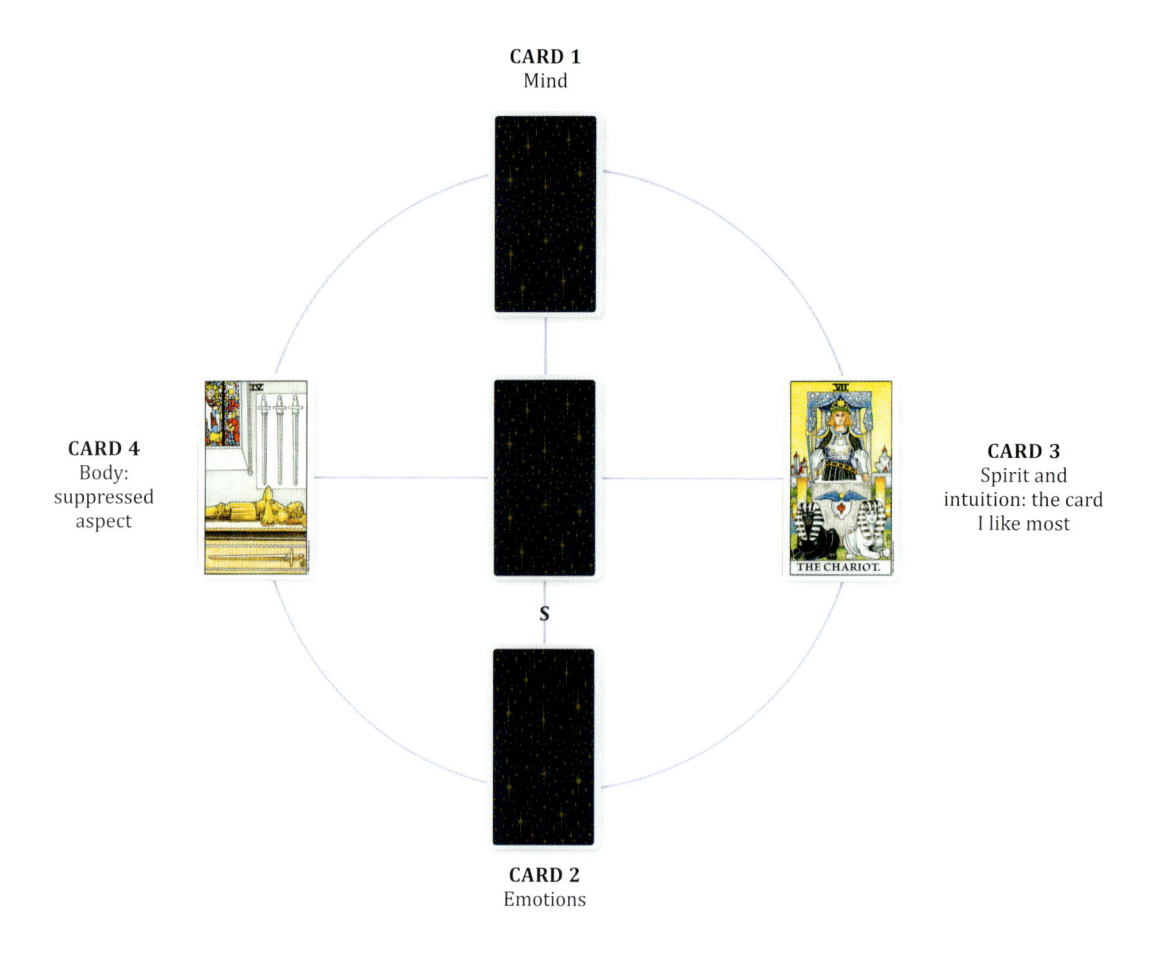

CARD 1
Mind

CARD 4
Body:
suppressed
aspect

S

CARD 3
Spirit and
intuition: the card
I like most

CARD 2
Emotions

If you chose card 3 as your favorite, then you may be feeling a strong spiritual connection to something at the moment—but you may also be forgetting about your body's needs. Symbolized by card 4, the "body" card is opposite card 3 on the wheel (and perhaps this is why there's a focus on grounding and being present to the body during some meditative and spiritual practices).

By paying attention to the suppressed aspect of the self, we help heal and rebalance *all* aspects of ourselves. Here's an example from everyday life: Move a single picture on your wall, and you'll end up moving your other pictures around to accommodate the new dynamic!

Of course, as the introduction to this book explains, tarot can reveal to us where we are right now. So, know that this reading doesn't predict permanent patterns of behavior. Instead, it helps you become more aware of your needs on a day-to-day or week-to-week basis.

THE LOVING-KINDNESS SPREAD

Loving-kindness is compassion that begins with the self; when you're kind to yourself, you can be authentically compassionate toward others. This spread invites you to explore any imbalances in your life that may be blocking your access to loving-kindness: What do you need more of—and what do you need less of—to meet your personal needs?

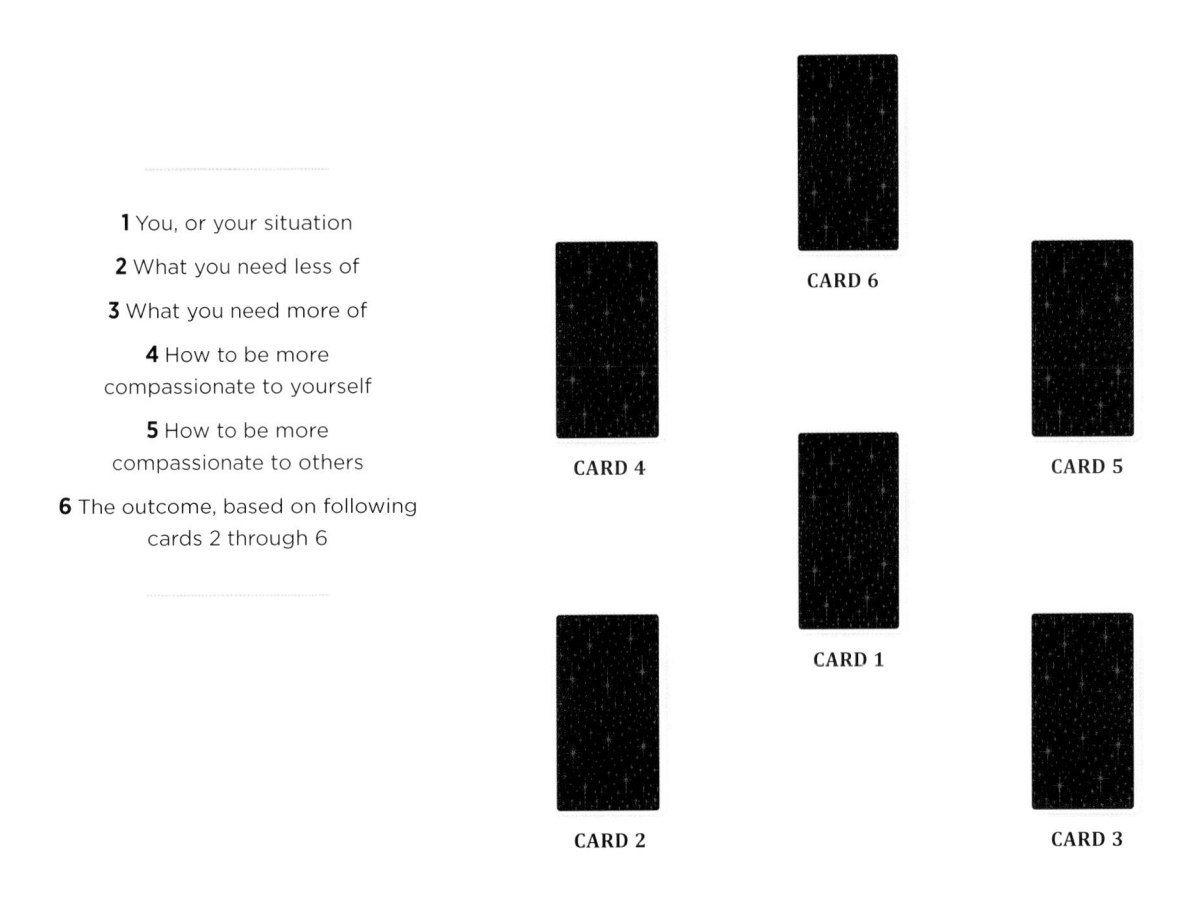

1 You, or your situation

2 What you need less of

3 What you need more of

4 How to be more compassionate to yourself

5 How to be more compassionate to others

6 The outcome, based on following cards 2 through 6

CARD 6

CARD 4

CARD 5

CARD 1

CARD 2

CARD 3

Shuffle and choose your cards (see page 16), laying them all face down in the sequence shown above. Turn them all face up and begin your interpretation. After the reading, you might like to take cards 3 and 4 and meditate on their images with an attitude of loving-kindness toward yourself.

Example: Daisy's Reading

Daisy's short relationship had just ended, but she felt more upset than she'd imagined she would: She'd had real hope that this one would last. She was beginning to berate herself for failing at love yet again. At thirty-five, she was beginning to lose faith that she would ever attract the right partner. Here is her reading:

CARD 6
Outcome based on cards 2 through 6

CARD 4
Self-compassion

CARD 1
Situation

CARD 5
Compassion for others

CARD 2
Need less of

CARD 3
Need more of

1 XIII Death (situation): Death confirmed Daisy's sense that the ending of this relationship felt profound—but perhaps it would help her clear away other issues that were holding her back in relationships.

2 Ten of Cups reversed (need less of): Daisy interpreted this as self-pressure to start a family. She also thought it represented poor communication with her own family, who were constantly asking her why she wasn't in a serious relationship at her age.

3 Ace of Wands (need more of): Daisy agreed that she needed a new start, but she had been putting off applying for a more rewarding job; with the right man, she would have a baby to care for, and wouldn't have to think about that.

4 XV The Devil (self-compassion): The Devil indicates issues of control in relationships. I asked Daisy to really connect with this card. What did it mean for her? In her past relationships, could she have been the one who was trying to remain in control because she was so ready for "The One"—regardless of how her partners may have felt? Since The Devil can also represent addictive behaviors, perhaps Daisy's way of being in relationships was actually perpetuating failure.

5 Queen of Pentacles (compassion for others): Daisy's way of supporting others was to offer practical help, including money, when she could. She was generous and giving, qualities she could really begin to value in herself in order to boost her self-esteem.

6 Two of Cups (outcome): If Daisy could recognize her strengths and let go of the need to control, a happy partnership would be on the cards—and, even more important, a happier relationship with herself.

SPREADS FOR CHARACTER INSIGHT

THE TWELVE HOUSES OF ASTROLOGY: YOU, YOU, YOU

This spread will help you look in detail at twelve life aspects that correspond to the twelve signs of the zodiac. You can also use this as a predictive spread for each month of the year ahead.

S Significator: the theme of the reading

Shuffle and choose your cards (see page 16). First, lay down a Significator card, face down, then lay cards 1 through 12 in the arrangement shown here, all face down. Then turn all the cards face up, and begin your interpretation.

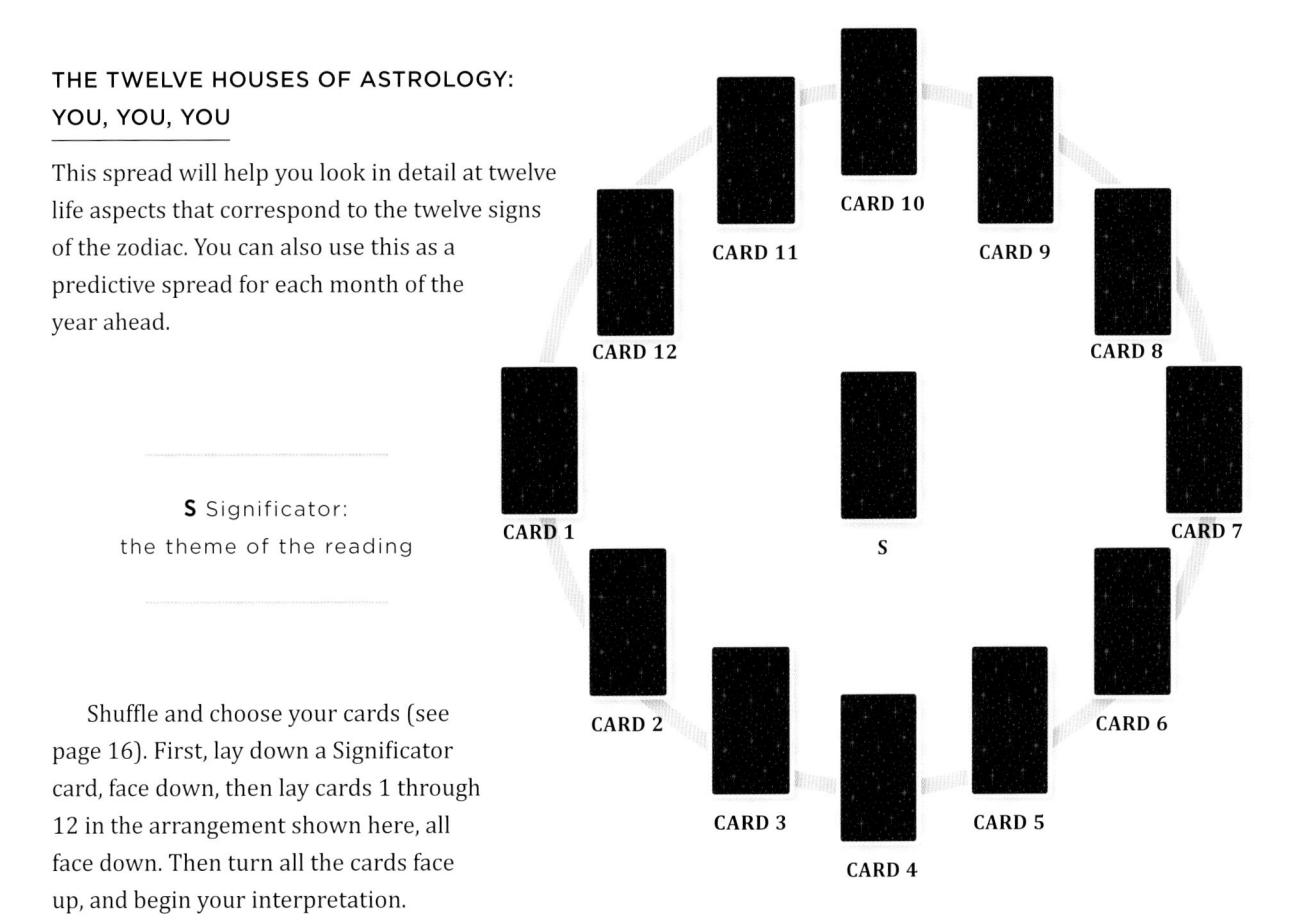

CARD 10
CARD 11
CARD 9
CARD 12
CARD 8
CARD 1
S
CARD 7
CARD 2
CARD 6
CARD 3
CARD 5
CARD 4

INTERPRETING THE ZODIAC SIGNS

CARD	ZODIAC SIGN	INTERPRETATION
1	Aries	How you appear: your personality
2	Taurus	What you need: possessions and security
3	Gemini	How you interact: communication and trips
4	Cancer	How you settle: home and childhood
5	Leo	How you express yourself: fun, confidence, and children
6	Virgo	How you think: work and health decisions
7	Libra	How you respond to others: relationships and associates
8	Scorpio	How you evolve: business, investment, and sexuality
9	Sagittarius	What you learn: travel, religion, and philosophy
10	Capricorn	What you aspire to: plans, career, and the future
11	Aquarius	How you share your vision: social life and community
12	Pisces	How you survive and thrive: dealing with adversity

Developing the Reading: Find the Motives

You can also lay an additional ring of cards in order to glean more insight into each of the cards from the first ring. Cards from this "second" ring can help reveal the motivations behind the corresponding cards from the first ring. For example, they may shed light on why you think a certain way, or may reveal the reasons that underpin your particular goals.

Shuffle the cards after the first layout, and set the intention to find out more about your cards as you do so. Then choose twelve more cards and lay them out as shown below. Interpret them in pairs: Look at cards 1 and 13 together, for instance. In this case, 13 will indicate the reasons for, or background behind, card 1. The same applies to 24 and 12; 23 and 11; and so on.

THE SPREAD OF THE SEVEN PLANETS: WHAT DO YOU VALUE?

This spread reveals aspects of our lives that correspond to the values associated with the seven classical planets of antiquity (that is, those that could be seen in the sky without the aid of a telescope). The seven planets were divided into two groups: the "personal" planets, which consist of the Sun, Moon, Mercury, Venus, and Mars (although today, of course, the sun and moon are not classed as planets); and the "transpersonal" planets, Jupiter and Saturn. These groups probably reflected the planets' proximity to earth; since Jupiter and Saturn are farther from Earth than Mercury, Venus, and Mars are, they were considered "impersonal."

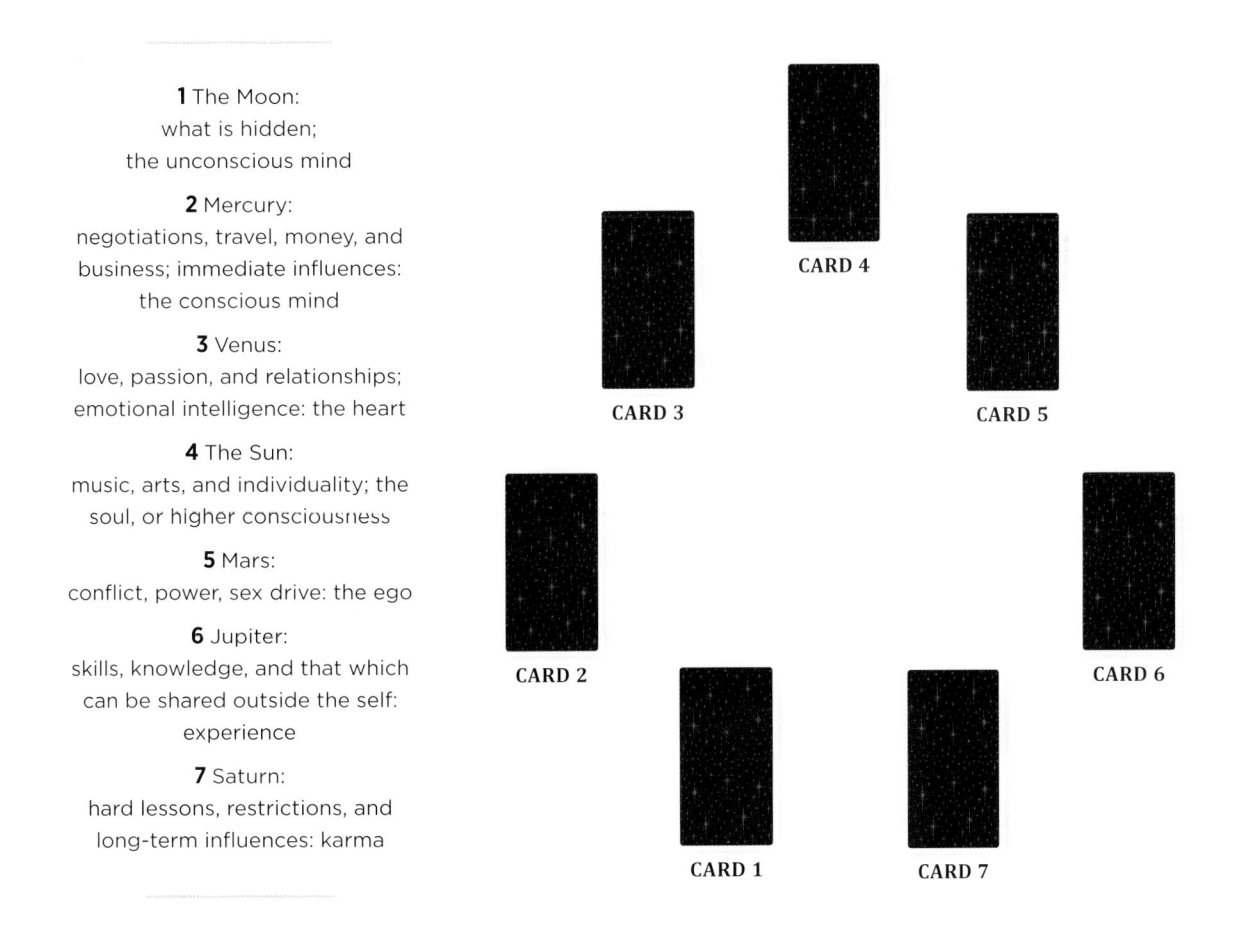

1 The Moon:
what is hidden;
the unconscious mind

2 Mercury:
negotiations, travel, money, and
business; immediate influences:
the conscious mind

3 Venus:
love, passion, and relationships;
emotional intelligence: the heart

4 The Sun:
music, arts, and individuality; the
soul, or higher consciousness

5 Mars:
conflict, power, sex drive: the ego

6 Jupiter:
skills, knowledge, and that which
can be shared outside the self:
experience

7 Saturn:
hard lessons, restrictions, and
long-term influences: karma

Shuffle and choose your cards (see page 16). Lay them out face down, then turn all the cards face up and interpret each planet's card.

This spread follows the three major lines on the palm: the Head line, the Heart line, and the Life line. It also includes two minor lines: the Intuition line and the Fate line. When you're reading, there's no need to interpret the card meanings as fixed; instead, try to view this spread as a glimpse of how your life, relationships, and personality traits are developing at this particular moment in time.

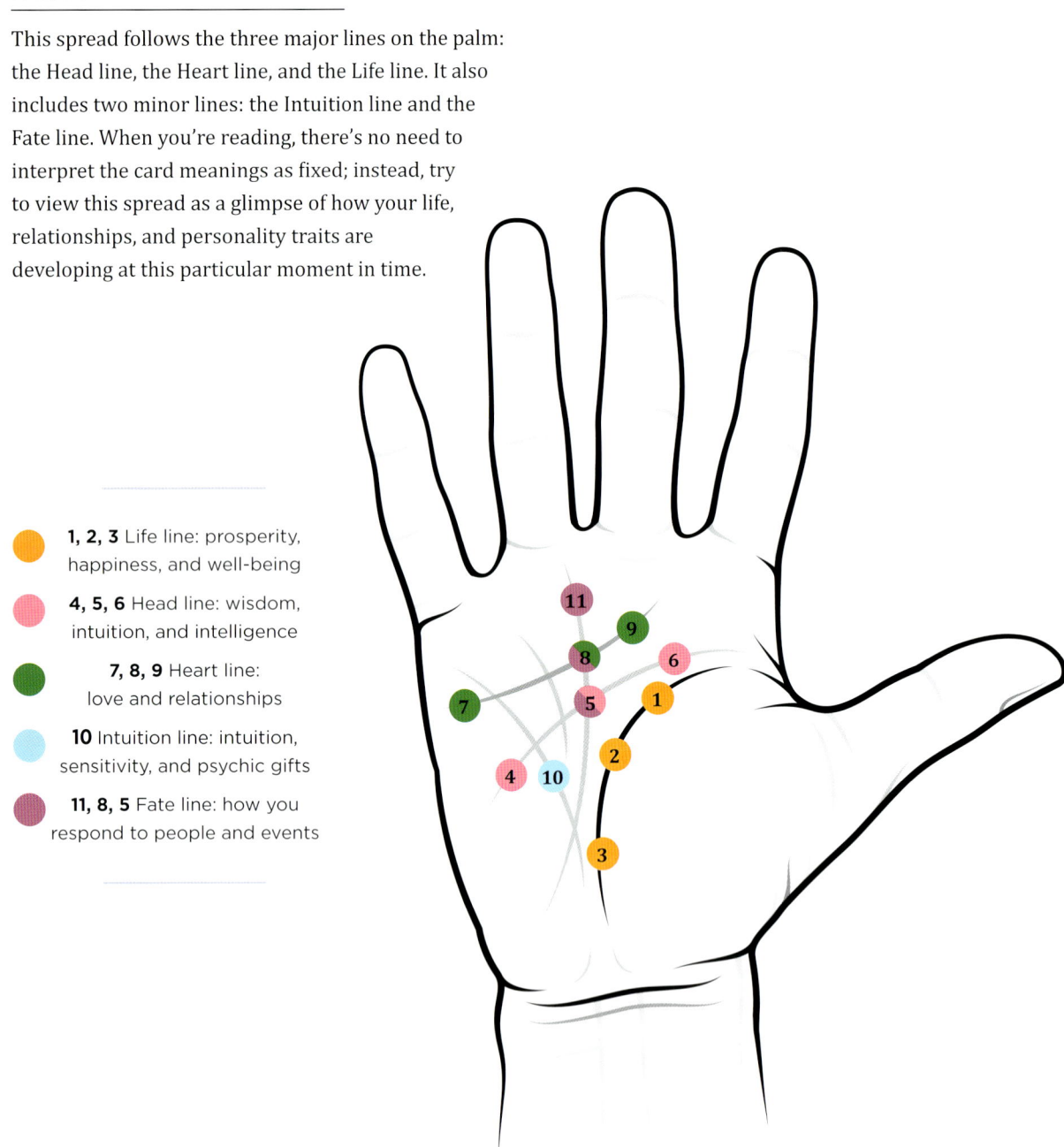

1, 2, 3 Life line: prosperity, happiness, and well-being

4, 5, 6 Head line: wisdom, intuition, and intelligence

7, 8, 9 Heart line: love and relationships

10 Intuition line: intuition, sensitivity, and psychic gifts

11, 8, 5 Fate line: how you respond to people and events

Shuffle the deck and choose your cards (see page 16). Lay out all the cards face down in order as shown above, then turn over all the cards and begin your interpretation.

CHINESE ASTROLOGY:
WHAT DO I NEED TO KNOW ABOUT MYSELF?

This spread is inspired by the personality traits of the twelve signs of the zodiac in Chinese astrology: the rat, ox, tiger, rabbit, dragon, snake, horse, sheep or goat, monkey, rooster, dog, and pig or boar.

As you shuffle the cards, ask, "What do I need to know about myself?" Choose your cards (see page 16), and lay them out face down as shown here. Turn over all the cards, and begin your interpretation.

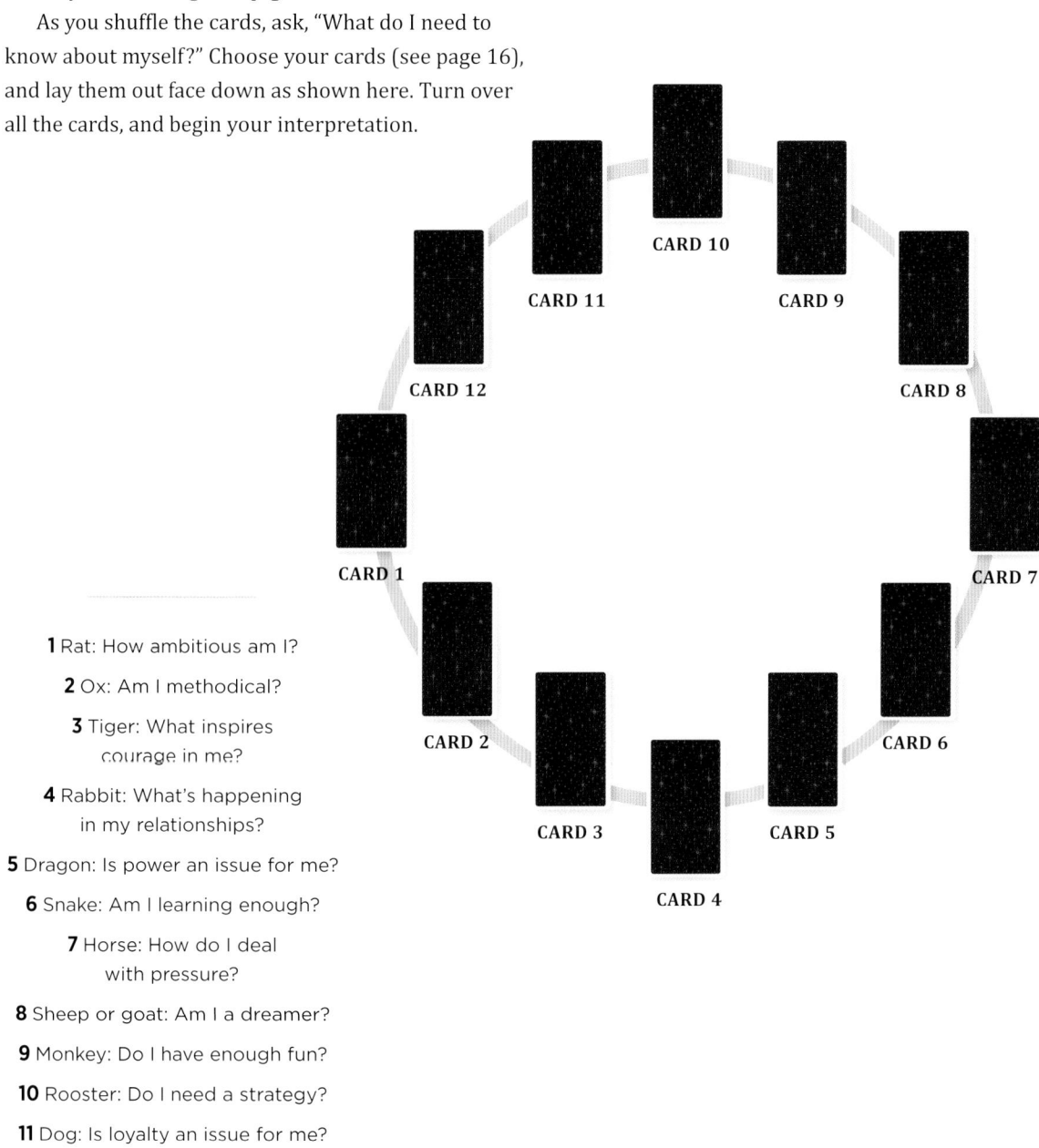

1 Rat: How ambitious am I?

2 Ox: Am I methodical?

3 Tiger: What inspires courage in me?

4 Rabbit: What's happening in my relationships?

5 Dragon: Is power an issue for me?

6 Snake: Am I learning enough?

7 Horse: How do I deal with pressure?

8 Sheep or goat: Am I a dreamer?

9 Monkey: Do I have enough fun?

10 Rooster: Do I need a strategy?

11 Dog: Is loyalty an issue for me?

12 Pig: Can I be positively self-indulgent?

9

CROSSROADS: CRISES, DECISIONS, AND CHANGE SPREADS

WHETHER YOU'VE GOT A BRAND-NEW BUSINESS IDEA, a corporate structure to navigate, or a new job to find, the spreads in this chapter can help. Offering a variety of approaches to decision making, they'll guide you as you assess immediate concerns and options when it comes to work and career. When we pause, reflect, and make our decisions from a place of inner wisdom, we're more able to see opportunities when they arise, and have the courage to walk away when we need to. Often, we feel we must wait for the next best thing before turning away from draining work or people; however, sometimes we may need to make that jump to create space for new possibilities to present themselves. From beginning a new business to dealing with crises and letting go so you can move on, here are insightful ways to help you explore the path ahead. Oh, and if you're suffering from horrible-boss syndrome? Never fear: There's a spread for that, too.

KEY CARDS FOR CRISIS, DECISIONS, AND CHANGE

LOOK FOR:

III The Emperor: Strong management; organization

VI The Lovers: A major turning point: making a mature decision for long-term benefits

VII The Chariot: Progress; new work or career

XI Justice: A fair decision, usually to your advantage

XX Judgement: Self-judgement; decisions about the past

Minor arcana Aces: Auspicious beginnings

Two of Pentacles: Weighing options

Three of Pentacles: Acknowledgment for work; also job interviews or presentations

Seven of Pentacles: Endurance; potential for success

Eight of Pentacles: Hard work, perfectionism, professionalism; can also indicate graduation

Two of Wands: A positive partnership; vision; also future plans

Six of Wands: Success and reward

Eight of Wands: Travel, news, flow; communication

Page of Swords: Contracts and documents

Page of Pentacles: A job offer or opportunity within your current job

Page of Wands: A creative person or activity: writing, acting, dance, or music; also job applications

Kings and Queens of Swords, Pentacles, and Wands: Business leaders, managers

WATCH OUT FOR:

XII The Hanged Man: Waiting around; stasis

XV The Devil: Unreasonable demands, unfair contracts, ego

XVI The Tower: Events beyond your control

XVIII The Moon: A crisis of faith; illusion

Five of Pentacles: Unemployment, or being excluded at work

Two of Swords: Procrastination, stalemate

Five of Swords: Opposition, confrontation

Eight of Swords: Restriction

Ten of Wands: Pressure, feeling overwhelmed

Reversed Court Cards: Mismanagement, manipulation, opposition

SPREADS FOR NAVIGATING WORK ISSUES

PAGES SPEAK: WILL I FIND WORK SOON?

In this spread, we examine the next three months to see whether job offers are forthcoming. It's an easy spread to try, because you get to ignore all card meanings apart from five cards: Take note of the position of the Page of Wands, the Page of Pentacles, the Page of Swords, and the Ace and Three of Pentacles.

Use only the minor arcana cards. Think about future work as you shuffle the deck: Then, dealing from the top of the deck, lay three rows of three cards in the order shown on the next page, all face up. Each row represents one week. When you've laid down the first three rows, continue to lay more rows of three underneath in order to see more weeks ahead. If you don't have much room on your table, lay the cards for week 4 onward on top of the existing three rows, as shown here. When you see one or more of the five Career Cards, make a note of the week or weeks in which they fall—and there you have your answers.

FIVE CAREER CARDS

Ace of Pentacles:
a new job begins

Three of Pentacles:
an interview or trial

Page of Wands:
the job application

Page of Pentacles:
the job offer

Page of Swords:
the contract of employment

CARD 1   CARD 2   CARD 3   Weeks 1, 4, 7, 10

CARD 4   CARD 5   CARD 6   Weeks 2, 5, 8, 11

CARD 7   CARD 8   CARD 9   Weeks 3, 6, 9, 12

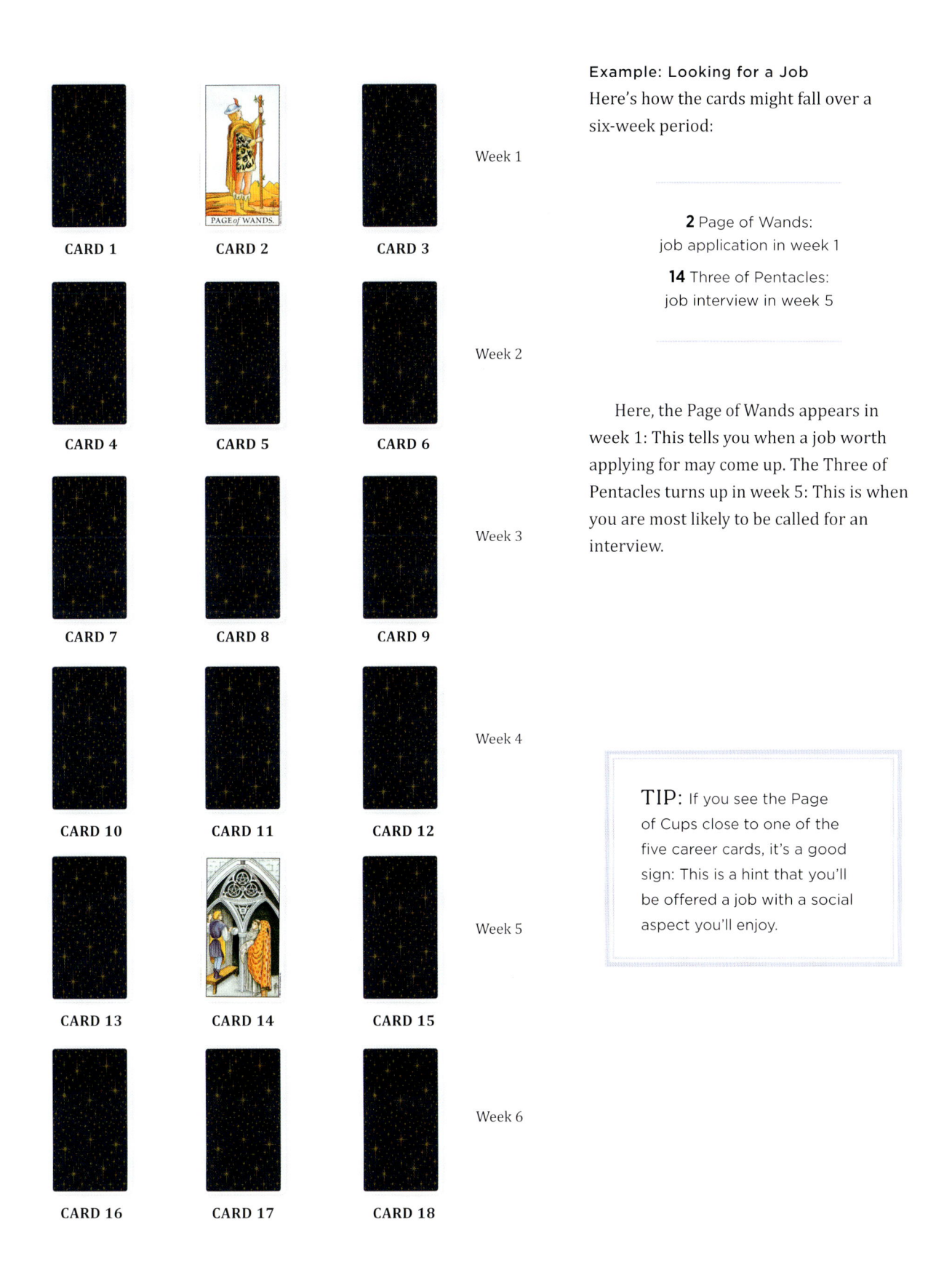

CARD 1	CARD 2	CARD 3	Week 1
CARD 4	CARD 5	CARD 6	Week 2
CARD 7	CARD 8	CARD 9	Week 3
CARD 10	CARD 11	CARD 12	Week 4
CARD 13	CARD 14	CARD 15	Week 5
CARD 16	CARD 17	CARD 18	Week 6

Example: Looking for a Job

Here's how the cards might fall over a six-week period:

2 Page of Wands:
job application in week 1

14 Three of Pentacles:
job interview in week 5

Here, the Page of Wands appears in week 1: This tells you when a job worth applying for may come up. The Three of Pentacles turns up in week 5: This is when you are most likely to be called for an interview.

> **TIP:** If you see the Page of Cups close to one of the five career cards, it's a good sign: This is a hint that you'll be offered a job with a social aspect you'll enjoy.

TWO PATHS: SHOULD I STAY OR SHOULD I GO?

This is a great spread for a very common career question (we've all been there!). It allows you to explore the potential of a career move alongside current blocks and opportunities.

1 Present work situation

2 Is anything blocking me from moving on?

3 What are my strengths?

4 Is there any reason to stay?

5 What are the benefits of staying?

6 Is anything blocking me from progressing where I am?

7 Which strengths shall I play to?

8 Outcome: Should I stay?

Shuffle and choose your cards (see page 16), laying them all face down as shown here. Then turn over all the cards, and begin your interpretation, from cards 1 through 8.

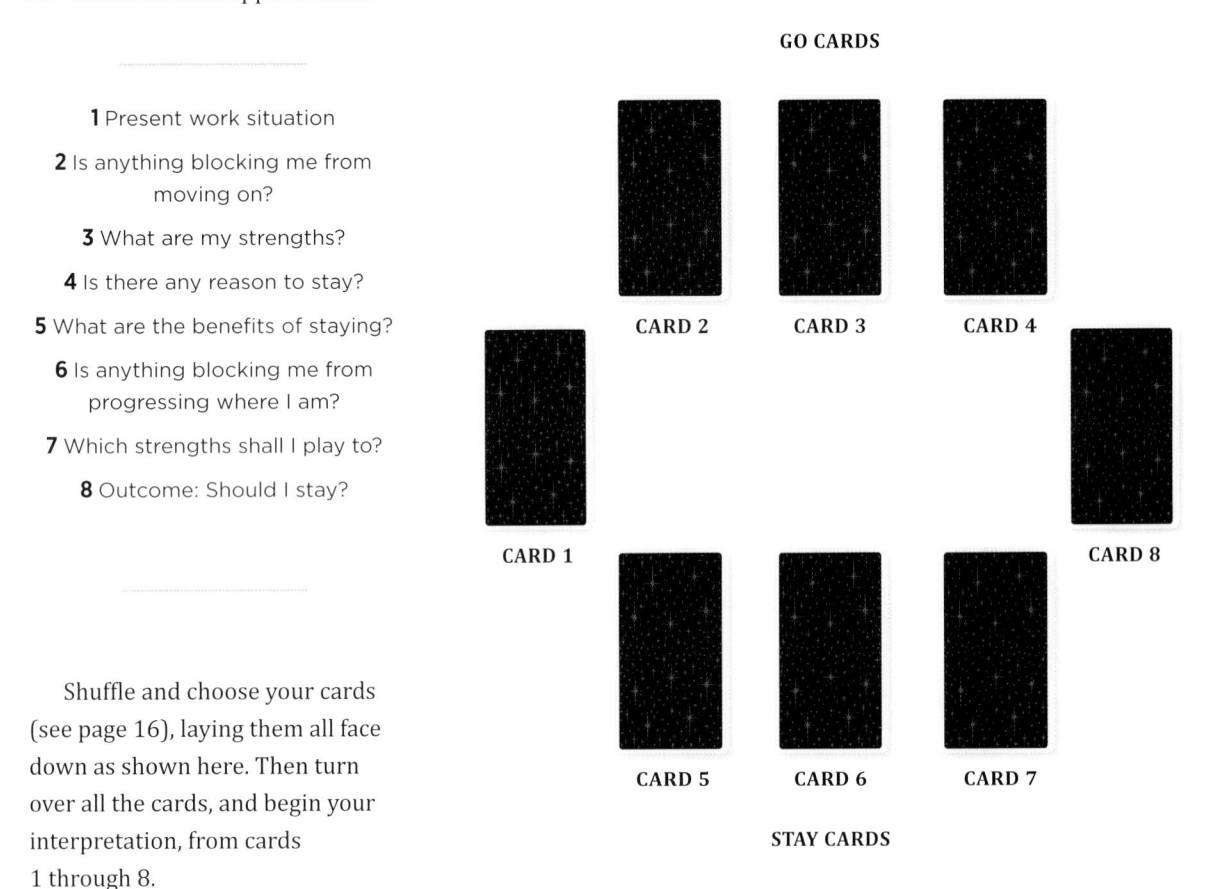

GO CARDS

CARD 2   CARD 3   CARD 4

CARD 1   CARD 8

CARD 5   CARD 6   CARD 7

STAY CARDS

TIPS

• If you need help interpreting the outcome card, refer to page 23 the "Yes or No?" reading, for a list of cards and their yes-or-no interpretations.

• If you draw the Ten of Wands as your first card, take a deep breath and clear your mind; then shuffle and lay again. This Ten often indicates that there's too much going on just now, and you may be feeling overwhelmed about making a decision. Readings work best when you're feeling relaxed. If it appears anywhere when you lay the cards a second time, leave the reading for three days before you try again.

The Ace of Wands is the tarot's entrepreneur card. It denotes beginnings, ideas, and energy.

1 What kind of business can I create?

2 When could I to do this?

3 Lessons learned from past experience

4 What other skills I may need

5 What or who is on my side?

6 Outcome: Will I succeed?

First, remove the Ace of Wands from the deck and place it at the top, as shown. Then shuffle the remainder of the deck and lay out the cards as shown here, face down. Then turn over all the cards from 1 to 5. Interpret them first, then turn over the outcome card.

To figure out a timeline for card 2, use the minor arcana to suggest a season of the year: Swords for winter, Pentacles for fall, Cups for summer, and Wands for spring. If you have a major arcana card for card 2, deal another card from the top of the deck: The first minor arcana card you see suggests the season in which you might start your venture.

CARD 6

CARD 5

CARD 4

CARD 3

CARD 2

CARD 1

BOSSES: DEALING WITH THE DEVIL (IN PRADA)

The apparent omnipresence of the power-crazed boss or coworker has engendered many a novel and movie. And this spread is based on the movie *The Devil Wears Prada* (2006), which is the story of Andrea, a young journalist beholden to her magazine-editor boss, Miranda Priestly (rather a wonderful name for the devil!). It isn't long before Andrea's life becomes controlled by her boss's ridiculous twenty-four-hour demands—and she loses her partner and friends in the bargain. Unfortunately, this drama isn't always fiction: For many of us, it's a very real past (or current) experience. Worse still, the devil-as-boss trope becomes a repeating theme: We leave one devil-boss job only to meet another bully or manipulator in the next. But by understanding the role the devil plays in our lives—and by figuring out who can help us break his or her spell—we can recognize the old pattern before it takes a firm hold. Then we can take steps toward change—whether it's to assert our boundaries within our current position or to escape from the situation for good.

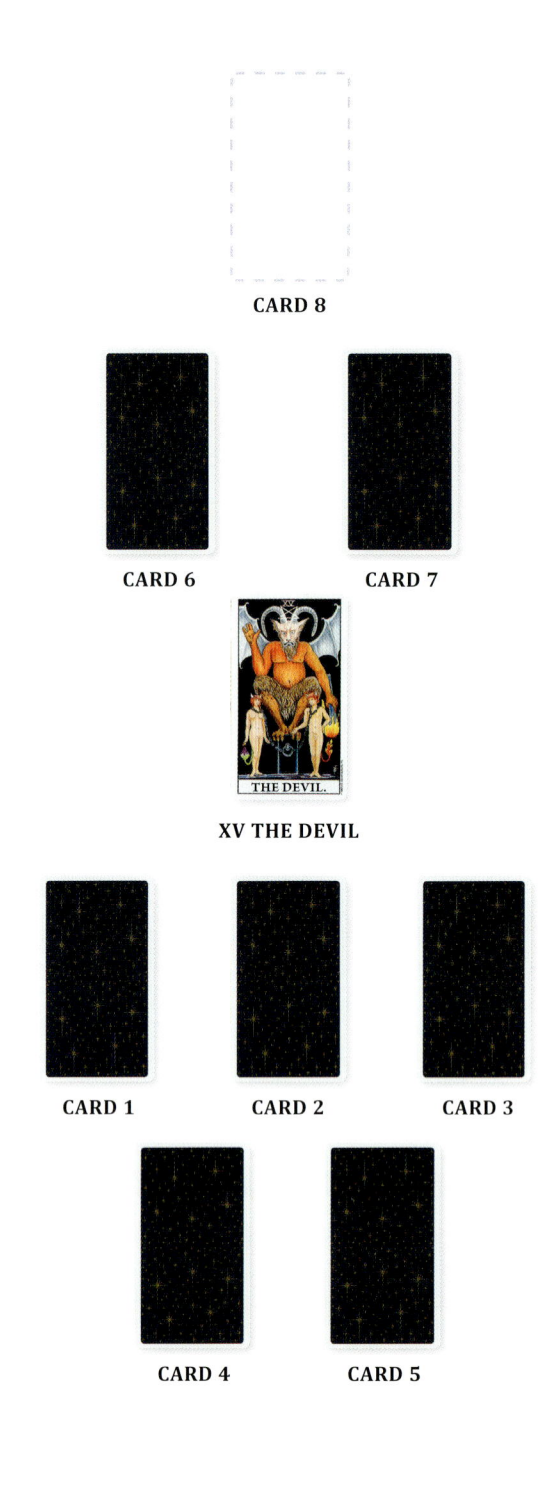

1 You: how you feel at work now

2 Your boss: their personality or actions

3 How your boss impacts your career

4 Colleague 1: advice and/or attitude: what to do

5 Colleague 2: advice and/or attitude: what to ignore

6 Lesson to be learned

7 Outcome

8 Alternative outcome

Begin by taking card XV The Devil from the deck and placing it face up in the center, as shown above. Place cards 1, 2, and 3 below it, then cards 4 and 5 below those, followed by 6 and 7 above it. Don't lay down card 8 until you've finished interpreting the first seven cards. Card 8 represents an alternative future that's possible when you've considered what action to take—and which messages to ignore.

Lisette disliked both her boss and her work environment in general. Here's how she interpreted her cards:

CARD 8

CARD 6
Ten of Swords

CARD 7
Five of Pentacles

XV THE DEVIL

CARD 1
Ten of Wands

CARD 2
Four of Swords

CARD 3
XII The Hanged Man

CARD 4
I The Magician

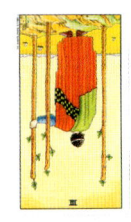

CARD 5
Three of Wands

1 Ten of Wands (Lisette's situation): Lisette was overwhelmed with work and felt belittled and couldn't see a way to gain perspective on her situation. She was beginning to feel she was at fault.

2 Four of Swords (her boss): Appeared to do nothing, while she did all the work.

3 XII Hanged Man (boss's impact): This meant her career was in limbo; her boss was either absent or didn't acknowledge her input. She found herself getting used to this behavior, and in danger of losing control of her career.

4 I The Magician: The card for colleague 1, who encouraged her to stand up to the Devil or take action to leave. He reminded her of all her untapped skills.

5 The Three of Wands reversed: The card for colleague 2, who threatened to leave for months, but did nothing. She was a constant source of negativity.

6 The Ten of Swords: The lesson card. Lisette felt this was a warning: if she continued on like this, she could walk out of her current position without a new job lined up. Or, if her job suddenly ended for some reason, she'd be so bruised that she would find it hard to present herself well in a job interview.

7 The Five of Pentacles (outcome): This is the most likely outcome, if the current situation doesn't change—and it reflected Lisette's worst fears: She'd be unemployed and cash-poor.

Lisette considered her tarot reading and focused on an alternative future. What would happen if she took her supportive colleague's advice and made changes, as suggested by the presence of The Magician? She drew another outcome card:

8 XXI The World (alternative outcome): Here, the World represents order restored, plus endings and new beginnings. Lisette saw this as a way to approach her situation: that is, to accept that she had to move on and appreciate all she had achieved—and, with that positive focus, look for a more rewarding work environment.

Here's a simple spread to try when you're considering changing your profession or working within a different industry rather than examining specific issues surrounding your current job situation. Is this the right path for you on a long-term basis?

S Significator: King of Wands, Swords, Cups, or Pentacles

1 My recent experience in this career

2 What's the most I can gain if I stay on this path?

3 Most likely outcome, or advice to self

CARD 3

CARD 1

S
King

CARD 2

Begin by taking the four Kings from the deck, then look at the list below to see which King most closely represents the type of work or work environment in which you're presently engaged. Place that King in the center, face up, as shown above. Return the other Kings to the deck, then shuffle and choose your cards (see page 16), laying them face down. Turn all the cards face up, then begin your interpretation.

KINGS IN THE WORKPLACE

King of Wands	Entrepreneurship, inventor; business; media, communications and travel; coaching
King of Cups	Counselor, negotiator, charities, health, human resources, teaching, the arts
King of Pentacles	Banking and finance, building industry, real estate, agriculture, manufacturing, sport, food industry
King of Swords	Medicine, law, science, psychology, research, politics, training, protection services (military, police, security)

HOW CAN I ATTRACT MORE CLIENTS?

This is a common dilemma for freelancers. From stylists to writers, promoters to retailers, keeping up a steady flow of clients is essential. Try this layout to discover what might enhance your success as a freelancer in your industry.

Shuffle and choose your cards (see page 16), and lay them all face down as shown here. Turn cards 1 to 5 face up and interpret them, then look at the outcome card. View each card as direct advice.

1 Your situation now

2 What's detracting from your success

3, 4, 5 Three new approaches to your business

6 Outcome

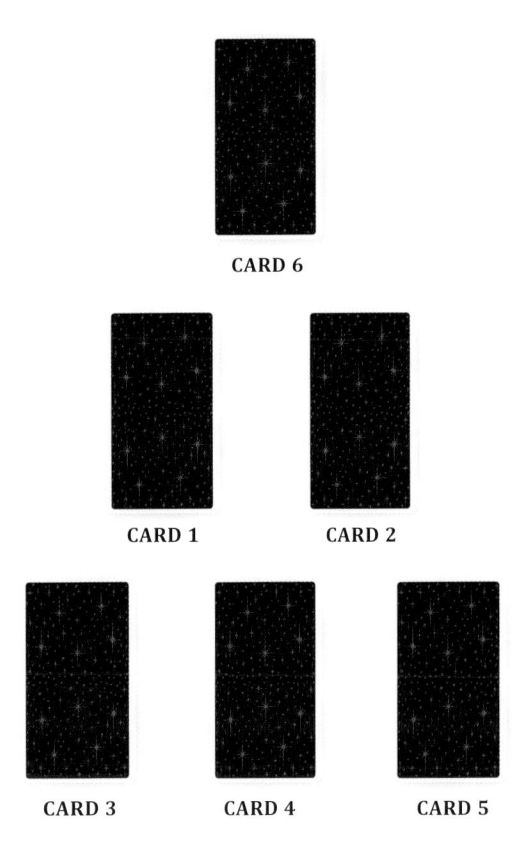

CARD 6

CARD 1   CARD 2

CARD 3   CARD 4   CARD 5

Example

If you got the Ten of Swords, the Eight of Wands, and the Knight of Pentacles Reversed for cards 3, 4, and 5, they could be interpreted as:

Ten of Swords: Accept the end of a business relationship. Look elsewhere for what you need.

Eight of Wands: Travel and/or promote what you do more actively through your network.

Knight of Pentacles reversed: Look again at your business plan. Is it still viable?

SPREADS FOR LIFE CHOICES

THE FOUR ACES: WHAT'S MY DIRECTION?

This spread is an enhancement of a Four Aces spread shared by the late author and astrologer Jonathan Dee. The Four Aces are the gifts of each minor arcana suit, and they denote a different aspect of our lives. By laying two cards on either side of each Ace, we can see which life area and skills are likely to be most productive for us, and aspects in which we may be blocked. I've added the directions associated with the four suits if you'd like a literal steer as to where you might go geographically, too, but the spread works perfectly well without this dimension.

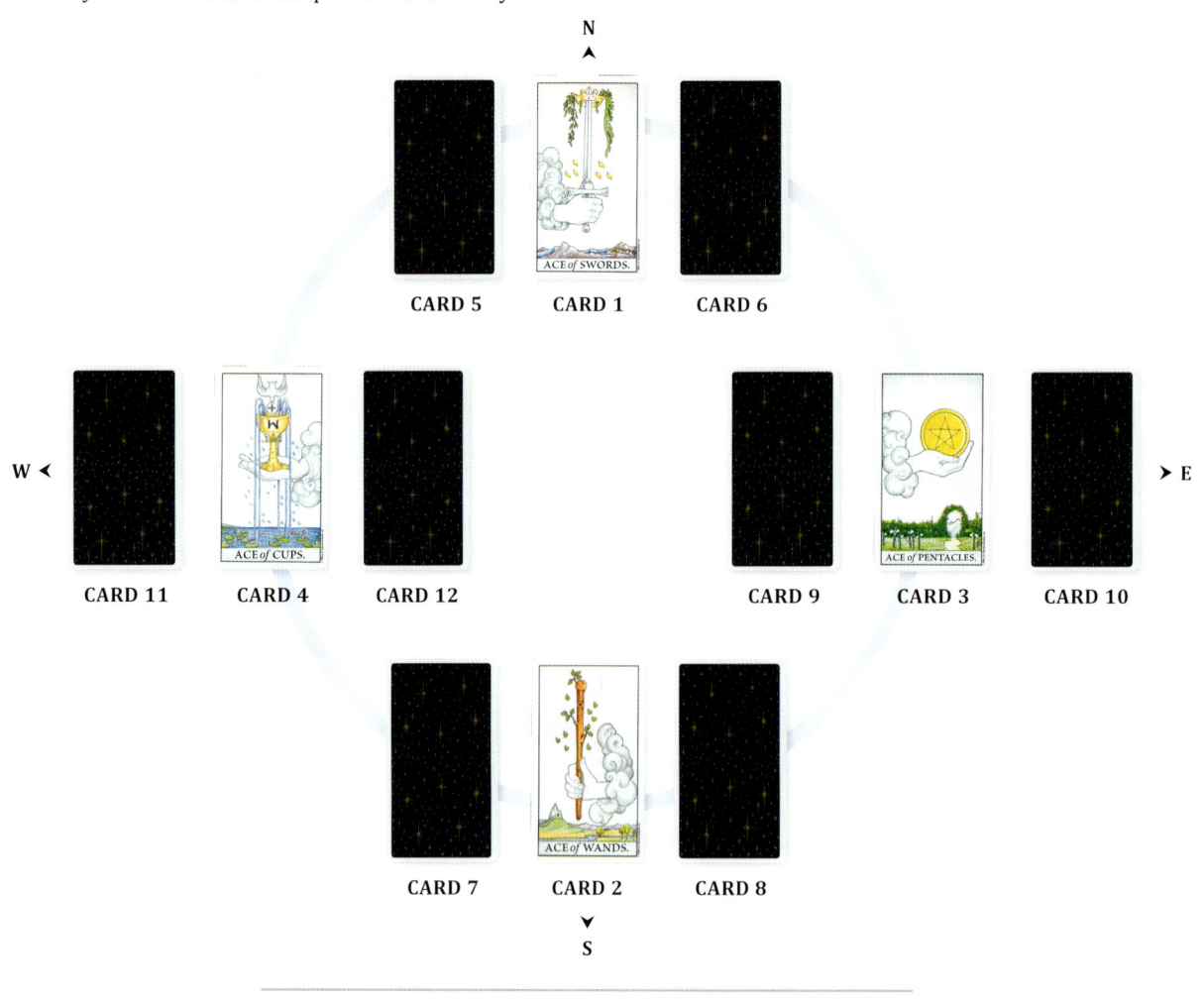

1 Swords: decisions, analysis: the mind

5, 6 past and future

2 Wands: intuition and desire: projects, communication: the soul

7, 8 past and future

3 Pentacles: money, property, security: the body and the physical world

9, 10 past and future

4 Cups: love and relationships: the emotions

11, 12 past and future

Take the Aces from the minor arcana and lay them in a circle as shown on the previous page, face up. Now take the major arcana and shuffle the cards. Lay a card on each side of each Ace, face down. Now turn over the first Ace. The major card to the left is the past; the one to the right is the future. Turn over the cards around each Ace, and interpret them.

Developing the Reading: Taking Action

Look at the Ace that you want to investigate further. For example, if you got XVII The Star in the future position for the Ace of Cups, you might want to know what you can do to activate the benefits associated with that card (for The Star, this would be guidance, creativity, and healing). Take the Ace and its future card to a new place on your table with enough room to lay more cards around it.

Now shuffle the remaining cards in the deck and lay two more cards, as shown below.

The Six of Swords (card 1) shows an opportunity to move on emotionally or physically through a move or traveling. The Six of Pentacles represents support and generosity, giving and receiving, and, in relationships, staying open to new love and friendship.

1 Who or what can help me move forward?

2 What action can I take?

CARD 1

CARD 2

THE LION: HOW CAN I MAKE THE BEST OF A BAD SITUATION?

We use card VIII Strength as the focus for this reading. The maiden on this card is calm and patient in the face of great danger from the lion; she holds his jaws apart, accepting his power while standing her ground. This spread is helpful if you've faced difficult times recently. It can give you insight into the causes of the issue and your reactions to it, and can suggest choices you might make in order to heal and move forward.

Take out card VIII Strength from the major arcana and place it face up in the center as shown. Then shuffle and choose the remaining cards (see page 16), and lay them out in a row in the order shown above, face down. Turn over cards 1 through 5 and begin your interpretation.

1 Present situation

2 How the lion roared: past causes of the situation

3 What could I release in order to move on?

4 What could I hold on to?

5 Outcome

VIII STRENGTH

| CARD 2 | CARD 3 | CARD 1 | CARD 4 | CARD 5 |

TIP: Add up the numbers of the five cards you've laid down and reduce it until you have a major arcana card (for more details on how to do this, see page 27). This card offers a way in which you might approach the situation as a whole. For example, if your numbers reduced to II The High Priestess, then discretion will be an important factor, while XIX The Sun tells you to protect and nurture yourself in a safe place.

POWER OF THREE: WHAT DO I NEED TO LET GO OF TO MOVE ON?

The ritual of laying and choosing cards in rows is part of a transformational process: In it, you physically and mentally move through the cards and select the pieces of your life you'd like to let go of—people, memories, projects, responsibilities—and the pieces you'd like to hold on to as you move forward.

Shuffle and choose your cards (see page 16) and lay them all face down as shown here.

Begin with the first row; turn only these cards face up.

Interpret the card meanings and choose one card to let go of. Turn it face down.

Do the same for the next two rows, so that you have six cards face up, with two on each row, for example:

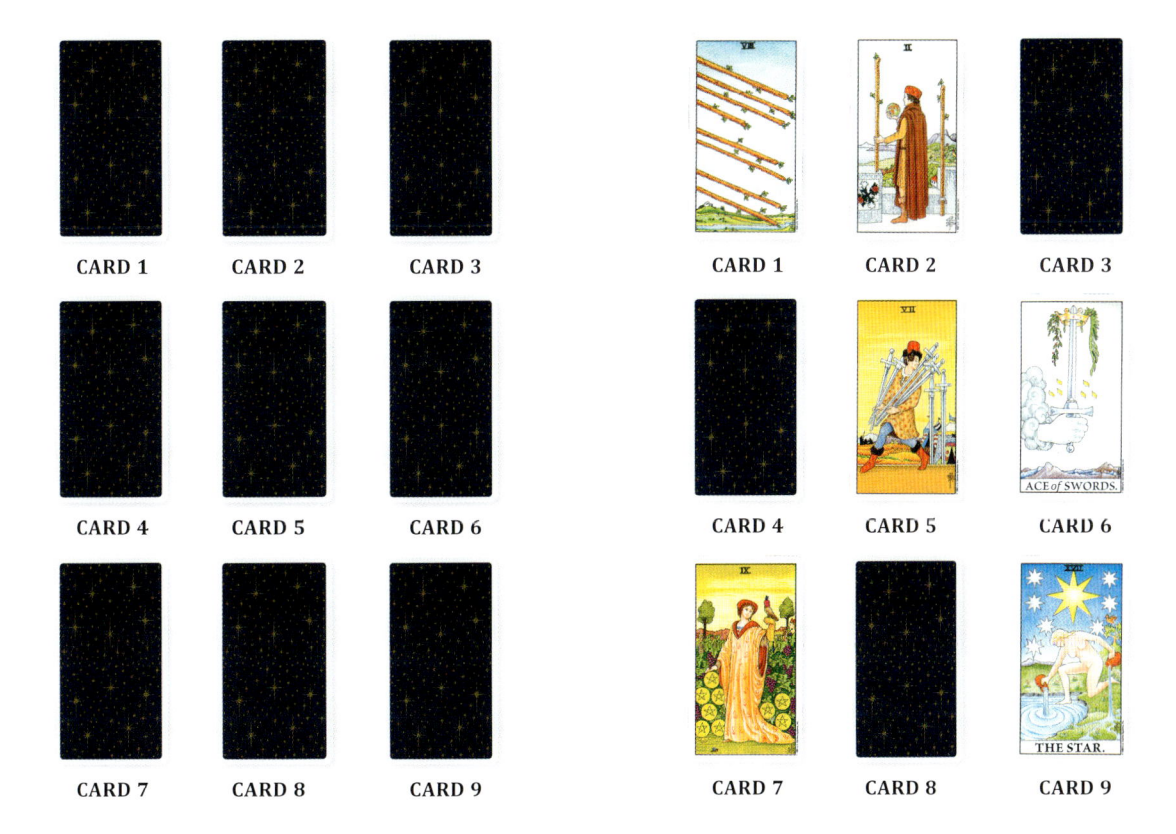

CARD 1 CARD 2 CARD 3

CARD 4 CARD 5 CARD 6

CARD 7 CARD 8 CARD 9

(continued)

Now take the three cards that are face down and place them in a row:

1 The circumstances that led to the situation

2 The situation itself

3 The impact it made upon you

CARD 1
Card from row 1

CARD 2
Card from row 2

CARD 3
Card from row 3

Now refer back to the original layout, which has six cards left, face up. Focus on what you want to keep in your life: As you do so, choose one card from each row that you like. (Card 4 comes from row 1 of the original nine-card layouts; card 5 from row 2; card 6 from row 3.) These cards show you how to let go of each of the issues revealed in cards 1, 2, and 3, so place them above each card.

CARD 4

CARD 5

CARD 6

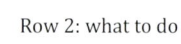 Row 2: what to do

CARD 1

CARD 2

CARD 3

Row 1: what happened

Now interpret cards 1 and 4 together as a problem or an event and a way forward; then do the same for cards 2 and 5; and, finally, for cards 3 and 6.

Are you struggling to choose between two different paths? This layout can help. Use it to divine the possible outcome of each option.

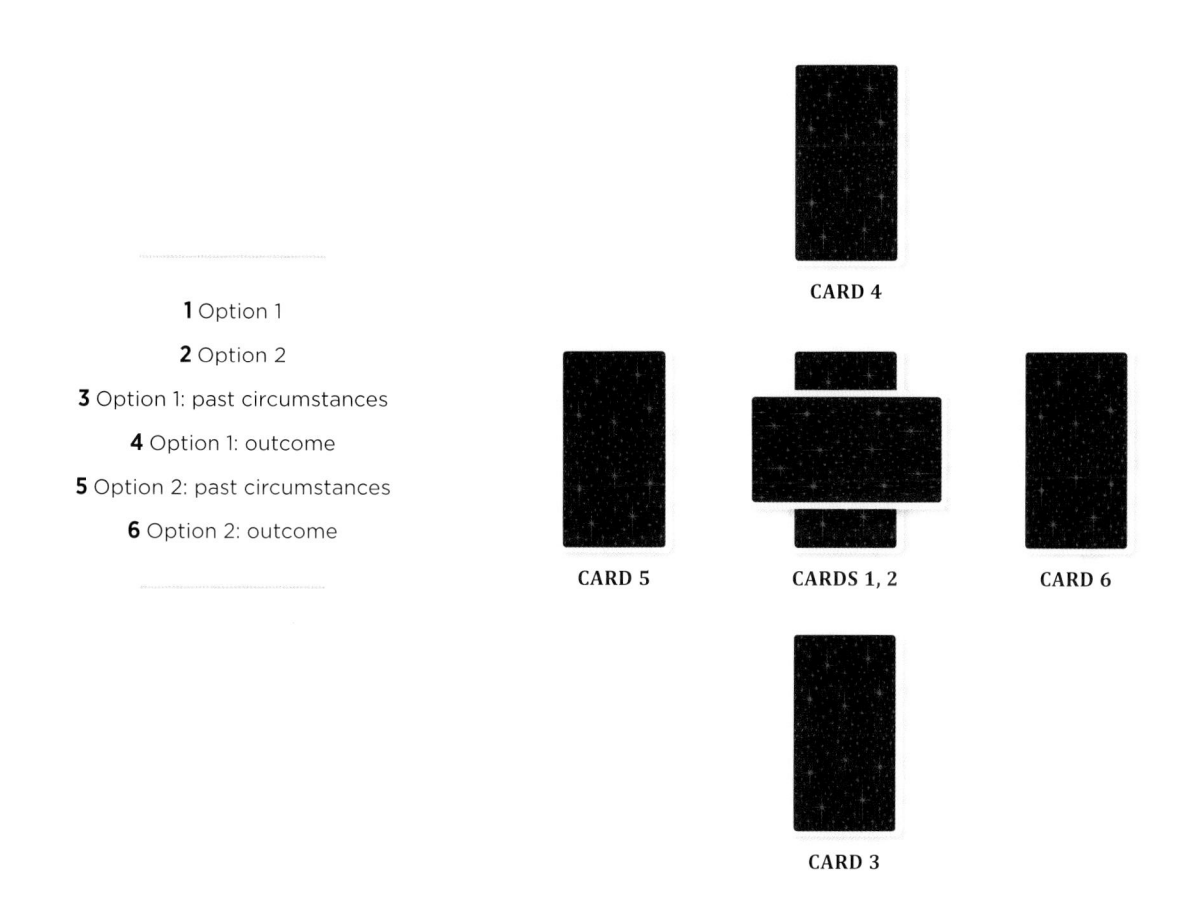

1 Option 1

2 Option 2

3 Option 1: past circumstances

4 Option 1: outcome

5 Option 2: past circumstances

6 Option 2: outcome

CARD 4

CARD 5

CARDS 1, 2

CARD 6

CARD 3

Shuffle and choose your cards (see page 16), placing them all face down in the positions shown. Turn all the cards face up and begin your interpretation. The option 1 and option 2 cards reveal the two choices you have; the remaining cards show the past circumstances surrounding each situation and the most likely future outcome given the present circumstances. When you've interpreted each card, compare your two outcome cards, 4 and 6. Which do you prefer?

Hecate was the Greek goddess of the crossroads, often depicted with her three symbols: the dog, the snake, and the horse, represented in this spread as your instinct (dog), wisdom (snake), and willpower (horse).

Card XVIII The Moon is central in this layout, because the card's two towers signify the threshold between your comfort zone and the potentially threatening territory beyond. The crayfish, a symbol of the soul, is emerging from the water. To move forward, it will have to writhe on the earth, encounter the wolf-dogs who protect the tower gateway, and survive to discover what lies ahead. This is a great spread to try when you're procrastinating and losing faith in your ability to decide. The cards reveal what's going on beneath the surface, and help you see the potential outcome of any decisions you may make.

1 You or your situation

2, 3 The pillars: the environment

4, 5 The wolves: risks and challenges to confront

6 Your instinct

7 Your wisdom

8 Your willpower

9 Potential gain

10 Outcome

Remove card XVIII The Moon from your deck, and place it in the center as shown above. Shuffle and choose your cards (see page 16). Lay out cards 1 through 10 face down, then turn over all the cards and begin your interpretation.

CARD 10

CARD 9

CARD 2

XVIII
THE MOON

CARD 3

CARD 4

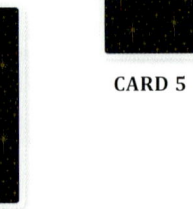

CARD 5

CARD 1

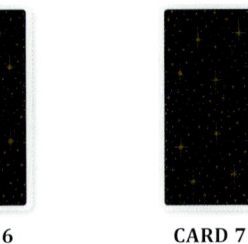

CARD 6

CARD 7

CARD 8

10

SPIRITUAL DEVELOPMENT: SACRED SYMBOLS AND DIVINE BEINGS SPREADS

THESE SPREADS OFFER A HOST OF WAYS TO EXPLORE your spiritual path through sacred symbols and traditions. Symbols include the pentagram of Wicca, the lightning flash symbol of the mystical system of Kabbalah, and the infinity symbol, along with the ancient spiral spread; all of these are insightful ways to look more deeply at your spiritual connection and development.

Here, too, are layouts inspired by divine beings. If you're attracted to angels, then the angelic guidance spread is for you; then find the Ascended Masters, or great teachers in spirit with whom you connect in the "Spread of the Seven Rays" on pages 298 and 299.

KEY CARDS
FOR SACRED SYMBOLS AND DIVINE BEINGS

LOOK FOR:

II The High Priestess: Mentor, keeper of spiritual law: hidden or esoteric knowledge; the psychic; the afterlife; the goddesses Isis and Hathor, associated with magic, life, and fertility

III The Empress: The mother; the goddesses Demeter (the harvest), Venus (love and fertility); also Hathor and Isis (see above)

IV The Emperor: The father; order and protection

V The Hierophant: Orthodox beliefs and religion

IX The Hermit: The monk; the spiritual seeker; meditation, reflection, wisdom

X The Wheel of Fortune: Destiny; a turn for the better

XVII The Star: Hope, spiritual healing

XVI The Tower: A collapse of the ego, bringing illumination

XIX The Sun: Enlightenment, the divinity within

XX Judgement: The past; spirit guides and people in spirit

XXI The World: Spiritual ascension

The three Tarot Angels:

   VI The Lovers: Archangel Raphael, for healing

   XIV Temperance: Archangel Michael, for truth and protection

   XX Judgement: Archangel Gabriel, for news and creativity

Page of Cups: The young psychic

WATCH OUT FOR:

II The High Priestess and V The Hierophant reversed: Corruption, egotism, false prophets

XV The Devil: Ego and manipulation

XVIII The Moon: A crisis of faith

SPREADS FOR SPIRITUAL DEVELOPMENT

THE PENTAGRAM: ALL OF ME

As an ancient symbol of protection, the pentagram's five points represent the four elements—earth, air, fire, and water—and the fifth element of ether, or spirit. A pentagram spread helps you view yourself holistically from an elemental perspective.

S Significator

1 Water: Emotions and love. What do you need more, or less, of?

2 Fire: Intuition and desires. What is your intuition telling you?

3 Earth: Security. What grounds you? What are you "growing" for the future?

4 Air: Thoughts and influences. What's your focus?

5 Spirit: The cumulative effect of cards 1 through 4; all of you

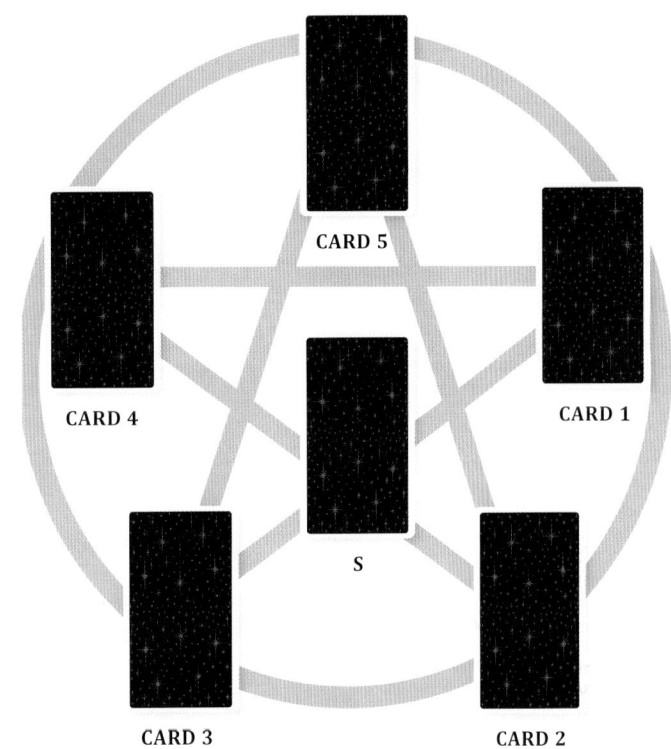

Separate the major and minor arcanas: You will only need the major arcana cards for this reading. Shuffle the major arcana and choose your cards (see page 16), then lay them out as shown, face down, beginning with the Significator in the center. Next, turn them all face up, and begin your interpretation.

James needed to reflect on an on-again, off-again relationship. He had been involved with someone who seemed to be dismissive of his belief in spirituality, but the attraction between them still felt powerful. Here are his cards:

CARD 5
Spirit

CARD 4
Emotions

CARD 1
Security

S
Significator

CARD 3
Intuition

CARD 2
Thoughts/influences

James identified card 1, The Sun, as the future he wanted in terms of a relationship: a loving partnership with a soul mate and true kindred spirit. The Empress, in the thoughts and influences position, represented his on-again, off-again partner. His intuition, in the form of The Chariot, was telling him he needed to move on, and The Lovers, in the emotions position, revealed that the relationship he'd hoped would be serious was now in jeopardy. He also said that he'd been putting off making a final decision because he still hoped it might be worth trying again. This is indicated by Judgement, the Significator card, which is all about reviewing the past and the possibility of second chances. The Spirit card, The Emperor, showed James as he is, as a whole person—according to his interpretation, a man ready to take responsibility and embrace his position in society, possibly as a husband and leader. He said, "Actually, seeing that card means I know I'm ready for the next step in my life—whether or not my ex is. And maybe it's time to find someone who wants to make that commitment, too: physically, emotionally, and spiritually."

This layout reflects the pattern of the ten sephirot, or spheres, of the Tree of Life, the central motif of the mystical Judaic system of teachings called Kabbalah. The sephirot express the story of creation: They speak of the divine will that flowed from the source, creating the top three sephirot, which overflowed in turn and created more sephirot beneath. The lightning flash, a symbol of spiritual awakening, is the movement between the sephirot in their numbered order. The paths between each sephira show approaches to divinity, or ways of understanding God. In a tarot reading, you might read the cards as a journey, beginning with card 1—that which is unconscious or unmade—to card 10, or what *is* made or manifested. As you journey, you're traveling through layers of self-awareness, examining the male and female aspects of yourself, love, power, rebirth, relationships, the mind, and, ultimately, what's happening in your material world.

1 Kether: Your divine purpose

2 Chockmah: Your wisdom and values

3 Binah: Your creative power

4 Chesed: Love and self-support

5 Geburah: Issues of power: what opposes you

6 Tiphareth: Achievements

7 Netzach: Attractions and relationships

8 Hod: Work, intelligence, and communication

9 Yesod: What is hidden; dreams and the psyche

10 Malkuth: The future environment; the outcome

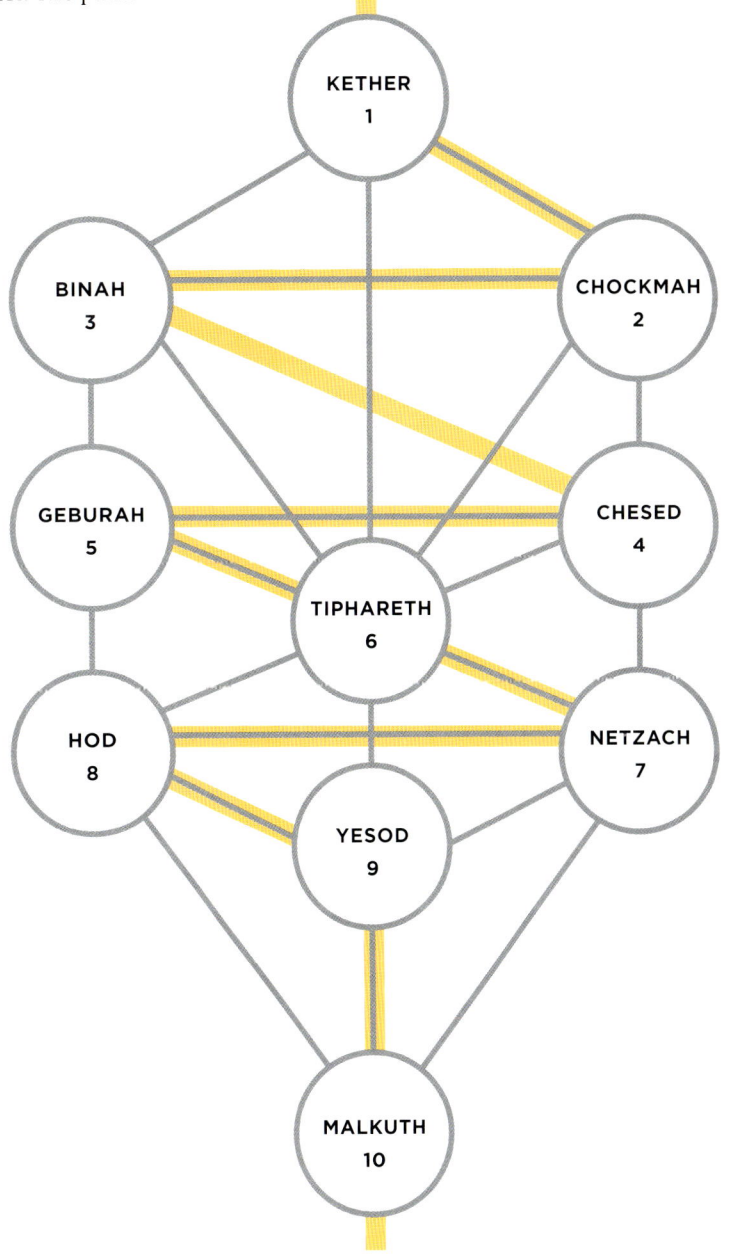

Developing the Reading:

Linking in the Major Arcana

Traditionally, the major arcana cards are linked with pathways—the routes between two sephirots—on the Tree of Life. However, we can also link these cards with the sephirots themselves. Below is a list of my associations: You might also want to devise your own. In a reading, if any of these cards appears in the sephirot positions, take particular note of each card and prioritize its meaning in your reading. For example, if you got The Empress as card 3, which is linked with 3, Binah, then compassion and creativity are key issues for you right now.

FURTHER SEPHIROT MEANINGS AND THE MAJOR ARCANA

SEPHIROT	ASSOCIATIONS	MAJOR ARCANA CARDS
1 Kether	The crown; divine light	0 The Fool, XII The Hanged Man
2 Chockmah	Wisdom, action; the male principle	IV The Emperor, VII The Chariot
3 Binah	Understanding, compassion, creativity; the female principle	III The Empress
4 Chesed	Universal love, peace, the law	V The Hierophant, XI Justice
5 Geburah	Power, destruction, judgement	XVI The Tower, XIII Death
6 Tiphareth	Beauty, the child, rebirth	XVII The Star, XIX The Sun, XX Judgement
7 Netzach	Endurance, relationships, instinct, desire	VIII Strength, VI The Lovers, XV The Devil
8 Hod	The mind, communication, intelligence	I The Magician
9 Yesod	The unconscious; dreams, intuition, psychic ability	II The High Priestess, XVIII The Moon, IX The Hermit
10 Malkuth	The earth, physical reality	X The Wheel of Fortune, XXI The World

Three Archangels are depicted in the tarot: VI The Lovers, XIV Temperance, and XX Judgement. These cards share a common meaning: They ask us to weigh a situation and make a decision. Need a little angelic guidance to help you come to your decision? Try this simple spread.

VI The Lovers: Shows Archangel Raphael, the Holy Healer.

Meaning: Love, and choices that bring long-term happiness.

Advice: Choose love over gratification.

XIV Temperance: Shows Archangel Michael, the warrior-angel of truth and protection.

Meaning: Negotiation, reconciliation, and finding balance.

Advice: Be strong; hold your integrity. You are protected.

XX Judgement: Shows Archangel Gabriel, the messenger of the Annunciation.

Meaning: A spiritual wake-up call; renewal, self-judgement, and second chances.

Advice: Accept the past. It's time to begin again.

Remove The Lovers, Temperance, and Judgement from your deck. Place them face down in a row. Close your eyes and ask any question you might have. If you don't have a specific question, you might simply like to say, "Please show me the angel who can guide me today." Open your eyes and touch the first card you are drawn to, then turn it over. This is your angel tarot card for the day. Now see the card meaning and advice, as shown to the left.

Developing the Reading:
Meditating on Your Card

Close your eyes, hold the card to your heart, and ask for a message from the angel of your card: Raphael, Michael, or Gabriel. An image may form in your mind, or you may see or hear words; or, you might find that, over the next few days, you are compelled to notice particular words or images or to pay special attention to certain conversations. This is the angel's way of guiding you toward a message.

THE SPREAD OF THE SEVEN RAYS

The seven rays relate to the mystical system of Theosophy. The seven rays are emanations of the divine will of God, the universe, or All That Is. They are held by Ascended Masters, beings who once lived in human form and who have taken initiations, or undergone spiritual transformations. Each Master is associated with a number of qualities, represented by the card positions.

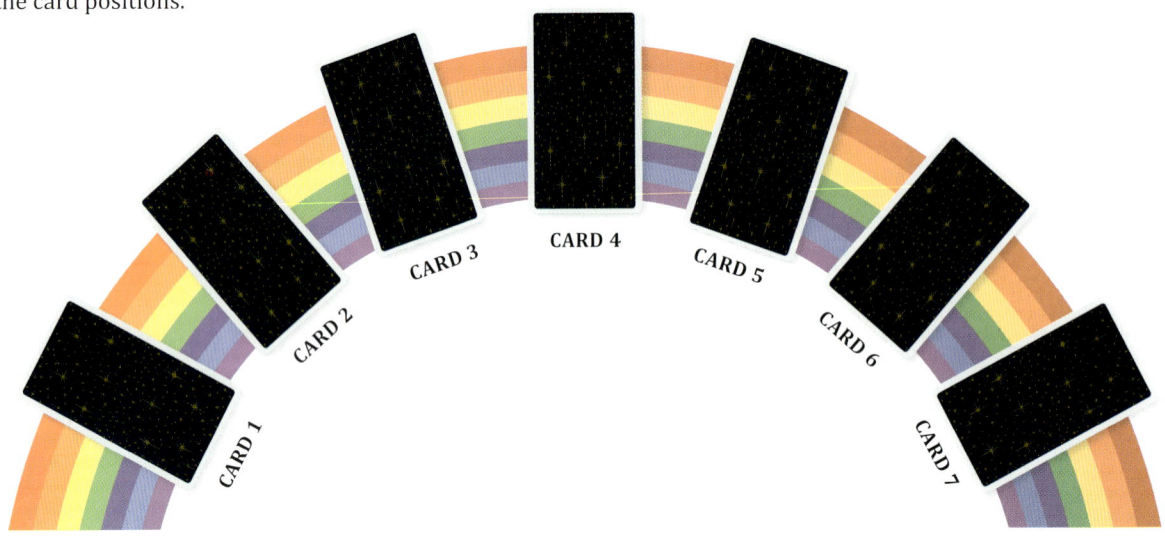

1 Faith

2 Willpower

3 Creativity

4 Peace

5 Health and healing

6 Sacrifice

7 Change and progress

Shuffle the deck and choose your cards (see page 16), and lay them out face down as shown above. (Note that in this spread we don't use reversals, so if any reversed cards appear, turn them upright.) Turn over all the cards and begin your interpretation. Take note of any major arcana cards, as these can reveal an Ascended Master (see the chart on the next page); you might like to find out more about that Master's teaching.

A Daily Ascended Master's Reading

As you shuffle the major arcana cards only, ask, "Which Ascended Master's teaching do I need today?" (Again, we don't use reversals for this reading.) You might like to visualize that Master's color, too: See the chart below for associated colors and meanings.

THE WORLD.

The World is associated with the Ascended Master Serapis Bey, who guides us toward peace and spiritual ascension.

THE SEVEN RAYS, MASTERS, AND MAJOR ARCANA ASSOCIATIONS

RAY	COLOR	ASCENDED MASTER	MEANING/TEACHING	MAJOR CARD OF THE RAY
1	Blue	El Morya, the god Thor, and Elohim Hercules	Faith	0 The Fool, II The High Priestess, V The Hierophant, IX The Hermit
2	Yellow	Master Lanto	Willpower, self-discipline	I The Magician, IV The Emperor, VII The Chariot, VIII Strength, XI Justice
3	Pink	Master Roweena	Creativity, kindness	XVII The Star, XIX The Sun
4	White	Master Serapis Bey	Peace, ascension, light	XX Judgement, XXI The World
5	Green	Pan, Hilarion	Abundance, nature	III The Empress, X The Wheel of Fortune
6	Red	Master Jesus Christ, Master Virgin Mary	Sacrifice	VI The Lovers, XII The Hanged Man, XIII Death, XV The Devil, XVIII The Moon
7	Violet	Master Saint Germain	Transmutation, progress	XIV Temperance, XVI The Tower

THE SPIRAL

The spiral is an ancient symbol of life, mapping the journey from the outer world (the outer ring of the spiral) through personal consciousness to inner consciousness, or the soul, at the center. In this reading, we take card position meanings from the first ten cards of the major arcana (see below) to create a progression through earthly experience toward the realization of our higher purpose.

1 You and your situation

2 Mentors and helpful people

3 What can you nurture now?

4 Spiritual boundaries; do you need more self-protection?

5 How you express your beliefs

6 The gifts your spirituality brings you and others

7 Moving forward; is this the right time for spiritual growth?

8 How you respond to criticism or opposition

9 Spiritual learning available to you now

10 Your highest purpose at this time

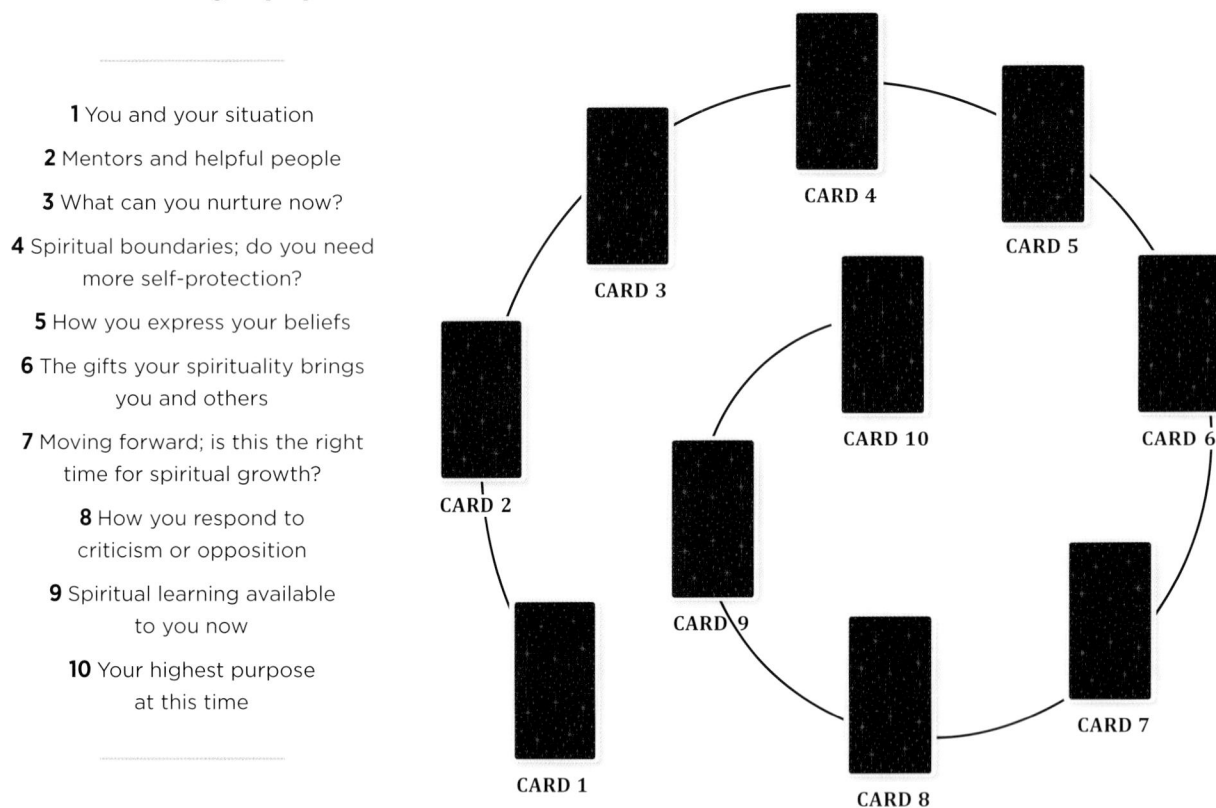

Shuffle the whole deck, and choose your cards (see page 16). Lay them all out face down, following the card positions as shown. Turn the cards face up, and begin your interpretation.

Developing the Reading:

Extending the Spiral

The card positions are based on selected meanings of major arcana cards 1 through 10:

I The Magician	The individual
II The High Priestess	A mentor, wisdom
III The Empress	Productivity
IV The Emperor	Order through knowledge
V The Hierophant	Orthodox religion
VI The Lovers	Love
VII The Chariot	Journeys
VIII Strength	Courage
IX The Hermit	Self-knowledge
X The Wheel of Fortune	Destiny

You can continue the spiral by creating card positions inspired by the next major arcana cards in the sequence. To do this, select the highest-numbered major arcana card and place it in the center of the spiral. The outer circles (which are laid face down) will still hold the lowest-numbered cards. For example:

XI Justice	Divine law
XII The Hanged Man	Spiritual sacrifice
XIII Death	Rebirth, reincarnation
XIV Temperance	Balance
XV The Devil	The shadow
XVI The Tower	Breakthrough, enlightenment
XVII The Star	Divine guidance, healing
XVIII The Moon	Crisis of faith; doubt
XIX The Sun	The Divine Child; spiritual growth
XX Judgement	Self-judgement, review
XXI The World	Wholeness, ascension

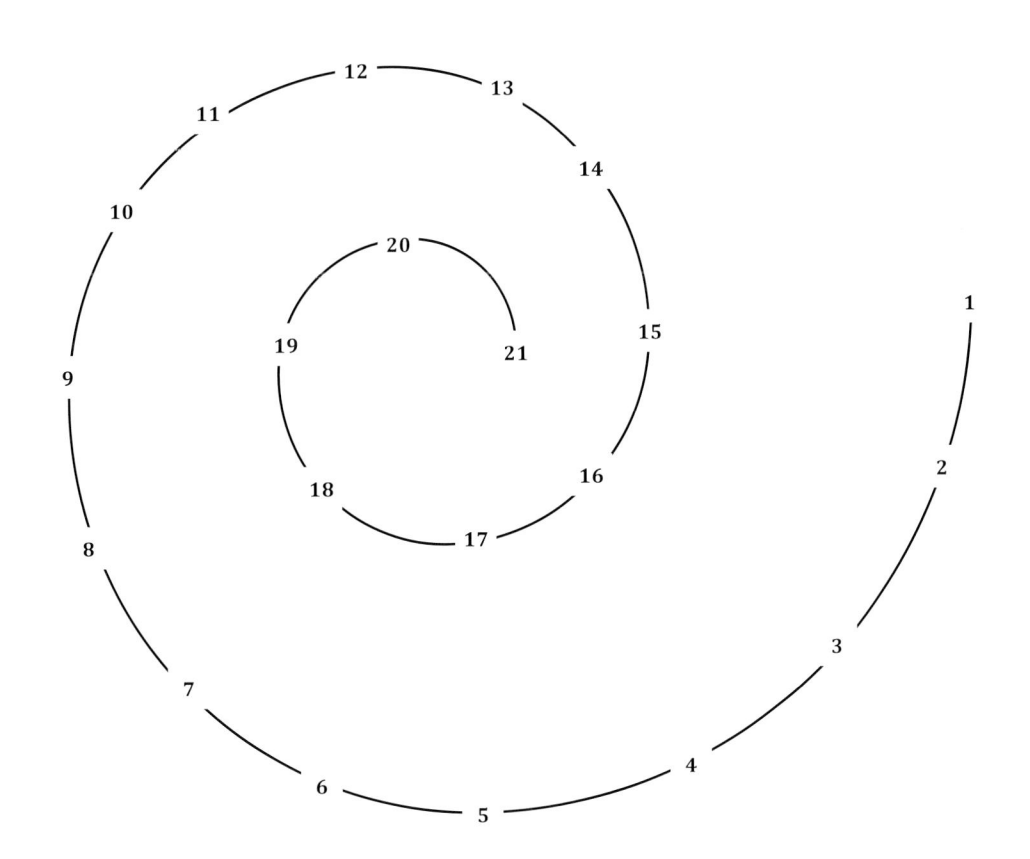

THE INFINITY READING: THREE REASONS I ATTRACT REPEAT SITUATIONS

The infinity symbol, also known as the lemniscate, is a sacred symbol in tarot, signifying continual change and the flow of life. Its shape, a sideways figure eight, encompasses two opposing loops, and it's the tension between these two opposites that maintains the flow of the life force. At a more mundane level, this is a reflection of the energy we invest into negative situations: When tension persists, situations persist.

This spread lets us see why certain experiences repeat themselves. The two cards in the center of the figure eight reveal the ongoing, or recurring, situation. The other cards in the spread help reveal how and why this is happening. You might interpret this as karma that you need to work out, or as current beliefs that are keeping you trapped in a cycle. Although this doesn't mean you are responsible for the actions of others, it is always possible to respond with greater awareness and to change the type of situations you attract.

1, 5 Your situation now and what perpetuates it

2, 6 Aspect of the situation and reason or lesson

3, 7 Aspect of the situation and reason or lesson

4, 8 Aspect of the situation and reason or lesson

TIP: Eights in the minor arcana are cards that denote change. If an Eight comes up in your reading, it's a sign that the time is right to break old patterns.

Shuffle and choose your cards (see page 16), laying them all face down in the order shown. Then turn over all the cards, interpreting cards 1 and 5 first: These cards reveal the issue, while cards 2, 3, and 4 show three reasons you're in the situation in question. Cards 6, 7, and 8 reveal why: that is, the lesson to be learned or the action you need to take in order to break the cycle. When reading, look at the cards in pairs: So, interpret cards 2 and 6 together, then cards 3 and 7, followed by cards 4 and 8.

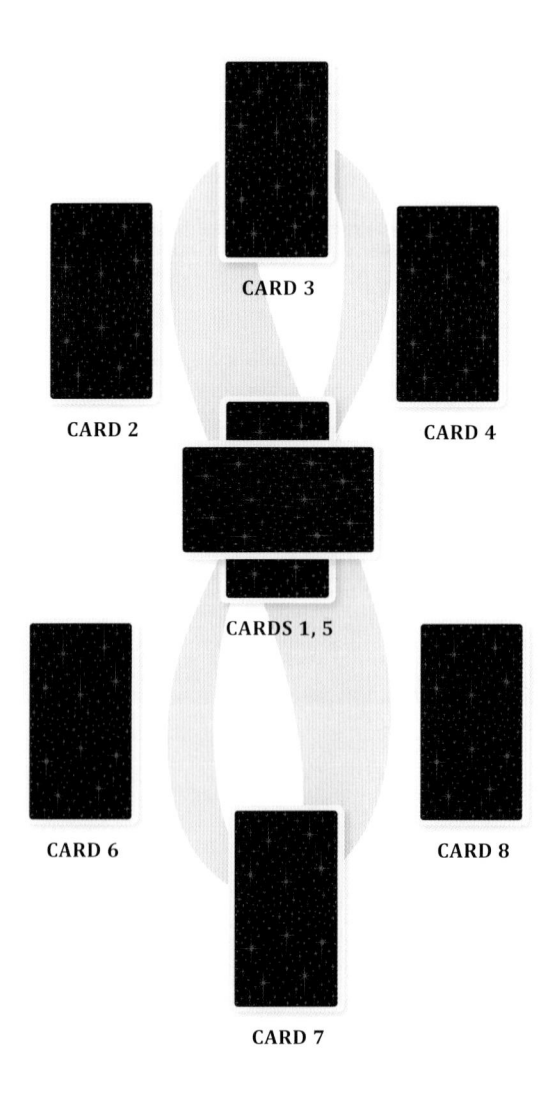

CARD 3

CARD 2   CARD 4

CARDS 1, 5

CARD 6   CARD 8

CARD 7

Example: Jennifer's Reading

1, 5 The Three of Pentacles crossed with the Eight of Swords. Indicates restriction around issues of career or work. Jennifer felt that every time she began to get recognition or earn some success (Three of Pentacles), she hit a brick wall, and her career path became blocked (Eight of Swords) in terms of promotion or advancement. This had happened three successive times in her past positions.

2, 6 The Two of Swords (aspect of the situation) and III The Empress (reason). Jennifer identified these cards as, firstly, her blocked progress (Two of Swords; having no clear perspective on her predicament) being connected with her Empress qualities; she tended to give to others easily, even in a highly competitive workplace. Considering the card again, Jennifer also became aware of the possibility that, in her efforts to be liked and to show compassion to others at work, she gave away her power. She often let others lead or take credit for her work, and she also attracted a "bully" character in every job she'd had: a human representation of her block to success.

3, 7 The Four of Pentacles and I The Magician. Jennifer saw the Four of Pentacles as a sign of security, or smugness; if she didn't leave her unfulfilling job, surely she'd end up like this—financially secure, but institutionalized and unambitious. The Magician gave her the sense that it was time to take action and to push herself forward as an individual with worth instead of playing the role of compliant team member.

4, 8 The Ace of Swords and XI Justice. Jennifer saw the Ace of Swords as her cut-and-run attitude: She felt unable to assert herself enough to negotiate better terms, and just walked away, starting from scratch in a new workplace after having spent a respectable length of time at her previous job. Justice suggested that she needed to find a balance between being herself—a compassionate soul—and being unafraid to stand out. With this attitude, the "bully" characters, too, would disappear from her life.

CARD 3
Aspect

CARD 2
Aspect

CARD 4
Aspect

CARDS 1, 5
Repeating situation

CARD 6
Reason/
lesson of 2

CARD 8
Reason/
lesson of 4

CARD 7
Reason/lesson of 3

11

CREATIVITY: NURTURING PROJECTS AND DEVISING YOUR OWN LAYOUTS

TAROT READING NATURALLY INSPIRES CREATIVITY. Interpreting your cards calls upon your intuition and imagination, exercising your ability to visualize and create stories—and that's why practicing tarot can help your creativity grow and grow. The images on the cards can inspire new avenues to explore, or point you toward ideas and influences that may affect your work in progress, so trying a tarot reading before you begin creative work is a great way to get into the zone. This is because working with tarot cards stimulates your right brain, the seat of the unconscious and your inner creative resources—the memories, images, and beliefs that often guide and inform our creative projects. And you may find that looking at the cards' images alone, without referring to card meanings, sparks new stories and ideas.

These ten spreads will not only help you explore where you are in your projects, but also new ways to devise your own spreads, transforming creativity into action.

KEY CARDS FOR NURTURING YOUR CREATIVITY

LOOK FOR:

0 The Fool: Curiosity and wonder

I The Magician: The drive to create

III The Empress: Productivity

VIII Strength: Self-discipline; staying the course

IX The Hermit: Writers' or artists' solitude

X The Wheel of Fortune: Going with the flow

XII The Hanged Man: Incubation of an idea

XVI The Tower: Creative breakthrough

XVII The Star: Guidance

XIX The Sun: Safety, growth, and playfulness

XX Judgement: Editing

XXI The World: Success and completion; also, ideas for new projects

Ace of Wands: A new idea; a passion

Six of Wands: Deserved success

Three of Pentacles: Acknowledgment for work or ideas

Eight of Pentacles: Hard work and attention to detail

Nine of Cups: A wish come true

Ace of Swords: Success; good decisions

WATCH OUT FOR:

XII The Hanged Man reversed: Procrastination, self-sabotage

XV The Devil: Restrictive agreements

XVIII The Moon: Self-doubt

Seven of Cups: Fantasy, inability to choose a project and see it through

Five of Pentacles: Money issues and/or creativity blocked by fear

Two of Swords: Procrastination

Three of Swords: Lack of trust

Five of Swords: Stressful confrontation

Eight of Swords: Restriction

Nine of Swords: Anxiety, pressure

SPREADS FOR CREATIVITY

HOW CAN I BE MORE CREATIVE?

We're all naturally creative. Without time pressure, perfectionism, and other creative blocks, we would be able to create unhindered—right? Try this little spread to see if and what you could change to unleash the artist within.

1 You or your situation

2 Time: Is time an issue now?

3 Expectations:
What do you hope to achieve?

4 Who or what is blocking you?

5 Inspiration: Are you motivated?

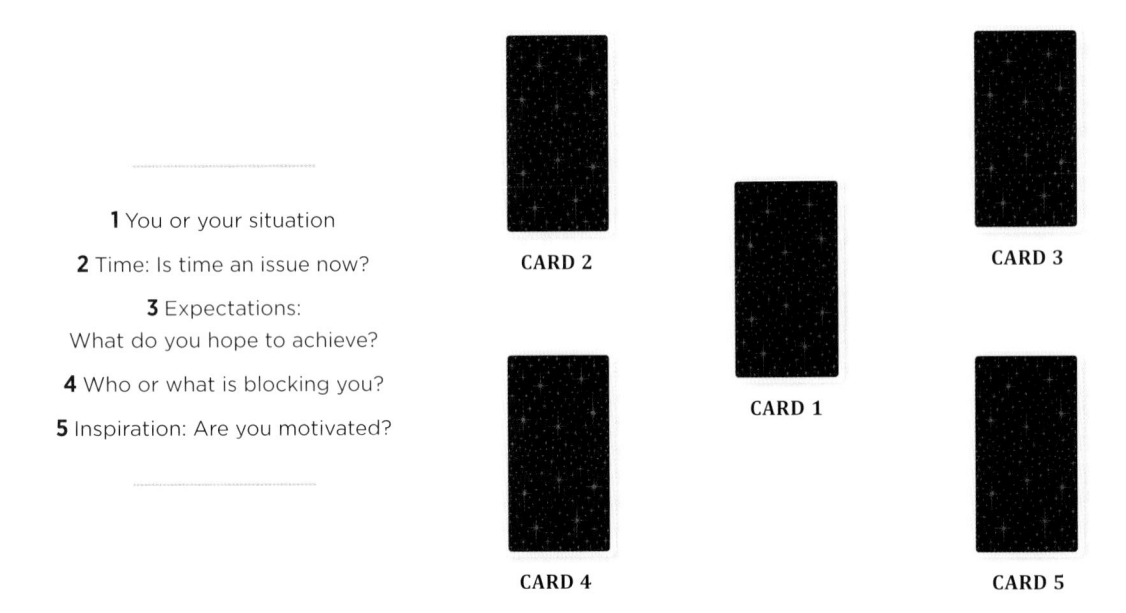

CARD 2

CARD 3

CARD 1

CARD 4

CARD 5

Shuffle and choose your cards (see page 16), then lay out all the cards as shown above, face down. Turn over all the cards and interpret them in order.

Developing the Reading: Transformational Tarot

Take card 4, the block card, away from the spread. Move card 5 into card 4's position, keeping its meaning as inspiration, and taking a new card 5 from the deck. This card represents what the outcome would be if the block were removed.

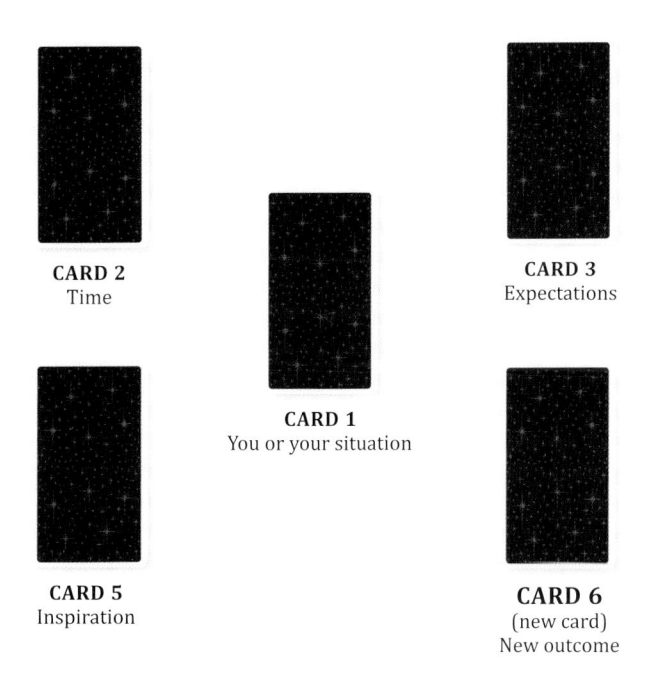

CARD 2
Time

CARD 3
Expectations

CARD 1
You or your situation

CARD 5
Inspiration

CARD 6
(new card)
New outcome

Moving cards around within a reading is known as "transformational tarot." By physically moving a card out of a reading, or by changing a card's position within a reading, you're manifesting an intention to explore a different option or another way of being. When you do this, you get a sense of how it feels not to have a block, so you can remember and relive this feeling to generate positive energy when you're doing creative work. It's a great way to shift the stubborn block at the back of your mind that conditions your expectations. After all, the more free you feel when you're creating, the more enjoyable—and productive—the experience will be.

Example: Ruth's Reading

Ruth drew the following cards to help her understand why she couldn't begin a creative project. She'd fantasize about taking photos, making artwork, learning the cello, or taking French classes—but somehow she never seemed to get around to *doing* any of these things. Here are her cards:

CARD 2
Time

CARD 3
Expectations

CARD 1
Self

1 **Queen of Cups (self)**: Ruth explained that she could relate to this card. She saw herself as a very sensitive person who often put others' needs before her own.

2 **IX The Hermit (time)**: Ruth did have time to devote to her projects, but she often gave away this time to others instead of beginning her own work.

3 **Two of Pentacles (expectations)**: Ruth wasn't sure whether she could succeed. "I'm a procrastinator, to be honest," she admitted.

4 **V The Hierophant reversed (block)**: "If this relates to education—and I feel that it does, for me—this card reminds me of a teacher at school who criticized my art. He was sarcastic and I knew he didn't like me. No one else in my family was particularly interested in art, so he was the only person who gave me feedback—and all of it was negative."

5 **The Seven of Cups (inspiration)**: Ruth's issue, along with the "bad mentor" Hierophant, was that she was inspired (and distracted) by everything. Ideas were no problem, but she thrived on the fantasy of being a great creator without actually doing anything about it. The fear of criticism stopped her in her tracks every time.

CARD 4
Block

CARD 5
Inspiration

CARD 6
Final outcome

When Ruth removed her block card, she chose an outcome card:

XX Judgement: This card asks us to be fair judges of ourselves and our past actions. Ruth reflected on what it meant to be her own judge, rather than to allow The Hierophant's opinion to dominate. Judgement is also a card that signifies resurrection, and it called Ruth to recover her creativity on her own terms.

THOTH'S MANIFESTING SPREAD FOR WRITERS

Thoth was the Egyptian god of knowledge who gifted humanity with art and the sciences. He was known as Ur heka: *Ur* means "first" or "original," while *heka* means the "principle of magic," so we can think of Thoth as the first, or original, magician. Thoth was also believed to have invented the system of hieroglyphics.

Since writing can be described as a sort of magical flow, we use I The Magician, as the center card in this spread, which helps you take a closer look at how your writing might evolve. You can apply this layout to any other creative project, too.

CARD 6
Heaven card

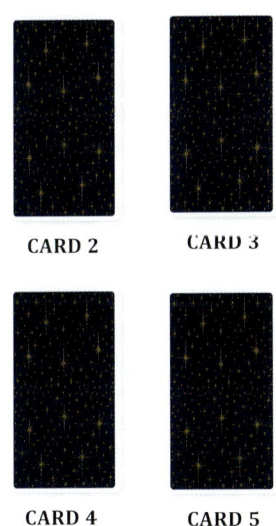

I THE MAGICIAN

CARD 2 **CARD 3**

CARD 4 **CARD 5**

CARD 1
Earth card

EARTH

1 Present situation or environment

I THE MAGICIAN'S RESOURCES

2 What I possess

3 What I know

4 What I love

5 What I desire

HEAVEN

6 What I manifest, given my resources

First, take The Magician from the deck and place him face up, as shown. Then shuffle the remaining cards, choose them (see page 16), and place them face down. Turn all the cards face up, and then begin your interpretation.

THE PYRAMID: WHAT DO I NEED TO SUCCEED IN MY PROJECT?

If you feel that your creativity is being blocked or dammed, or if you find that external issues are keeping you from doing the work you need to do, try this great spread. It'll help you understand and overcome those blocks, letting you move forward with your project.

Shuffle and choose your cards (see page 16), and lay them all out in the order shown, face down. Turn the bottom row of cards face up and interpret them first, followed by the second and third rows, and, finally, the outcome card.

1, 2, 3, 4 What advantages do I have?

5, 6, 7 What challenges do I face?

8, 9 What do I need to overcome these challenges

10 Outcome: If I can do this, can I succeed?

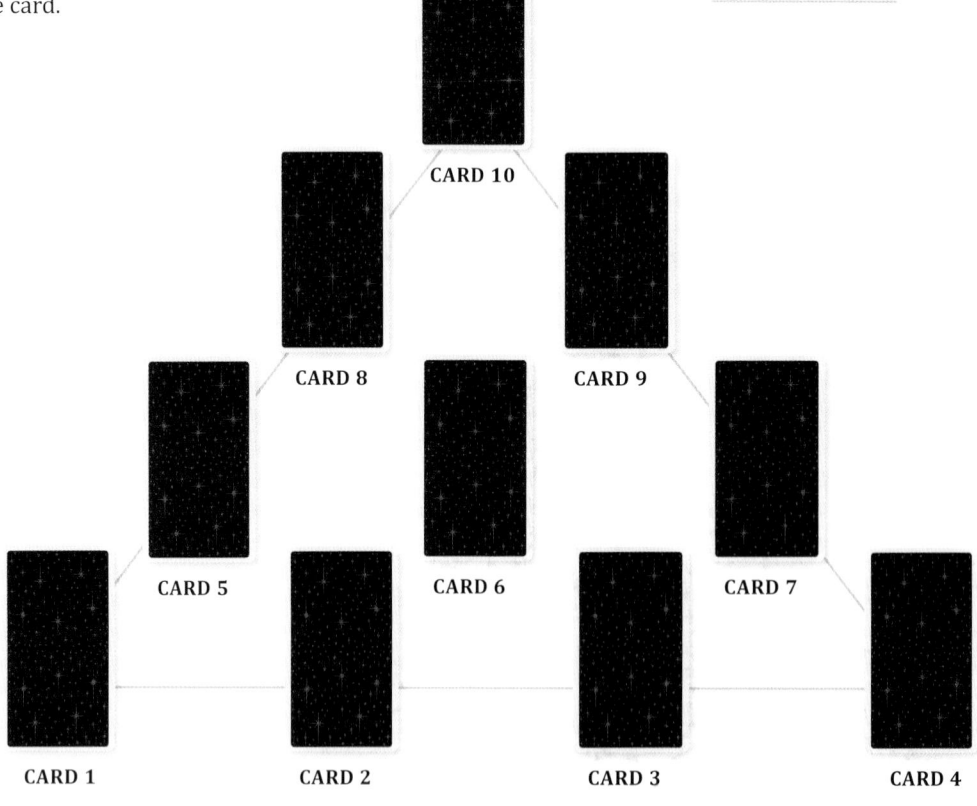

CARD 10

CARD 8   CARD 9

CARD 5   CARD 6   CARD 7

CARD 1   CARD 2   CARD 3   CARD 4

Example: Jeanne's Reading

Jeanne had received harsh criticism about a half-finished project by a colleague she thought she trusted. Not only had the conversation damaged their relationship, but also she was seriously beginning to wonder whether those comments had a nugget of truth in them. Should she continue on with her project anyway, or should she question the whole basis of her work—possibly even abandoning her project completely?

Here are the cards she drew:

Outcome — CARD 10

What I need to overcome — CARD 9

Challenges — CARD 7

Advantages — CARD 4

CARD 8

CARD 5 CARD 6

CARD 1 CARD 2 CARD 3

Advantages: Jeanne saw the Hierophant as her education level and her body of knowledge. She saw the Chariot as her determination and ambition; the Hermit as the writer-aspect of herself, the way in which she was following her own path; and the Queen of Pentacles as a sign that her work had been, and could still be, well received and rewarded.

Challenges: She felt the loss of the friendship that the Five of Cups signified, and saw the danger of the Seven, which suggested that she might not have a good steer on the situation: Was she overreacting? The Devil showed Jeanne that her colleague might be trying to control her through criticism—but, ultimately, Jeanne herself was giving her colleague that power.

What I need to overcome: The Four of Wands indicated that it was time to stop analyzing and to do something that gave her pleasure: Perhaps she needed to take a short break or spend more time with her children and with her partner, the King of Cups, who had a very different perspective on the situation. He believed that her colleague had been unfair and that Jeanne should ignore the remark; she should stop questioning herself and simply move on.

The outcome: The Four of Pentacles reminded Jeanne of all the stable things in her life, and reassured her that she could overcome the situation with her colleague. While Jeanne could no longer regard her as a friend, she could try to become the observer at work rather than the victim: She could try to distance herself from the situation—and her colleague—and reclaim some power for herself in that way.

THE STORY SPREAD: GETTING INTO THE FLOW

This spread is a fabulous way to warm up before you begin a creative project. Spend five minutes on it before you pick up your pen or paintbrush (or any other creative tool!) or use it to help devise plots if you're writing or illustrating.

First, take the major arcana cards and look at them all, face up. Then, look at the list of suggested archetypes, on the next page. (Many other archetypes can be associated with each card; these are the principal associations. Feel free to add your own, if you like.) Lay out the cards according to the framework of your story, then change or add cards to see how you might change or develop your plot or characters.

Example: The Fairy Tale

In this example, I've chosen Little Red Riding Hood (RRH) to illustrate how storytelling works when it's paired with tarot. Fairy tales contain obvious archetypes—the language of the tarot itself—so it's easy to identify characters through the cards.

CARD 1
The Fool
(young heroine):
"I'm going to
Grandma's house
in the woods."

CARD 2
The Empress
(mother):
"Don't leave
the path!"

CARD 3
The Devil
(temptation):
RRH leaves the
path to smell the
flowers: The
hungry wolf sees
her and knows
where she is going

CARD 4
Death
(transformation):
Wolf runs ahead to
Grandma's house,
eats Grandma, and
lies in bed to wait
for RRH

CARD 5
The Chariot
(hero): A woodcut-
ter rushes to help,
kills the wolf...

CARD 6
The Tower
(destruction): ...
and cuts open its
stomach.

> TIP: If you're looking for inspiration for a story, choose some cards at random and create your opening line around the theme of the first card. Then continue to lay cards and invent your narrative as you go. You might begin with three cards (beginning, middle, and end), and then add more cards to create intervening events. Try using both the major and the minor arcanas.

CARD 7
Judgement
(second chances):
Grandma and Red
Riding Hood are
saved

CARD 8
Justice (justice):
Justice is done, and
all ends well

We could create a different kind of fairy tale by rearranging the same cards:

The Empress finds a foundling child. The Empress loves the child, but the villagers say that the child is cursed, which is why she is ugly—and that **The Devil** cursed her.

STORY ARCHETYPES

MAJOR ARCANA CARD	ROLE IN YOUR STORY
0 The Fool	The adventurer, or young hero or heroine
I The Magician	The magician; the inventor
II The High Priestess	The wise woman: the mystic, the intellectual, the teacher, the virgin
III The Empress	The mother, wife, ruler, or queen
IV The Emperor	The father, husband, ruler, or king
V The Hierophant	The teacher; the mystic; the judge
VI The Lovers	The divine couple
VII The Chariot	The hero; the warrior; the rebel
VIII Strength	The martyr; the heroine
IX The Hermit	The wise man: the intellectual, the teacher, the monk
X The Wheel of Fortune	The gods; the workings of Fate
XI Justice	The rule-maker
XII The Hanged Man	The martyr; the victim
XIII Death	The destroyer
XIV Temperance	The mediator
XV The Devil	The controller; the tempter; the rebel
XVI The Tower	The avenger
XVII The Star	The maiden, the artist, the healer
XVIII The Moon	The madman or madwoman
XIX The Sun	The child or children; the mystic
XX Judgement	The hero returned; the rescuer
XXI The World	The hero rewarded

The Fool (a village boy) must find The Devil, who cursed the child in vengeance because he envied the girl's beauty. The Fool must vanquish The Devil, or the child will die by her sixteenth birthday; he must do **Justice** by her. He finds The Devil and answers his impossible riddle by completing three tasks. Completing these tasks successfully makes him the hero, signified by **The Chariot**.

The Fool/Chariot happily rides back to the village on the girl's birthday, but The Devil has tricked him: The girl is dying, just as the curse foretold (The Devil has become **Death** and **The Tower**). But the shock of The Tower brings a breakthrough; The Fool/Chariot remembers his trials by The Devil, and gives the girl a magic potion he discovered while completing The Devil's three tasks. The Fool/Chariot now evolves into **Judgement** as the girl returns to life. The curse is lifted: The girl is transformed into a beautiful young woman before his eyes . . . and (guess what?) they all lived happily ever after.

DIVINING YOUR THEMES

At times, a little limitation can actually stoke your creativity instead of restricting it. Too many choices can be overwhelming: Faced with a wealth of possibility, where do we start? This spread asks you to choose between a select number of themes and to base your project, or a narrative, around only those themes.

It takes time to run through the deck and place the cards into themed piles, but the very process of organizing the cards helps open up a creative pathway. This might sound familiar: Completing a manual task (washing the dishes, filing, or shuffling cards) before getting into the groove of a creative project helps us be more productive when we begin our work. Practical rituals can help you make an effective shift into the creative zone.

First, take the whole deck and remove all the Court cards. Place them in a pile. Next, take out the three "wild cards" (X The Wheel of Fortune; the Nine of Cups; and the Six of Cups) and put them to one side: You'll need them later. Then, take the remaining deck and arrange the cards into the themes shown on the chart to the right (see page 316 to see which cards belong with which themes). When you've done this, you'll have one pile of Court cards, the three wild cards, and twelve small piles representing each theme.

Take the Court cards. Look at these cards face up and pick one to represent you or your hero in your story. Now look at the remaining twelve piles. Shuffle each pile, then lay them in front of you as indicated here.

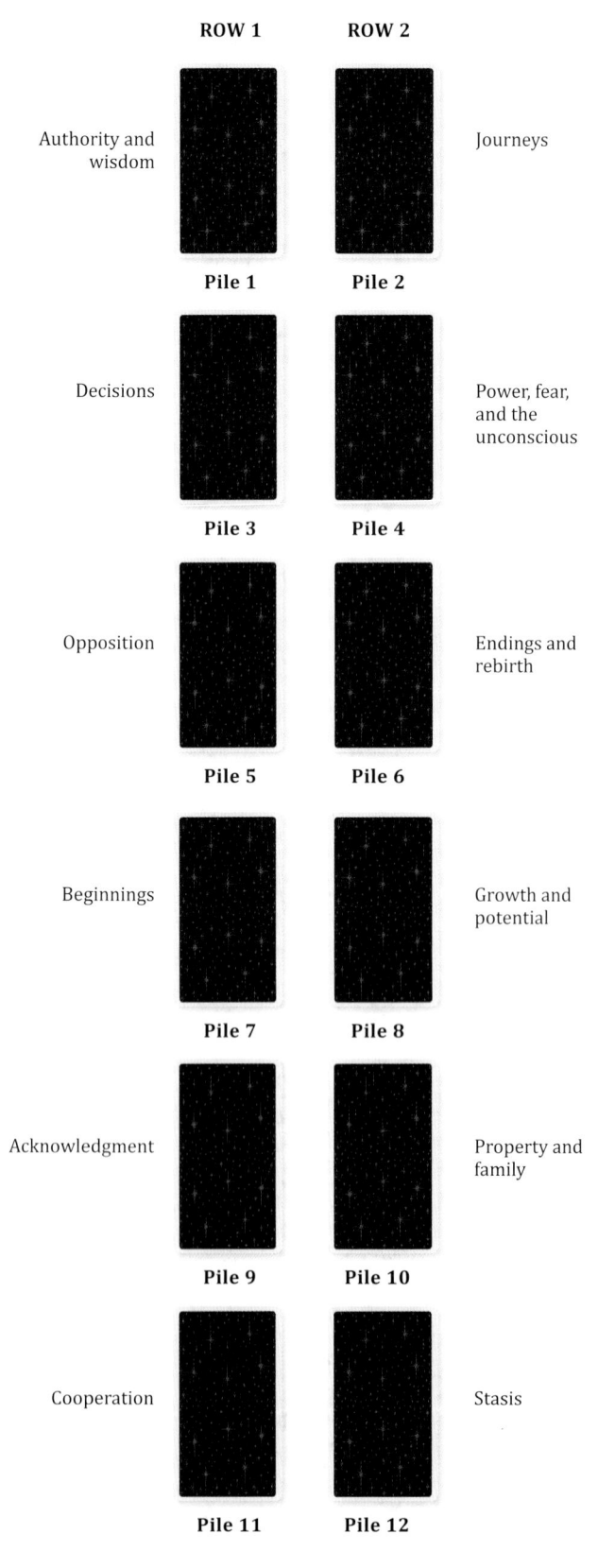

ROW 1	ROW 2
Authority and wisdom — **Pile 1**	Journeys — **Pile 2**
Decisions — **Pile 3**	Power, fear, and the unconscious — **Pile 4**
Opposition — **Pile 5**	Endings and rebirth — **Pile 6**
Beginnings — **Pile 7**	Growth and potential — **Pile 8**
Acknowledgment — **Pile 9**	Property and family — **Pile 10**
Cooperation — **Pile 11**	Stasis — **Pile 12**

Take one card from the top of a pile in either Row 1 or Row 2, and work your way down: Take a card from either pile 1 or pile 2, then another from either pile 3 or pile 4, and so on, until you have six cards in front of you, still face down. By choosing your themes in this way, you're divining which themes attract you and are therefore worth exploring in your creative project.

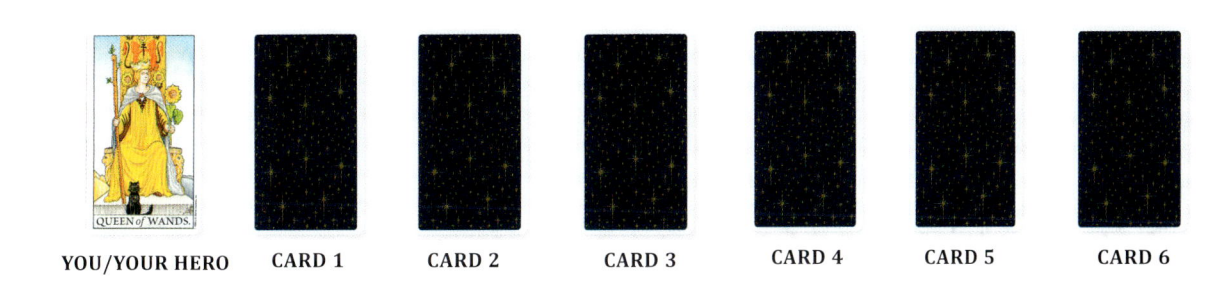

YOU/YOUR HERO   **CARD 1**   **CARD 2**   **CARD 3**   **CARD 4**   **CARD 5**   **CARD 6**

Now take your hero card and lay it down on the left side of your table. Now pick up the six cards you've laid down and add the three wild cards (the magic wish is the Nine of Cups; the divine message is The Wheel of Fortune; and the visitor from the past is the Six of Cups). Shuffle them together, and then lay the first six cards from the top of the pile face down, as shown above:

Turn over cards 1 through 6 and create a narrative around these cards. One way to do this is to move your hero card along the row under each card in turn as you ask, "What happens when my hero meets this person or situation?"

Tarot Narrative Themes

People
The Court cards: Pages, Knights, Queens, and Kings

Authority and Wisdom
II The High Priestess, IV The Emperor,
V The Hierophant, XI Justice

Journeys
0 The Fool, VII The Chariot, IX The Hermit, Six of
Swords, Eight of Cups, Three of Wands, Eight of Wands

Decisions
VI The Lovers, XIV Temperance, XVIII The Moon, Seven
of Cups, Two of Swords, Two of Pentacles

Power, Fear, and the Unconscious
XII The Hanged Man, XVI The Tower, XV The Devil,
Nine of Swords, Five of Pentacles

Opposition
Five of Wands, Seven of Wands, Nine of Wands, Ten
of Wands, Three of Swords, Five of Swords, Seven of
Swords, Eight of Swords

Endings and Rebirth
0 The Fool, XIII Death, XVII The Star, XX Judgement,
XXI The World, Ten of Swords, Five of Cups

Beginnings
The four Aces, I The Magician

Growth and Potential
III The Empress, XIX The Sun, Seven of Pentacles

Acknowledgment
Six of Wands, Three of Pentacles, Eight of Pentacles

Property and Family
Four of Wands, Four of Pentacles, Nine of Pentacles,
Ten of Pentacles, Ten of Cups

Cooperation
VIII Strength, Two of Wands, Two of Cups, Three of
Cups, Six of Pentacles

Stasis
Four of Cups, Four of Swords

Wild Cards

The Magic Wish
Nine of Cups

The Divine Message
X The Wheel of Fortune

The Return of a Person from the Past
Six of Cups

TIP: The narrative themes list is a useful aid when it comes to learning the cards'
meanings by theme, particularly if you're feeling overwhelmed by learning the individual
meanings of all seventy-eight cards. Begin by pulling out the cards and arranging them
into their themes, as above, and viewing the similarities by group.

American occultist Paul Foster Case (1884–1954), founder of the Western mystery school BOTA (Builders of the Adytum), connected major arcana cards to the musical scale and to colors. He made these associations on the basis of the Hebrew letter, planet, astrological sign, and, in some instances, chakra colors linked with each card.

NOTE	MAJOR ARCANA CARD	COLOR
C	IV The Emperor, XVI The Tower, XX Judgement	Red
C♯	V The Hierophant	Red-orange
D	VI The Lovers, XIX The Sun	Orange
E♭	VII The Chariot	Orange-yellow
E	0 The Fool, I The Magician, VIII Strength	Yellow
F	IX The Hermit	Yellow-green
F♯	XI Justice, III The Empress	Green
G	XIII Death	Green-blue
A♭	II The High Priestess, XII The Hanged Man, XIV Temperance	Blue
A	XV The Devil, XXI The World	Blue-violet
B	X The Wheel of Fortune, XVII The Star	Violet
B♭	XVIII The Moon	Violet-red

Ways to Use the Notes

If you're musically inclined, you might compose a melody generated by the notes of the cards that turn up in your readings, or you could put together a sequence of chords. Or explore the tarot-music theme by choosing a simple melody you like, then divining which card links with each note. Arrange the cards from left to right, reflecting the order of notes, to create a spread and give yourself a reading.

Ways to Use the Colors

Look around your home—and in your closet—and take note of the colors you choose for your home décor and your wardrobe. To which cards do they correspond? Because we often subconsciously choose the colors we need in our lives, you might take the meaning of each card as an indicator of the qualities you value or hope to attract. For example, if blue is a favorite of yours, consider what these cards might mean for you: II The High Priestess (truth, wisdom, and privacy); XII The Hanged Man (time and sacrifice); or XIV Temperance (reconciling demands).

DEVISING YOUR OWN LAYOUTS

SIMPLE LAYOUTS OF THREE

Because they're so easy to remember, three-card readings are the simplest way to begin when you're devising your own layouts. The classic three-card reading is the Past, Present, and Future spread (see page 21 and below, "Creating a Layout Using the Cards' Facing Directions"). Others include Mind, Body, Spirit, and this little gem:

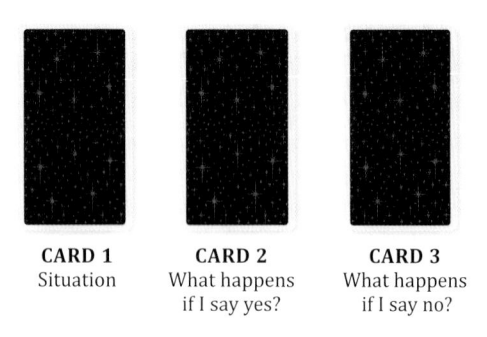

CARD 1
Situation

CARD 2
What happens
if I say yes?

CARD 3
What happens
if I say no?

You might begin by contemplating which areas of life are important for you right now, then you can create a three-card layout around these areas. For instance, you might choose Money, Children, and Travel; or Love, Projects, and Home. Before you begin, establish both what you want to know and what you would like your spread to reveal, such as:

The situation now

Advice

Future prediction

Issues at present

Obstacles in your path

Past issues

You might also like to focus on one key area—such as money, for example—and devise a spread around it as follows, using the categories below:

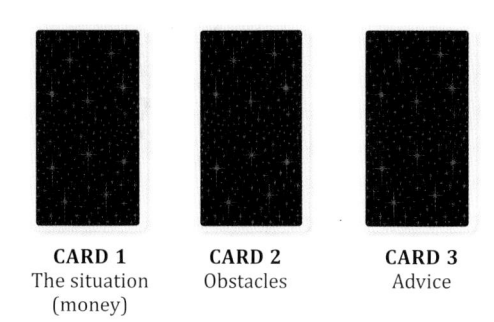

CARD 1
The situation
(money)

CARD 2
Obstacles

CARD 3
Advice

When you're placing the cards, experiment with how the cards feel to you when they're placed in a row, or in a column, or in two rows. As a general rule, we place cards that relate to the past to the left side; we place cards related to the present in the center; and we place cards related to the future on the right. So, we can read the spread as a timeline that runs from left to right.

Developing the Reading: Expanding Your Themes
You can add more categories and/or cards to your layout. For example, ask, "Who can help me?" or "What should I avoid?"

CREATING A LAYOUT USING THE CARDS' FACING DIRECTIONS

The facing direction of objects or people depicted in the minor arcana cards allows you to create past, present, and future card positions. This technique comprises two steps: First, you create "marker positions" with the minors, and then you lay majors under them to yield a reading. This technique works best with a general question, such as "What do I need to know now?"

Here's how to do it. Separate the major and minor arcanas. Take the minor arcana cards, shuffle them, and choose three cards (see page 16). Place them in front of you, face up.

Interpret them according to their facing directions (see the chart on page 321). Because these cards act as markers for past, present, and future card positions only, don't interpret their meanings. For example:

Three right-facing cards: Future, future, future
Two right-facing cards, one left-facing card: Future, future, past
Two forward-facing cards, one right-facing card: Present, present, future

And so on. For example:

PAST	PRESENT	PAST

Next, arrange the cards so that they fall into this pattern: past cards to the left, present cards in the center, and future cards to the right. In this example, you'd move the two past cards together to the left and place the present card to their right:

PAST	PAST	PRESENT

(no future card)

Take a note of any timeline—past, present, or future—that doesn't appear in the cards you draw. If it's not there, it's not relevant in your reading just now. If you drew the cards in the example above, which doesn't contain a future card, you're being asked to focus on the past reasons for your present situation.

Here's another example:

FUTURE	PAST	FUTURE

(continued)

Arrange them as before according to past, present, future:

PAST   **FUTURE**   **FUTURE**

(no present card)

Here there's no present card: Instead, notice that there's a strong emphasis on the future.

Now take the major arcana cards and shuffle them. Then choose three cards: Place one under each minor arcana card, laying them face up from left to right. This gives you an interpretation for the past, present, and future—or whatever your combination might be. For example:

PAST   **FUTURE**   **FUTURE**

First, designate what the major cards will mean in your reading. They may, for example, stand for the impact of the person or event shown in the minor card above it.

In the past position, we have the Nine of Wands—strength and hard-won achievement—paired with the major arcana card IX The Hermit; The Hermit, the card of solitude and contemplation, shows the need for quiet time and reflection to conserve energy.

In the two future positions are the Five of Pentacles with VIII Strength, and the Nine of Swords with XVI The Tower. The Five, the card of fear of poverty and exclusion, paired with VIII Strength reminds you that you are strong enough to overcome your fears. The Nine of Swords, the anxiety card, twinned with XVI The Tower reveals the reason, perhaps, for your stress—that you're on the cusp of a breakthrough; pent-up anxiety and energy gets released, and you re-create your life as you need it to be.

Developing the Reading: Laying More Majors
Continue to lay more major arcana cards under the first row for more insight into the situation.

CARDS' FACING DIRECTIONS: PAST, PRESENT, OR FUTURE

The facing directions are exactly as you see them on the cards, not from the point of view of the characters on the cards.

RIGHT-FACING CARDS: THE FUTURE	LEFT-FACING CARDS: THE PAST	FORWARD-FACING CARDS: THE PRESENT
Ace of Cups	Five of Cups	Two of Cups
Six of Cups	Page of Cups	Three of Cups
Seven of Cups *(the hand is outstretched to the right)*	Queen of Cups	Four of Cups
		Nine of Cups
Eight of Cups	Ace of Swords	Ten of Cups
Knight of Cups	Five of Swords	
King of Cups	Seven of Swords *(the body is turned to the left, although the face looks to the right)*	Two of Swords
		Three of Swords
Six of Swords	Page of Swords	Four of Swords
Nine of Swords	Knight of Swords	Eight of Swords
Queen of Swords	King of Swords *(forward-facing, but his sword—his suit emblem—is held to the left)*	Ten of Swords
Five of Pentacles		Two of Pentacles
Eight of Pentacles		Three of Pentacles
Page of Pentacles	Ace of Pentacles	Four of Pentacles
Knight of Pentacles	Six of Pentacles	Nine of Pentacles
	Seven of Pentacles	Ten of Pentacles
Ace of Wands	Queen of Pentacles	King of Pentacles
Six of Wands		
Eight of Wands *(wands appear to be flying to the right, but you may prefer to categorize this card as center)*	Two of Wands	Three of Wands
	Nine of Wands	Four of Wands
	Knight of Wands	Five of Wands
Ten of Wands	King of Wands	Seven of Wands
Page of Wands		Queen of Wands

CREATING A LAYOUT BASED ON YOUR FAVORITE SYMBOL

Symbols are statements of our values, compressed into signs; we wear them as jewelry, fabric designs, or tattoos. For many of us, they represent who we are or what we love and wish to protect. Devising a tarot spread in the shape of your symbol is a powerful way to awaken its meaning, reconnecting you with its values. You might like to choose one of the symbol spreads from this book, such as the heart, protective pentagram, or infinite figure eight (see pages 234, 293, and 302) and create a layout with your own unique card positions. Or you might want to devise a spread from scratch. Here's an example from a feline-loving friend:

Example: The Cat Spread

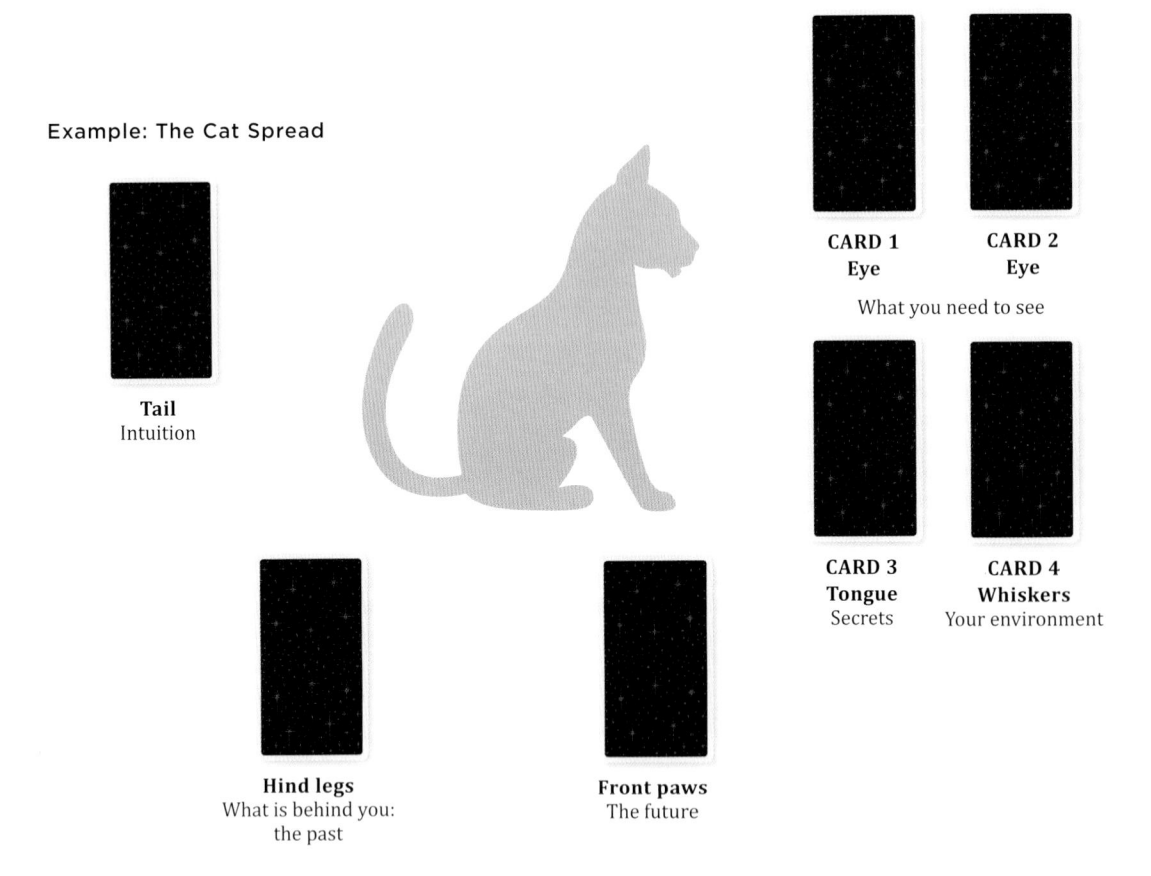

Tail
Intuition

CARD 1
Eye

CARD 2
Eye

What you need to see

CARD 3
Tongue
Secrets

CARD 4
Whiskers
Your environment

Hind legs
What is behind you:
the past

Front paws
The future

To create your own spread, draw your symbol, then contemplate the kind of reading you'd like, using the example above and the layouts in chapter 3 (page 20) as a starting point. Shuffle your cards, choose them, and begin your layout.

CREATING A LAYOUT BASED ON YOUR LIFE PATH NUMBER

In numerology, your Life Path number reveals your innermost character, or the personal qualities you carry with you throughout your life's journey. This layout design is based on the major arcana card associated with your number. Here's how to begin.

Write down the numbers in your date of birth and add them together until you reach a single number, or numbers 11 or 22.

Relate that number to the major arcana card numbers. For instance, if your number were 3, your card would be III The Empress; if it were 11, your card would be XI Justice; and if it were 22, you'd take 0 The Fool (in the major arcana sequence, some tarot scholars consider The Fool to be both 0 and XXII).

Look at your card and choose an image, then draw it in a simple shape. This forms the basis of your layout.

LIFE PATH NUMBERS AND TAROT SYMBOLS

LIFE PATH NUMBER	MAJOR ARCANA CARD	SUGGESTED IMAGES
1	I The Magician	Figure eight; lily; rose; wand
2	II The High Priestess	Two pillars; cross; moon
3	III The Empress	Venus symbol; tiara with 12 stars; tree
4	IV The Emperor	Throne; ram's head; scepter
5	V The Hierophant	Crozier; triple crown; crossed keys
6	VI The Lovers	Triangular shape of angel; man and woman; earth, mountain, cloud, and sun
7	VII The Chariot	Chariot; river crossing; charioteer's staff, the charioteer and sphinxes
8	VIII Strength	Figure eight; lion
9	IX The Hermit	Lantern and star; Hermit's staff
11	IX Justice	Two pillars; sword; scales; three crenelations of crown
22	0 The Fool	Dog; cliff

Next, choose a question based on your card. For example, if your Life Path number is 7, your card is VII The Chariot. This card's meaning (see page 58) is about control and determination—your character traits—so you might investigate these traits by asking, "What do I need to get where I need to be?" or "Where am I going?" Then, you might choose the symbol of the chariot from the card and devise the following spread, beginning with the charioteer, which represents you. Choose features of the card to establish a shape for your spread. Now that there's a shape to your spread, you can assign meanings to the staff, wheels, outer chariot, and sphinxes. In tarot spreads, we often create timelines based on card positions—so, the sphinxes would be future cards, because they are coming forward, while the wheels are behind the sphinxes, so they could represent past issues. Consider the symbolism within the image: For instance, because a staff is associated with strength, The Staff card could reveal your personal strengths. Wheels are associated with time, so this card might represent the lessons you've learned with the passage of time. The crest is an emblem of recognition, so a card in the Crest position could reveal information about your reputation. Use your intuition and free-associate to get your card meanings.

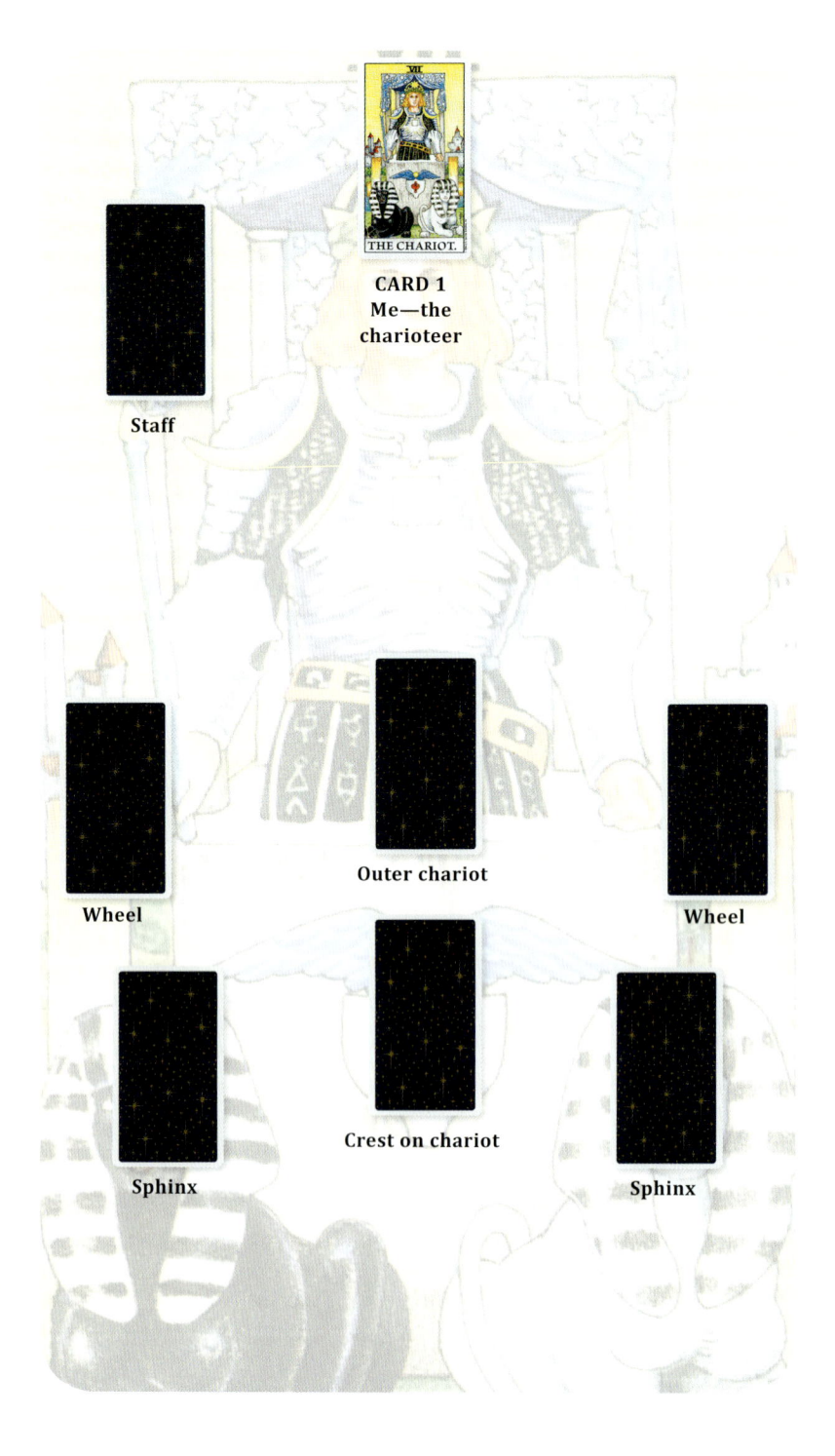

CARD 1
Me—the charioteer

Staff

Wheel

Outer chariot

Wheel

Sphinx

Crest on chariot

Sphinx

The Chariot's card layout meanings, therefore, could be:

CARD 1
Me—the
charioteer

Staff
My strengths

Outer chariot
What protects me?

Wheel
Past lessons

Wheel
Past lessons

Sphinx
Future
outcome

Crest on chariot
What's my reputation?

Sphinx
Future
outcome

Finally, determine the order in which you'll lay down the cards. The "You" card is card 1, then you might lay the remaining cards from left to right under the Chariot, as shown to the right.

It's important to experiment with card positions to see which feels right to you. You might want to add a new card position or remove one, or change a card's meaning: It's your spread, so go ahead and invent freely.

CARD 1
Me—the charioteer

CARD 2
Staff
My strengths

CARD 3
Wheel
Past lessons

CARD 5
Outer chariot
What protects me?

CARD 4
Wheel
Past lessons

CARD 7
Sphinx
Future outcome

CARD 6
Crest on chariot
What's my reputation?

CARD 8
Sphinx
Future outcome

APPENDICES

ASTROLOGY, KABBALAH, AND THE MAJOR ARCANA: THE GOLDEN DAWN SYSTEM

CARD	ELEMENT	SIGN OR PLANET	TREE OF LIFE PATHWAY	HEBREW LETTER
0 The Fool	Air	Uranus*	1	A (*Aleph*)
I The Magician	Air	Mercury	2	B (*Beth*)
II The High Priestess	Water	Moon	3	G (*Gimel*)
III The Empress	Earth	Venus	4	D (*Daleth*)
IV The Emperor	Fire	Aries	5	H (*Hei*)
V The Hierophant	Earth	Taurus	6	U, V (*Vau*)
VI The Lovers	Air	Gemini	7	Z (*Zain*)
VII The Chariot	Water	Cancer	8	Ch (*Heth*)
VIII Strength	Fire	Leo	9	T (*Teth*)
IX The Hermit	Earth	Virgo	10	I, Y (*Yod*)
X The Wheel of Fortune	Fire	Jupiter	11	K (*Kaph*)
XI Justice	Air	Libra	12	L (*Lamed*)
XII The Hanged Man	Water	Neptune*	13	M (*Mem*)
XIII Death	Water	Scorpio	14	N (*Nun*)
XIV Temperance	Fire	Sagittarius	15	S (*Samekh*)
XV The Devil	Earth	Capricorn	16	O (*Ayin*)
XVI The Tower	Fire	Mars	17	P (*Peh*)
XVII The Star	Air	Aquarius	18	Tz (*Tzaddi*)
XVIII The Moon	Water	Pisces	19	Q (*Qoph*)
XIX The Sun	Fire	Sun	20	R (*Resh*)
XX Judgement	Fire	Pluto*	21	Sh (*Tav*)
XXI The World	Earth	Saturn	22	Th (*Tau*)

* The astrological associations initially linked the cards with the seven classical planets: The Sun, Moon, Mercury, Venus, Mars, Jupiter, and Saturn. Uranus, Neptune, and Pluto were later additions.

KABBALAH: THE TREE OF LIFE PATHWAYS AND THE MAJOR ARCANA

Each major arcana card is linked with a pathway on the Tree of Life, the major motif of Kabbala.

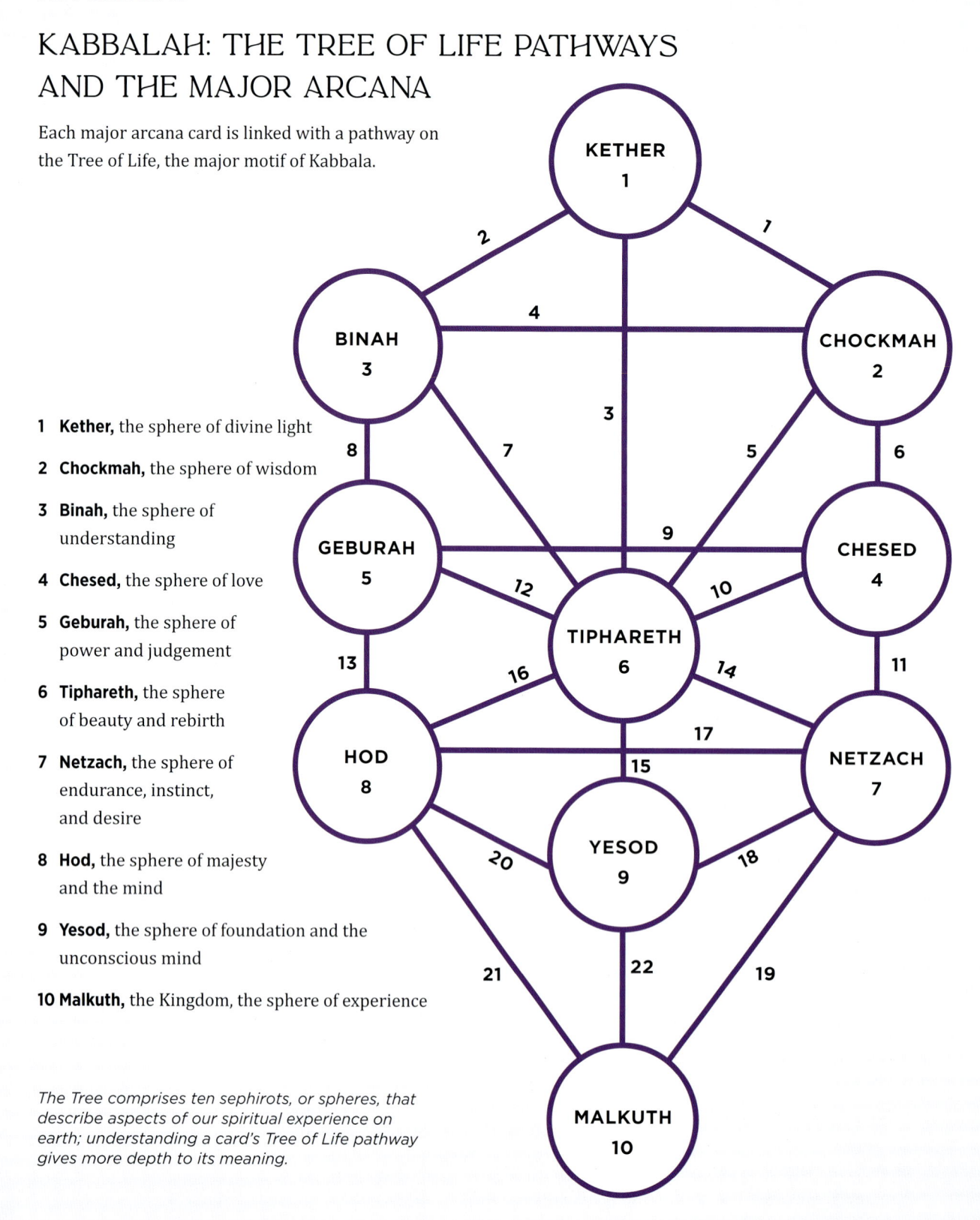

1 **Kether,** the sphere of divine light

2 **Chockmah,** the sphere of wisdom

3 **Binah,** the sphere of understanding

4 **Chesed,** the sphere of love

5 **Geburah,** the sphere of power and judgement

6 **Tiphareth,** the sphere of beauty and rebirth

7 **Netzach,** the sphere of endurance, instinct, and desire

8 **Hod,** the sphere of majesty and the mind

9 **Yesod,** the sphere of foundation and the unconscious mind

10 **Malkuth,** the Kingdom, the sphere of experience

The Tree comprises ten sephirots, or spheres, that describe aspects of our spiritual experience on earth; understanding a card's Tree of Life pathway gives more depth to its meaning.

APPENDIX C

ASTROLOGY, KABBALAH, AND THE MINOR ARCANA

THE ASTROLOGICAL SIGNS OF THE KNIGHTS, QUEENS, AND KINGS

Knight of Wands - - - - - - - - - Scorpio and Sagittarius

Queen of Wands - - - - - - - - - Pisces and Aries

King of Wands - - - - - - - - - - Cancer and Leo

Knight of Cups - - - - - - - - - - Aquarius and Pisces

Queen of Cups - - - - - - - - - - Gemini and Cancer

King of Cups - - - - - - - - - - - Libra and Scorpio

Knight of Pentacles - - - - - - - Leo and Virgo

Queen of Pentacles - - - - - - - Sagittarius and Capricorn

King of Pentacles - - - - - - - - - Aries and Taurus

Knight of Swords - - - - - - - - - Taurus and Gemini

Queen of Swords - - - - - - - - - Virgo and Libra

King of Swords - - - - - - - - - - Capricorn and Aquarius

TREE OF LIFE CORRESPONDENCES

Aces: Kether

Twos: Chockmah

Threes: Binah

Fours: Chesed

Fives: Geburah

Sixes: Tiphareth

Sevens: Netzach

Eights: Hod

Nines: Yesod

Tens: Malkuth

APPENDIX D

CHAKRAS, CRYSTALS, AND THE MAJOR ARCANA

I have attributed a chakra and crystal to each major arcana card. These attributions are my own and relate to my personal experience of tarot and healing work. You may have alternative suggestions or attachments.

Along with the seven principal chakras—the base, sacral, solar plexus, heart, throat, third eye, and crown—I refer to the new chakras becoming available to us during this time of spiritual shift: the higher heart, for universal love; the alta major chakra, for past lives; the palm chakras, for manifesting; the angelic, or fifth-eye chakra, for spiritual activation; the fourth eye, for spiritual connection; the heart seed, for soul remembrance; the soul star, for soul connection; the earth star, for spiritual grounding; and the stellar gateway, or cosmic doorway.

Tarot cards also have crystal attributions, and again, these largely depend on the author's preference. You can also allocate your own crystals to the cards.

TAROT CRYSTAL RITUALS

Crystals magnify and balance the energies of their associated tarot card. For example, if you want to manifest more abundance in your life, select the Magician from your deck and place one of his crystals on the card and then display the card and crystal where you can see them when you are working to make your projects happen. If you are experiencing the confusing, destructive impact of the Tower, carry a red carnelian in your pocket or bag to help you feel more secure.

The crystals listed on page 331 are those traditionally associated with each chakra point, along with some that are my personal suggestions.

THE BODY'S CHAKRA POINTS

There are seven principal chakra points on the body. As we ascend to higher levels of consciousness, new or "developing" chakras open up.

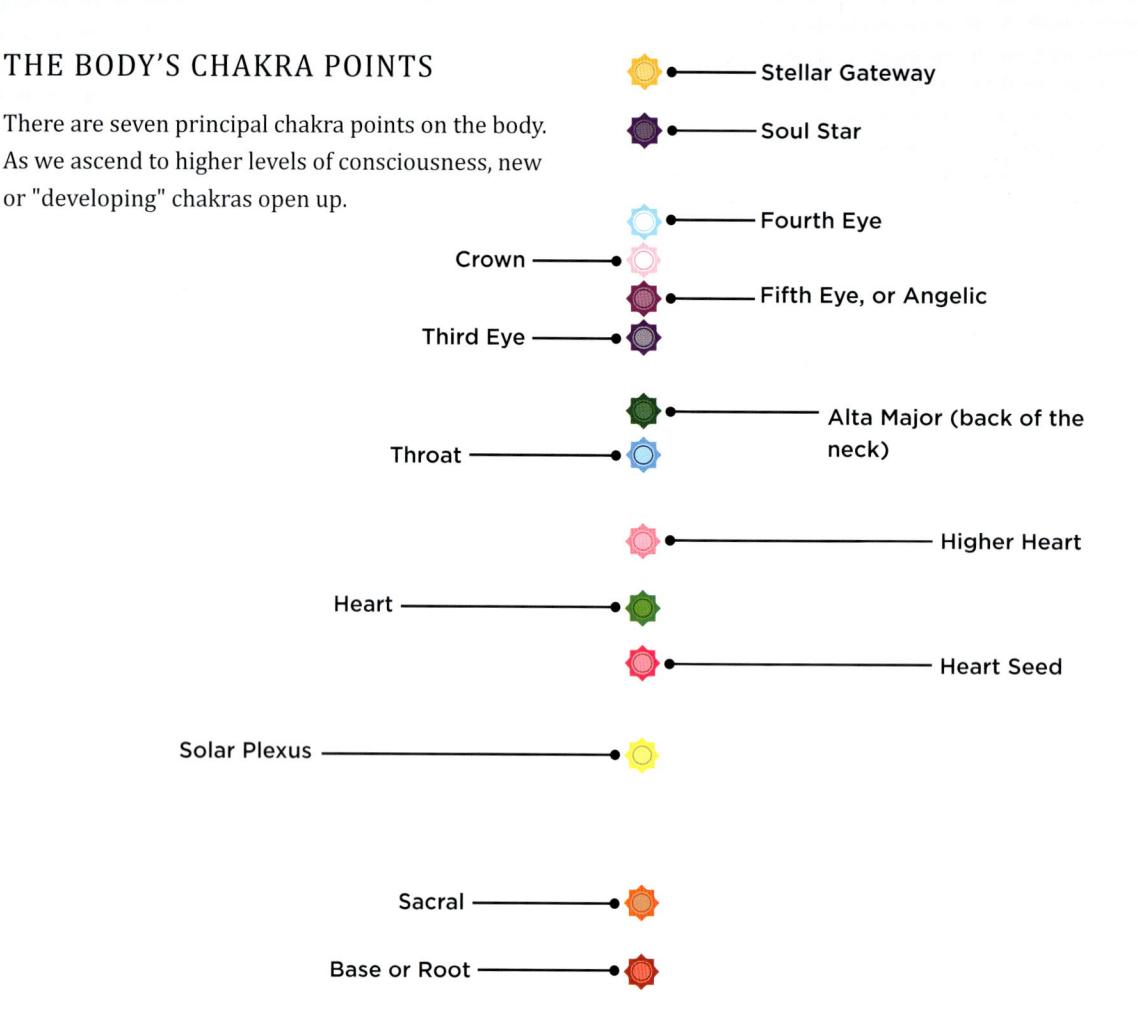

Stellar Gateway

Soul Star

Fourth Eye

Crown

Fifth Eye, or Angelic

Third Eye

Alta Major (back of the neck)

Throat

Higher Heart

Heart

Heart Seed

Solar Plexus

Sacral

Base or Root

THE SEVEN PRINCIPAL CHAKRAS

Base or Root: security
Sacral: creativity
Solar Plexus: energy and wisdom
Heart: love and relationships
Throat: communication
Third Eye: intuition
Crown: connection with guides and the spiritual realms

THE DEVELOPING CHAKRAS

Stellar Gateway: cosmic connection
Soul Star: karma and soul wisdom
Fourth Eye: spiritual direction
Fifth Eye, or Angelic: angelic contact
Alta Major (back of the neck): past lives, expanding consciousness
Higher Heart: universal love; the seat of the soul
Heart Seed: soul memory
Earth Star: grounding and connection

Earth Star

TAROT, CHAKRA, AND CRYSTAL CORRESPONDENCES

MAJOR ARCANA CARD	CHAKRA	CRYSTALS
0 The Fool	Crown Base	Clear quartz Red carnelian and red jasper
I The Magician	Palm chakras	Aquamarine and fire agate
II The High Priestess	Angelic (fifth eye)	Lavender quartz, selenite, and moonstone
III The Empress	Heart Sacral	Rose quartz, emerald Orange carnelian and orange calcite
IV The Emperor	Base	Red jasper, red calcite, and garnet
V The Hierophant	Fourth eye	Apophyllite, celestite, and sapphire
VI The Lovers	Heart	Aventurine, agate, and rose quartz
VII The Chariot	Throat	Blue lace agate
VIII Strength	Solar plexus	Citrine and tiger's eye
IX The Hermit	Heart seed	Tugtupite
X The Wheel of Fortune	Soul star	White topaz
XI Justice	Earth star	Hematite, obsidian, and bloodstone
XII The Hanged Man	Third eye	Amethyst and sapphire
XIII Death	Alta major	Blue moonstone
XIV Temperance	Solar plexus	Citrine, amber, and yellow topaz
XV The Devil	Base chakra	Carnelian and ruby
XVI The Tower	Crown Base	Clear quartz Red carnelian, and red jasper
XVII The Star	Higher heart	Kunzite, dioptase, and red tourmaline
XVIII The Moon	Third eye	Amethyst and lapis lazuli
XIX The Sun	Solar plexus	Citrine and golden topaz
XX Judgement	Alta major	Blue moonstone
XXI The World	Stellar gateway	Lemurian seedquartz

ACKNOWLEDGMENTS

With thanks to my agent, Chelsey Fox; my editors, Jill Alexander, Renae Haines, Leah Jenness, Jennifer Kushnier, and Liz Weeks; my husband, Michael Young; and in memory of Jonathan Dee, mentor extraordinaire.

ABOUT THE AUTHOR

Liz Dean is a professional tarot reader and divination teacher working with the Rider-Waite Smith deck. Her 24 books and tarot decks include *The Ultimate Guide to Tarot*, *The Ultimate Guide to Tarot Spreads*, *Tarot By Numbers*, HBO's *Game of Thrones Tarot*, and *The Magic of Tarot*. She has taught at the Omega Institute and Reader's Studio, New York; in Perth, Melbourne, and Sydney for the Tarot Guild of Australia; and at tarot conferences in the UK, amongst others. She also teaches her own groups online, with classes bringing to life the knowledge within Sacred Tarot.

Liz began reading tarot professionally at Psychic Sisters within the famous Selfridges department store, London, and now reads privately for a global client list. Formerly, Liz was an editorial director in book publishing, and was co-editor of the UK's leading spiritual magazine, *Kindred Spirit*. She lives by the sea in Sunderland in northeast England.

Learn more at: lizdean.info

INDEX